Creative FLOWER *and* PLANT PHOTOGRAPHY

tips and tricks for taking stunning photos

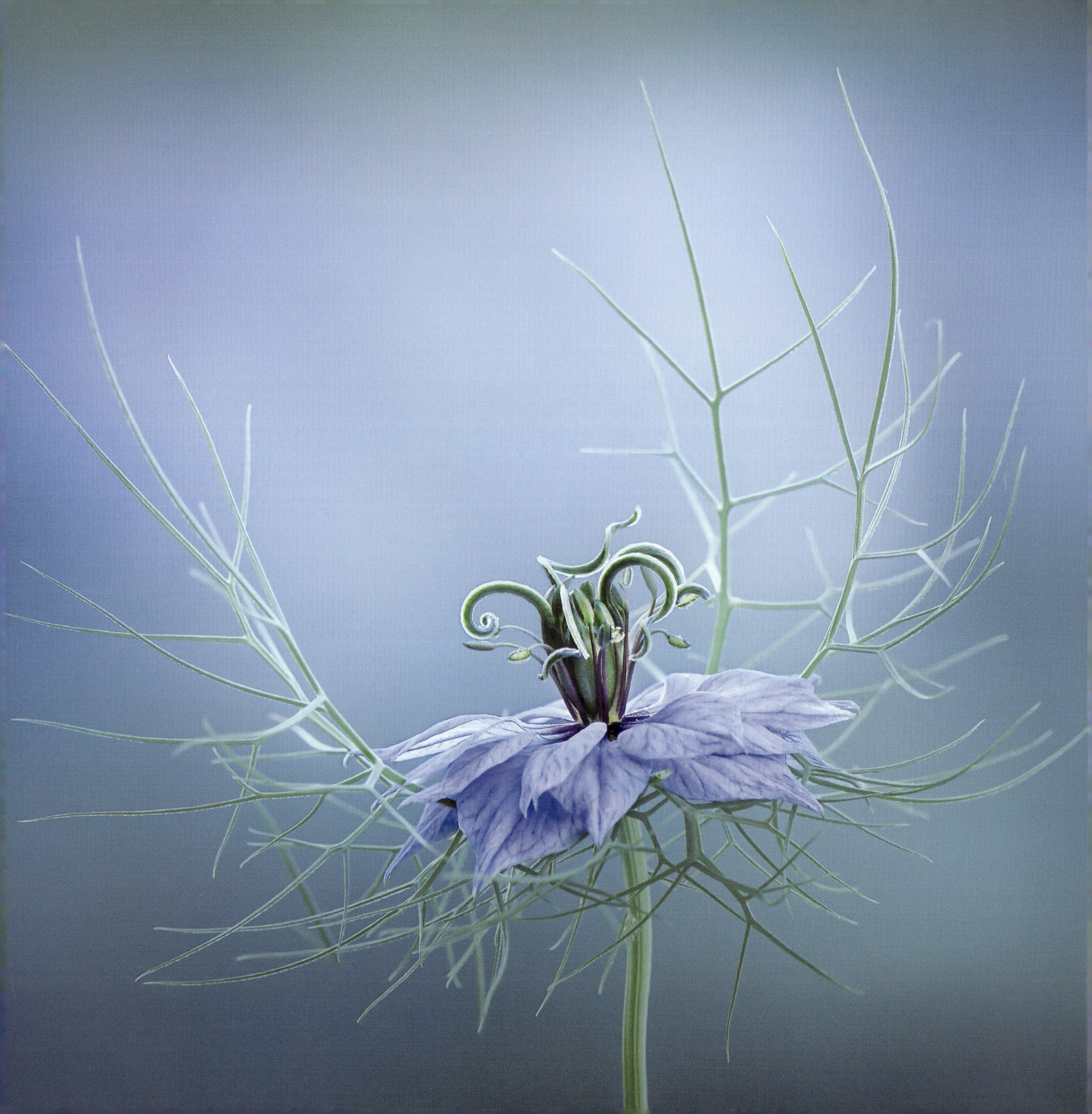

Molly Hollman

Creative FLOWER *and* PLANT PHOTOGRAPHY

tips and tricks for taking stunning photos

THE CROWOOD PRESS

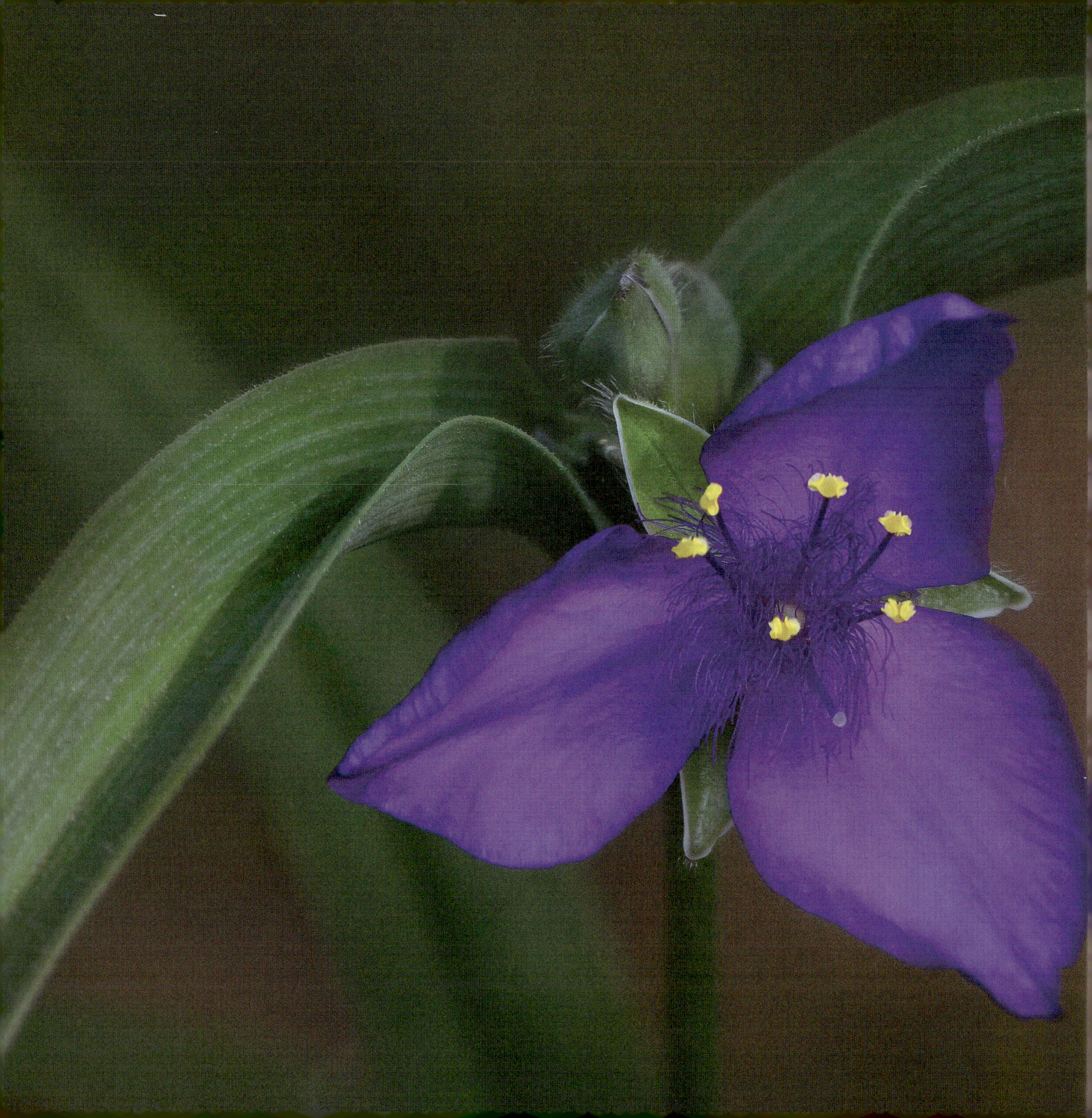

Contents

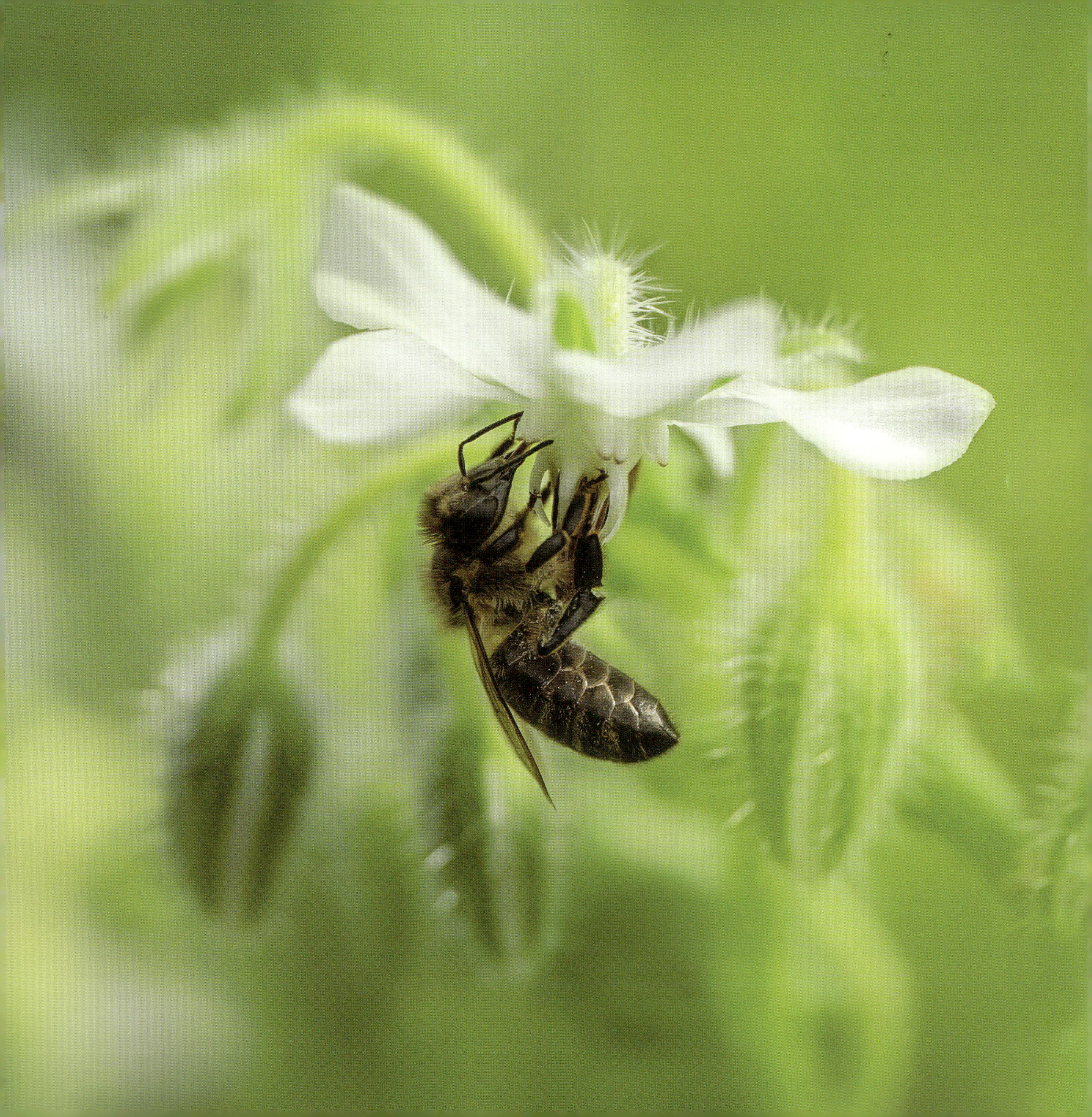

Introduction

I love being outside in nature.

About fifteen years ago I decided that I would take a camera when I was out walking or visiting local gardens to record some of the things I was seeing and the rest, as they say, is history. Much of my free time since then (often with two children in tow) has been spent trying to photograph the flowers and gardens I see in a way that comes close to representing their true beauty, and this isn't easy. Part of this journey has been learning to edit my photos on a computer so that I can bring light levels and colours back to the way I observed them in nature.

The stillness required to closely observe and find the best composition means that you become totally immersed in nature and are able (usually) to forget the rest of the world, if only for a few seconds. More and more people are turning to photography in this and similar ways to improve their mental health and well-being and I cannot recommend the benefits enough. As a teacher, I'm fully aware that no one person can know everything and I still feel that I'm on a journey with my photography but I also feel that I've learnt enough to know what I like and enjoy, and want to photograph more. When Covid-19 hit I invested a lot of time replanting my own garden and am proud that some of my favourite photos were taken there.

Not everyone is lucky enough to have a garden but we can all be close to nature, even if that means a botanical garden in the middle of a city or some pots on a balcony. During the winter months I visit local florists and buy flowers to photograph indoors. Even this can bring some cheer to the dark winter.

I hope some of the ideas in this book will inspire you and that your time spent taking photographs of flowers and plants will bring you joy, as it does me.

Each chapter of this book will conclude with a selection of flowers, plants or garden landscapes that may be available to photograph in each particular month, depending of course on where you live and the climate. All of these photos were taken in the month that they are listed in and plants are usually labelled with their botanical name to avoid the confusion with the myriad of common and regional names that now exist.

◀ Honeybee on white borage flowers.

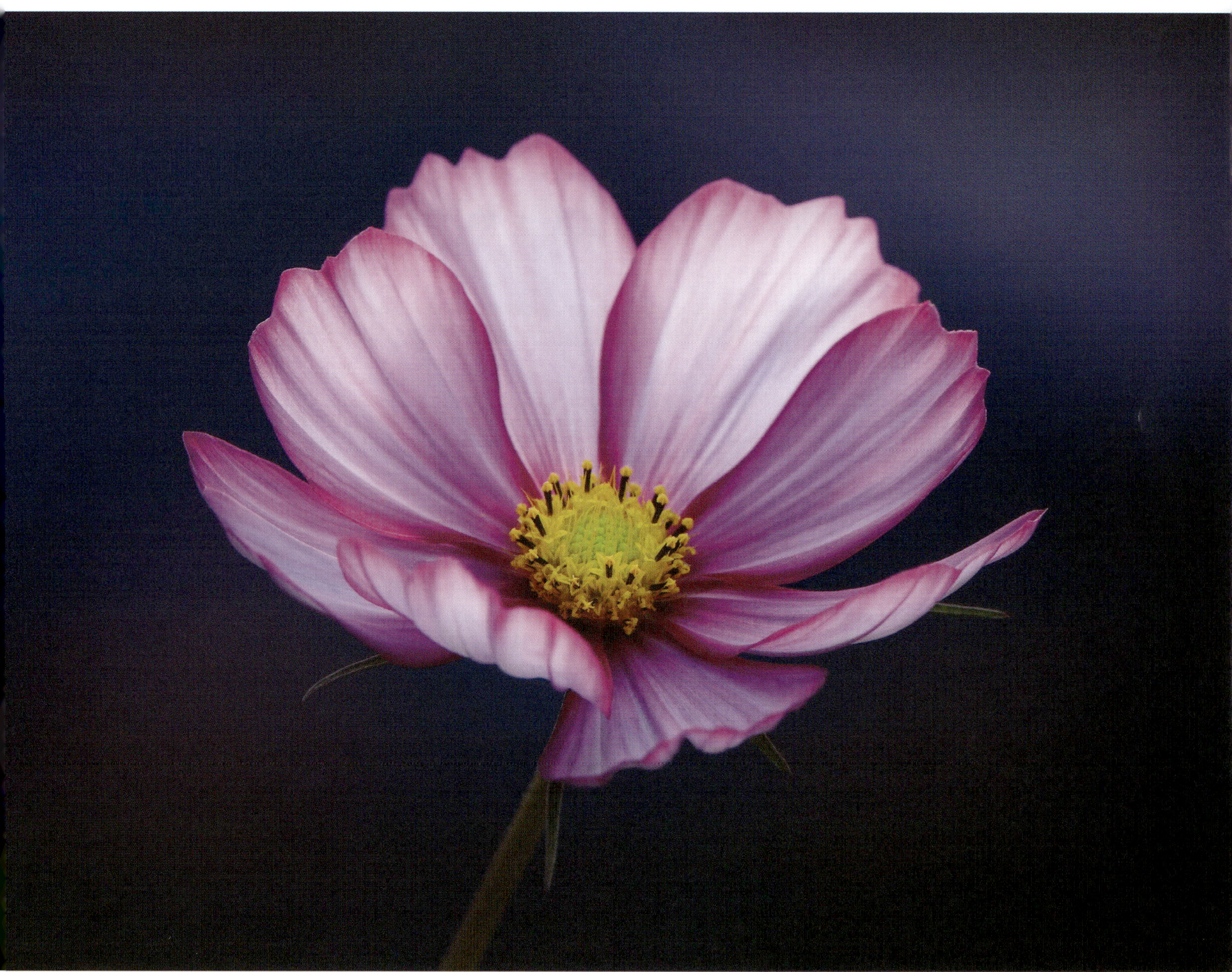

Cosmos bipinnatus in evening light.

CHAPTER 1

Equipment and Setting up your Camera

> You can love a good camera the same way that you can love a good fountain pen. It moulds to your hands in the same way and just feels right. It will not make you a better photographer, but it might make you use it more and, critically, with more care. However, regardless of your choice of camera, the way to take good pictures is by looking. If you cannot see the shot then neither will the lens.
>
> MONTY DON

In this chapter I'll discuss the equipment that I use to get the most out of my flower and garden photography, but it's never been my aim to 'exclusivize' garden photography and to this end I'll try to cover everything, including budget options. I'll also discuss how you can use just a mobile phone and still get great photos.

Finally, I'll talk about the basics of setting up your camera, with a brief explanation of shutter speed, aperture and ISO, as a secure understanding of these will make a big difference to your approach to flower and plant photography.

CAMERAS

If you're reading this book it's likely that you'll have a digital interchangeable lens system camera, be it a DSLR (a single lens reflex camera with an optical viewfinder) or a mirrorless camera (with an electronic viewfinder or screen), although almost everything within the following chapters will work for film cameras (excepting obviously the digital post-processing) and mobile phones.

There are pros and cons for both mirrorless and DSLR cameras and I'll discuss those here briefly, but for me it's important that flower and garden photography should not mean an equipment upgrade and if you've bought your camera within the last ten years and it functions properly, it should be more than suitable.

There has been rather a 'pixel race' in recent years as camera companies have tried to persuade the camera-buying public that the more megapixels (MP) the better. In reality, pixel count is not really that important unless you'll be printing your photos at large sizes, such as A3 or above, or wanting to crop into an image a great deal in the edit. A camera or phone that has 8MP or above is usually more than ample to print at A4 size, or 8 × 10 inches (the size of many frames) and for sharing on social media or via email 1MB is more than enough. If you have money to spend it would usually be much better spent on a lens, new or second-hand.

DSLR cameras are beginning to wane in popularity as the trend for mirrorless increases, but they are still used by many photographers due to the enormous range in lens choice. At the time of writing it will be some years before mirrorless systems

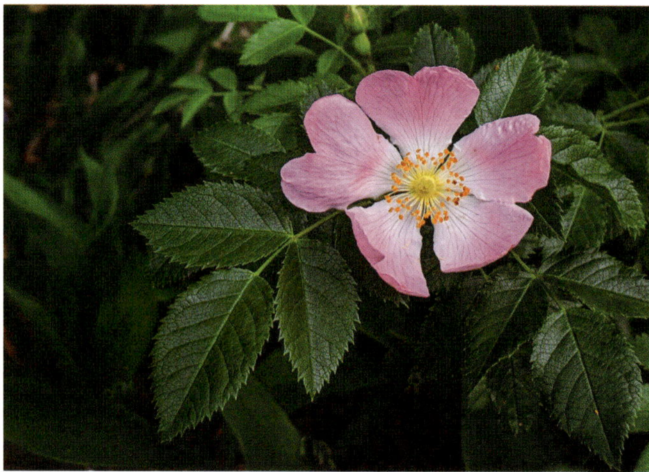

I took this photo of a rambling rose in a cemetery using my mobile phone as it was the only camera I had with me at the time. I edited it using Snapseed, which is a great free app for mobile phone editing, and is fairly straightforward to use.

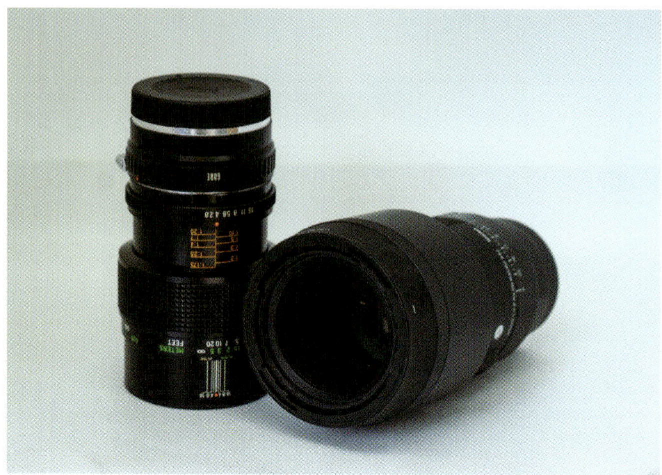

A manual-focus vintage macro lens (left) next to an auto-focus modern macro lens (right). I love both for different reasons.

catch up on this score. The battery life on most DSLRs is usually longer than that of mirrorless cameras and users with larger hands often prefer them as they 'fit' better.

Mirrorless cameras are increasing in popularity and most of the major brands now make them. Photographers are often preferring them because they are lighter and can sometimes have very advanced features, such as the ability to track human and animal eye movement. However these cameras can be more expensive than DSLRs and lenses made especially for mirrorless cameras are often still quite heavy, thus offsetting the lower weight of the camera.

Bridge cameras which have a single unchangeable lens can actually be very useful in flower photography as they often have very powerful zooms, which can enable you to zoom in to a distant flower that is out of reach, and will also blur the background nicely when at full or near-full zoom, something that can be very useful in flower and garden photography. However, good versions of these can also be quite expensive. Bridge cameras make good travelling cameras as they are very versatile, the only downsides being that they can struggle more in low light and can have difficulty focusing if the background is quite patterned.

Mobile phone cameras

If you're going to make good use of your mobile phone camera, read up on the various settings in the manual or on YouTube so that you can get the best possible photos. It's more than possible to get great photos from a mobile phone, and as the saying goes 'the best camera is the one that you have with you at the time!' Just remember to switch any softening or background blurring filters off as this can create a false-looking separation of the subject and background.

Lenses

The lens market is even wider and more diverse than the camera market, but here I can give more focused advice (no pun intended!) as we are concentrating solely on the genre of garden and flower photography.

I use lots of vintage lenses in my photography as I prefer the colours and bokeh (background light blur) of older lenses, and these will often be manual focus. For me, autofocus is not essential as I like to manually place the focus of my photo anyway (autofocus will often focus on the nearest petal to the lens for example, rather than the centre of the flower, which is often more desirable).

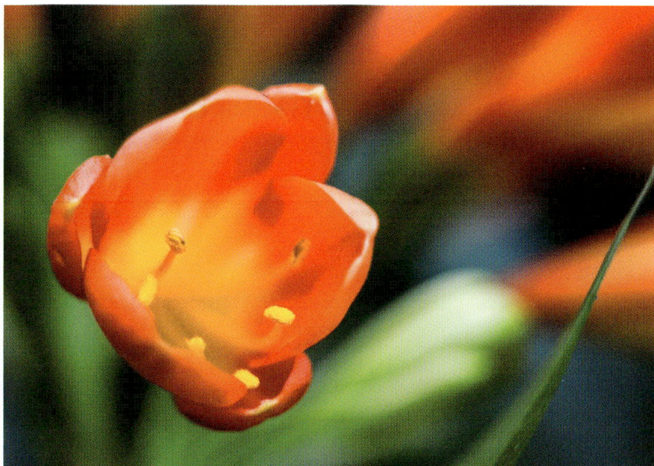

Tulips, taken with an inexpensive vintage 50mm f/1.7 prime lens shot wide-open; this image has not been edited.

Prime (fixed lenses that do not zoom) lenses are often sharper and give better picture quality, but a set of primes covering the same range as a zoom lens will cost more so this may be something else to weigh up.

Mobile phone lenses

You can actually buy lenses that clip on to mobiles and this might be worth investigating if you don't have a camera or a mobile with a macro setting. Some of them are especially designed to enable your phone to take more 'close-up' photos, which is ideal as mobile phones usually have a very wide field of view and when zoomed in the picture quality usually drops. The quality of these can however vary greatly so definitely take personal recommendations or read lots of reviews.

Camera bag

If you're going to be visiting lots of gardens make sure your camera bag is up to the job and won't strain your back or other muscles. Invest in one that is comfortable with the most pockets you can find, as these are essential for all the accessories I'll be talking about next. Of course if you're mostly photographing at home or in your own garden this is less essential, but always store lenses and accessories in an organized way so that you can grab things quickly if you need to.

Useful lenses to have in your bag

- A mid-range prime lens, such as a 50mm or 85mm lens.
- A long-range, or telezoom lens, such as a 180mm, 300mm or even longer (provided it's not too heavy). You will get excellent results with very long lenses (such as 600mm) but it's a trade-off in terms of how heavy they are.
- A macro lens for very close-up pictures – some lenses offer this as a switch on the side of the lens. For *very* close-up pictures look for a macro lens that is 1:1, which means that the object is real size or bigger in the camera's sensor. There are many vintage manual macro lenses of excellent quality and it's not necessary to buy 'new'.
- A wider zoom (or prime) lens covering a distance of about 24–70mm if you want to do more photography of garden vistas and views.

Many flower photographers use 'specialist' lenses that give creative effects, such as Lensbaby composer lenses and vintage Helios lenses, which whilst hard to get to grips with initially can give good results. I will leave you to do your own research into these before purchasing. Some particular ones to explore if you want to develop your photography in this area would be the Lensbaby Velvet 56, the Helios 44-2 58mm/f2, the Meyer-Optik Oreston 50mm f/1.8, the ISCO 35mm f/2.8 (unusual bokeh), the Super-Takumar 55mm f/1.8 and for very swirly backgrounds the Fujian 35mm f/1.6 (CCTV C-mount lens). You'll probably need an adapter for some of these, depending on your camera type.

Remember that you can buy adaptors for lenses to fit your camera if the lens is of a different brand; these are fairly inexpensive for a manual adaptor (the autofocus will not work) or, for some lenses, you can buy a more expensive adaptor that will allow autofocus. Again, do your research to decide if this is necessary for you.

I use old vintage lenses quite a bit and three of my most-used lenses cost me under £250 altogether; there are definitely bargains to be had. Only purchase from reputable sellers – on eBay that means sellers with over 99.4 per cent satisfactory feedback.

Accessories

I carry around many small accessories with me and although I may not use them all regularly, it's still nice to know they're available if I need them. Only acquire, second hand if possible, as many or as few as you feel you'll need, maybe adding to your collection over time.

Spare batteries and memory cards

There is nothing worse than driving for an hour to make that visit to a beautiful garden you've been planning for months, only to realize that your battery is low or that there's no memory card in the slot of your camera. Definitely keep a spare of both in your camera bag, just in case.

Reflector/diffuser (or home-made versions)

Possibly my most used accessory. I have a small one and a larger one, and they have a double function: reflecting light from the sky back up onto the flower you're photographing or diffusing sunlight to avoid harsh shadows on the flowers you're photographing. I'll talk about this more in Chapter 3. There are many 'recipes' for homemade versions on the internet, for example tin foil stuck to some card is commonly used as a cheap homemade reflector, and tracing or baking paper makes an effective diffuser.

Tripod

Really, the smaller the better to minimize the weight you're having to carry around, but you'll often need a tripod to hold the diffuser or the camera itself. If you can, buy one that allows your camera to be close to the ground when mounted on it, for lower shots.

Light/s

A small LED light or ring-light that can be mounted onto the top of the camera with the hot shoe (the slot for a flash). Sometimes I handhold an LED light whilst mounting the camera on a tripod. A mini torch can also be useful to pinpoint light onto your subject.

I also have a set of 'sunlight' lamps for my indoor photography of the type that gives plants and seedlings simulated sunlight to stop them becoming 'leggy'. These clamp to the table and are multi-directional, very useful for when I'm working indoors. I sometimes use a diffuser with them if they're too bright for my needs.

A double-ended clamp or plamp

A plamp (sometimes called a 'studio flex arm' or 'duel spring clamp') is a sturdy but bendable metal rod with a crocodile clip at each end. You would usually fix one end to your tripod while the other end grips your reflector, or backdrop. The most-used brand is the Wimberly Plamp.

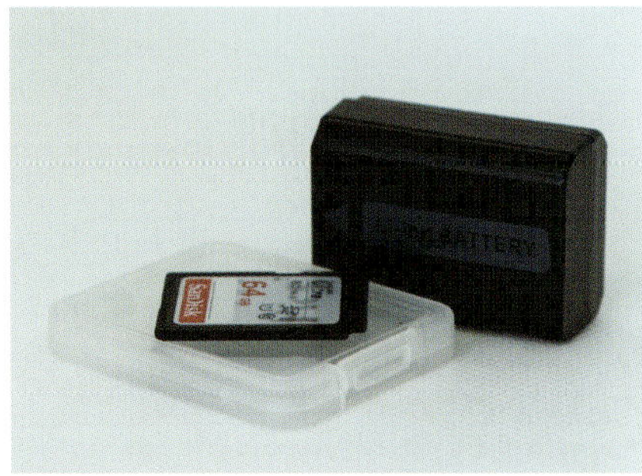

Always try to keep a spare battery and memory card in your camera bag – they could potentially save you a wasted trip.

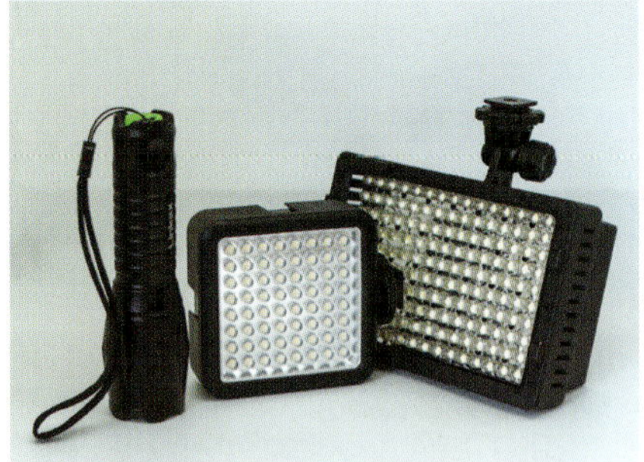

I have several small and inexpensive LED lights and will often put one in my camera bag on dull days, or use them in my indoor photography.

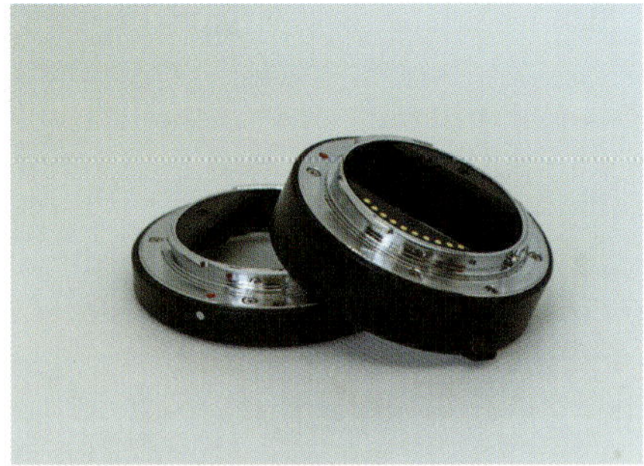

I often take extension tubes in my camera bag when visiting a garden so that I don't have to carry my heavy macro lens. They are also an inexpensive way of trying out macro.

A set of extension tubes or macro close-up lenses if you want to try macro photography without a macro lens

These can be bought generically fairly inexpensively from well-known internet shopping sites – just make sure that they're compatible with your camera.

Extension tubes fit between the lens and the camera – you need to buy the correct type for your camera and lens although I do have a set that I use with an old vintage Pentax lens and my Sony camera, so you can sometimes connect 'incompatible' types.

Macro close-up lenses screw onto the front of your lens like a filter and add magnification this way. Just check you have the correct filter thread size when ordering (the filter size is always listed in mm on the front with the Φ symbol, e.g. Φ50mm).

Memo clips or a 'third hand'

Third hands (sometimes called 'helping hands') are metal clips, usually with a magnifying glass, that are often used for needlework, or close-up work of varying kinds. I use mine to hold stems of delicate flowers that would be crushed by the arms of a bigger plamp or clamp. They are useful as they can be angled in all directions (unlike memo clips) although the magnifying glass could be removed as it's redundant. They are also usually on a weighted base for stability.

Glycerin

An alternative to water if you're getting creative with your macro – a drop of glycerin will look and 'hang' like a water droplet but last much longer before falling off. A small bottle won't cost much on the internet. Like water, I would only use this in an indoor set-up as I feel it's wrong to start disturbing flowers when you're somewhere other than your home. I have a small plastic pipette to dispense the glycerin onto a flower petal.

UV torch

If you're interested in trying out ultraviolet photography you can buy a small UV torch on the internet – they are usually fairly inexpensive. Some flowers glow brightly under UV light and this is always an interesting project to research and try; do have a look at some examples on the internet.

Clothes pegs or clips

Useful for gently holding leaves out of the way. It's best not to do this in a garden that is not your own as you may damage the foliage, but you may be able to ask a gardener for permission. The larger clips in the photo below fix to a clamp to attach them to a tripod.

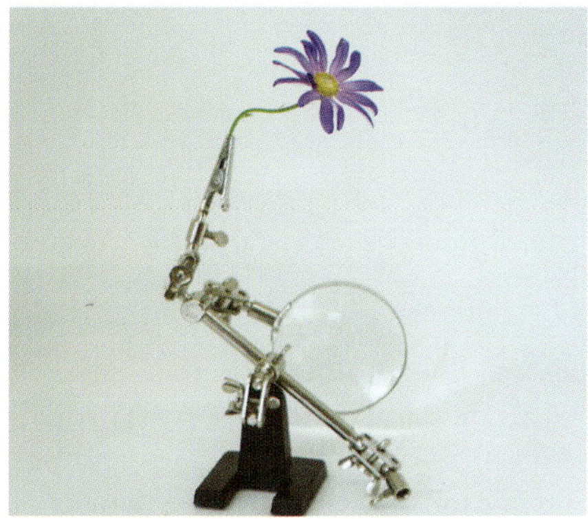

A 'third hand' clamp can hold cut flowers and can be angled in many different directions.

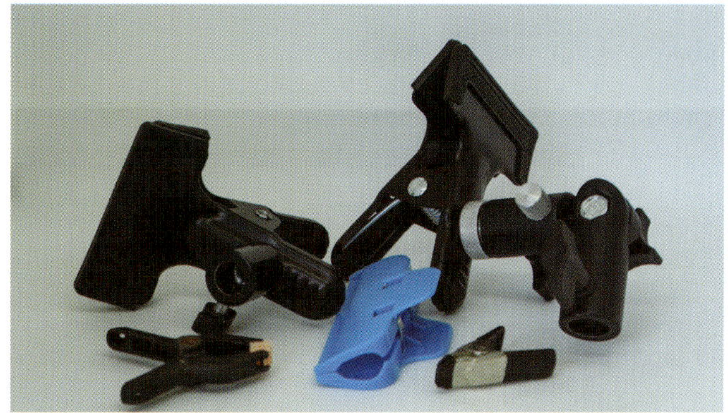

A selection of clips and clamps that I use in my photography; some attach to light stands or tripods and some are very small and are used with the flowers themselves.

Clear plastic bags and rubber bands
To waterproof your camera if showers happen. Attach the bag to your camera hood or lens using a rubber band, making sure that the plastic extends slightly beyond the hood or lens.

A plastic sheet/bin bag
When there is dew on the ground (as there often is in early mornings or evenings), or after rain, you'll probably feel more comfortable having something to sit (or lie) on. I also have a small padded baby-changing mat of the type that comes with a baby-changing bag to give my knees some extra comfort.

A small and very soft paintbrush
I use this to brush off or manoeuvre tiny insects from the flowers, very gently so that they're not harmed. Also useful for removing small bits of dirt and cobwebs.

Appropriate clothing
I know many people would assume that being a garden photographer is a seasonal activity: it most certainly isn't! Getting out on a bright January day is fantastic for feeling better in the middle of winter but you can't let yourself get cold or it will be a miserable experience. When I visit gardens in winter I wear ski trousers, fur-lined boots, thermal socks and lots of layers on my top half that I can remove If I get too warm. A hat, scarf and gloves without fingertips (or dedicated 'photography' gloves) complete the ensemble and I can stay out for hours without feeling the cold.

Garden membership cards
I have quite a few annual membership cards that give me access to a garden for a whole year and they're really worth their money if you're visiting gardens often.

My current membership cards (for use in the UK):

- The RHS (Royal Horticultural Society)
- The National Trust
- English Heritage
- Annual membership cards for your local gardens – find out about this on their websites.

Apps

I find some mobile phone apps extremely useful for my photography, both at the planning stage and then when I'm actually out at a garden. I wouldn't be without a weather app, and also regularly use plant and insect identification apps. The 'iRecord Butterflies' app not only tells you the species but can record your sighting and sends the results to Butterfly Conservation organizations; a lovely way to take part in the incredible work they do. Finally there are sunrise and sunset apps which tell you the time of day that the sun will rise and set and in which direction – some will even show you on a map. Snapseed is a good photo editing app for a phone and can also be used on tablets.

A more recent discovery of mine is the Historic Houses Association, which will give you a year's free entry to hundreds of historic houses and their gardens, and at the time of writing costs about the same as membership of the RHS or National Trust. Obviously the cost of these will quickly add up – use the internet to discover the ones worth getting for your local area and work out which memberships would give you the best value – you might only need one.

The National Garden Scheme website will show you the gardens in your local area, including smaller gardens that open for charity on a few occasions throughout the year.

SETTING UP YOUR CAMERA

Whatever camera you use it's always fine to shoot on auto, and you shouldn't worry about this. As you learn various skills and develop your eye you can move off the auto setting and see how the other options might suit your photographic needs; I'll discuss doing this later in the book.

Some cameras have presets for different situations, for example 'portrait', 'landscape' and 'sport' and there's often a 'flower' or 'macro' setting if your camera has these options. This will work well for close-up photos of flowers and plants but you'll need to switch back to a landscape setting if you're shooting garden vistas.

The information about the settings you have used on your camera is called EXIF data, and it's always useful to know this when you look at digital photos on the internet as you can then try out the same or similar settings to achieve similar results. If you follow photographers on internet forums such as Flickr or Facebook they will often give this information and if they don't, you can always politely ask if they would mind telling you.

I have given the EXIF data for many of the photos in this book, and to look it up on your own photos without an editing programme you can right click on the icon of a picture file and select 'properties' (or 'info' on an Apple device) and it will list all the settings (such as shutter speed and aperture). Some people refer to this as metadata, although the latter will usually include information about who created the file and possibly the shooting location. Your camera may also give you the option of setting up copyright and other information such as GPS coordinates in its menu.

Aperture priority

If you want to wean yourself off the green 'auto' setting, I would recommend switching to Aperture Priority or the A (or Av) setting on the dial first, before going fully 'manual'.

The word 'aperture' comes from a Latin word meaning 'hole' and it controls how much light you let into your camera onto the sensor. This amount of light is measured in 'f stops' and you'll be able to adjust this, either in-camera if the lens is more recent, or on the top of the lens if you are using an older lens.

By increasing or decreasing the aperture you change the 'depth of field' of the background of the photo, which basically means how much of the photo is in focus. If you are photographing a landscape with mountains in the background you'll need the mountains to be sharp and clearly in focus, so will need a narrow aperture (f number) of about f/8 to f/16 (or even higher). If you want to completely blur the background out to throw the focus solely on a close-up object such as a flower, you'll need a wider aperture of f/1.8 to f/2.8. At the time of writing, there are now lenses available that can have apertures as wide as f/0.75. My lens with the widest aperture goes down to f/1.7, and f/1.4 lenses are widely available. Depth of field is incredibly important with flower photography and this is definitely something to experiment with the next time you photograph a flower. I will refer to it throughout this book.

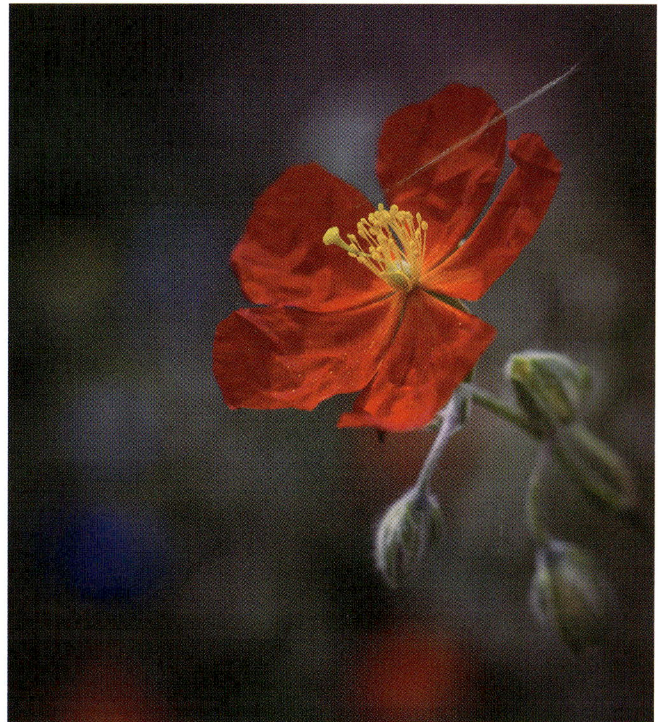

Helianthemum 'Henfield Brilliant' taken with a 55mm lens at f/1.8. Notice the blurs of colour (flowers) in the background created by a shallow depth of field.

Other things will affect depth of field such as the focal length of the lens (measured in mm) and how far your camera is from the subject you're photographing, but for now if you're fairly new to this use a wider (smaller in number) aperture such as f/1.4 to f/5.6 if you're photographing a single flower or plant and a narrower aperture such as f/8–f/16 if you're photographing a garden landscape.

Mobile phones and pocket cameras often struggle with depth of field – they cannot always achieve the same results as a DSLR or mirrorless camera due to the distance the lens is from the sensor. Many newer mobiles can digitally blur out backgrounds but, at the time of writing, this isn't always hugely successful. I'll talk more about aperture in the chapter about macro and close-up photography.

Shutter speed

Most of the time I shoot with the manual, or 'M' setting on my camera mode dial, which means I control both the aperture and the shutter speed, and usually the ISO too, though you can set this to auto. Controlling these three elements of a photo is often referred to as the 'exposure triangle'.

The shutter speed is the length of time the shutter is open for, therefore controlling the amount of light let into the camera. If you shoot on aperture priority, the camera will set the shutter speed for you, which will always give you perfectly reasonable photos, but sometimes I find it too bright for the look I'm after and want to have more control.

I think if you are going to be editing all your photos it doesn't matter too much as you can change the brightness of the photo in post-processing, but if you aren't then it might be nice to try shooting on the 's' or 'shutter priority' dial setting (or manual) and getting used to how the shutter speed can affect the light. You *can* achieve similar results in aperture priority mode by dialling in exposure compensation – (look for a +/- dial or button) but you might need to check your manual for this. In shutter priority mode the camera will set the aperture for you and of course you might not want this, in which case you can switch to the 'm' or 'manual' setting.

Sometimes I need to shoot an insect that's moving quickly and for this you'll need to use shutter priority (or manual) and a fast shutter speed; about 1/2000 of a second or even more if your camera allows. Because this is such a fast speed you'll probably need to boost the ISO to ISO400 or more so that the image isn't too dark; it will depend on the available light at the time.

Shooting in manual means that I can take very dark or 'low key' images if I wish – this can often suit a subject in shadow where there is just a very small point of interest in the frame.

ISO

Put simply, ISO is a camera setting that will brighten or darken a photo. As you increase your ISO number, your photos will get brighter. Because of this, a higher ISO can help you capture images in darker environments, or be more flexible about your aperture and shutter speed settings. Modern day cameras have ISO settings that go up to ISO102400 or even higher, but photos taken at more than 2400 ISO are likely to be 'noisy' and become more so the higher the ISO number (this does depend on the camera a great deal so do read up about yours).

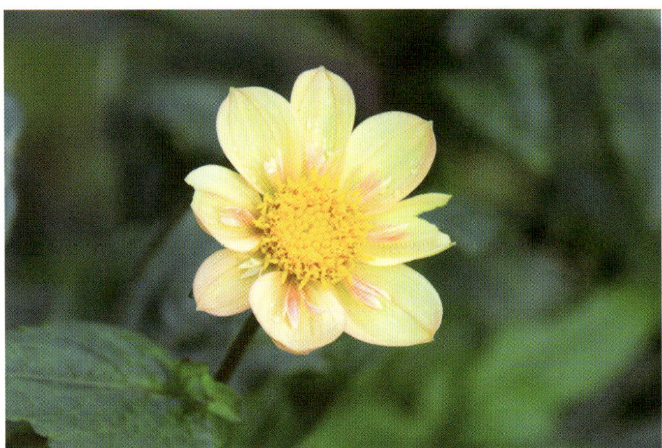

A photo of a dahlia taken with the aperture priority setting. The flower is a lighter yellow than it appeared in real life.

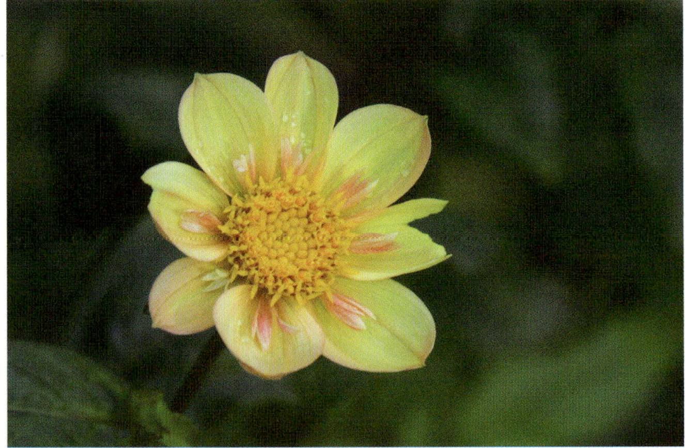

A photo of the same flower taken with the camera set to manual. I have set the shutter speed dial to be slightly faster (a higher number), letting less light into the camera and therefore darkening the image more. We can now observe more detail and richer colour; the water droplets for example can be seen more clearly. You can reduce your exposure when editing however if you want to stay on auto.

For a sunny day I would use ISO100 (or lower), a cloudy day would be 200–400 (depending on whether I was out in the open or under trees) and for dusk or evening photos I might push the ISO up to 1200.

Raising the ISO will have consequences though: a photo taken at too high an ISO will show a lot of 'digital noise'; a grainy or speckled effect on the photo. Because of this you should only really raise your ISO when you cannot brighten your image via the shutter speed or aperture instead. If you *are* stuck with a noisy photo, you can reduce it to a certain extent in Lightroom or Photoshop, or purchase additional 'de-noise' software.

I haven't generally listed the ISO data for each photo in this book as the majority of photos are taken between 100 and 400 ISO and this range should be a good starting point, or indeed setting your camera to auto ISO.

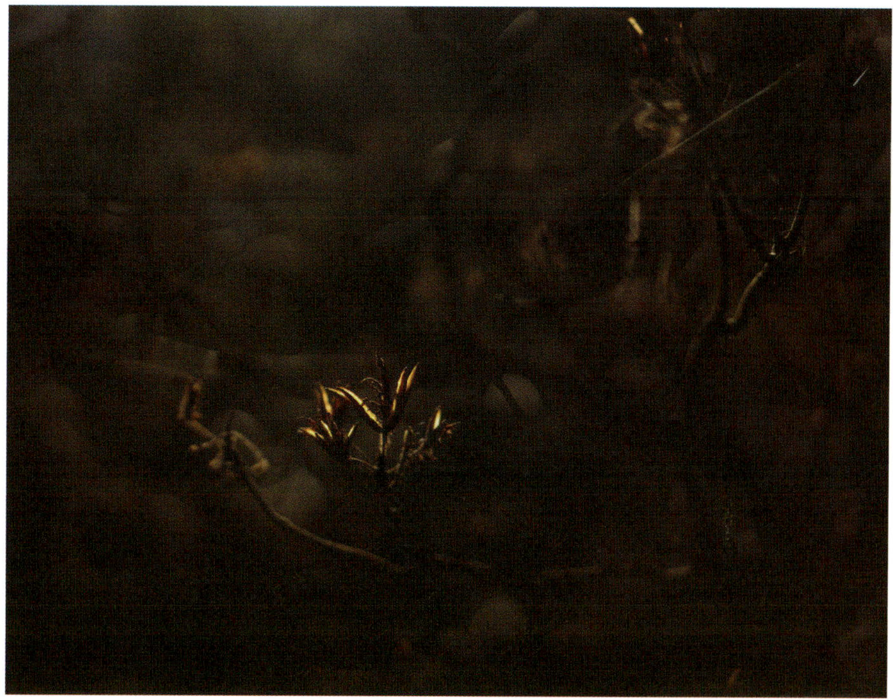

I photographed this weigela shrub in winter and wanted to capture the seedheads lit up by the low sun. A dark background draws all our attention to this with no distractions. Taken with a 55mm lens at f2 and a shutter speed of 1/5000 of a second – the fast shutter speed ensures that the seedheads aren't too bright.

Cleaning your camera

It's just so important to either get your camera cleaned once in a while or do it yourself. The sensor inside the camera can gather dust easily unless you're using a fixed-lens camera (where you never remove the lens) such as a bridge camera.

I use a dust blower weekly on my sensor (being careful not to touch any part of the camera with the blower). Some cameras have a dust removal vibrate setting that you can set to activate every time you turn off the camera. For more stubborn dust you may need to visit a local camera shop and have it removed professionally.

Dust inside your camera gives spots on your pictures – they are removable in Lightroom or Photoshop but it's a real pain, so it's best to clean your camera regularly to avoid this step. Further information about cleaning your camera sensor can be found online. Don't attempt it without knowing what you're doing as you can seriously damage your camera if you do it incorrectly. If you use your mobile phone for photography, make sure you wipe the lens at the back with a soft cloth regularly.

Flowers and plants to photograph in January

January is deepest winter but there is still botanical life to be found and colour to be seen, even on frosty and snowy days.

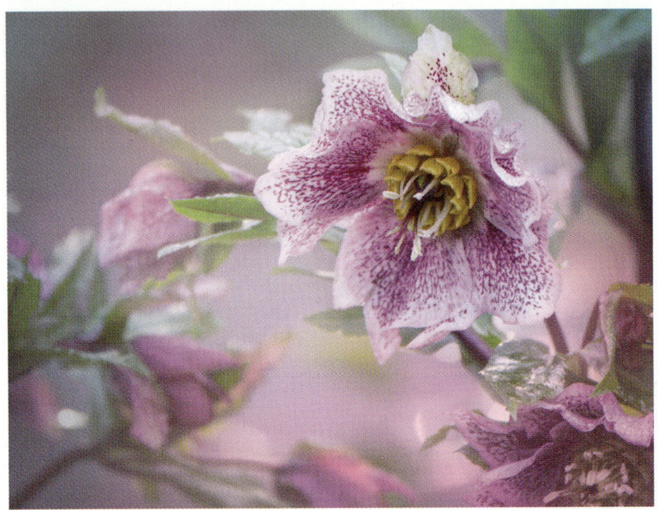

Helleborus – 1/60 sec at f/4, 220mm.

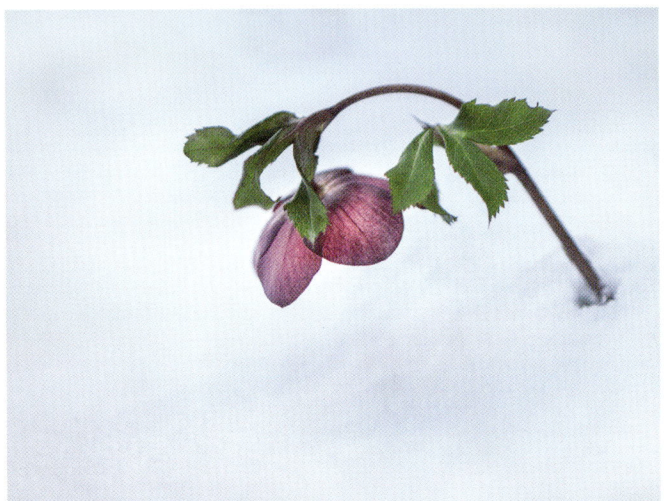

Helleborus in snow – 1/2000 sec at f/8, 55mm.

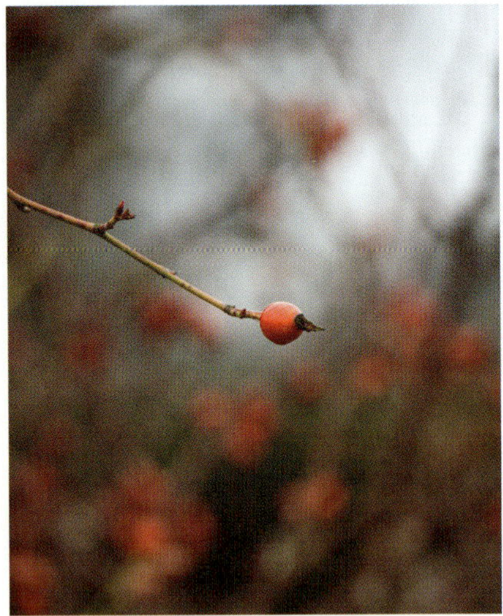

Rosehips (*Rosa*) – 1/400 sec at f/4, 200mm.

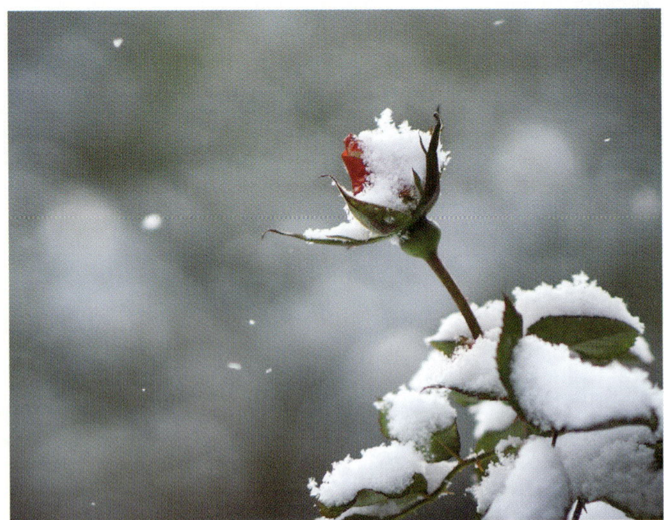

Rose in a snowstorm – 1/3200 sec at f/1.8, 55mm.

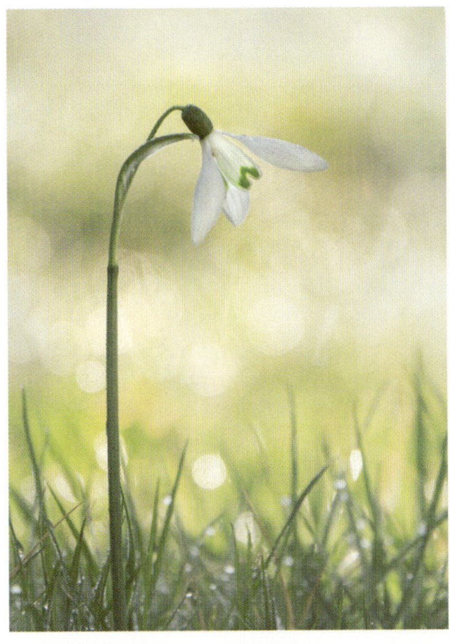

Galanthus nivalis (common snowdrop) – 1/400 sec at f/4, 200mm.

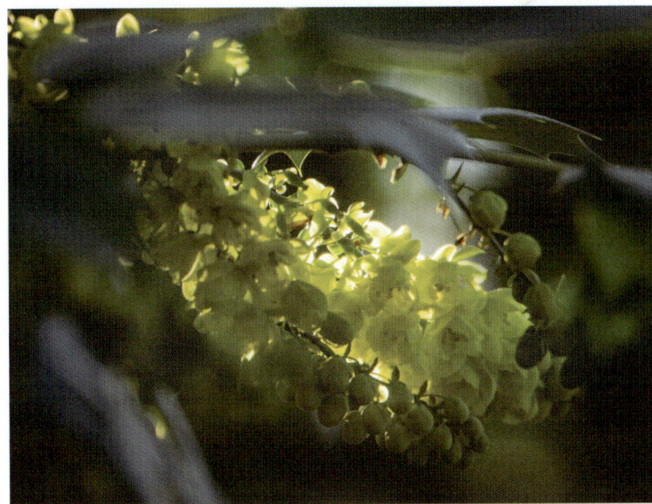

Mahonia – 1/400 sec at f/4, 220mm.

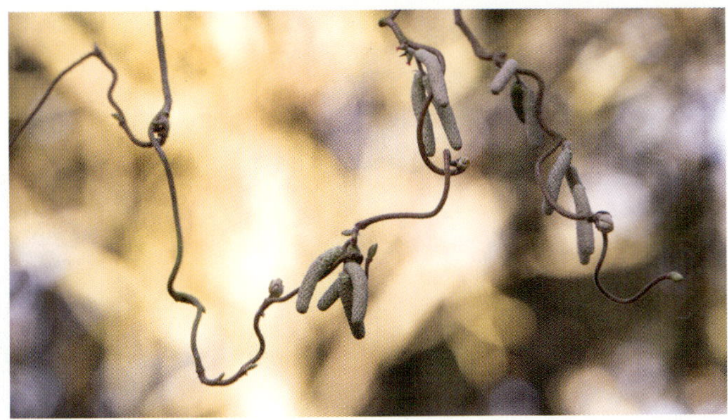

Corylus avellana 'Contorta' (hazel) – 1/500 sec at f/4, 90mm.

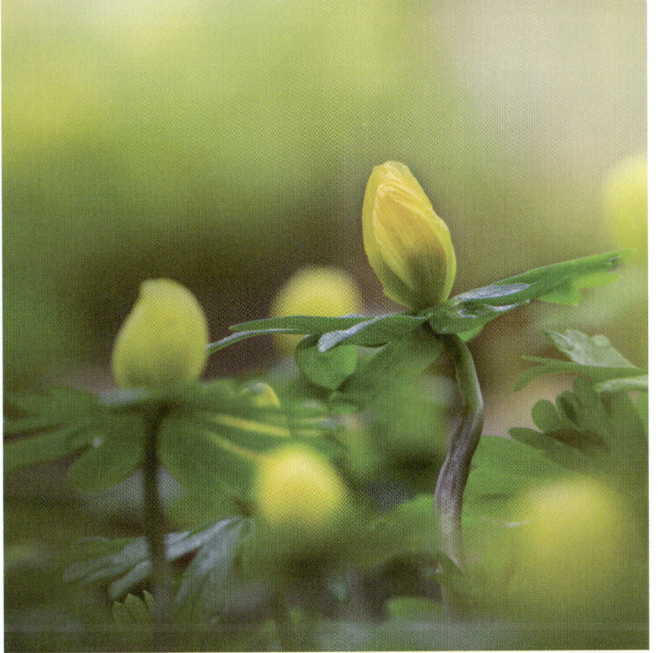

Eranthis hyemalis (aconites) – 1/200 sec at f/4, 155mm, overlay added in the edit.

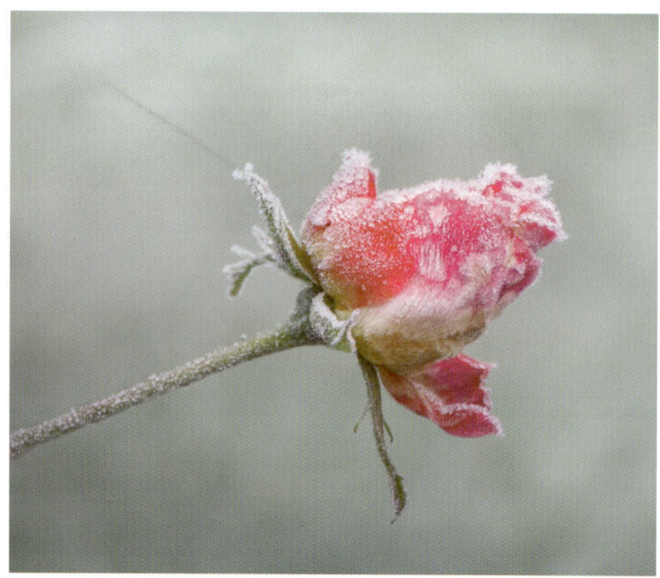

Rose after frost – 1/250 sec at f/4, 250mm, overlay added in the edit.

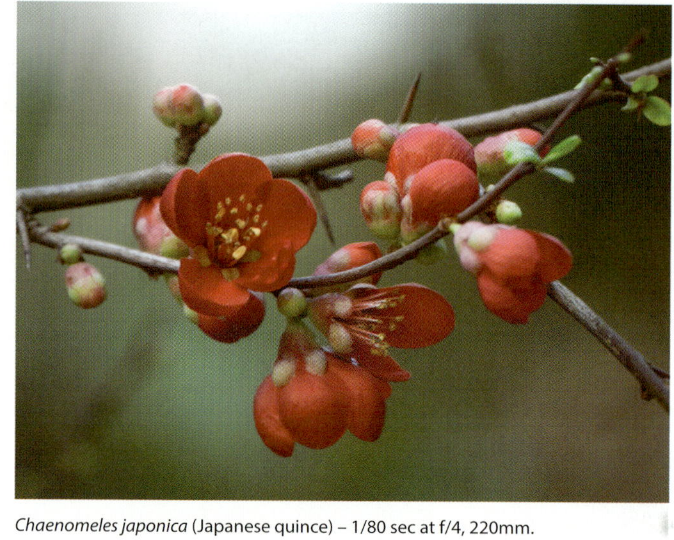

Chaenomeles japonica (Japanese quince) – 1/80 sec at f/4, 220mm.

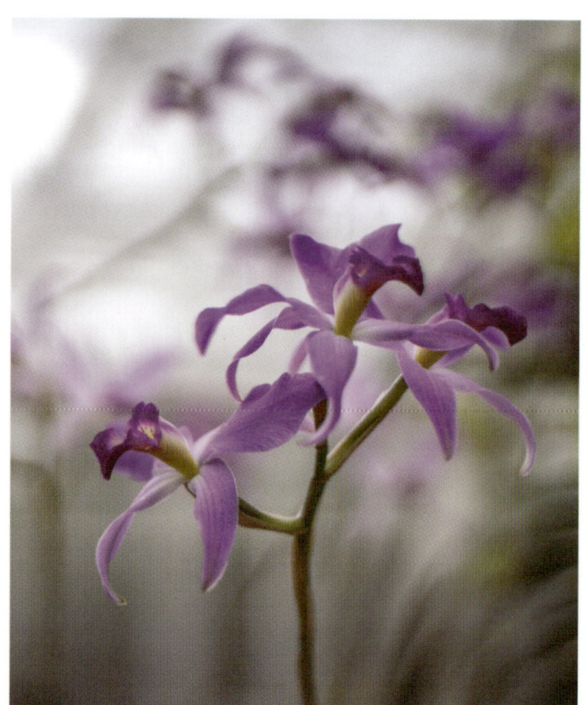

Laelia anceps in a glasshouse – 1/250 sec at f/1.7, 50mm vintage lens.

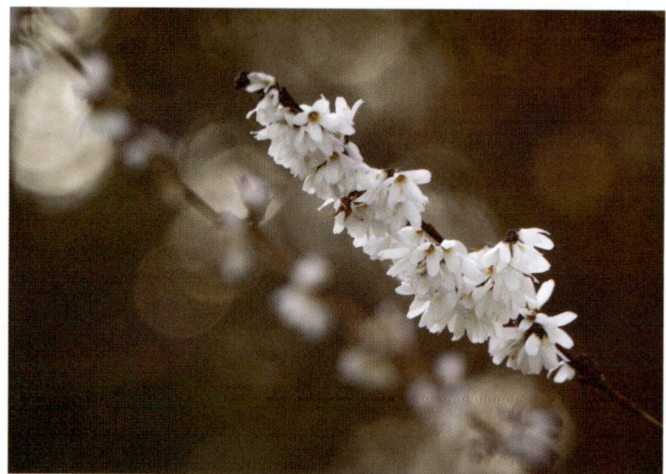

Abeliophyllum distichum – 1/200 sec at f/4, 135mm.

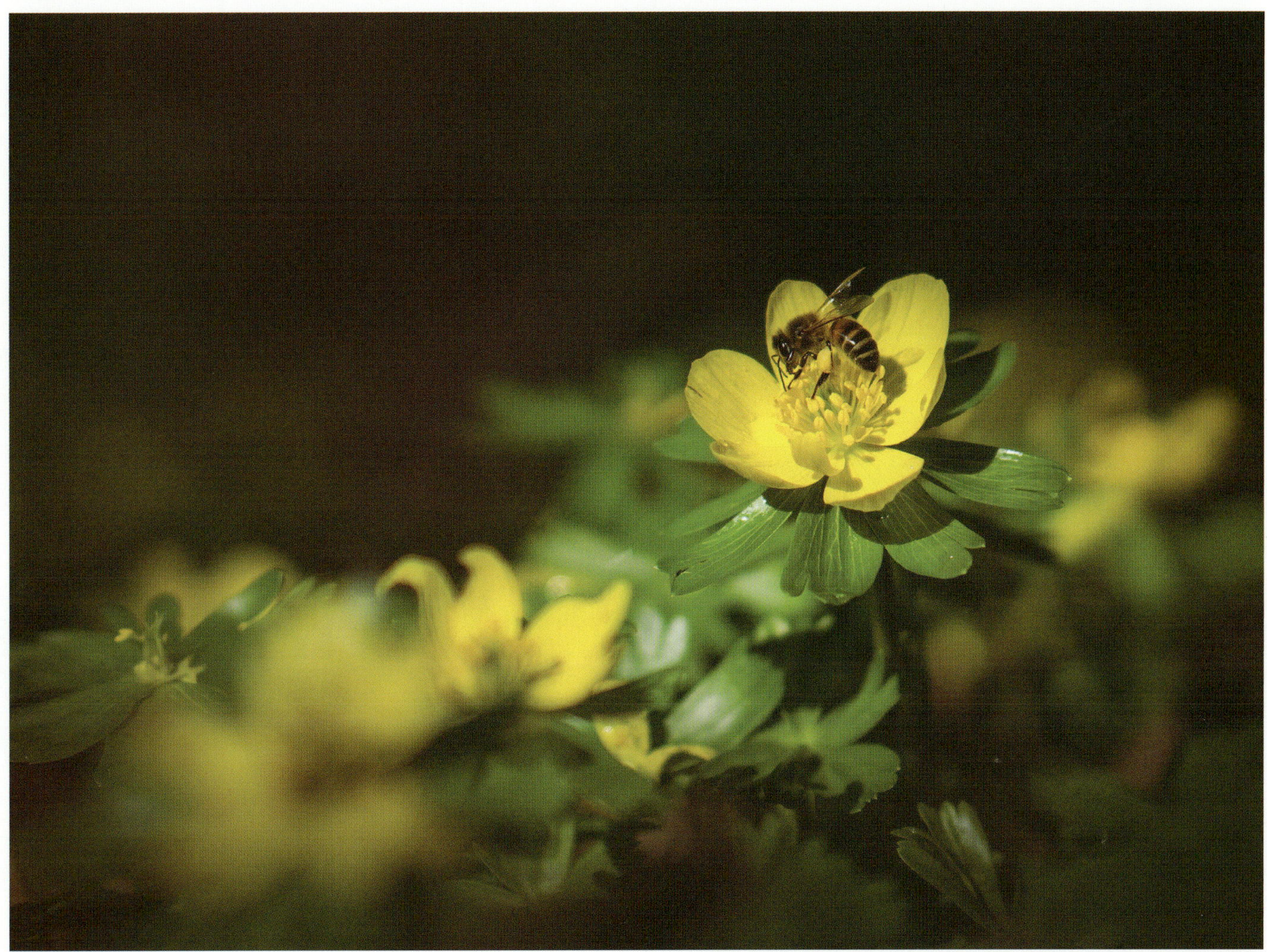

A honeybee on winter aconites, 1/4000 at f/2, 55mm lens.

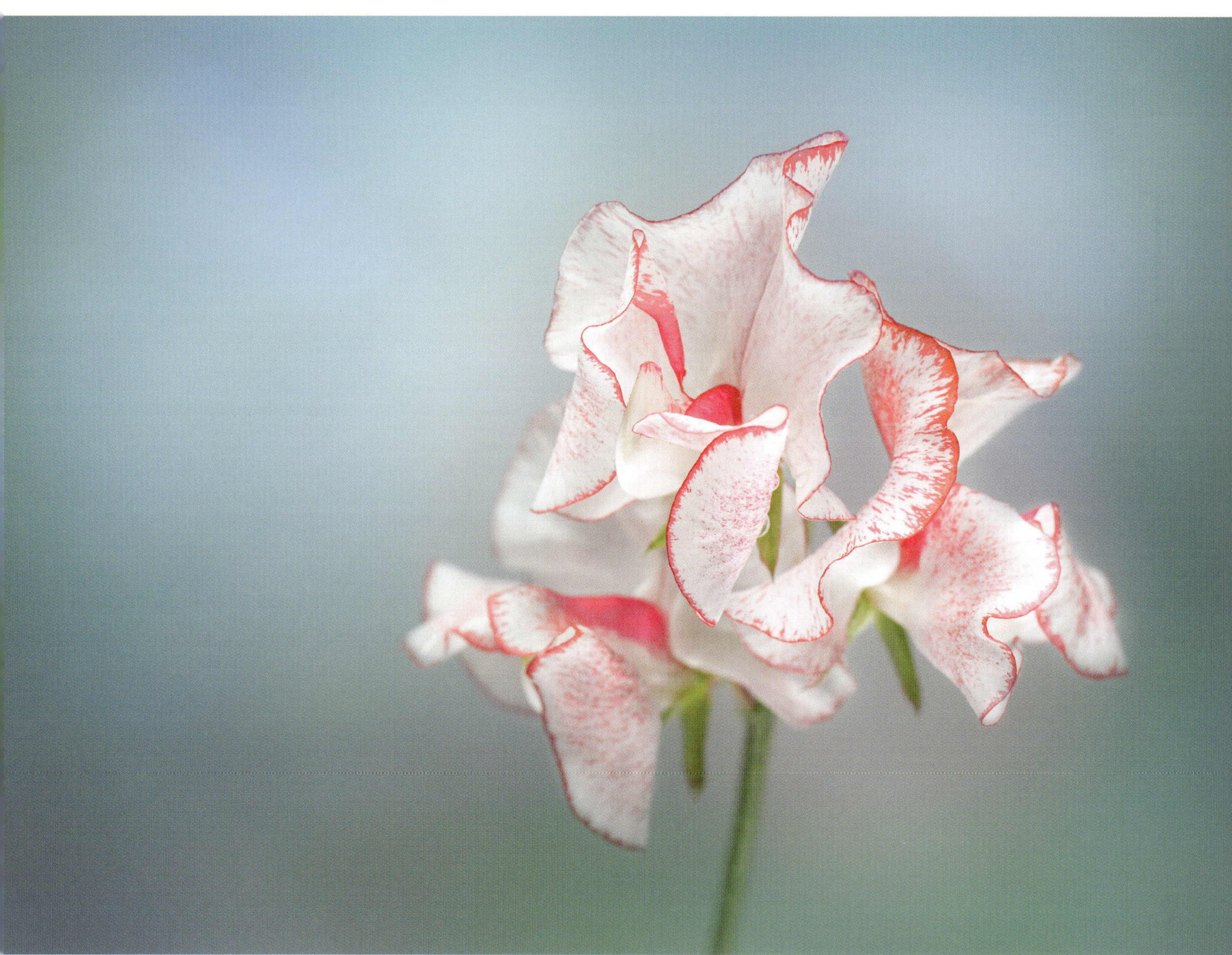

Lathyrus odoratus (sweet peas), photographed indoors with an overlay added in the edit.

CHAPTER 2

Composition

> A good photograph is knowing where to stand.
>
> ANSEL ADAMS

You could write a whole book devoted to just this topic, it's so important. I'm going to split this chapter into sections, discussing close-ups of flowers and plants and then trees and garden vistas.

CLOSE-UP COMPOSITIONS – FLOWERS AS FACES

I like to think of flowers as faces, and this helps me frame my composition considerably. Try to get the flower's 'face' – often the centre or best side of the flower – to be the focus of your photo. To do this you really need to walk around the flower (as much as is possible) and consider it from all angles – which position feels right to you? If you're photographing a small flower in its natural environment you'll often need to sit or even lie on the ground, so make sure you're not wearing your best clothes and perhaps take a padded mat or something else to kneel on. When viewing such a photo the eye is drawn to the sharpest part of the image, which you would normally want to be the centre of the flower, and for me, the stigma or anthers are usually the 'eyes' of the flower.

If no part of the flower is in focus it can be confusing, although occasionally (and more typically with groups of flowers) it can give an Impressionistic effect, which can work well.

Spend some time deciding on your best angle and don't forget to try out different viewpoints such as shooting from underneath or above. Non-photographers will almost always take a photo of a flower whilst standing above it, but getting lower, right down to the level of the flower, will give you more 'connection' with it, and thus the viewer of the photo will connect more too. For me, this is one of the most important things about flower photography – if you were photographing a person you wouldn't climb a ladder and look down on them, you'd (usually) take a photo at the same level as their face. You'll see photos in this book taken from different angles, but the viewpoint I try first is almost always this.

If at all possible, try to photograph flowers that are in good condition. Check them before you photograph them for stains, holes and other flaws as these will distract the eye more than anything else in the finished photograph. Brush off any small flecks of dust, cobwebs or dirt (I also use a soft paintbrush for this) and be careful not to damage the flower. Of course, if the photo is a quick snap for reference it doesn't really matter,

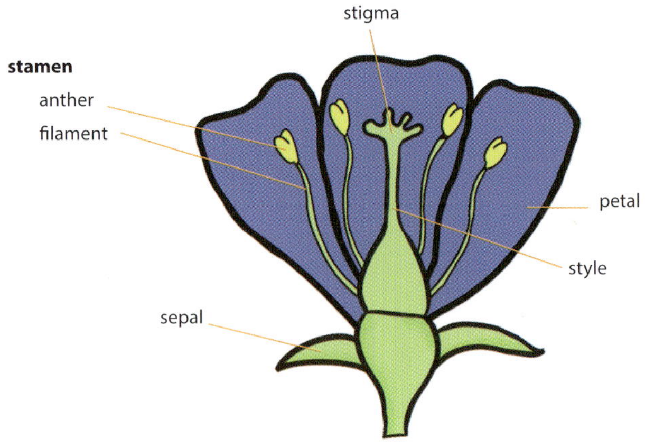

A botanical diagram of the parts of a flower.

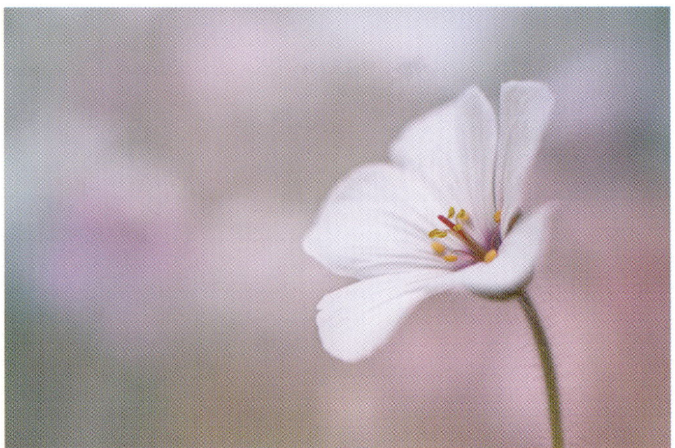

A pelargonium flower photographed at the level of the flower head. 1/500 sec at f/4, 220mm.

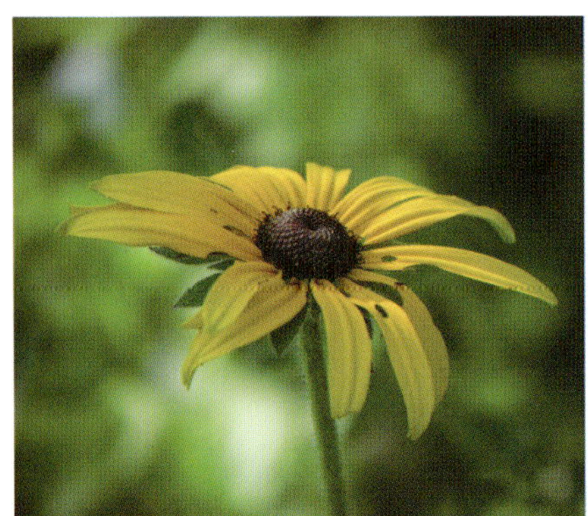

This rudbeckia flower is definitely past its best. Whilst I like the light in the background, the flower itself has holes, lots of pollen specks and even a small insect.

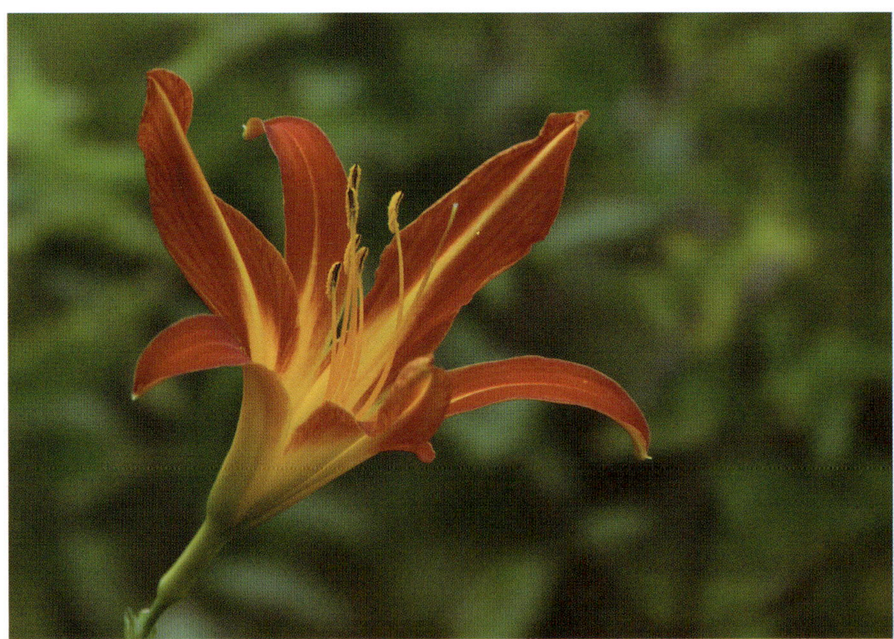

I didn't spot the spider's web coming from the bottom-right petal on this daylily until I viewed it later on the computer.

but if you are going to edit it and potentially print it or share with others do consider this, as the eye is immediately drawn to imperfections. Sometimes you won't notice a cobweb until you view the photo larger or on the computer which can be annoying, though fixable in most cases.

Sometimes there is no perfect flower in the clump of the flowers you wish to photograph, in which case I try to remove any imperfections when I edit (I explain how to do this in Chapter 11, 'Editing your Photographs'). This can be time-consuming, so if you find a good specimen to start with, all the better. Having said all this, I think it's often important to show nature in the raw, and not feel you need to process it too much. If a newly emerged bulb still has soil clinging to it, then that is part of the narrative of the flower's growth, and should be kept to tell the story. Imperfections can sometimes lend charm to an image.

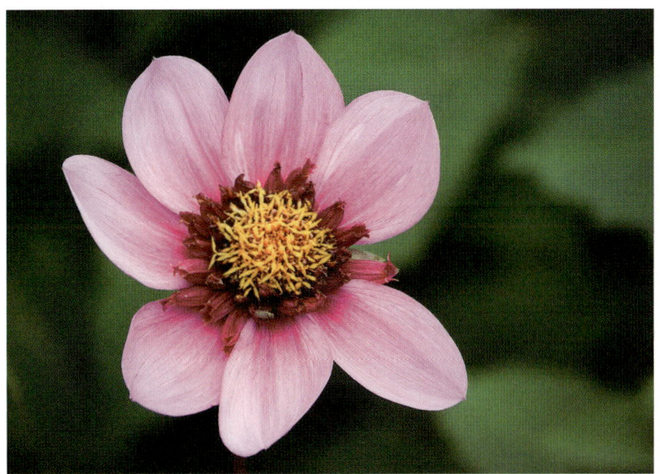

I have almost filled the frame with this dahlia and because of this, it has immediate impact.

Filling the frame

The most common 'mistake' that beginner photographers make when wanting a flower to be the main focus of a photo is not putting enough of the flower in the frame. Put another way, they include too much of its surroundings. The leaves of the flower that you are photographing are often useful and add to the composition, but the eye should not be distracted by nearby bushes or other things in the background if this is a 'close-up' photo. However, make sure to leave enough space around the flower for it to breathe and don't go so close that you accidentally crop off part of a petal, unless this is a deliberate choice.

Of course a flower's surroundings are often beautiful especially if there is good light, in which case you can include more of them. I will discuss this in the section on garden vistas further on in this chapter.

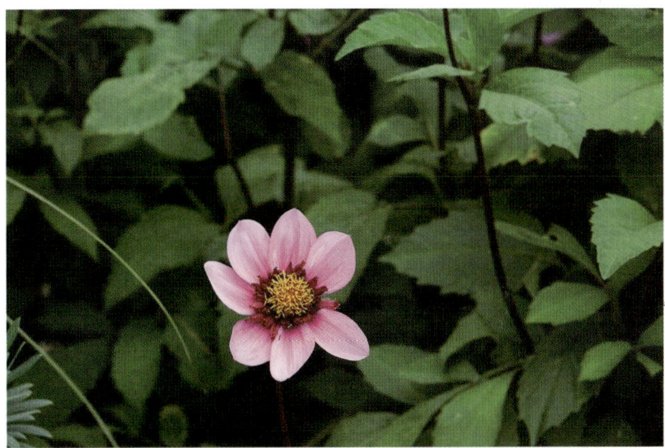

This photo of the same dahlia has been taken from further away and lacks the impact of the close-up version. Our eye is distracted by the grass on the left and the strong dark stems of other dahlias.

The rule of thirds

The 'rule of thirds' is a compositional device used by many photographers to get the viewer's eye to 'travel' into the photograph; sometimes if you put the subject of the photo bang in the middle the eye's journey is short and has nowhere to go. A grid is created by dividing a photo equally into nine rectangles (or squares) with two horizontal and two vertical lines – usually one would just visualize this but both cameras and editing software have the option to bring up an actual grid on the image.

By putting the focus of the photo on one of the thirds the composition often works better than when the subject is in the middle (although don't forget that rules are sometimes made to be broken – *see* Chapter 12, 'How to Move Forward').

If you haven't taken your photograph using the rule of thirds then don't forget that you can create this crop when post-processing the image, even on a mobile phone. Just leave a reasonable amount of space around the flower, as the crop will feel too 'tight' otherwise. Most editing software will be able to give you a grid of thirds when you choose the 'crop' option to help with the positioning. The rule of thirds is of course not the only option and later I will discuss other compositions, such as placing the subject more centrally.

A grid with lines placed on the third and two-thirds.

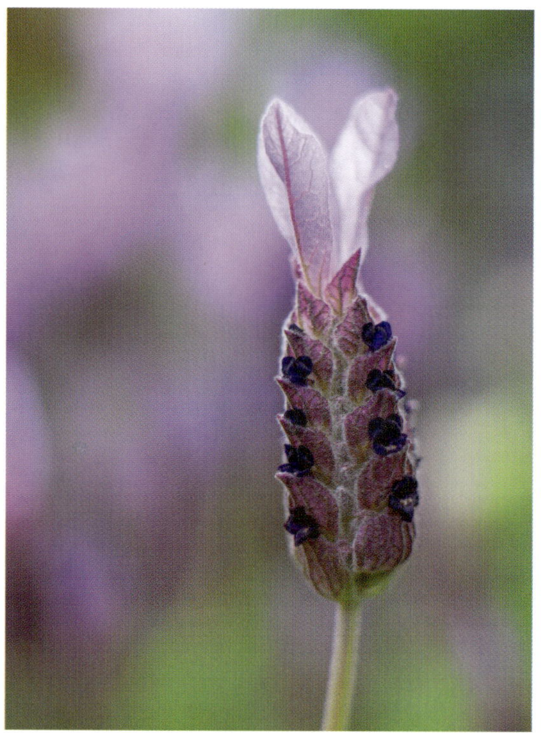

This *Lavandula stoechas* flower is placed on the right-hand third in portrait (rather than landscape) ratio. This works well as it echoes the shape of the flower, which is tall and slender.

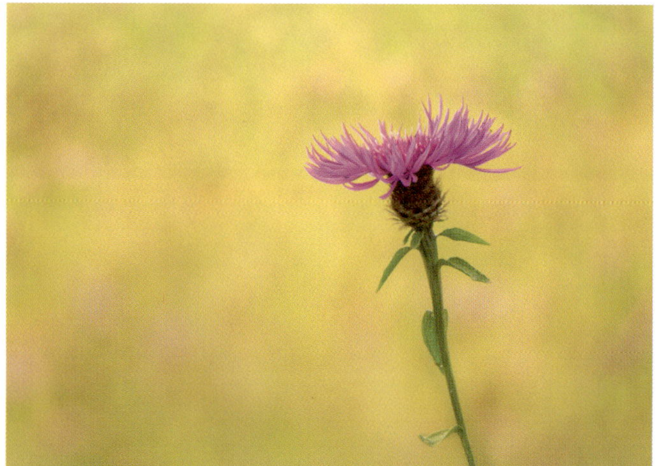

Imagine that this photo has a grid of thirds overlaid on top of it; the flower stem is on the right vertical third and the flower itself is on the top-right third (both horizontally and vertically).

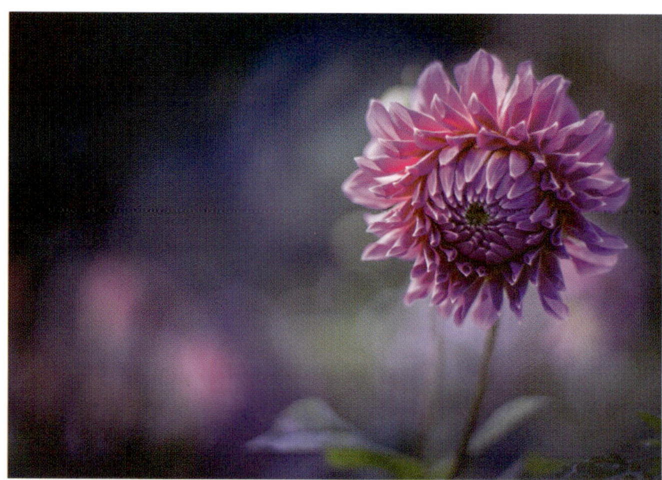

This dahlia is positioned on the right-hand third in landscape ratio. Notice how it leans into the frame slightly – if it were 'looking' in the other direction I would have positioned it on the left-hand third.

Sun-seeking flowers

Many flowers look towards the sun with their centres tipped slightly upwards. Try to get level with their 'faces' or slightly above in terms of where you sit or stand to take the picture. Then place the focal point of your flower, which is normally the middle of the flower (unless it's a really close-in macro shot) on a vertical third with the flower leaning into the photo. If the flower is upright, it will also work well to have its middle more towards the centre of the photo, especially if the stem comes in from the bottom-left third.

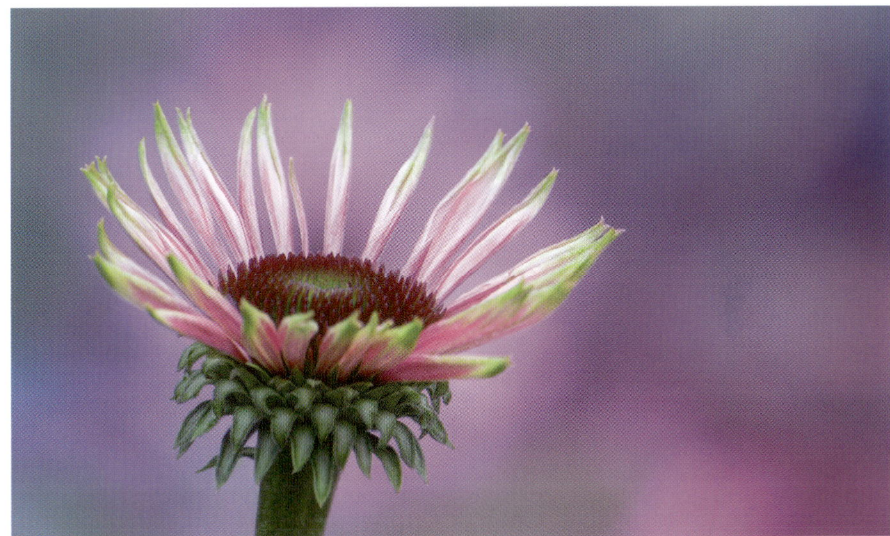

When I photographed this echinacea flower, I positioned myself at a point where I could see both the centre of the flower and its petals 'exploding' to the sky. It is on the left-hand third and leans to the right, into the photo.

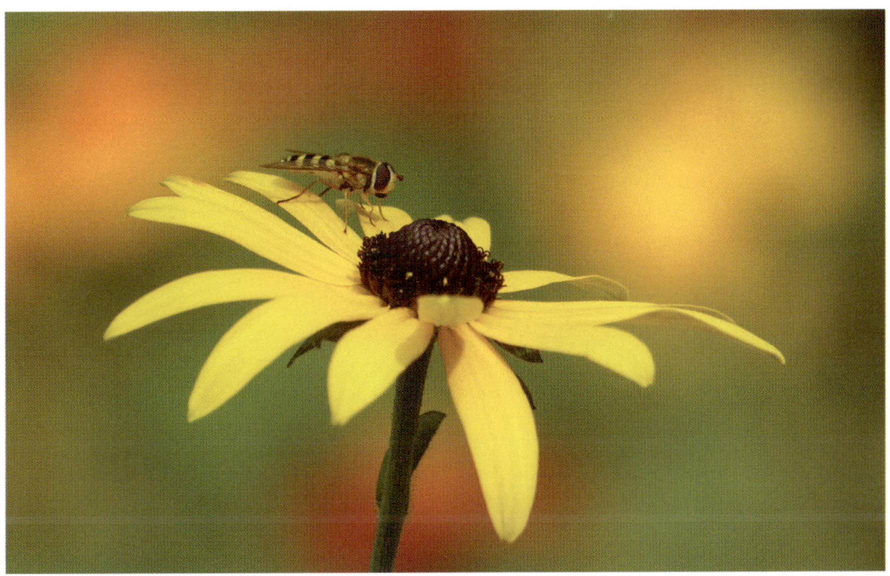

This rudbeckia leans into the photo slightly but the flower works well in the centre of the frame because of its elongated petals. The hoverfly also 'looks' into the photo and adds balance, and I waited for it to turn around before I took the photo.

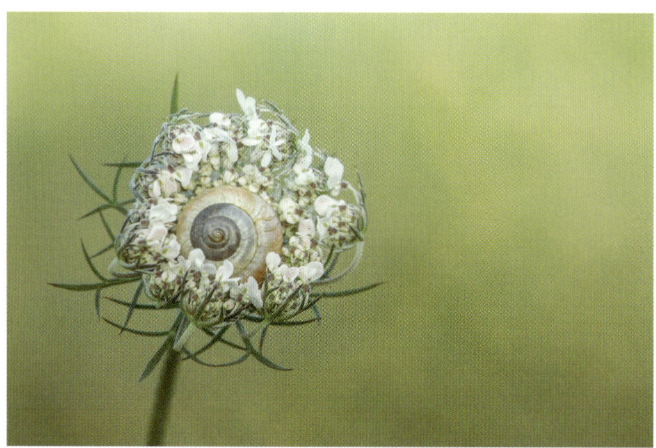

A snail, in its bed of *Daucus carota* (wild carrot), with negative space to the right giving context to the photo.

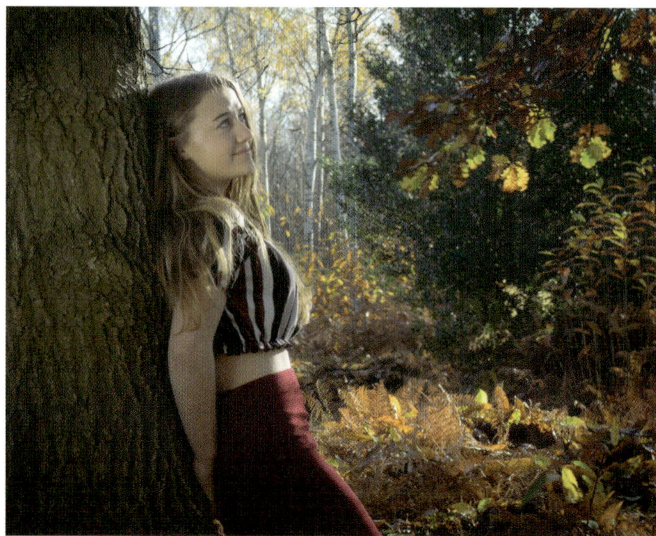

Hermione looks into her woodland surroundings and is positioned on the left third.

Negative space

The phrase 'negative space' is used to describe the area in the photo not occupied by your subject and it's good to have a little of this (or sometimes even a lot!) as it lets your subject 'breathe' a little and gives balance to a photo. Too much though and the flower will get lost in the frame.

Have the flower 'look' into the empty space, just as you would try to do if you were a portrait photographer and your subject was looking into their surroundings. Considering flower photography as being very similar to portrait photography will often really help with your composition and positioning of the flower in the frame.

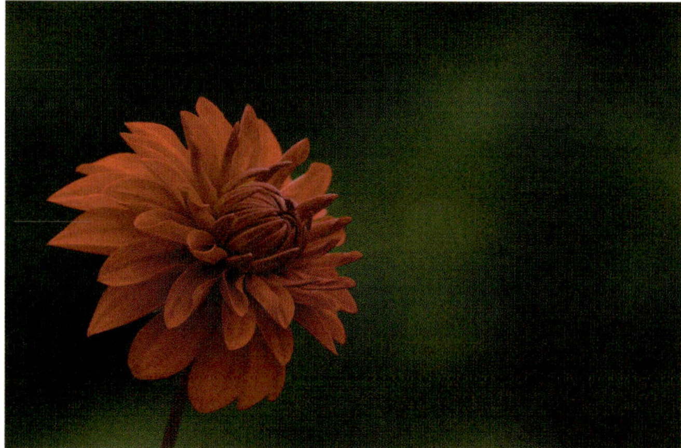

This red dahlia is also on the left-hand third and looking into the negative space.

Shy flowers

'Shy' flowers have nodding heads that droop and hang down. Whilst these flowers also look good photographed 'straight on', it's interesting to try to get underneath them if possible. Fritillaries, snowdrops and some bluebells can work really well this way. As they are slender, often with long stems, they tend to work better with a 'portrait' format.

If you are photographing in a woodland area and need to sit or lie on the ground to take the photo, please be extremely careful not to damage any flowers or foliage as some, especially bluebells, take many years to recover.

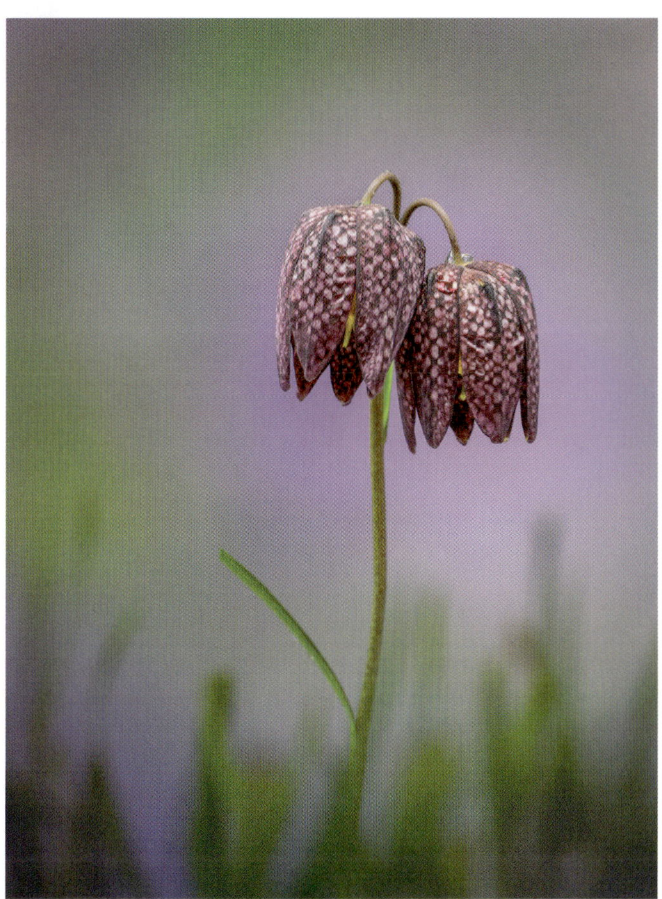

Fritillaria meleagris (snake's-head fritillaries) amongst long grass.

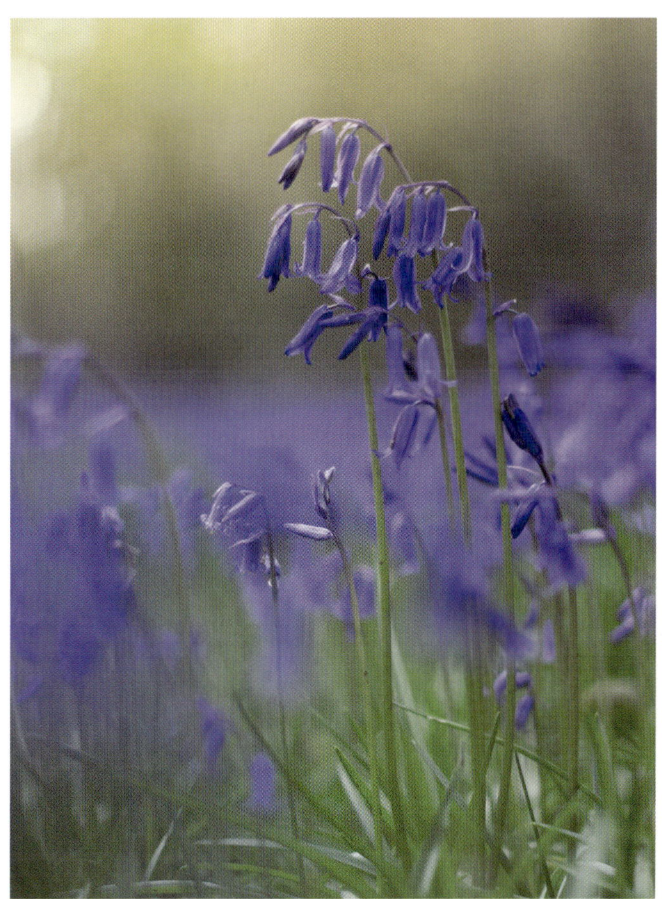

Hyacinthoides non-scripta (the native English bluebell) grows both in woodland and public gardens about an hour from my home; I have an annual pilgrimage to photograph them each year. I was lying on the ground when taking this photo.

Geometrical flowers

These are flowers that often have flattish 'faces' and can be photographed directly from above to take advantage of the intricate detail and geometrical patterns – usually very close up, and often with a macro lens. In this case the whole photo might just consist of a cropped-in flower face, exploiting its detail to the full. Even though they are not that flat, roses can work well this way, as can some daisies and osteospermum.

Every so often you'll notice a pattern that gives a really striking composition, and this will bring a whole new level of interest to your photograph – you can read about pattern within flower shapes and petals later on in the book. Flowers and plants with good geometrical patterns can often lend themselves well to monochrome. You can try this out when you edit the photo (*see* the section on black and white photography in Chapter 9, 'Colour and Pattern').

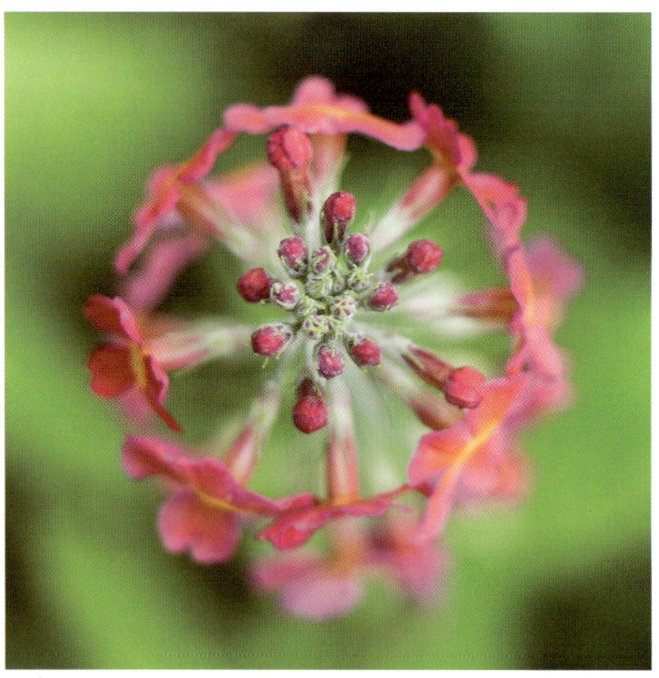

A primula shot from above to capture its 'explosion' and symmetry.

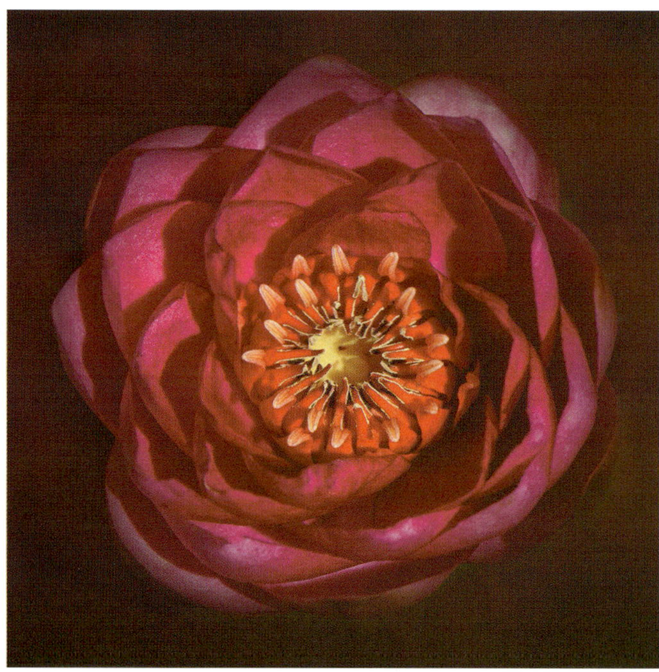

A water lily flower taken from directly above to exploit the beautiful patterns of its centre and petals.

A black and white conversion enhances the shapes of these sempervivums.

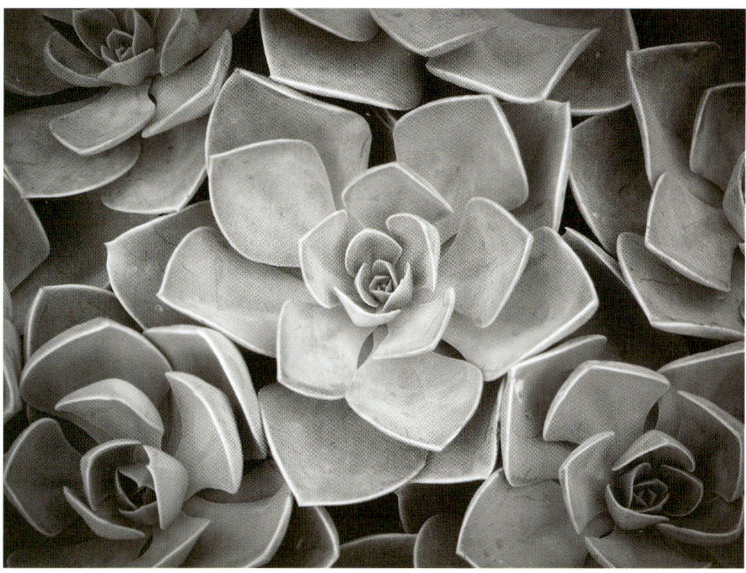

Background mirroring

Background mirroring is my term for the situation where you have a similar, but more out-of-focus flower than your subject in the background – it can work very well as a compositional trick but it's not often that you'll find flowers in a position that lends itself to this, so always study your backgrounds as carefully as your potential subjects.

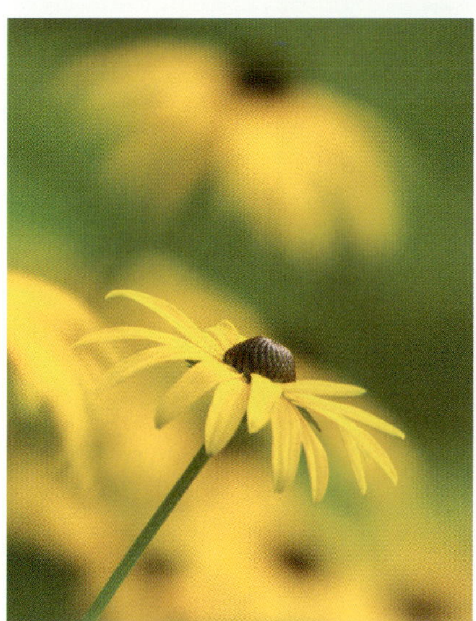

Two *Rudbeckias*, the one furthest away and out of focus mirrors the position of the one in the foreground.

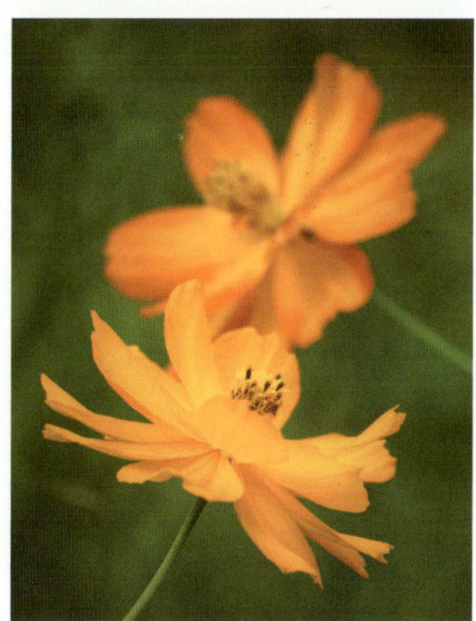

I found these *Cosmos polidor* at opposing angles to each other and darkened the one at the back slightly in the edit to throw the viewer's attention onto the one in focus at the front.

CROPPING – THE EASIEST WAY TO EDIT AND IMPROVE A PHOTO

The easiest way to make the biggest impact with a photograph, particularly one with a close-up subject, is to think about the crop. I don't just mean cropping slightly in on each side but actually changing the entire aspect ratio of the photo. There are so many different possibilities and ratios here, other than just the more obvious portrait and landscape rectangles. If you have a recent version of Photoshop it can actually crop *outwards* for you by filling the space outside the photo with a 'content awareness fill', thus 'faking' the background. This is very useful if you find, for example, that you need a little more stalk. Do this in the same way as you would for a normal crop but make sure that the 'content aware' box is ticked at the top, and then click the large tick to the right of it.

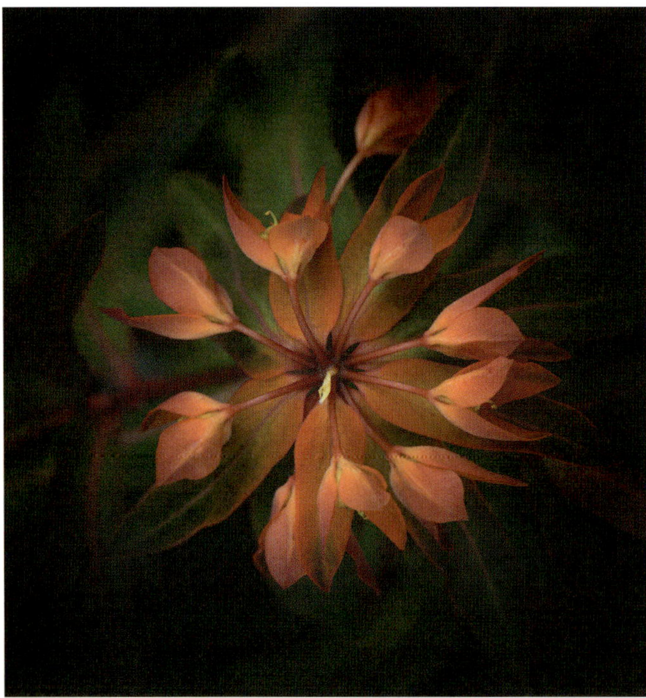

The square-ish shape of this *Euphorbia griffithii* flower is echoed in the square crop of the photo.

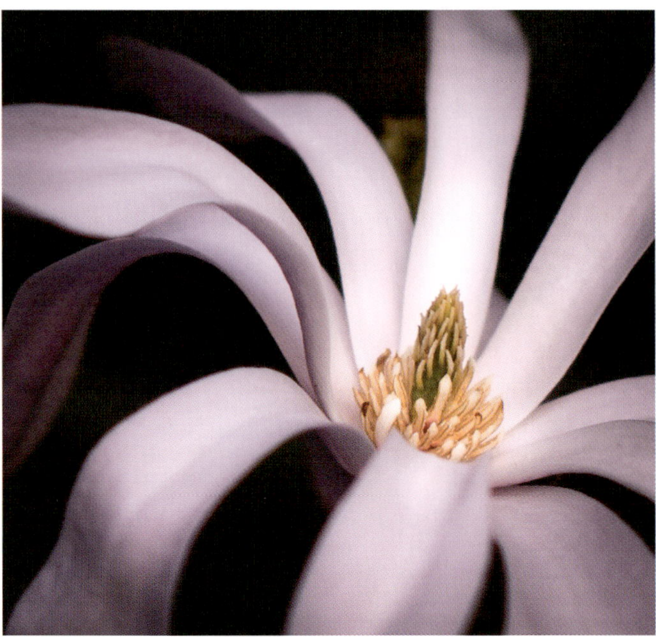

With this square crop I've placed the centre of the magnolia flower on the right third to lead the eye via the left-hand side petals into the image. The hard crop is softened with a slight vignette.

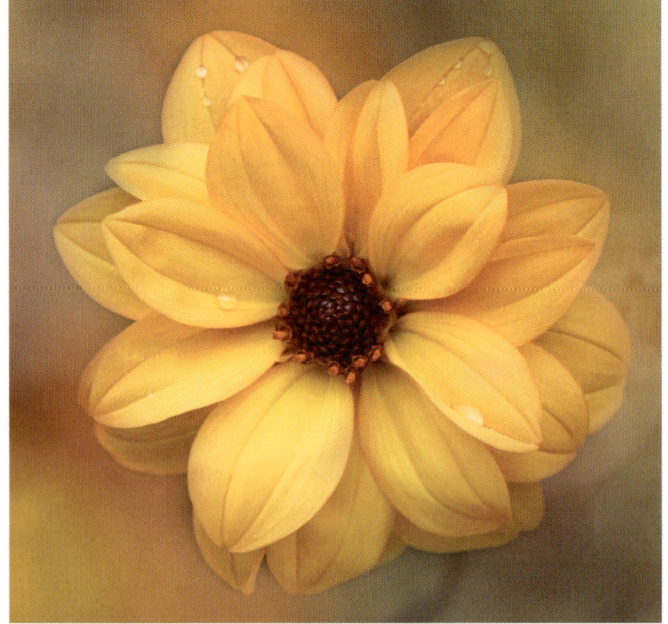

There was bare soil below this dahlia, so I added an overlay in the edit that I thought complemented the flower better without being a distraction.

Square crop

Some flowers work better with a square crop (done either in-camera or at the editing stage) than a more conventional rectangular one. Often this works for flowers shot directly from above, or more circular flowers, but sometimes the flower itself seems to have more of a square shape and a square crop will emphasize this nicely.

When you crop, always try to leave some breathing room around the flower or subject. If you need to print it at any point to specific measurements and it's too tightly cropped, you may lose some of the flower. If you want to crop right in so that parts of the petals are outside of the image, cropping hard on one or two sides usually works better than just clipping the tips of the petals off.

Roses often work well as square crops as their petals can often reveal square shapes within. It can be an interesting experiment to shoot the same flower over a period of days to observe how its natural shape changes and evolves; often the colours change too.

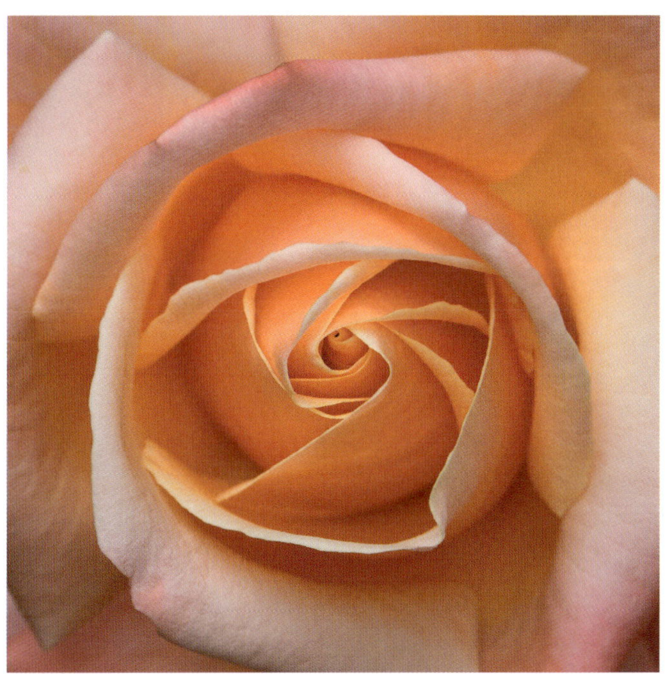

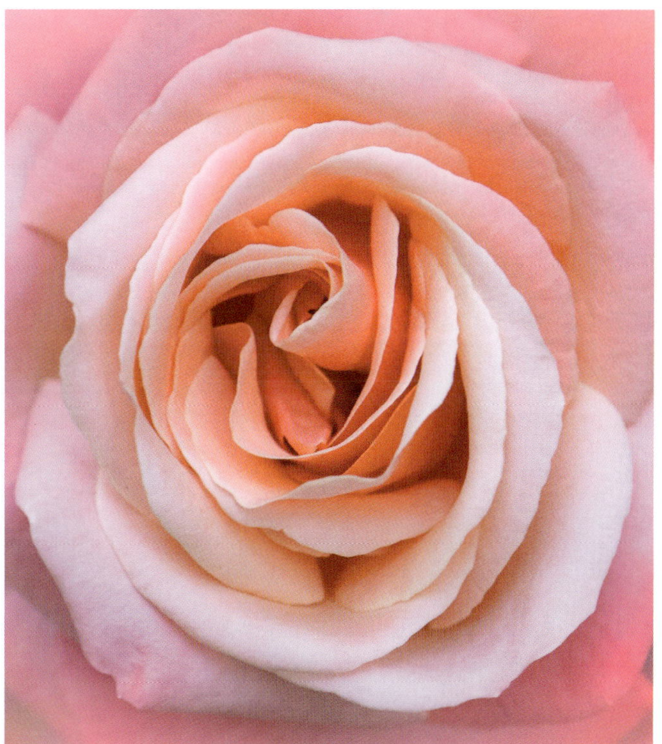

These two pictures feature the same rose in my garden and are taken with the same camera and settings outdoors just twelve hours apart. The colour is totally different: the first has the ambient light of sunset; the second is lit by diffused early morning light. It's also opened up considerably in just a short space of time.

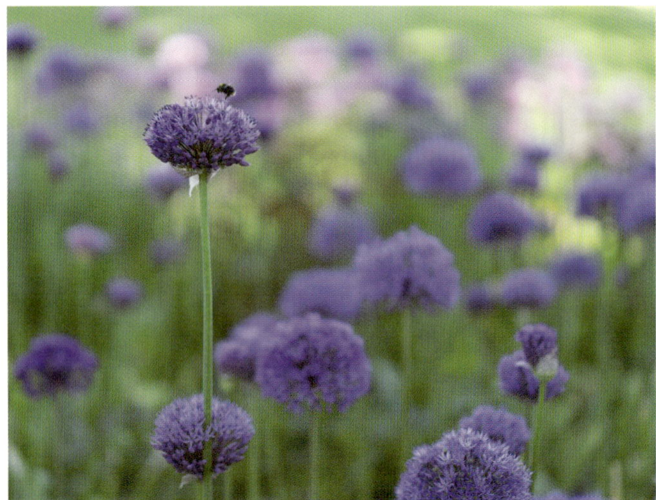

When I found this bed of alliums, I positioned the tallest one on the left-hand third and made sure that the focus was on this flower. The bee then came along and chose the very same flower – a happy accident!

Both Lightroom and Photoshop have alternative crop suggestions, and it can be really interesting to play with these crop and compositional ideas as your photography develops.

There are some more cropping suggestions in the final chapter.

PLANTS IN SMALL GROUPS

Usually I would treat this type of composition in a similar way to single flowers. Work out where you want the eye to focus and have that as your focal point, probably on one of the thirds. Groups of flowers will often have one flower that stands slightly taller than the others and I would use this flower as my subject and focal point.

Another approach would be to have the larger flowers near you, allowing the perspective to help your eye travel through the picture from the foreground to the background where the flowers are smaller.

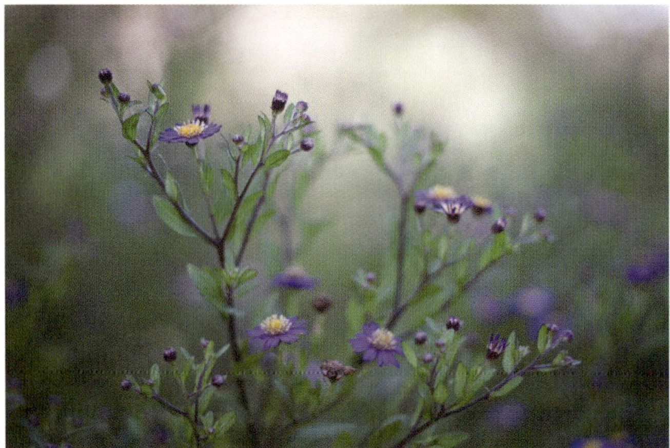

This photo of a group of asters has a shallow depth of field – only a few flowers are in focus on the left-hand third but the light in the background really glows as a result and helps the eye travel through the photo.

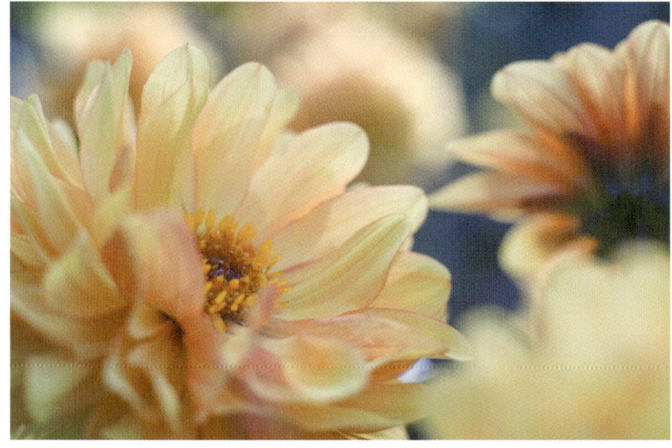

Another example of throwing the background flowers out of focus with a low aperture – here there is only focus on the centre of the left dahlia flower, but the others surrounding it give context to the photo.

LEAVES AND FOLIAGE

Some leaves are beautiful and are mini worlds of colour and structure in their own right, especially in the autumn. A nice way of photographing a leaf close up is to tape it to a glass window so that the light outside lights the leaf for you – then get in close and fill the whole frame with the leaf pattern – avoiding the sticky tape, or cropping it out in the edit.

Always keep an eye out for leaf colour – it's often more vivid when photographed at sunrise or sunset and in early spring or autumn.

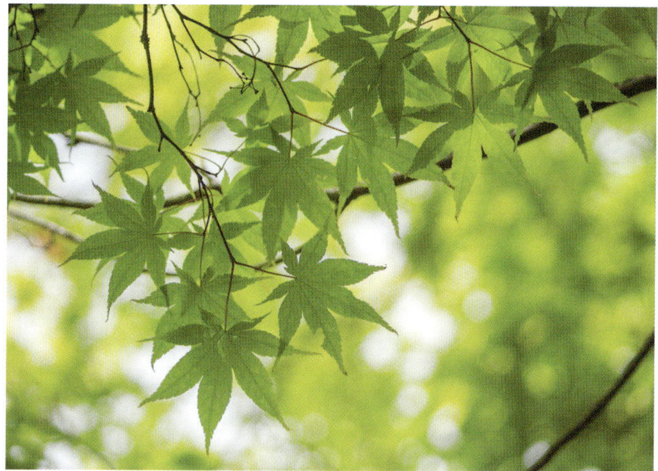

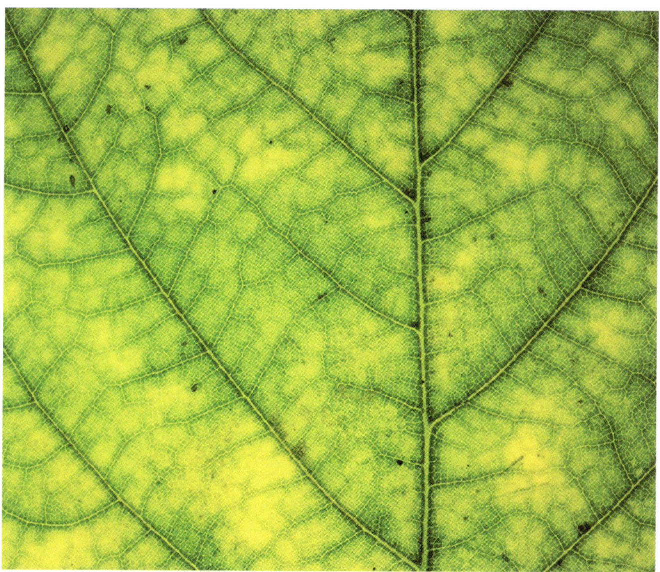

Backlit leaves show the intricate detail of veins and capillaries and work very well as macro subjects. The result can often be quite abstract.

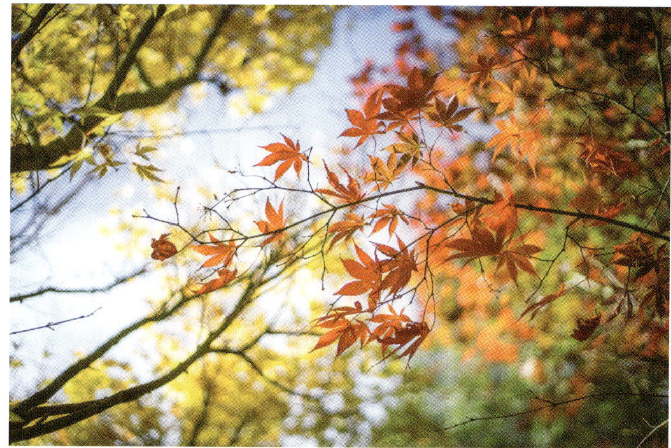

Acer japonicum leaves have stunning colours in spring and autumn and are always worth seeking out – if you photograph directly upwards you'll be able to backlight them with sunlight so that they glow.

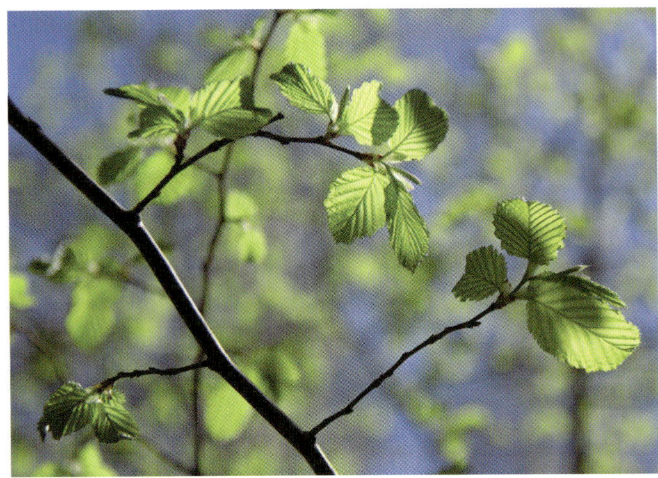

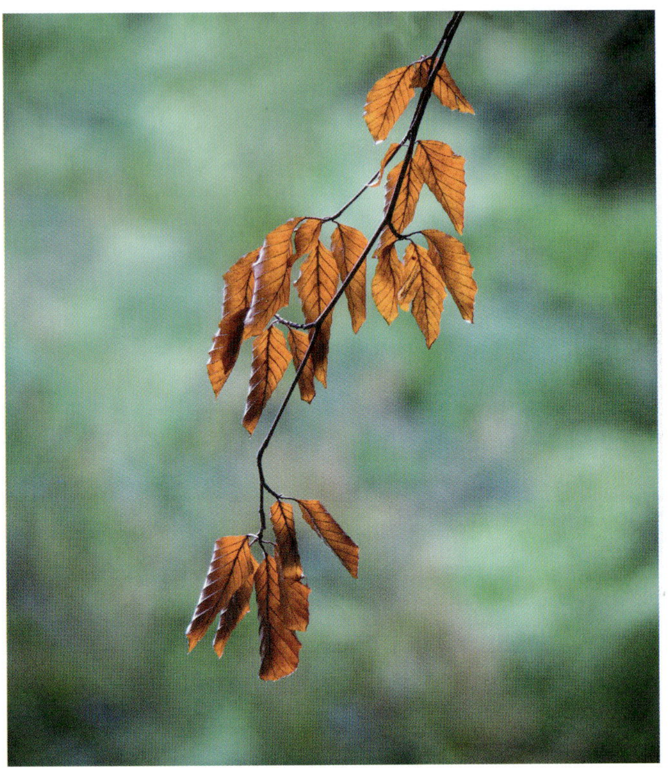

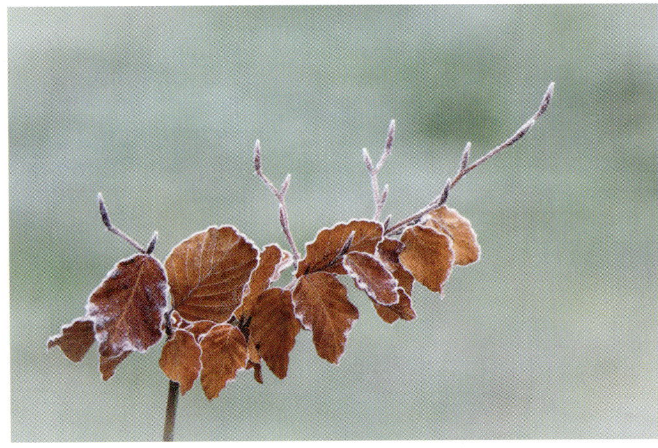

Fagus sylvatica (beech tree) leaves in spring, autumn and winter – these leaves can be beautiful all year round.

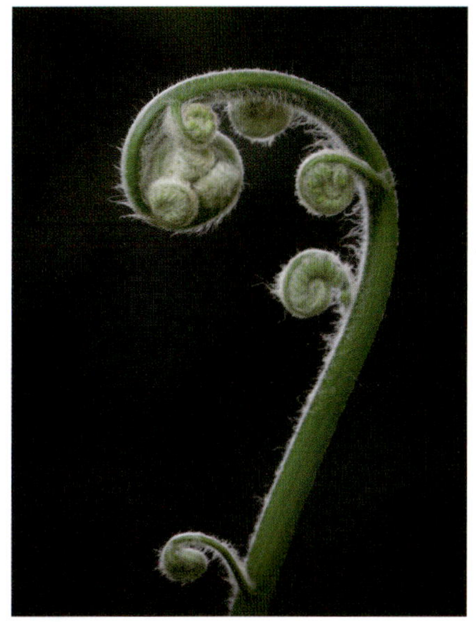
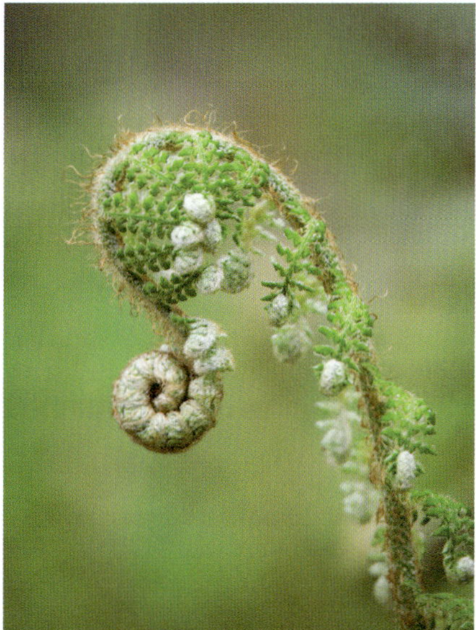
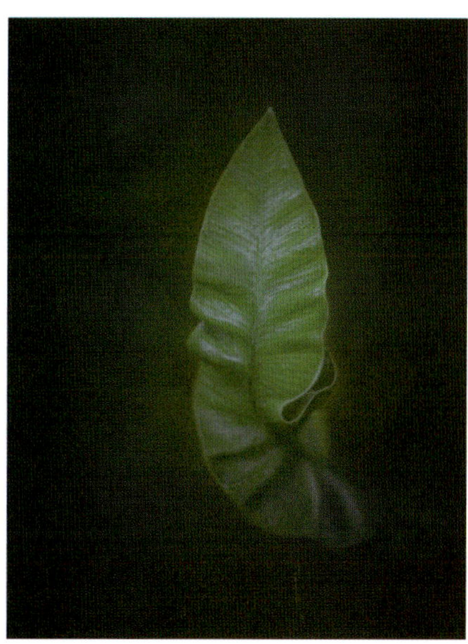

The beautiful spirals and shapes of ferns often work best when there are no other distractions in the photo, just the clean lines of the subject.

Some plants, such as ferns, can have beautiful curls and spirals – spend some time observing and working out the best possible angle to get the most from the pattern and then get in as close as you can. Look for them in spring and especially in glasshouses.

BLOSSOM

There are so many varieties of blossoms to find in spring, it's probably possible to find a new variety every day. Don't restrict yourself to gardens, as blossom is also to be found in our hedgerows. Many ancient and regional names still prevail; hawthorn blossom is commonly nicknamed 'May' in the UK as it emerges around the beginning of May.

The many varieties of *Prunus* (cherry blossom) and *Malus* (apple) prevail in spring and it's no surprise that they're a favourite subject of photographers. Experiment with close-up shots but also compositions with sections of branches and even whole trees. A wide aperture will blur out the background for a softer look.

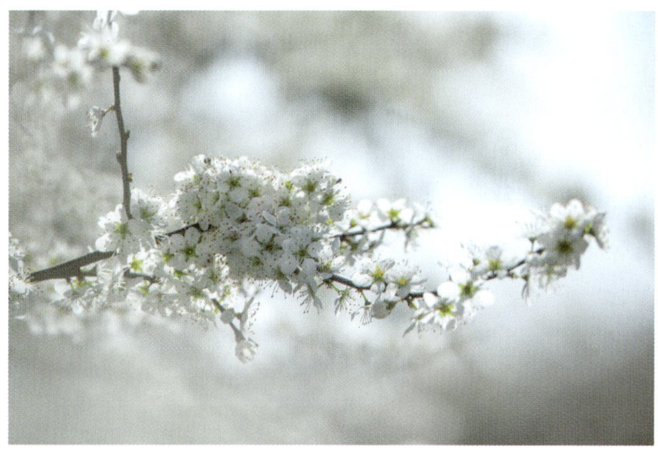

I photographed this blossom branch through more blossom in the foreground which is a technique called 'shooting through' that I explain further in a later chapter. It can give a very ethereal look, especially with light-coloured flowers.

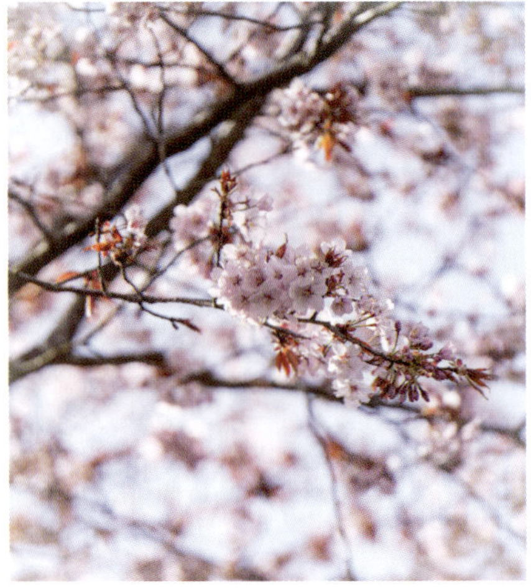

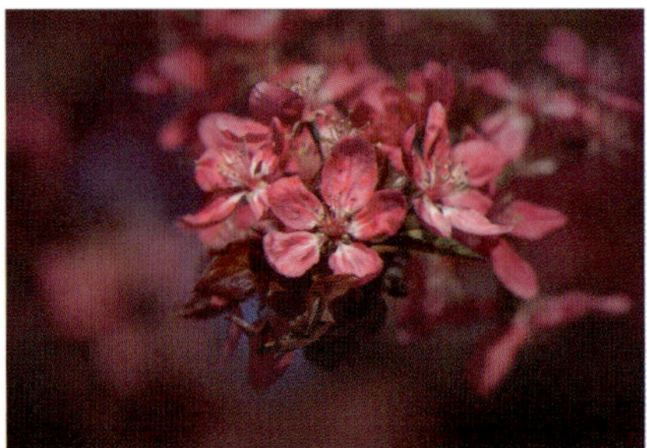

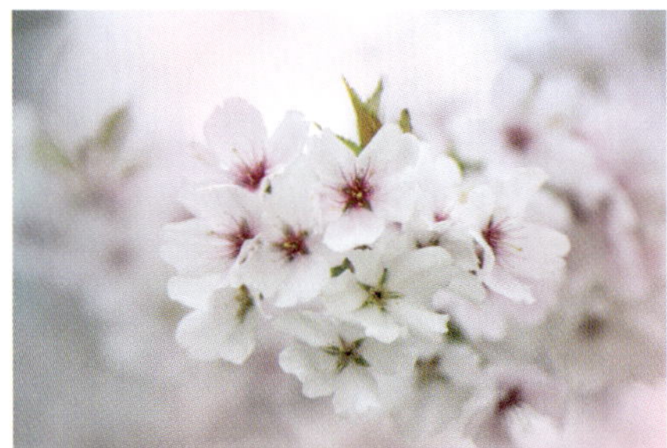

Rich-red malus blossoms (centre) between two pale pink flowering cherries.

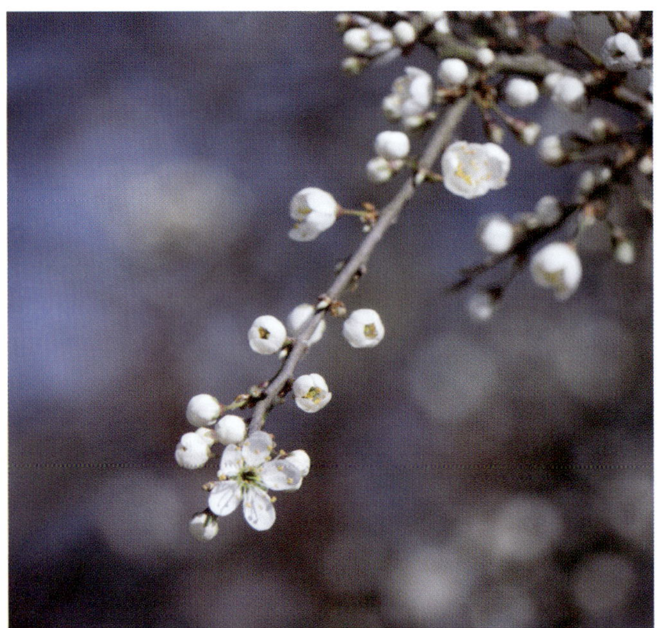

Apple blossom in sunlight, with out-of-focus circles of blossom behind.

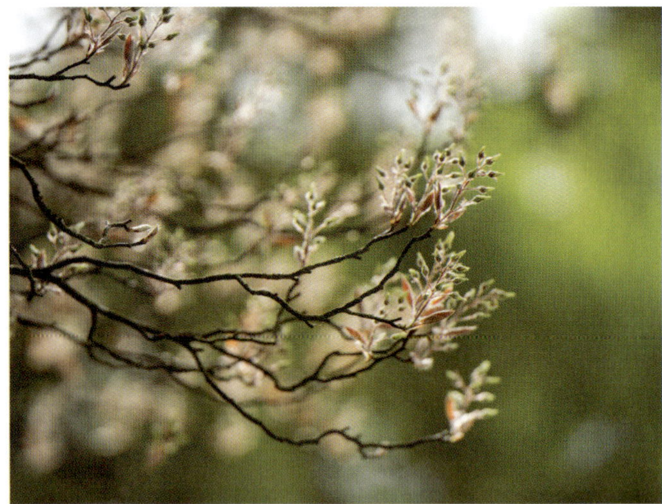

Amelanchier blossoms are backlit by the sun.

All blossoms can be photogenic but also lend themselves well to different styles; dark backgrounds contrast very well and give just as much interest as light-coloured ones. Observe from different viewpoints, looking for background colour and interesting shapes created by branches. As the sun is often low in early spring you can sometimes use it to back-light the blossom and make it glow.

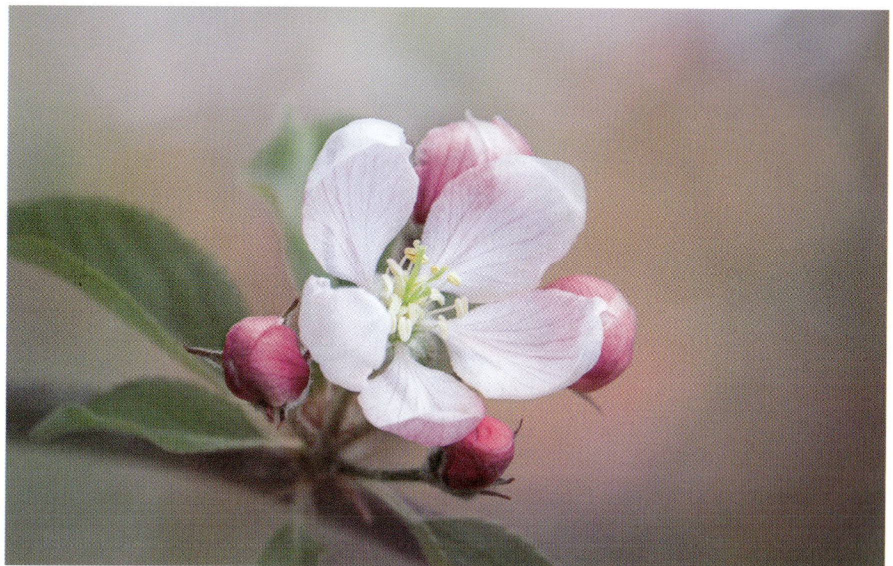

Don't forget that blossoms can work well close up or even macro – you can treat individual flowers as you would any other close-up flower subject.

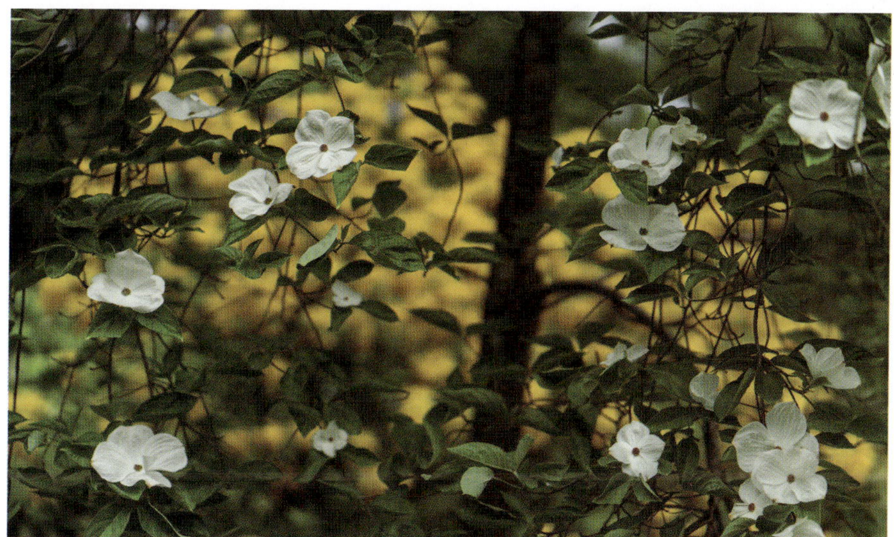

Some trees and shrubs have large flowers rather than many-petalled blossoms and these can be striking. With this cornus (dogwood) tree I found a position where I could use the yellow rhododendrons behind as a striking background.

TREES

It's often hard to use a whole tree for your image unless it features as part of a landscape or it's a small variety, such as a bonsai tree. However, if the tree isn't too large it's usually possible to create a good composition using branches as the main points of structure and leaves as decorative interest. Just as when photographing flowers and blossoms, try to walk around the tree to find the best composition. Look at how the branches interact, where the light is and how the colour of the leaves changes when the sun shines through them. Sometimes you'll find a composition that just works and the picture will jump out at you.

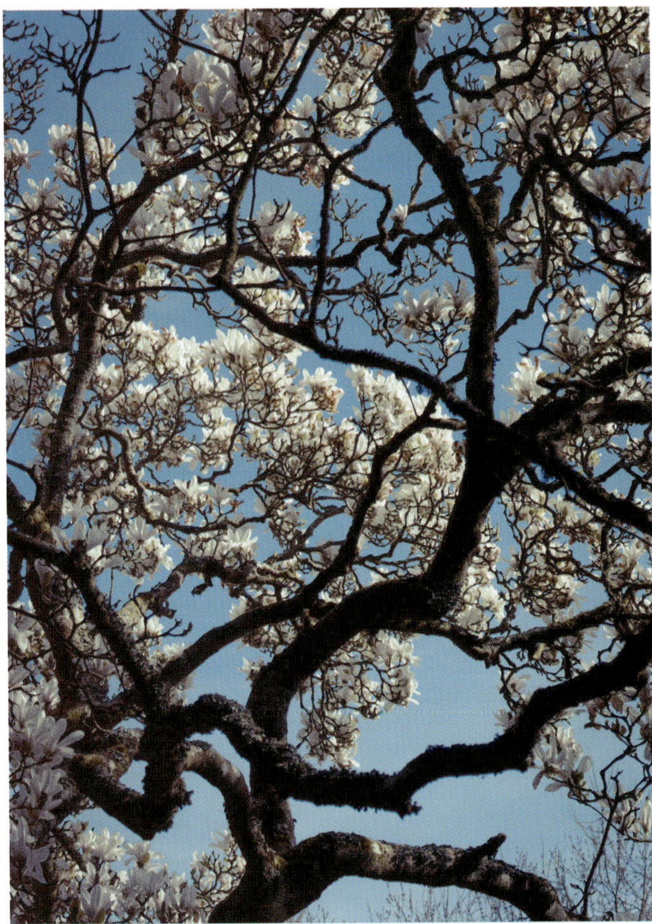

With this magnolia tree image the trunk comes from the bottom-left third and draws the eye to the top right third. This type of composition is sometimes seen in the Japanese woodblock prints that were an important influence on the Impressionist painters. I changed the colour of the blue sky in this photo slightly to remind me of a Van Gogh painting.

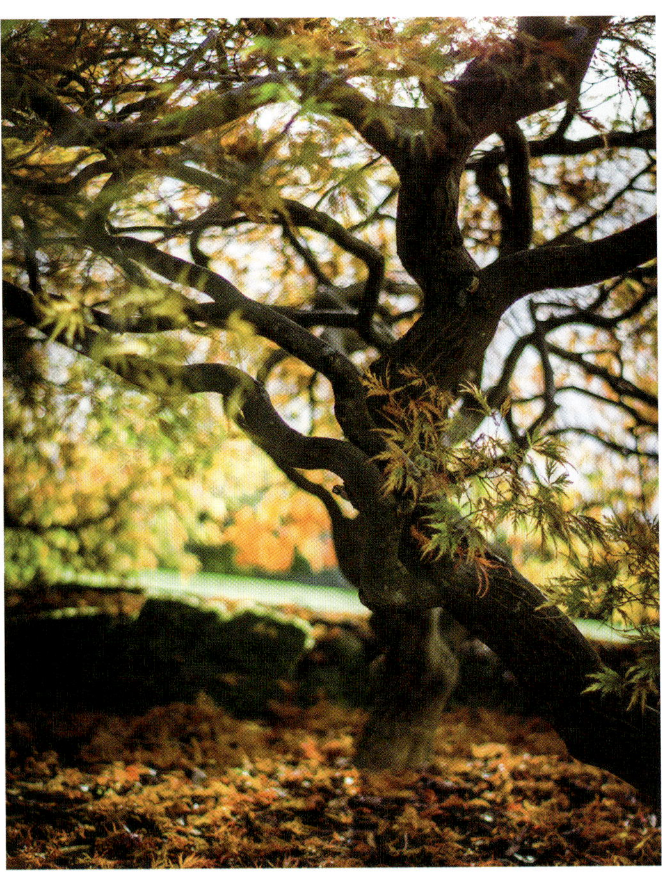

This photo of an acer in autumn places the trunk on the right third with most of the leaf interest in the top right, and this helps to lead the eye 'through' the photo. The out-of-focus blurs of colour are very appealing.

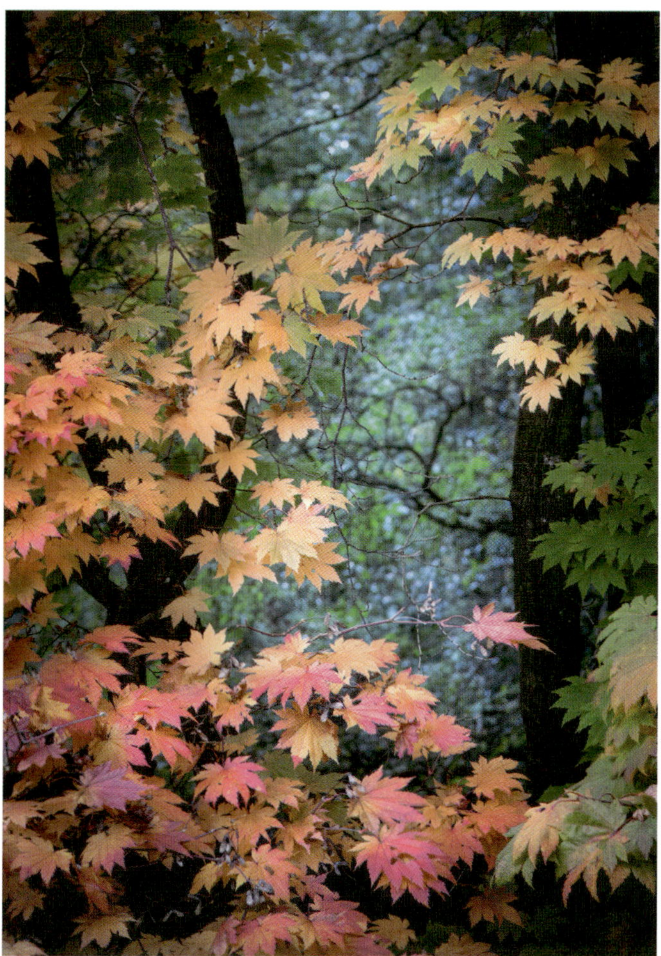

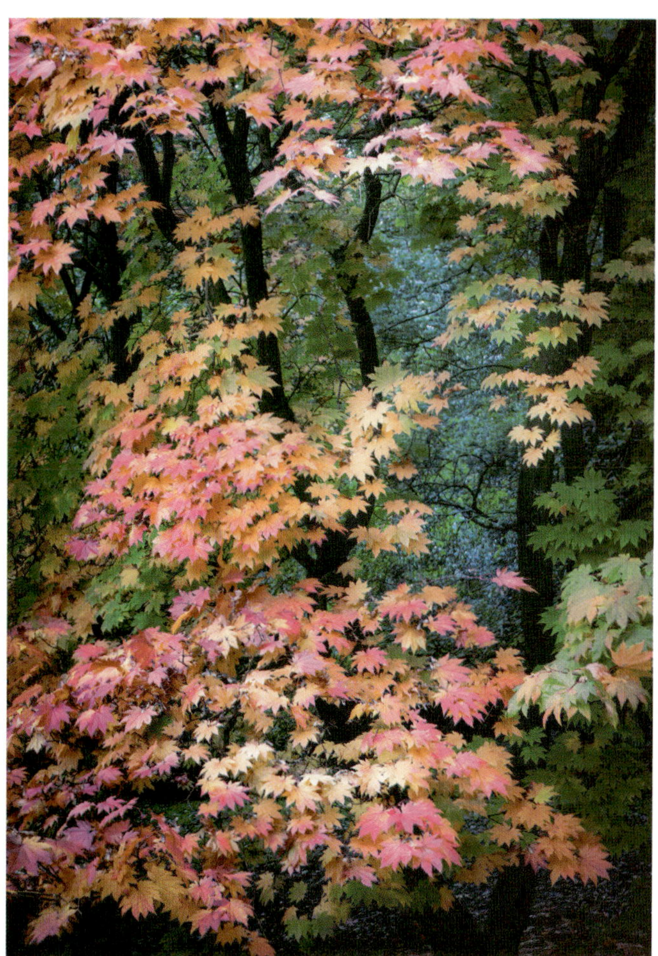

Try different compositions when you edit the photo too. Do you prefer the zoomed-in composition of these *Acer japonicum* or the wider aspect one?

Trees in winter often create beautiful sculptural shapes with their bare branches and as there is usually little colour to be found at this time of year, they may convert well to black and white images. Their branches create fractals, which can be found in some dead seed heads at this time of the year too.

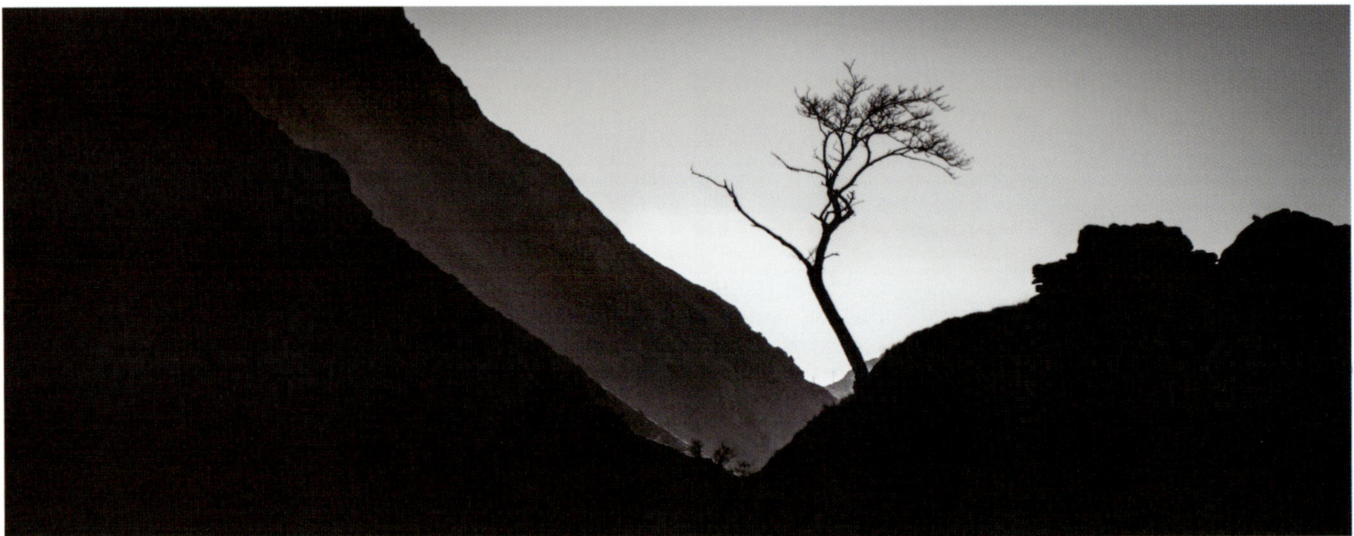

This tree silhouette was originally part of a much bigger image but I cropped in because I loved the parallel line it made with the mountain.

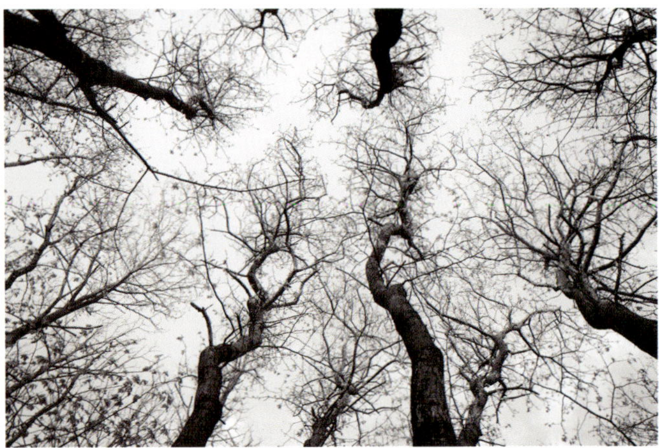

Don't forget to look up!

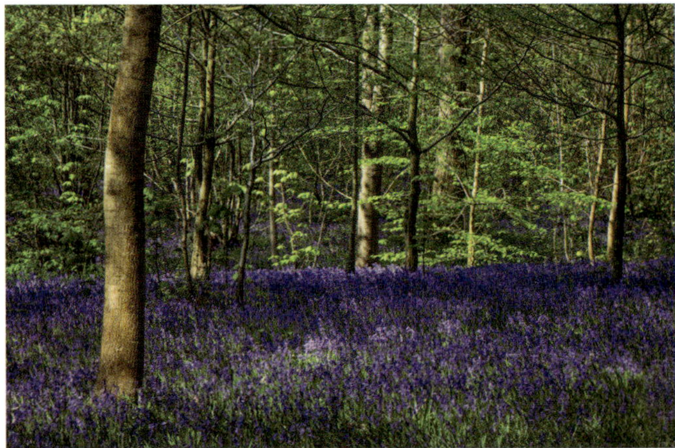

If photographing groups of trees, try and place a tree in the foreground to lead the eye in.

FUNGI

I've included fungi in this book as many of the flower and garden photographers I know do love to shoot fungi in the autumn. They are often at their best in September and October and the variety of species means they are always fascinating. Be aware that many are poisonous, so avoid touching ones you know nothing about.

I often see fungi in the public gardens I visit so it's not something that is purely restricted to a woodland or forest walk – if the gardens near you have a woodland section and you're visiting in the autumn months, have a good look around. If you want to take your fungi photography seriously then you can research on the internet where it is best to look – for example fly agaric mushrooms are most commonly found beneath birch trees. My one rule with fungi photography is to get down to the same level (or even beneath) as the mushroom you're photographing, this may mean carrying a bin bag or something to lie on, and resting your camera on the ground or a small bean bag.

Move around the fungus until you find a nice background – as much colour or light as possible is always the goal, although fungi have a habit of growing in darker and danker areas, so you

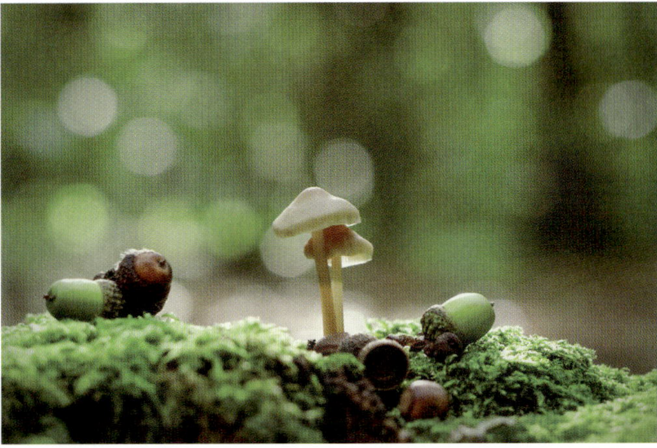

Mushrooms and acorns on a mossy log with out-of-focus circles of light (bokeh) in the background.

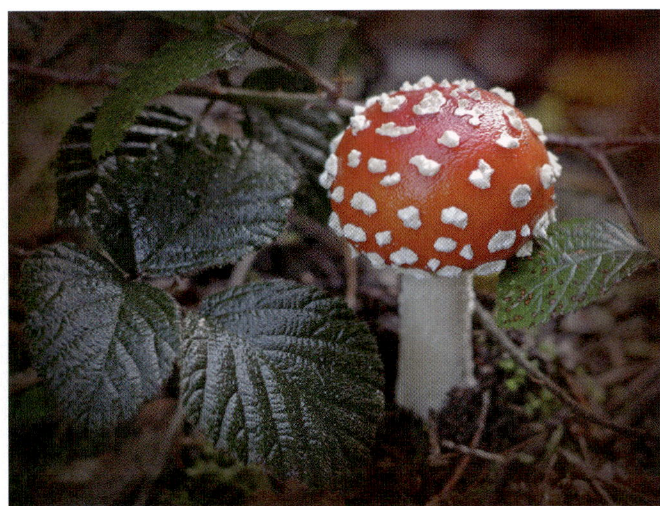

The famous red and white *Amanita muscaria* (fly agaric) fungi are very difficult to find intact, they are often full of holes or decaying. Move any surrounding twigs carefully so that you have a clear view but leave some of the wood floor to give context.

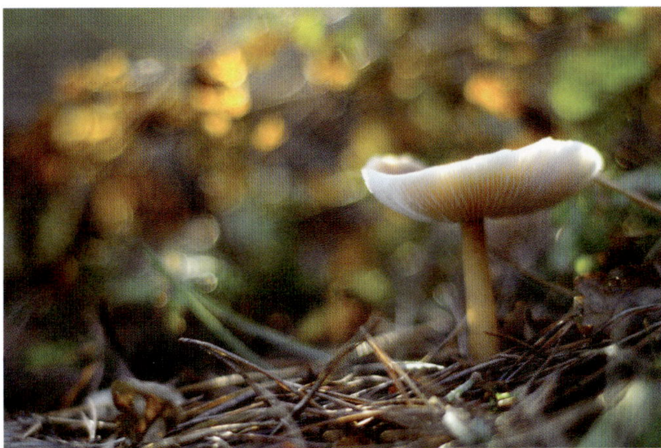

This fungi shot was taken using a vintage Pentax lens with the aperture 'wide open' (on its lowest setting) which gives good colour and background light.

might have to increase your ISO or use a small torch/LED light. Some photographers uplight the lamella or gills of a mushroom which will make them glow in the final photograph and this might be something to try with a small torch just out of shot. You will almost always have to carefully move surrounding stray twigs and leaves but avoid touching the fungus itself. Aside from possibly being poisonous they are incredibly fragile and I feel it's always best to leave nature undisturbed.

If you have a long lens you'll be able to get more of the mushroom in focus, but even with a 50mm lens and a low aperture you should be able to get the majority of it sharp and still have some nice light or bokeh in the background.

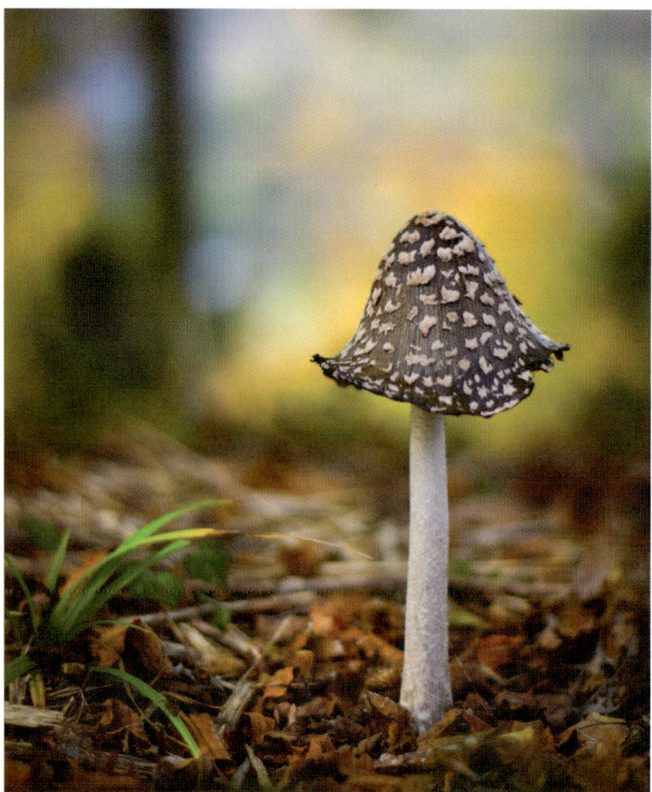

This *Coprinus comatus* (shaggy inkcap) mushroom was an easy find on the side of the path. I moved around it checking the possible backgrounds before I found a shrub with yellow leaves that blurred out really well in the final photo, adding good colour to the shot.

GARDEN VIEWS AND VISTAS

Regularly gracing the covers of garden and country living magazines, garden landscapes and vistas usually either have strong composition, beautiful light or both.

When I photograph garden landscapes I usually use a wide-angle prime lens (something between 18 and 30mm) to get as much into the frame as possible, with an aperture of about f/8 or higher, which should give you front-to-back sharpness. Strong lines play an important part here, leading the viewer's eye 'into' the photo; bold borders, paths or hedging work particularly well.

Remember that whilst it is a landscape, the image may not necessarily work best with a landscape orientation – I always try to take a photo in 'portrait' format too to see if it makes the composition stronger.

What many good garden vistas have in common is good foreground interest with something eye-catching behind that then creates a journey through the photo. Ideally there will be three 'stopping' points in the image – foreground, middle and finally background. Try to find colour or good light initially when framing your photo and if not, look for structural interest: tall or large plants that catch the eye.

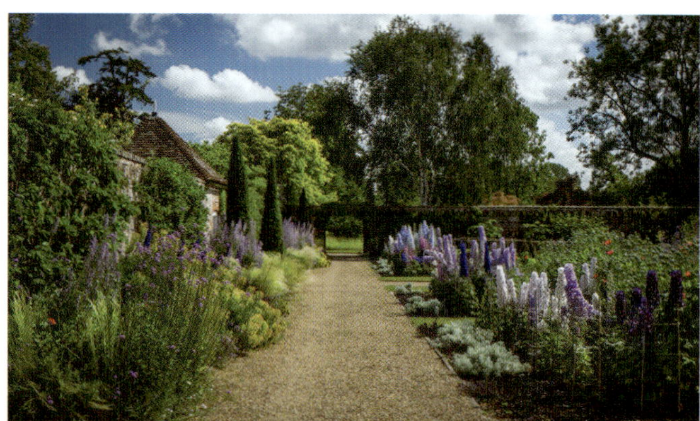

A shot of a walled garden where the path leads the eye into the photo.

In general, look at where the light is coming from. If it's fairly low in the sky (which is often preferable) try to use it as a feature of the photo, highlighting particular planting groups or other 'architectural' elements of the scene. Shooting garden landscapes in the golden hour (*see* Chapter 3, 'Light') will often produce great results with beautiful colours.

Here the eye follows not only the path, but the yellow *Eremurus* (foxtail lilies) in the foreground to the tall *Echium pininana* behind. The tall echium are echoed by the portrait ratio.

If you have strong horizontal lines (or actual horizons) in your photo do make sure that they are actually horizontal. A bit of a tilt can give the viewer an uncomfortable sense of 'sea-sickness'. You can straighten them in the edit if you don't notice at the time and all need not be lost.

Gardens can be just as interesting in winter, particularly if there is frost on the ground to give a magical touch. You might need to use your exposure compensation dial to lighten the photo a little in winter, especially if it features snow or frost. This will prevent scenes from becoming too dark, as the light is always weaker in winter than summer. Be careful that the bright parts of the photo (the highlights) don't become overexposed and 'burnt out', which can often happen with sunlight on snow.

If you have a local garden that you visit regularly it can be interesting to capture the same scene in different seasons. The difference in summer and winter will often be extreme and for me it's a joyous reminder in winter that things *will* grow again. You just need to make a note of the exact spot that you stand on, in order to replicate the scene at different times of the year. Some gardens open all year round – see if you can find some near you.

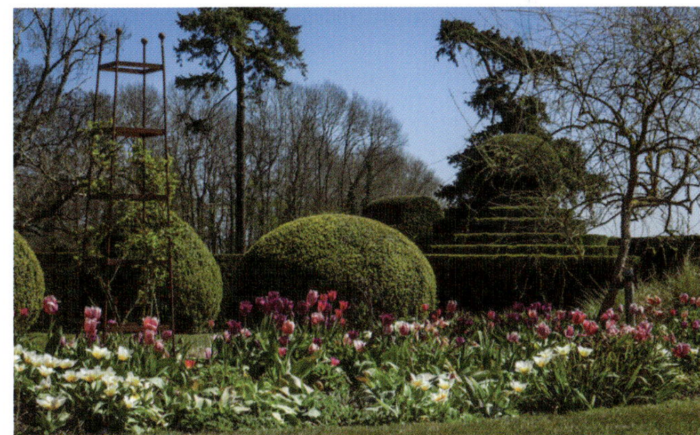

Photos of borders such as this one could be considered a little 'blocky' as it seems that there are no lines leading the eye into the photo, but the gardener's use of colour leads the eye in from the tulips at the bottom to the topiary hedges behind.

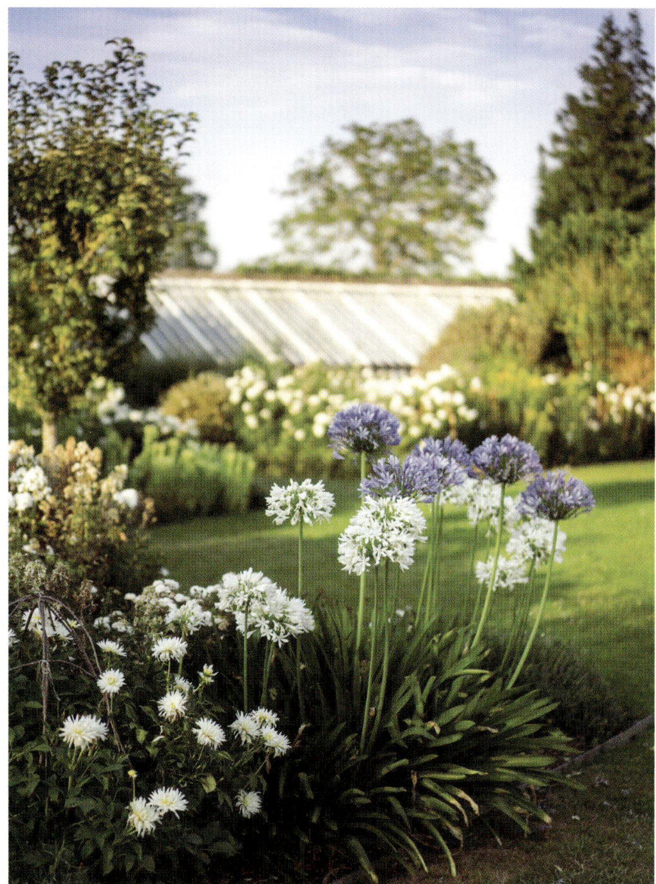

Our eye will usually travel to the brightest part of the photo. Here we notice the bold blue and white agapanthus in the foreground first and then the bright white dahlias and greenhouse behind.

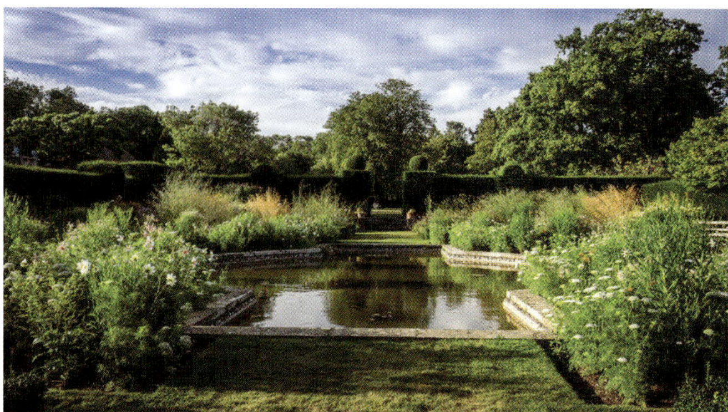

In this photo I made sure that the tops of the hedges, rather than the pond edge, were horizontal. This is because they are a focal part of the image, being where the eye travels to.

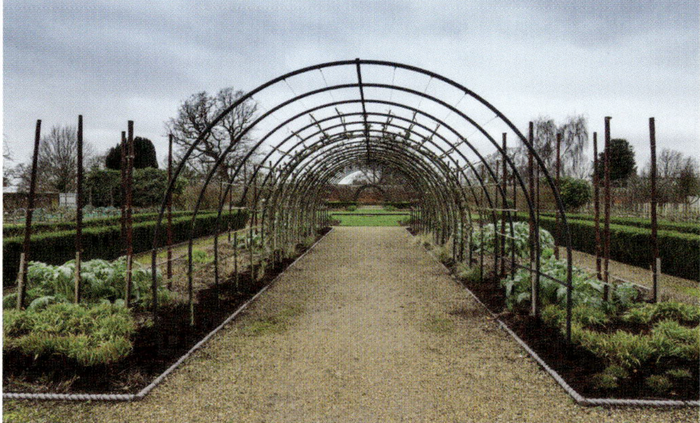

The apple pergola at Belmont Park Gardens in Kent in January.

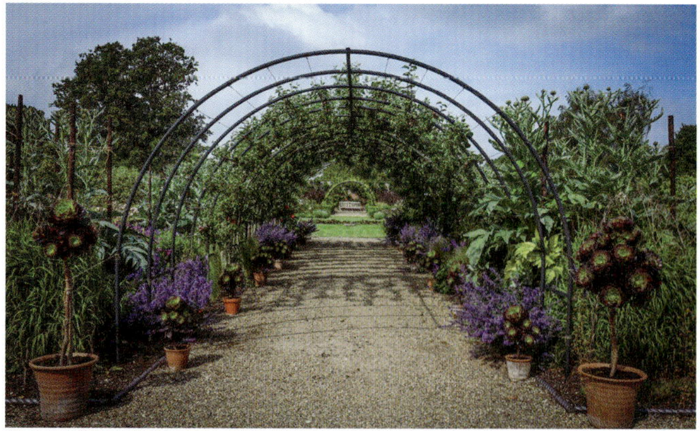

The very same view in June; the changes are extraordinary.

People

Gardens devoid of people can look peaceful, but sometimes a little sterile. For me, gardens are to be enjoyed and I have no qualms about featuring people in my garden photos (as long as I have their permission, or their parent's permission if they are under eighteen).

The presence of people can give a sense of scale to a picture and offer a focal point. However, do remember that if you want the *floral* content to be the main subject, adding a human element could detract from that.

As with flowers, you don't have to put human subjects dead centre. Try putting them in other parts of the picture where this strengthens the composition. I love the interactions that we have with plants and flowers and often try to capture the wonder of children and adults as they connect with nature.

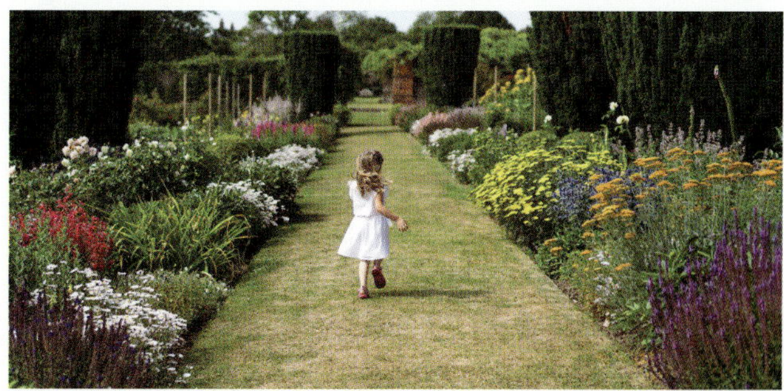

People can also add life and movement to a photo.

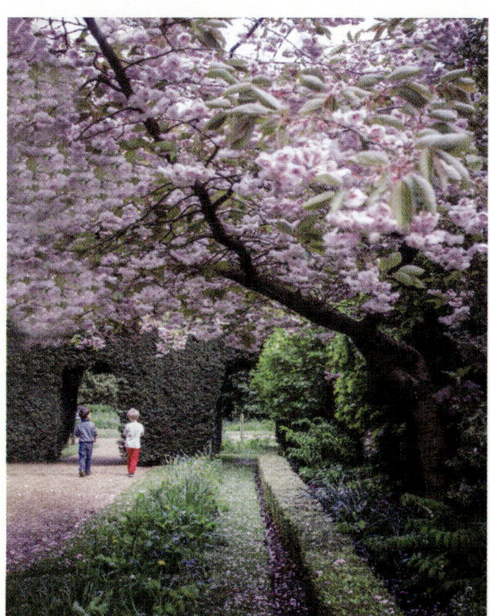

Our eye is drawn down the path to the two boys in the distance; the cherry blossom frames the photo.

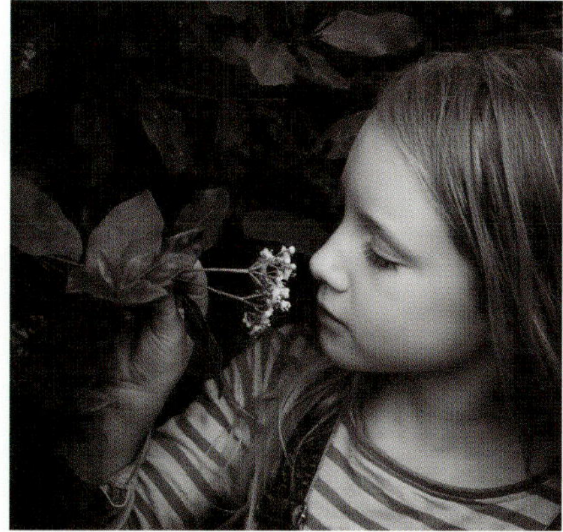

The smell of spring.

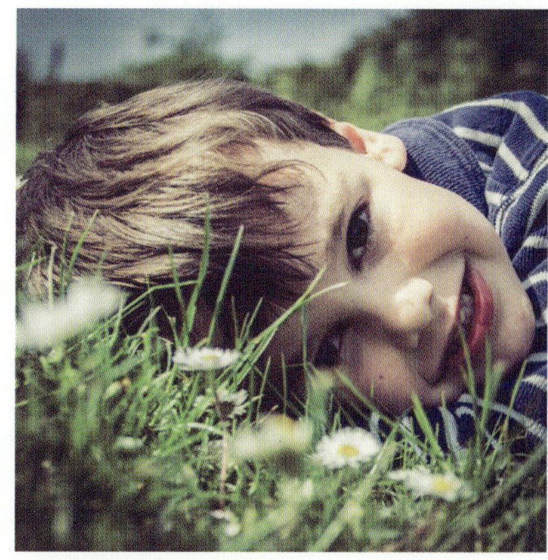

Don't forget that you can get down low with people and children as well as flowers.

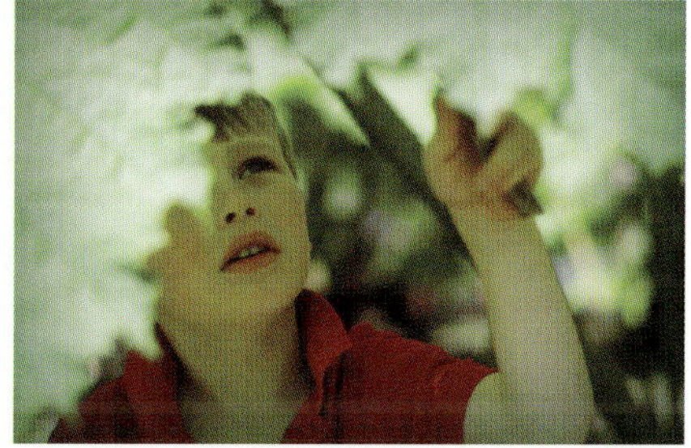

Underneath the gunnera.

Flowers and plants to photograph in February

February brings hope – bumblebees emerge on sunny days and we glimpse the first blossom.

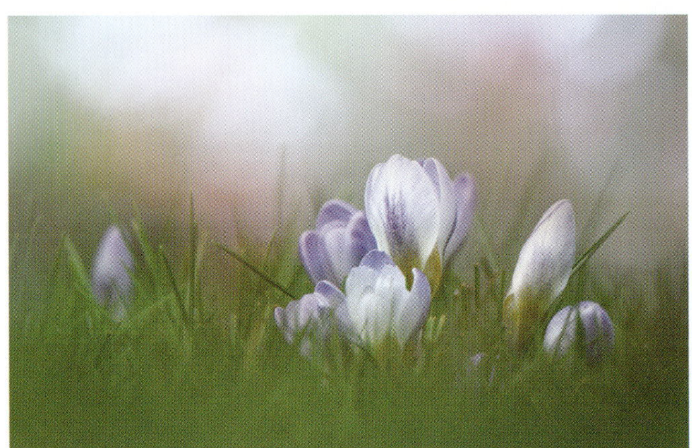

Crocuses – 1/400 sec at f/4, 220mm.

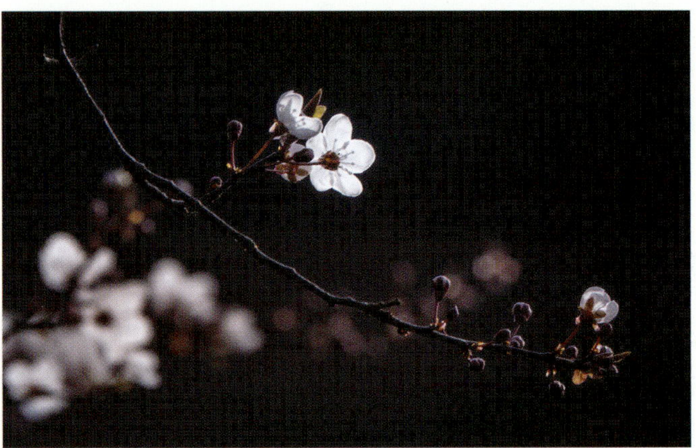

Prunus cerasifera (winter-flowering cherry) – 1/400 sec at f/4, 110mm.

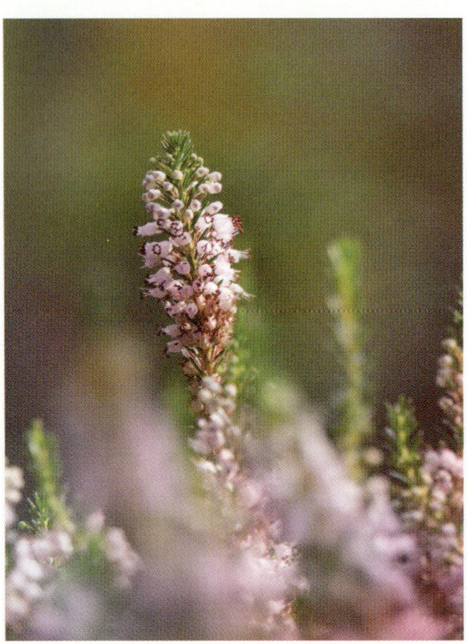

Erica carnea (winter heather) – 1/400 sec at f/4, 110mm.

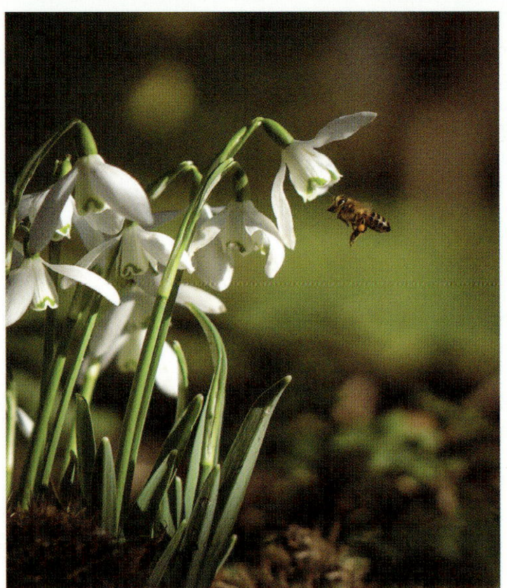

Galanthus (snowdrops) and honey bee – 1/5000 sec at f/2.8, 55mm.

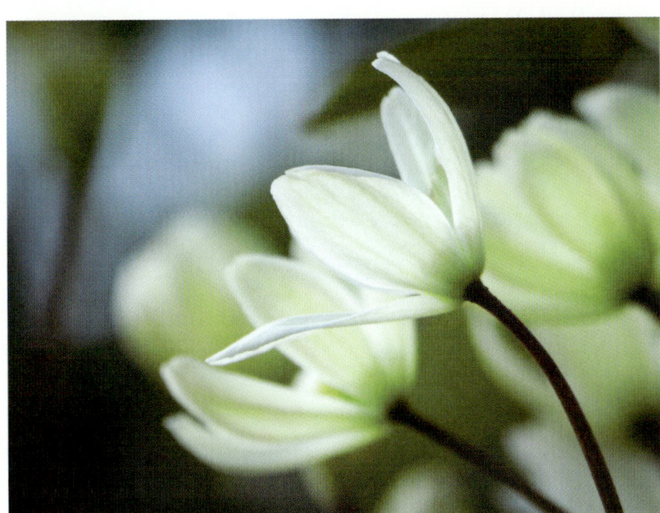

Winter-flowering clematis – 1/1000 sec at f/4 – 220mm.

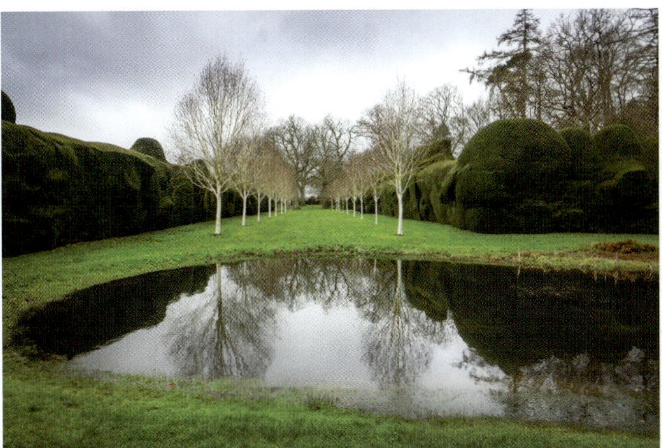

Betula pendula (silver birch trees) and pond reflections – 1/200 sec at f/5.6, 18mm.

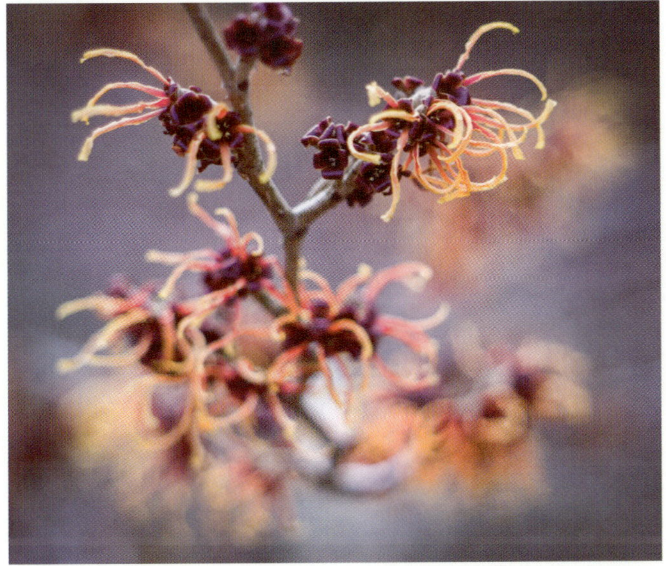

Hamamelis (witch hazel) – 1/100 sec at f/1.7 with a 50mm vintage manual lens.

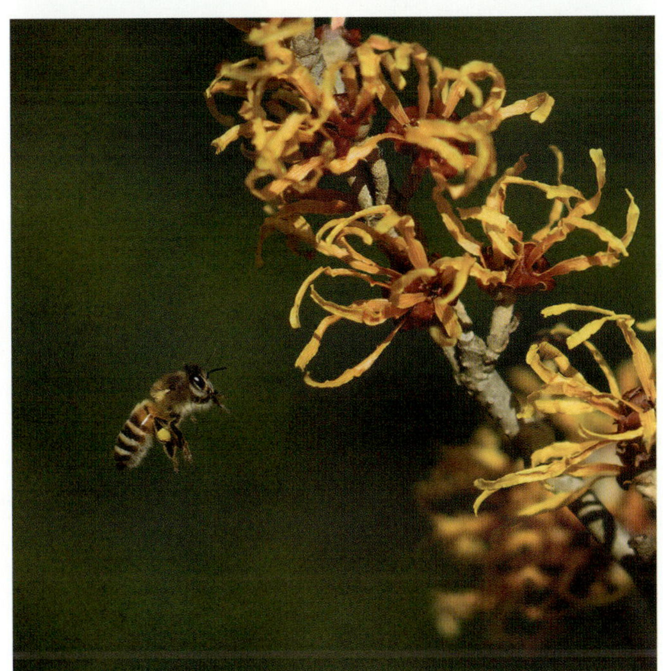

Hamamelis (witch hazel) and honey bee in flight – 1/5000 sec at f/2, 55mm.

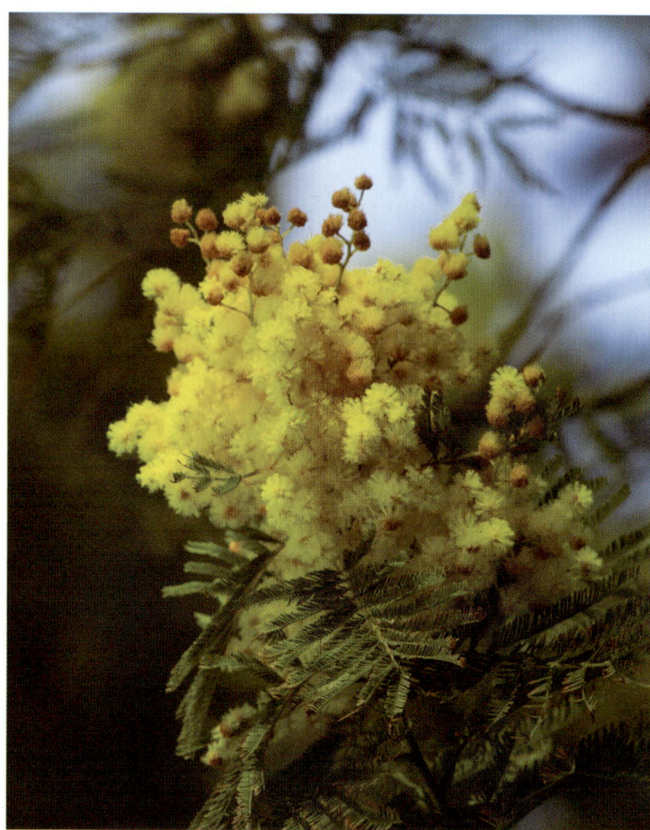

Mimosa – 1/320 sec at f/4, 320mm.

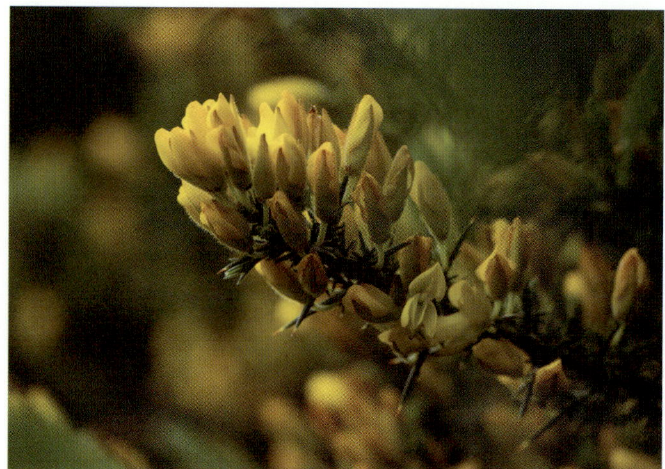

Ulex (gorse) flowers – 1/1000 sec at f/4, 180mm.

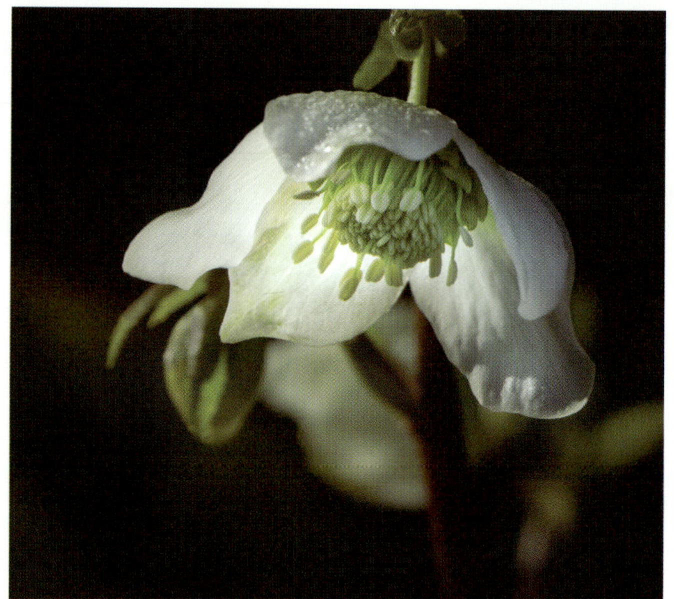

White hellebore – 1/2000 sec at f/4, 180mm.

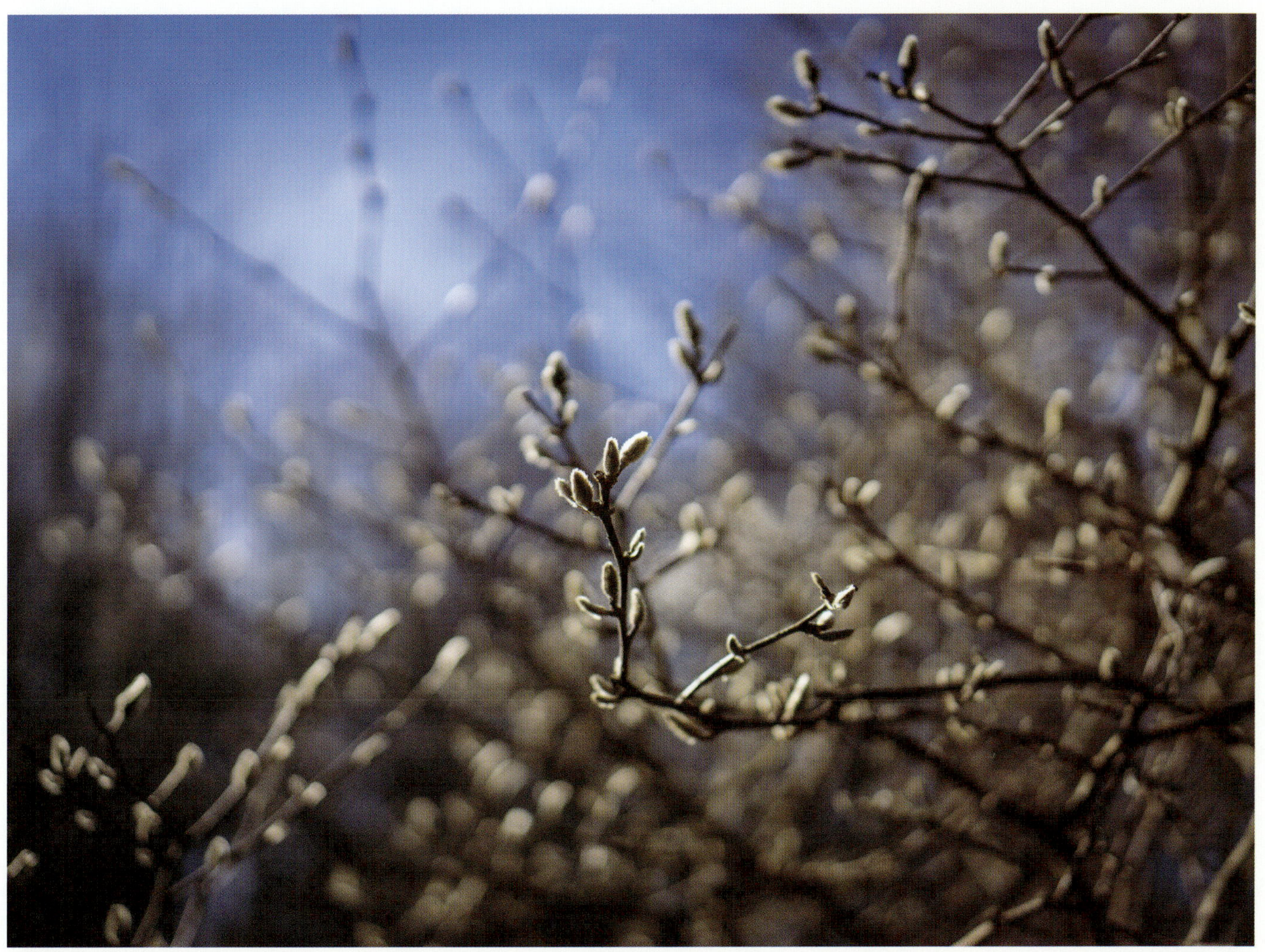

Emerging buds – 1/3200 sec at f/2, 55mm.

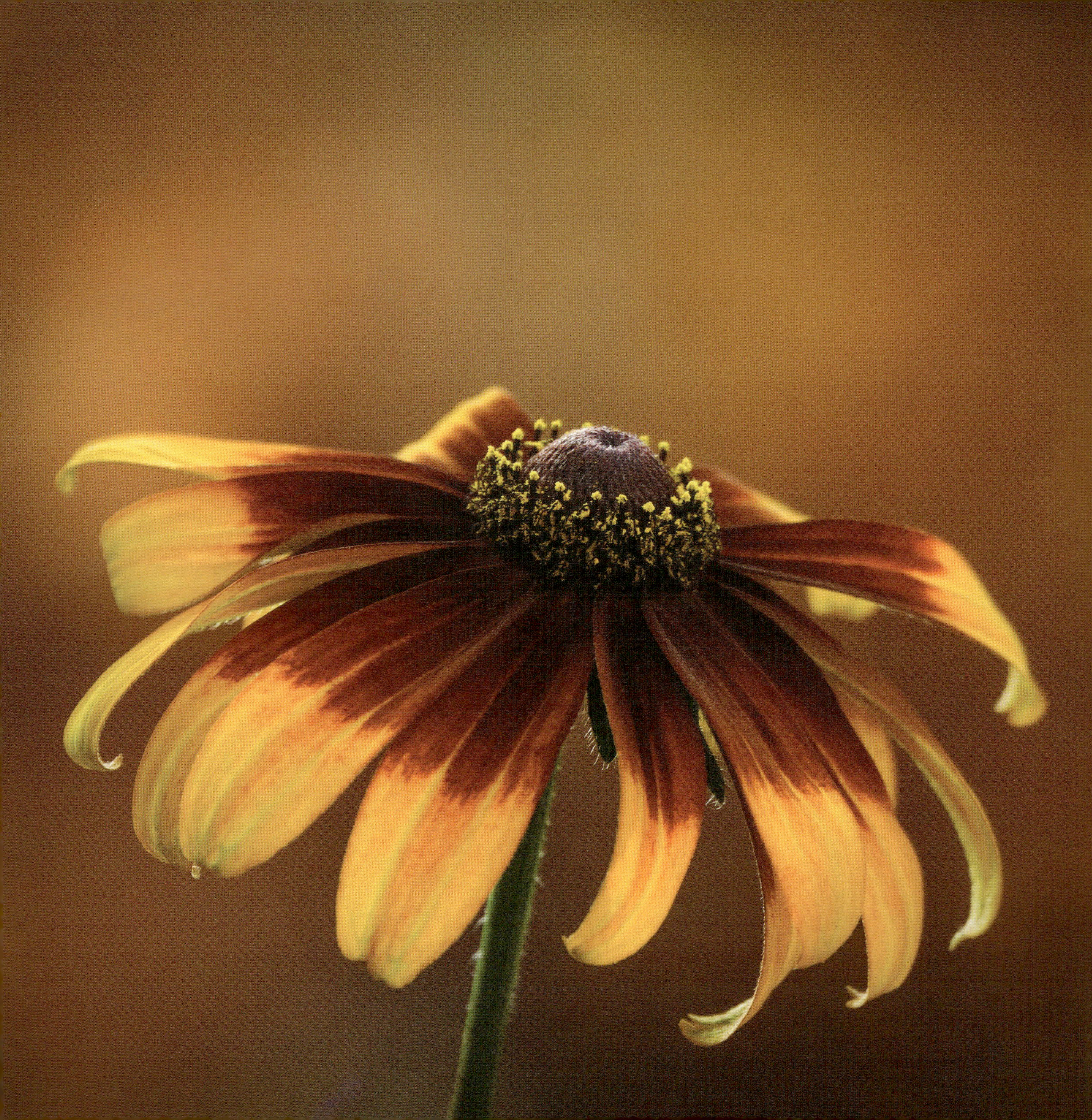

CHAPTER 3

Light

> The light constantly changes and that alters the atmosphere and beauty of things every minute.
>
> CLAUDE MONET

Light is one of the most important aspects of photography. Good light can transform an average subject into an amazing one. Garden photographers will try to use light as a tool to add another dimension to their photos and they employ many tricks to enhance it. Always look carefully to see how the light falls onto the subject and the background of your picture as it can make a huge difference. Move around as much as you can to assess the angle of the light and try to use this as another element of your composition.

DIFFUSED LIGHT

The best conditions for photographing single flowers are usually bright, overcast skies and *not* bright sunlight, as the latter creates harsh shadows on the flowers or plants. However we are often unable to choose our weather conditions, especially if we've planned a garden visit in advance, so we have to find ways to work around this.

A flower in bright sunlight will usually have shadows created by the petals or other flowers or trees. Cloudy skies diffuse the light, producing a much softer image which is usually preferable. I will often use a diffuser in bright sunlight to give a similar effect.

The diffuser doesn't need to be particularly large, just large enough to cover the flower. You could hand hold it yourself, ask a willing volunteer, or attach it to a tripod using a double-ended clamp. I also have a small diffuser that I can hold with one hand at the same time as taking a photo.

Position the diffuser between the sun and the flower/subject of your photo. Give yourself time to work out which angle achieves the effect you want.

◀ *Rudbeckia* 'Rustic dwarf mixed' at sunset.

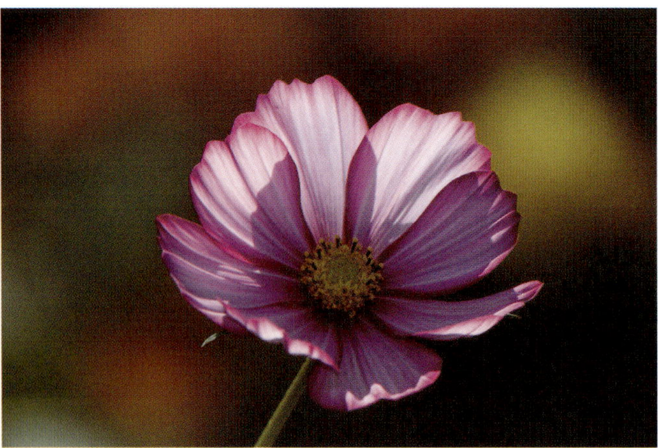

This cosmos was photographed in full sun. The lit-up petals are attractive but the lines the shadows make take our attention from the graceful petal shapes and centre.

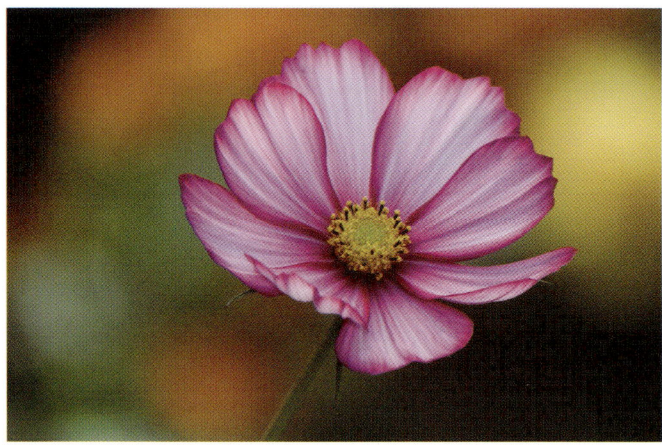

This is the same cosmos flower, photographed with a diffuser between the sun and the flower. I then lightened the flower slightly when editing it. The light falls evenly on the flower and we can see every detail.

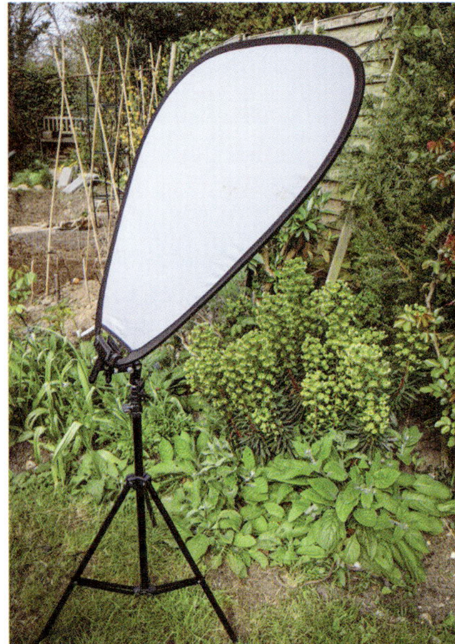

One of my diffusers attached to a light stand with a clamp in my garden.

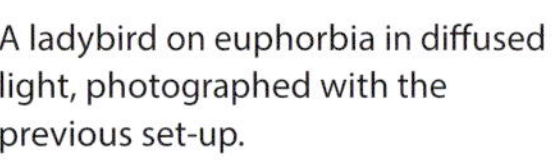

A ladybird on euphorbia in diffused light, photographed with the previous set-up.

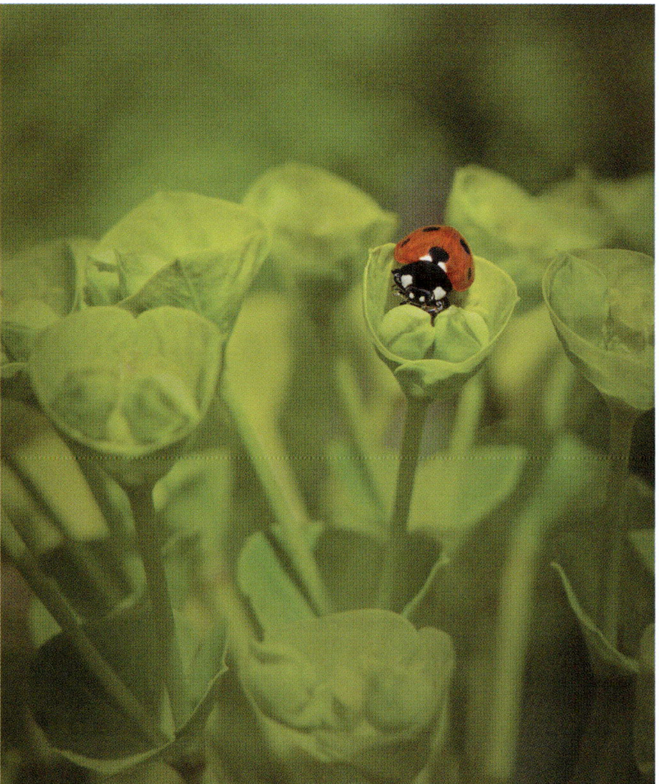

PHOTOGRAPHING ON SUNNY DAYS

If I'm out on a sunny day with some clouds in the sky, I will often wait for the sun to go behind the clouds before shooting close-ups of flowers, find other things to photograph when the sun is shining, or look for flowers in shade. If the flower is in deep shade you might want to use a reflector to bounce some light onto it; if you position a reflector at an angle under the flower or plant it will reflect light (even on cloudy days) from the sky back on to your subject. This gives a much more naturalistic light effect than having to resort to flash or another light source by holding it underneath and to the side of the flower. If you have an LED light with you, mounting this to the top of your camera will still give you even, soft light, and the background will appear quite dark, which is often effective for good contrast – light flower, dark background.

One of my favourite tricks on a sunny day is to search for a flower in the shade that has sunlight (preferably falling on colourful flowers) in the near or distant background. With a wide aperture you can blur the background and produce out-of-focus coloured light, which can look magical.

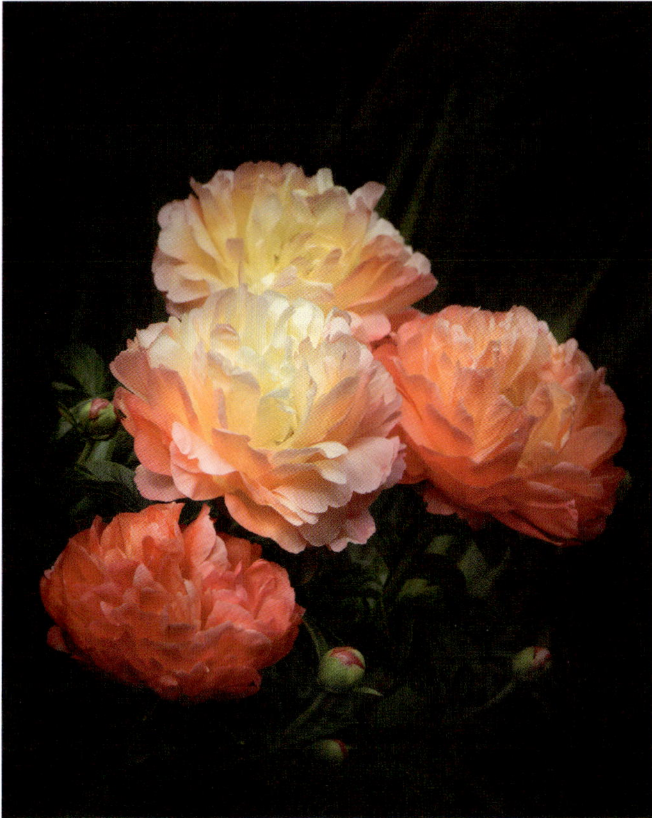

Because these peonies are in shade and lit by a reflector, their dark surroundings almost give the image the look of a classical oil painting.

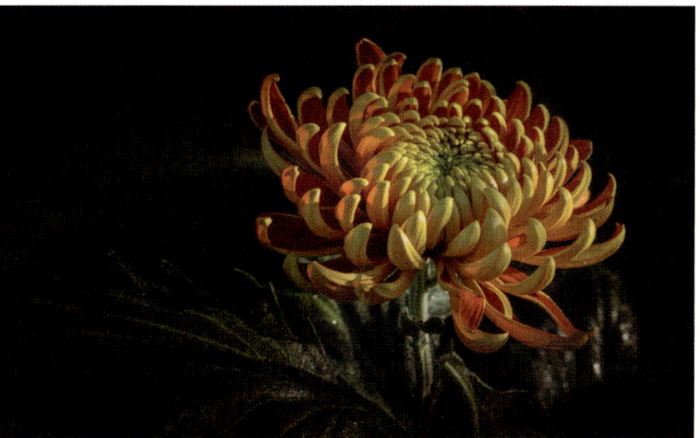

This chrysanthemum has the last rays of the evening sun falling on it, and the weak sunlight gives it a rich colour that contrasts well with the dark background.

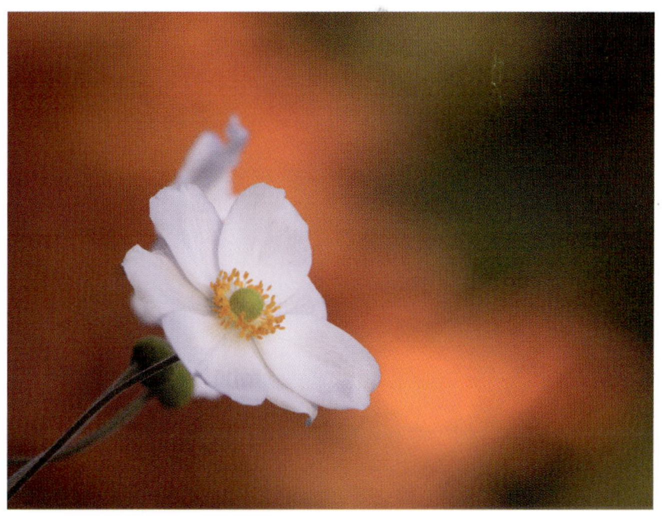

This Japanese anemone is in front of red maple leaves in sunlight.

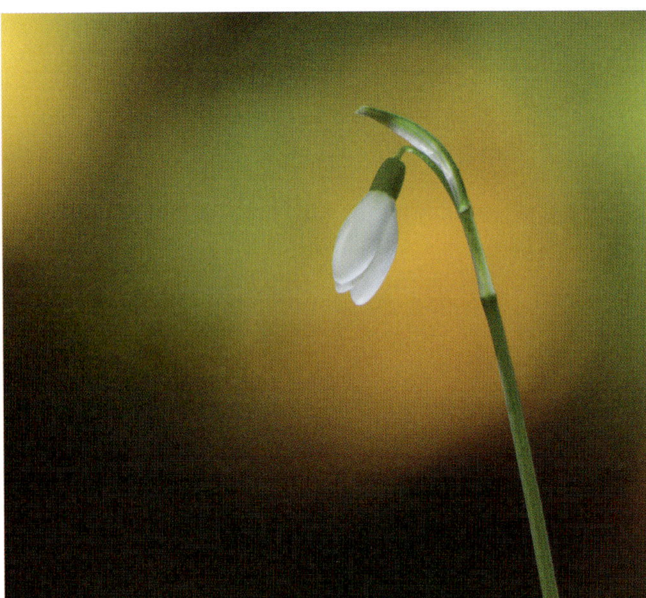

When I took this photo of the snowdrop it was in January at sunset (about 3.30pm) and the sun gave a lovely patch of colour to the hedge behind. The snowdrop itself was too dark in comparison, so I held a small torch in my left hand (whilst also holding the camera) to lighten it a touch.

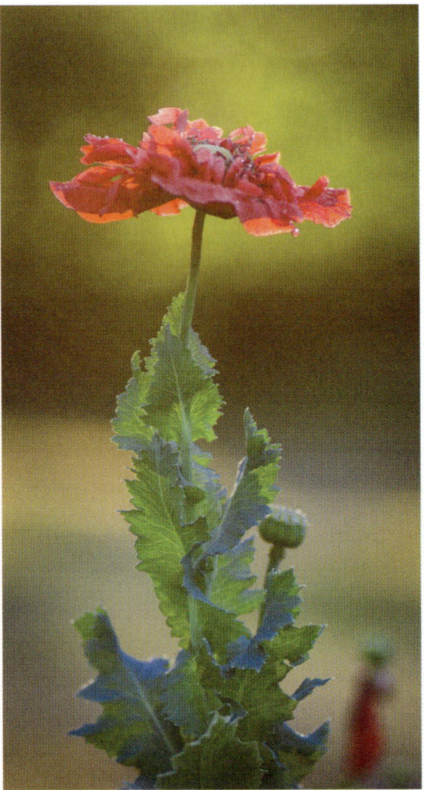

A poppy with hazy, early morning sunlight in the background.

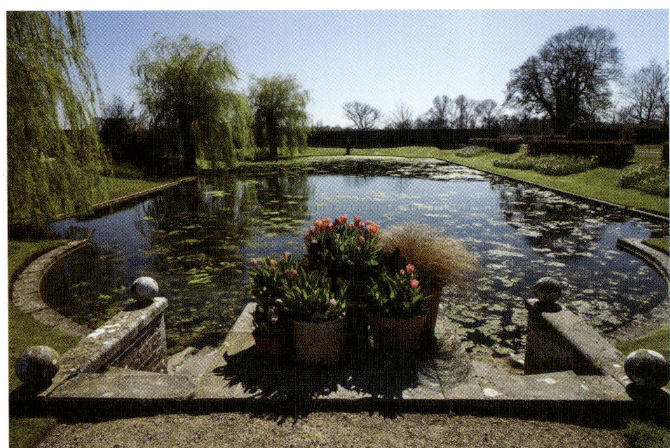

In this garden scene, which was taken at 2pm, the shadows of the pots, steps and trees are very harsh and almost fully black. By lifting 'shadows' and 'blacks' with the respective sliders in Lightroom you can lessen the effect to some extent.

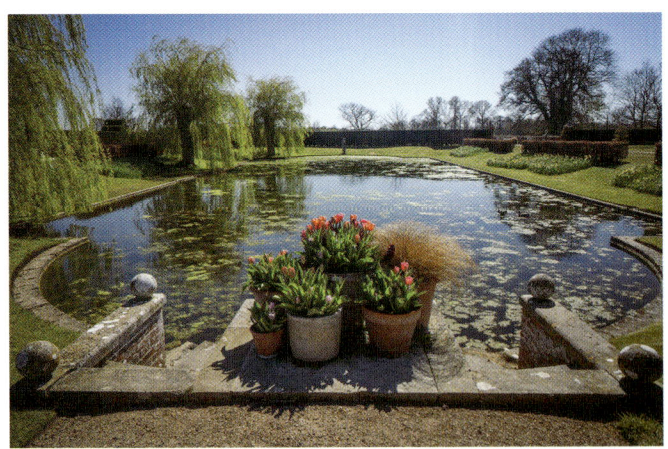

The same photo with shadows and blacks lifted in Lightroom.

If you find the flower itself is too dark in contrast with the background (the camera will probably expose the scene using the background light) you might need to throw a little light onto it with a torch or LED light.

I often grow flowers and bulbs in pots so that I can move them around the garden (sometimes putting them on tables) and find a nice position where the background light or colour is good. You can also use this method up-close to focus in on a part of the flower and have bright, out-of-focus light behind.

If you are photographing garden scenes in bright sunlight you might need to lift the shadows in post-processing (there is a 'shadows' slider in Lightroom). If your skies are very bright on sunny days you could fit a polarizing filter to your lens (make sure you buy the correct one for the width of your lens), which will give you richer, bluer skies and eliminate reflections to a certain extent.

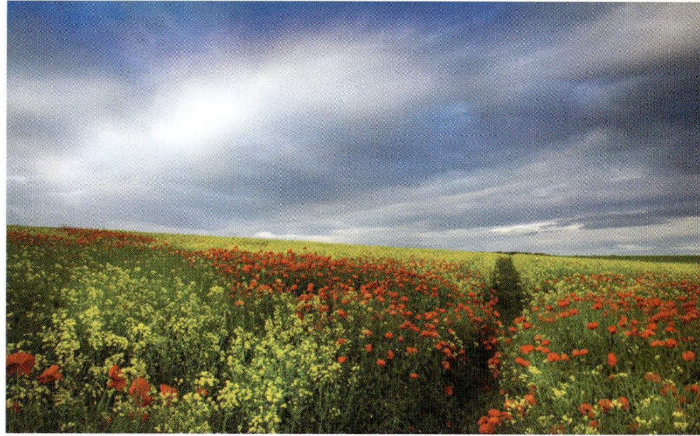

This photo of field poppies and yellow rapeseed flowers was taken with a circular polarizing filter. You can see that it has also added some definition and depth to the clouds.

The golden hour

The golden hour is the period of time before sunset or after sunrise when the sun is redder and softer because it is low in the sky, and comes from the side, rather than overhead. This can be a fantastic time to take photos, although in summer this is often at a rather inconvenient time of day – at 3am or 9pm many public gardens will not be open.

Flowers literally glow when caught in this golden light and background light can also be really magical. Colours are enhanced, to the point where you sometimes need to de-saturate them in the edit as they can look artificially over-cooked. The golden hour is especially good for broader vistas as the sun can light up whole borders and make them glow.

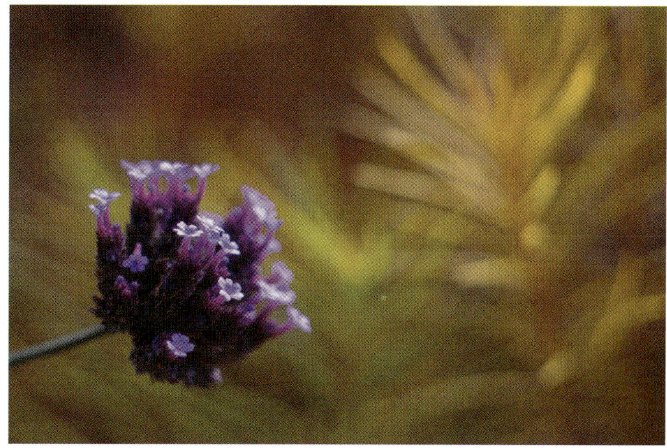

The *Verbena bonariensis* in the foreground has really delicate lighting from the low light and the leaves behind it have a golden glow.

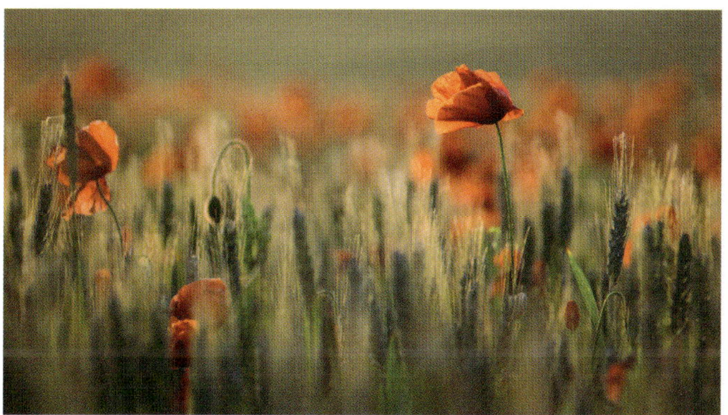

Poppies photographed about ten minutes before sunset, the colours are rich and the ears of wheat are backlit and glowing.

The blue hour

The blue hour is the period of time just before or after sunset when there is no 'direct' sunlight and everything has a softer, and often 'blueish' diffused light. When you're shooting in low light such as the blue hour you may need to lower your shutter speed (and/or raise your ISO) in order to compensate. Additionally, if you don't have a tripod with you, make sure your arms are tucked into your body, your feet are apart and then hold your breath before gently squeezing the shutter. Minimizing your own movement means you're less likely to cause camera shake (which would make the photo slightly blurry). I use this stance at all times if I'm standing rather than sitting.

If you're out when it's windy (regardless of the time of day), you'll probably need a higher shutter speed than normal, unless you want an impressionistic blur to suggest the idea of flowers swaying in the breeze.

Shooting towards the sun

If you position your subject between the camera and the sun the composition will be 'backlit'. The effect of having the sun (or another source of light) behind the subject is known in photography as contre-jour – literally 'against daylight' and is used a great deal in garden photography. It's certainly one thing to try on bright sunny days, especially when the sun is lower in the sky.

Never actually point your camera at the sun (and especially don't look into it when pointing it toward the sun) as it can seriously damage your eyes, and at the very least give you a headache. Even using the rear-view screen rather than the viewfinder can give you a headache after a while. Keep the camera low and shoot across the top of the flower. The background will sometimes appear completely black even though you may be shooting in the morning, as the camera will expose

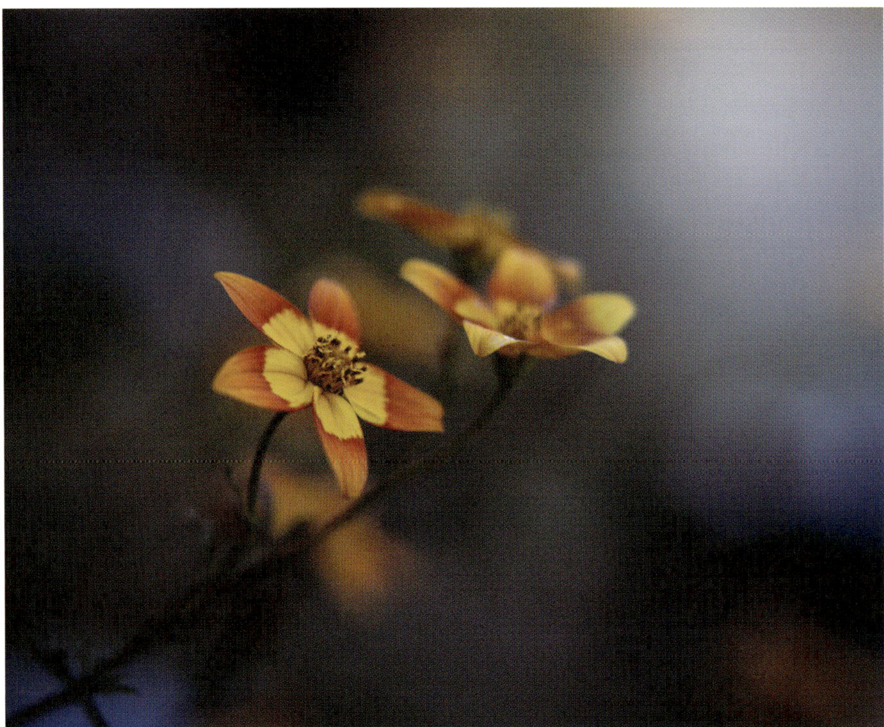

Bidens in soft, blue light taken post-sunset which gives a very ethereal effect. You might need to increase your ISO to keep the shutter speed high enough to prevent blurring.

Ferns in the blue hour with the only remaining light behind them.

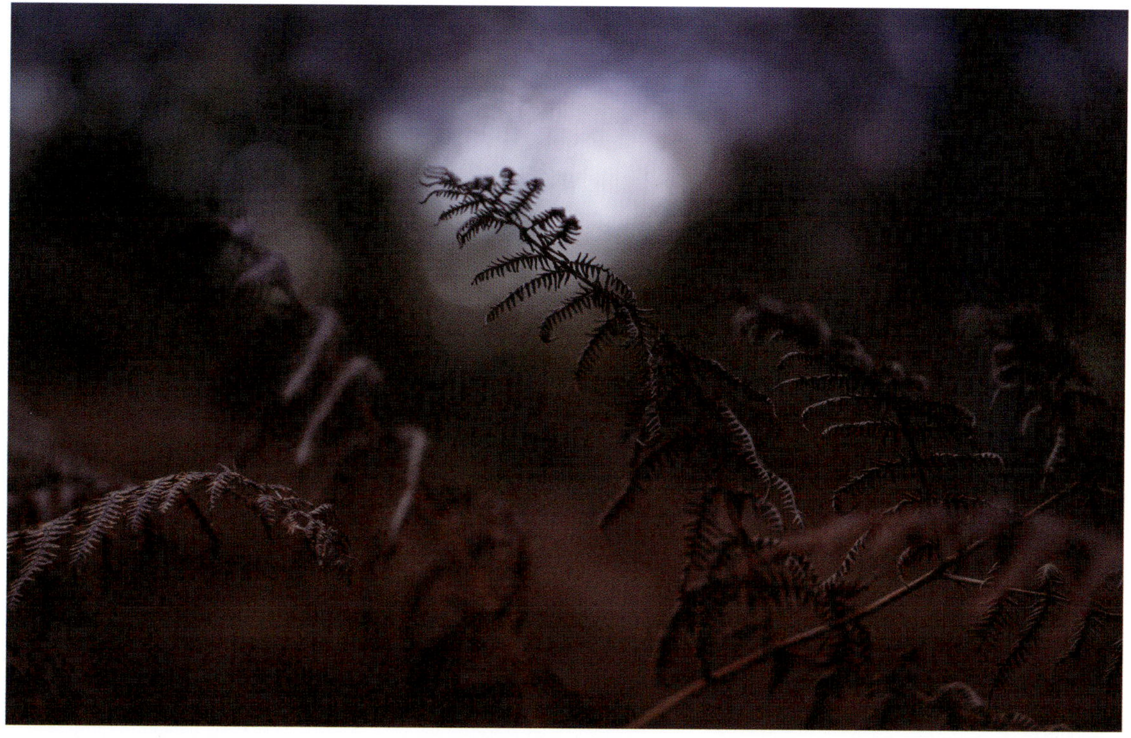

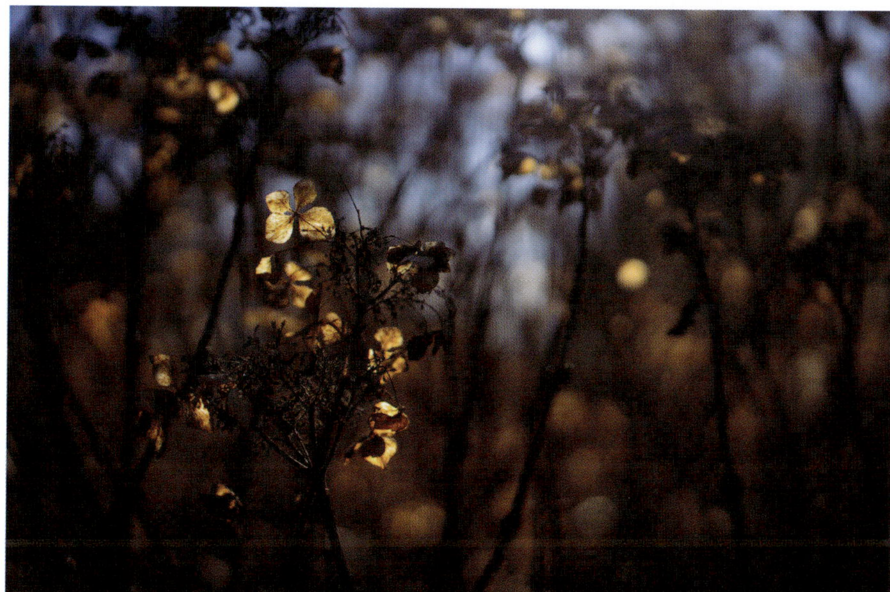

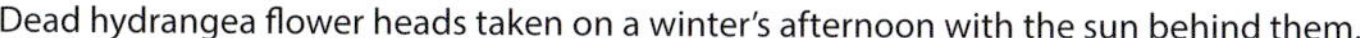

Dead hydrangea flower heads taken on a winter's afternoon with the sun behind them.

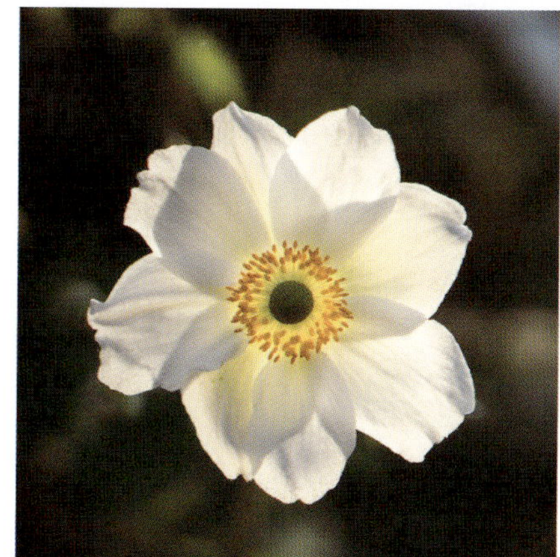

This *Anemone japonica* was photographed with the sun behind, on an August evening. I actually quite like the shadows created by the overlapping petals.

for the bright flower/s which will then throw the background into darkness.

If the sun itself shines directly into the lens you will get strong haze or even lens flare. Lens flare is when the sun's light enters the lens and subsequently hits the camera's film or digital sensor. This causes coloured spots or streaks in the photo, which can disfigure the image. Some lenses are more susceptible to lens flare than others but using a hood on your lens (which most lenses are now sold with) should considerably decrease the chances of it happening. Some photographers think lens flare can add magic to photos but it's a divisive issue, as other photographers hate it. I'll leave you to make up your own mind!

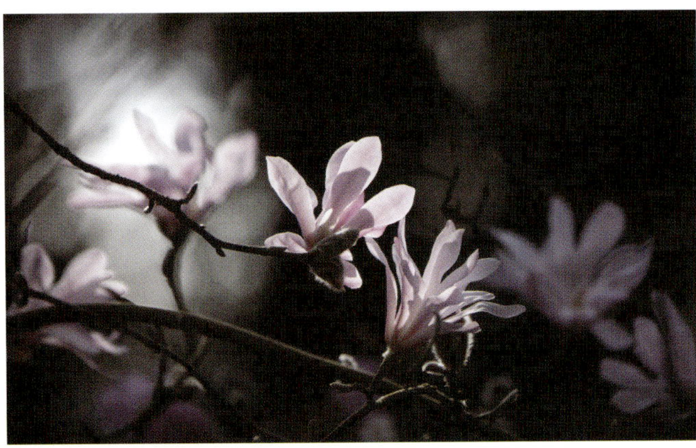

Shooting towards the sun in this magnolia branch photo has added all kinds of magical light effects.

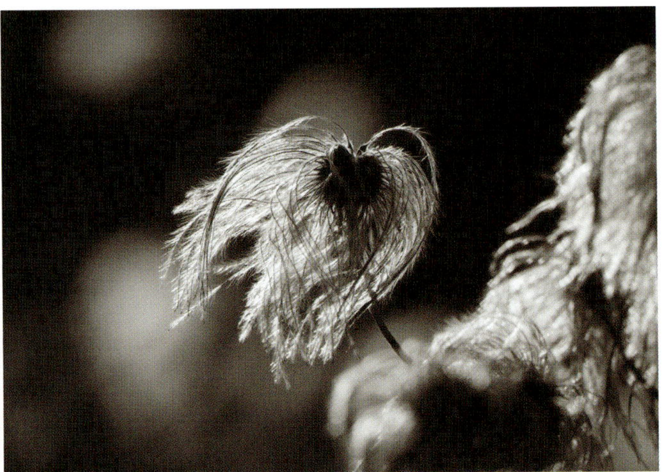

Feathery clematis seed heads in winter with the light behind them. As there was almost no colour in the scene I thought it worked well as a sepia conversion.

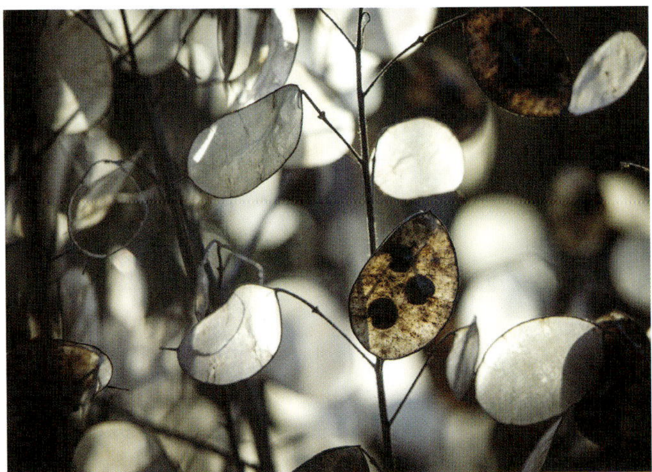

I particularly love seeking out flowers and seed heads that become translucent with the light behind them – the winter light in this photo has made these *Lunaria annua* (honesty) seed heads glow.

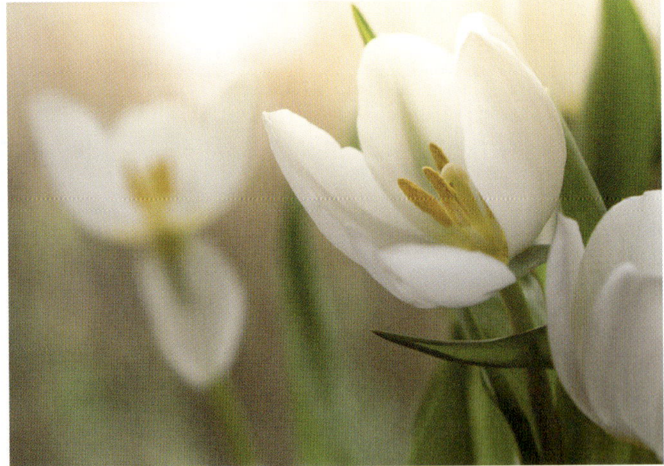

This backlit photo of tulips was shot on my windowsill (indoors) with the sun shining outside.

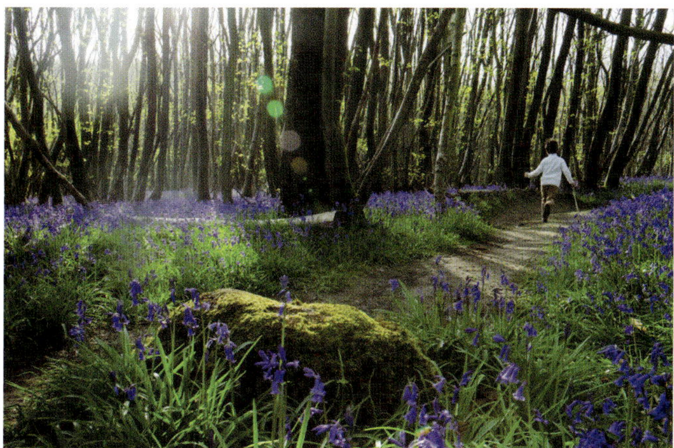

In this you can see lens flare (the green spots) in front of the largest tree trunk and a large white blob on the left.

Using the setting sun as part of your composition

If the flowers or plants you're photographing have thin and delicate petals or you can see through them in some way, you can even use the setting sun as part of your composition; use a high shutter speed to bring the light level of the sun right down so that it appears yellow or orange rather than bright white. Even so, I would still use the rear-view screen to compose a shot like this to avoid looking directly at it at all.

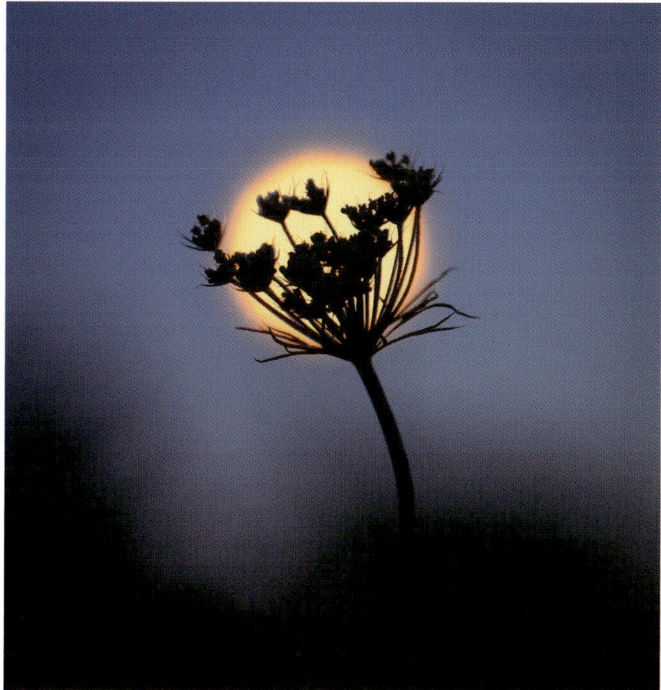

This is actually a cheat shot; what appears to be the sun is actually a street light outside my house! I mounted the fennel seed head (*Foeniculum vulgare*) on a tripod to line it up perfectly for the shot.

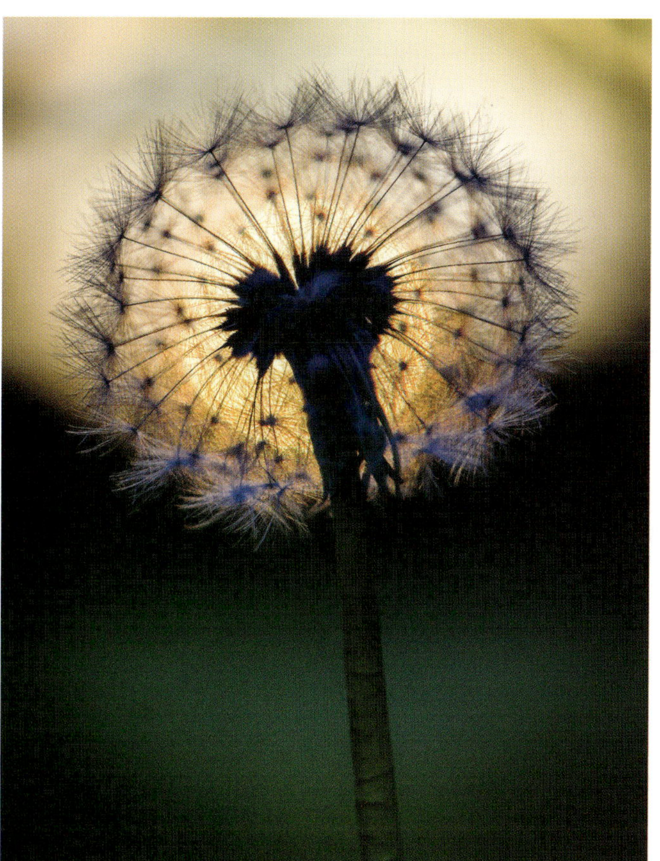

A dandelion with the setting sun behind it.

Starburst photography

An effect that landscape photographers sometimes employ is to turn the sun's rays into a star-like shape by using a very small aperture.

Putting your camera into aperture priority or manual mode, set the aperture to a high number, possibly as much as f/16. A very small aperture like f/22 will work, but may cause diffraction, which could cause your image to be less sharp overall. You'll probably need to use a tripod as the corresponding shutter speed will be quite slow. Try to get the sun just peeping through some foliage or around a tree trunk so that the effect appears more subtle. The more aperture blades your lens has, the more rays you will see in the starburst (you can look up your lens information in the manual or on the internet).

One thing that happens when you use a small aperture is that it will really show up any dust on your lens – you might have dust spots that you'll need to take out in the edit. It will obviously help somewhat if you give your sensor a careful blow beforehand with a camera dust-blower.

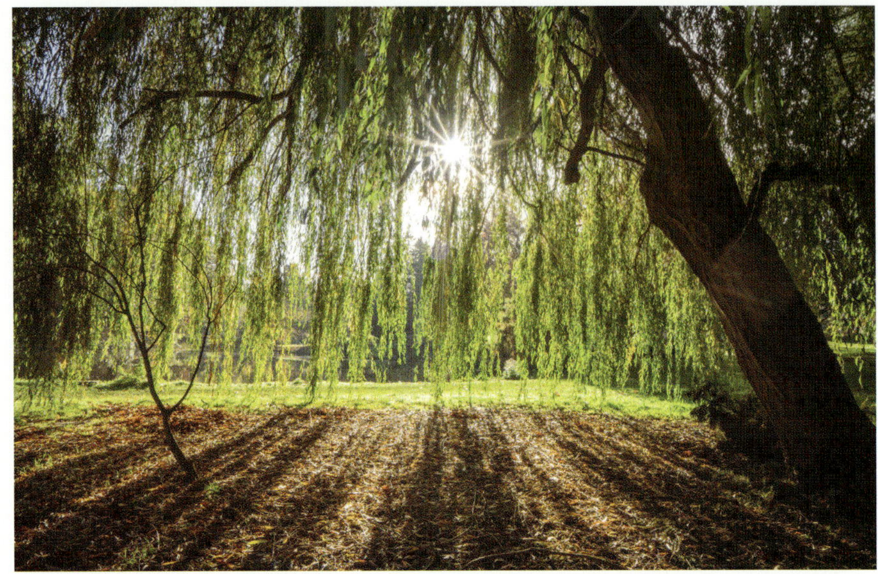

A *Salix* (willow tree) with the sunlight flared into a star shape by using a narrow aperture; f/22 in this case.

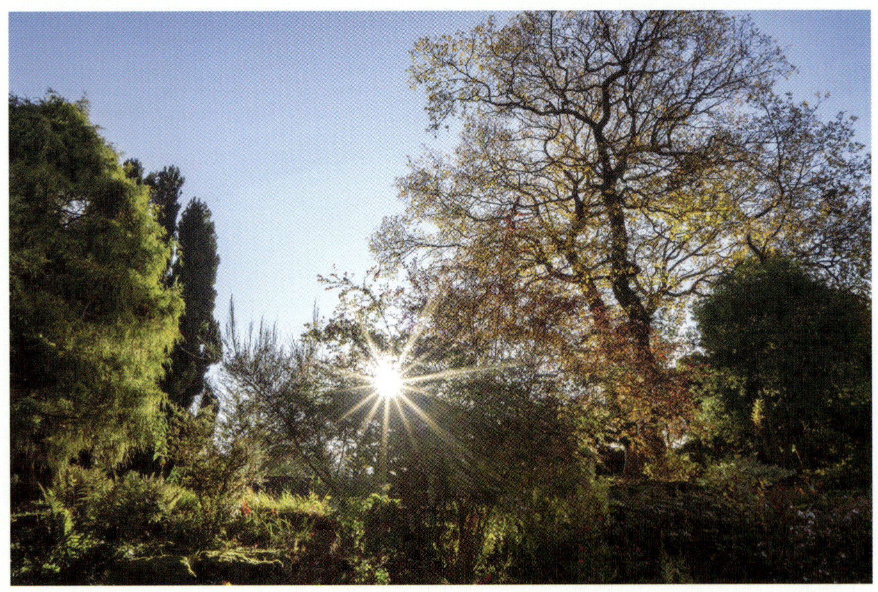

A starburst through trees and shrubs (also with the aperture set on f/22), the tree on the right is also backlit nicely. I had to take four dust spots out of the sky in the edit on this photo.

USING A SPEEDLIGHT OR YOUR IN-CAMERA FLASH

I rarely use flash in my photography – it will often give harsh reflections and 'shine' on photos that can make them look plasticky, and a soft, more natural approach is much better, most of the time.

However, whilst using a flash on a sunny or bright day might sound a little strange, a little extra light from the direction of the camera can often reduce shadows caused by harsh sunlight.

When I use flash in this way I use it on its lowest setting (sometimes called 'fill-in flash'), to bring out some of the shadows in the flowers if I'm standing well back and using a long lens. I dial the flash setting down to 2 or 3 on my camera. If you have a way of setting your camera flash so that you can reduce its strength in this way I would recommend experimenting to see what results it gives. You can also position your flash behind a small diffuser to soften its light – I have sometimes put masking or white tape over the flash 'window' to achieve the same effect. If your camera doesn't have an in-built flash you can buy a basic flash unit or speedlight to fit on the hot shoe on top of your camera.

Carefully used flash can also be useful to bring out the shadows on insects. Many close-up and macro photographers use flash, often with a diffuser over the flash to bring out details but avoid harsh highlights.

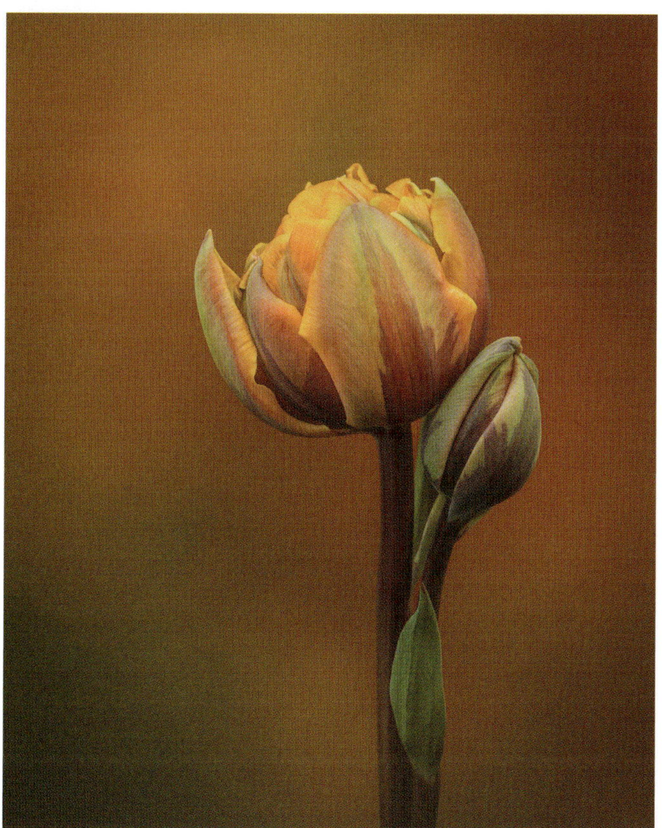

A tulip photographed using a flash with a diffuser to lighten the dark shadows on the stem and between the petals.

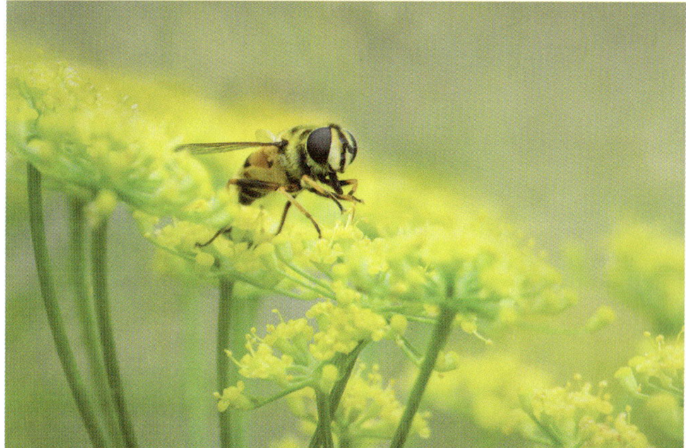

The details of this hoverfly on fennel have been brought out by using flash with a diffuser. I've added a texture in the edit to lighten the background above the flower.

USING AN LED LIGHT

Small LED lights can also be mounted to the camera using the camera hot shoe attachment and are often useful to bring out detail in close ups, or to reduce shadows caused by harsh sunlight. I often use them when photographing insects in the shade as it can give their eyes catchlights, which always give animals more 'life'. I prefer to use an LED light to a flash for flower and plant photography, as I can see the results before I press the shutter button.

When I'm photographing low-growing flowers I sometimes put an LED light on the ground to give more light to the flower/s if it's a very shady day.

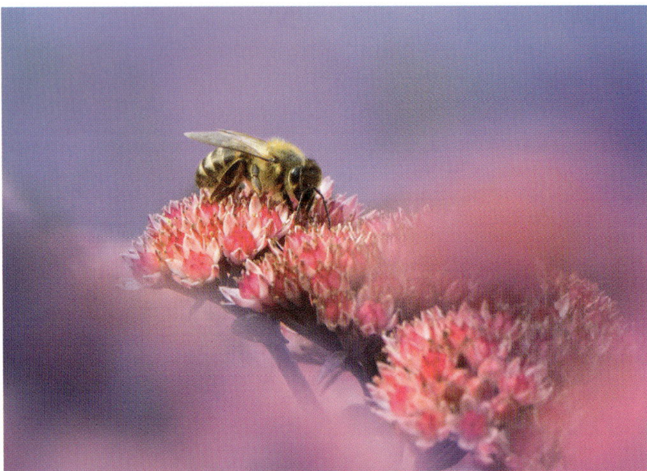

A honey bee on sedum in September with subtle catch-lights in its eyes. An overlay has been added in the edit to give the photo a more cohesive colour.

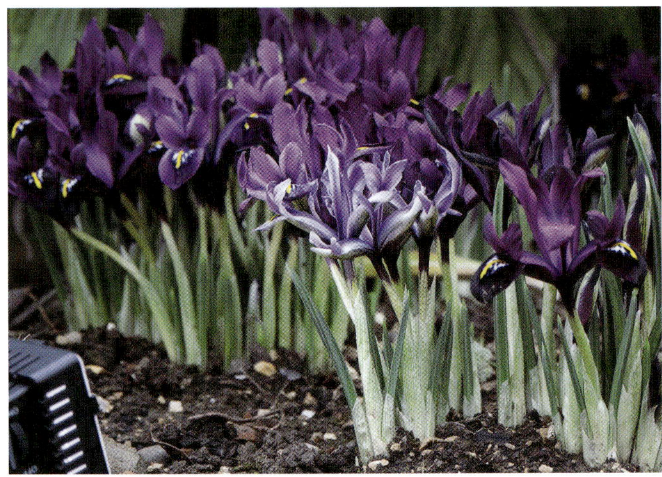

When I'm photographing lower-growing flowers I sometimes put an LED light on the ground to give more light to the flower/s if it's a very shady day. The *Iris reticulata* here were in a very dark part of the garden in January and the weather was grey and misty – adding light from an LED light to the left (shown in the picture) lifted the shapes and the colours.

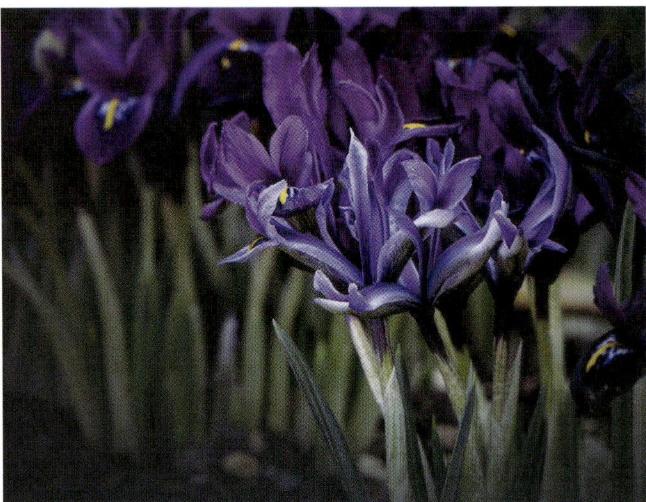

The final photo (which has a subtle texture and slight vignette added) has rich colours despite the inhospitable weather on the day.

Greenhouses and glasshouses

I love to photograph plants in greenhouses and glasshouses as they offer a beautifully soft, diffused light. Don't forget to venture inside if there is one in your local garden and see what you can capture. Often you'll find species of flowering cacti and orchids in glasshouses as they need a more temperate climate, so do go inside and experience the softer light.

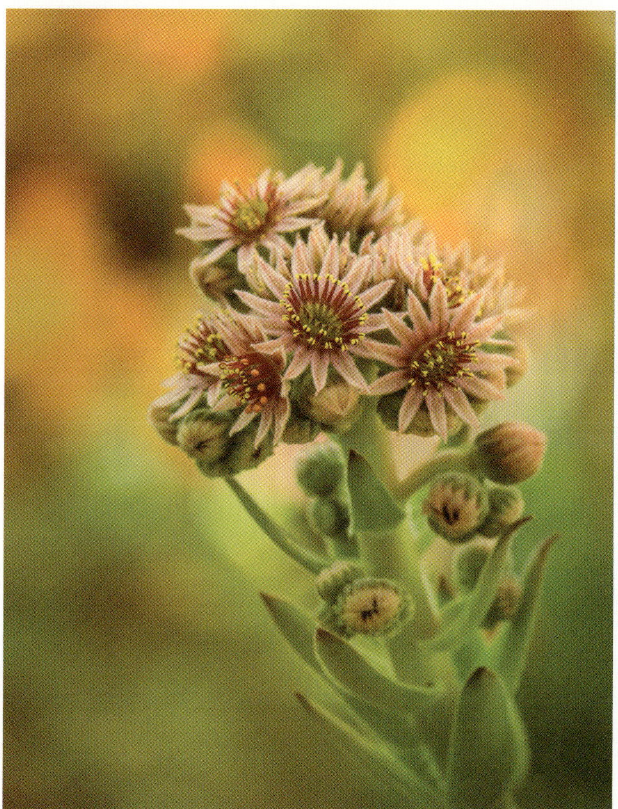

A *Sempervivum tectorum* (houseleek) flower inside a greenhouse. A subtle overlay has been added in the edit to enhance the colour of the background.

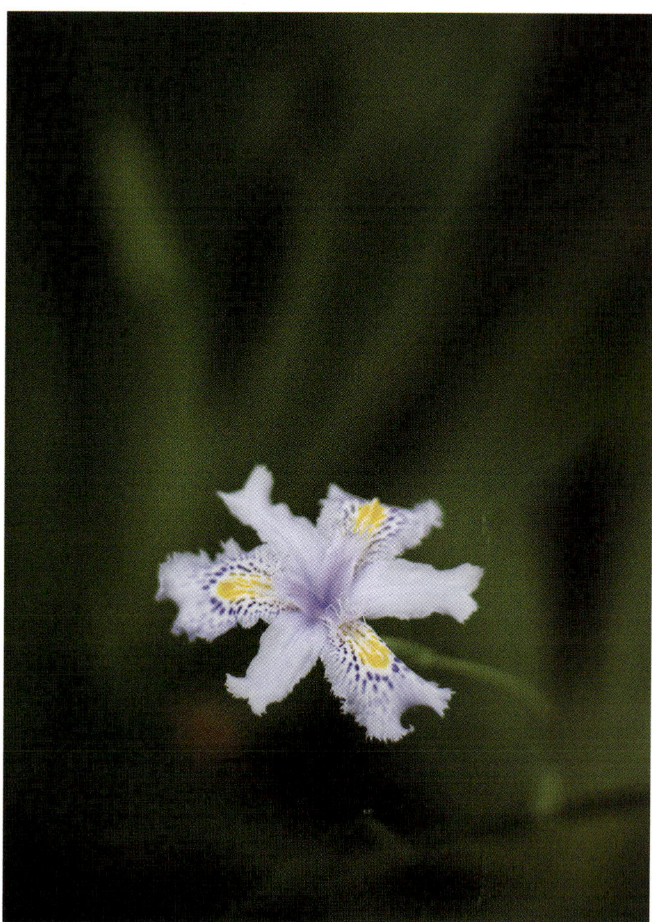

The diffused light of a glasshouse gives both this flower and its foliage a softness that compliments the delicate nature of the flower petals and leaves.

Histograms

If you have a camera that has a histogram setting I would definitely recommend using it. This gives a graphic representation of the pixels in the photograph. The height of the peaks represents the number of pixels of a particular colour or tone, and the tones are lined up from left to right from 0 (which is black) to 255 (which is absolute white). If the histogram goes beyond the top of the chart on the right-hand side then parts of your image will be too bright, or 'burnt out', which means that you will lose detail in that part of the photo. I can usually see by looking at the image that I need to reduce the exposure but it's nice to have the information in a histogram as reassurance. One can also change the exposure in the edit with the 'exposure' slider in Lightroom, or in Camera Raw in Photoshop. Exposure adjustment is also possible in some mobile phone apps. If the histogram was peaking on the left it would mean that the blacks were too black and 'crushed'.

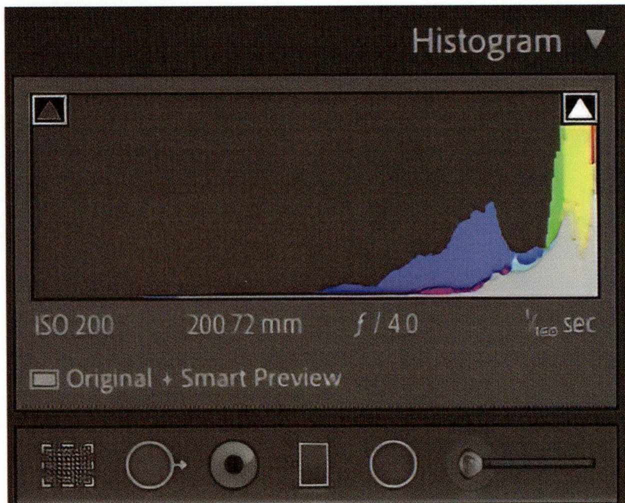

You can also see from the histogram in Lightroom that the peaks have gone way above the top of the rectangle on the right-hand side, indicating the same thing. You can also set most cameras to show you a histogram on the rear-view screen, which should help to get things right in-camera.

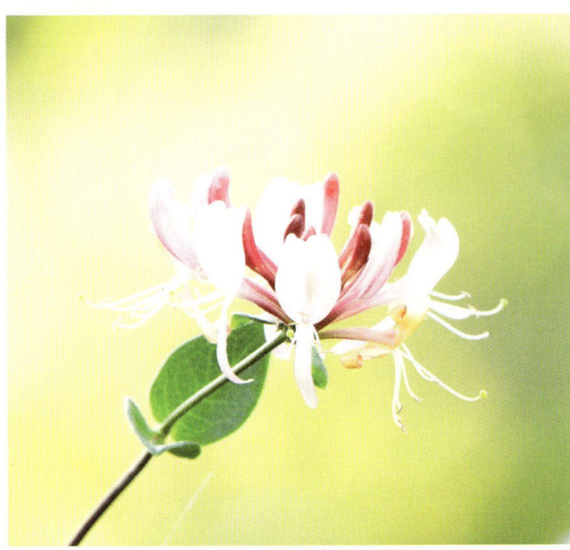

A photo of *Lonicera* (honeysuckle), which is very overexposed and has parts that are burnt out – Lightroom shows me this by marking red patches on the photo itself.

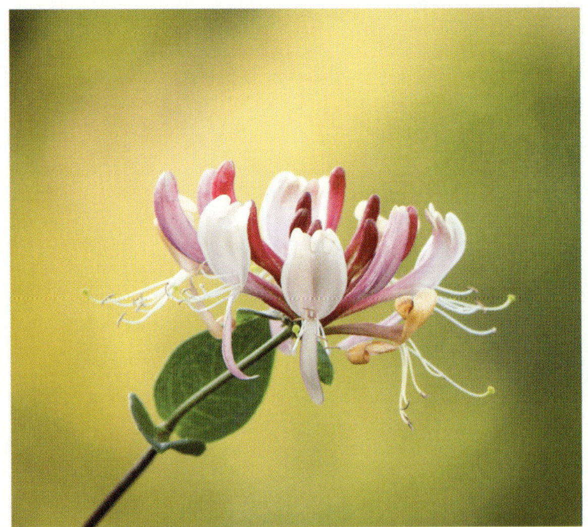

A correctly exposed photo of the same honeysuckle flower. If you shoot in raw it is fairly easy to adjust when you edit a photo such as this, which is way too bright or too dark.

Flowers and plants to photograph in March

March heralds the meteorological arrival of spring, along with daffodils, magnolias and unfurling buds of leaves.

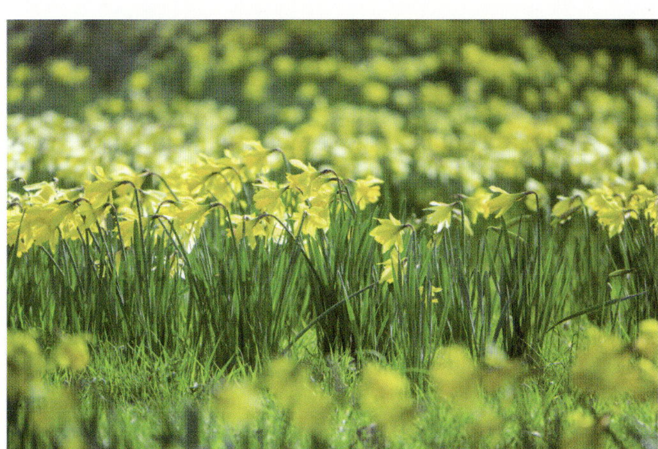

Narcissi in sunshine – 1/200 sec at f/4, 22mm.

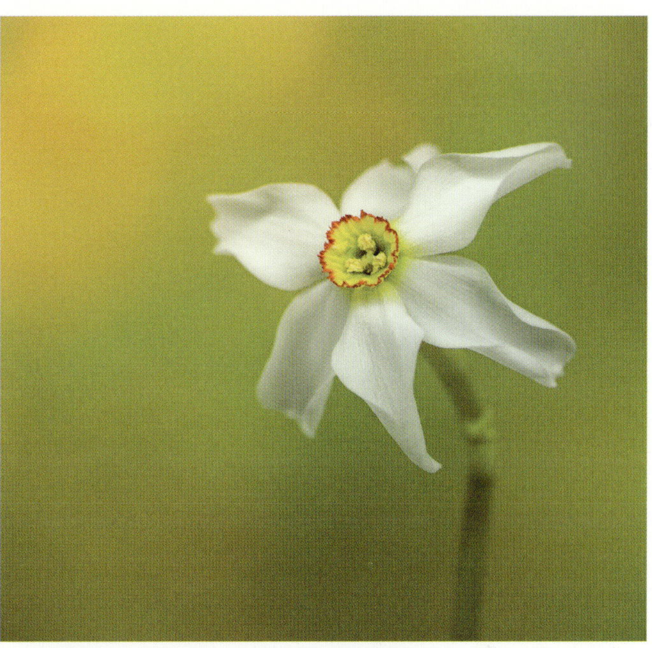

Narcissus poeticus – photographed indoors in a lightbox.

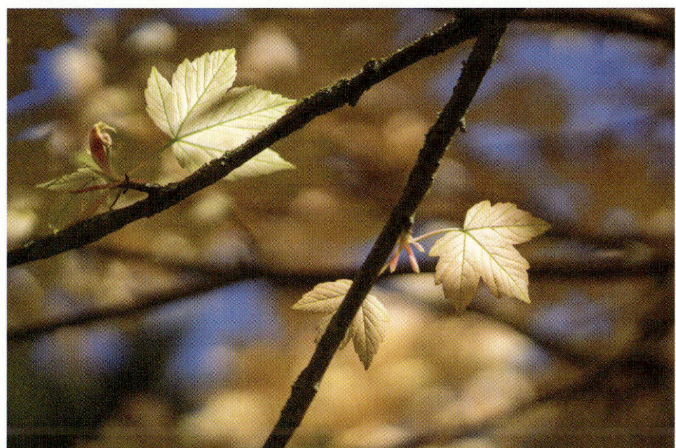

Leaves in sunlight – 1/8000 sec at f/1.8, 55mm.

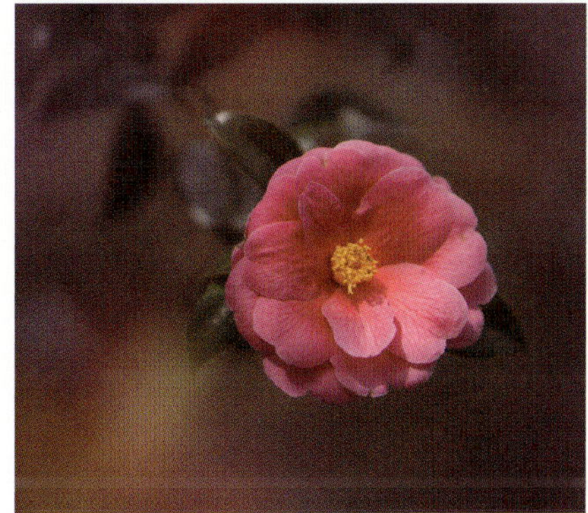

Camellia – 1/2500 sec at f/1.8, 55mm, overlay added in the edit.

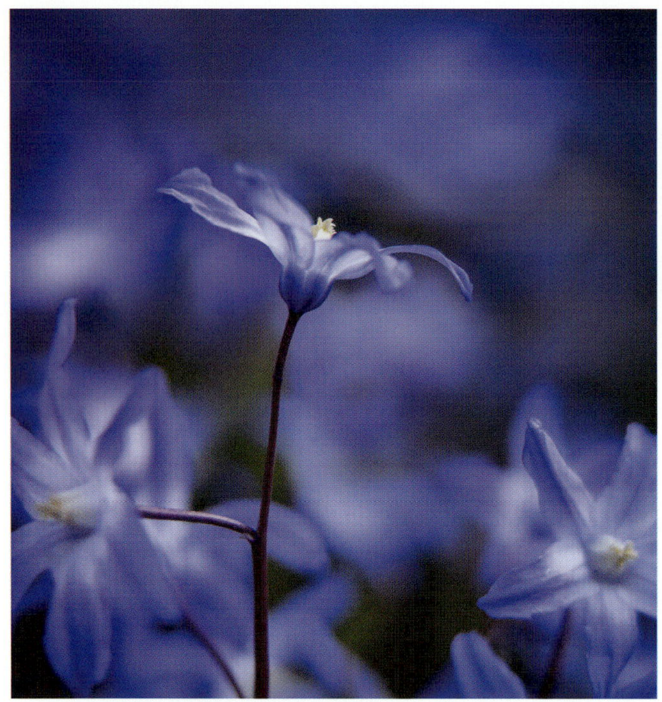

Chionodoxa flowers – 1/3200 sec at f/3.5, 55mm .

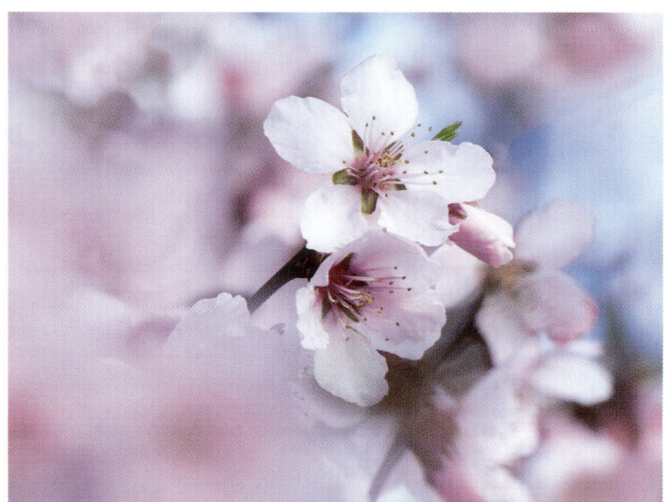

Prunus dulcis (flowering almond blossom) – 1/400 sec at f/4, 190mm.

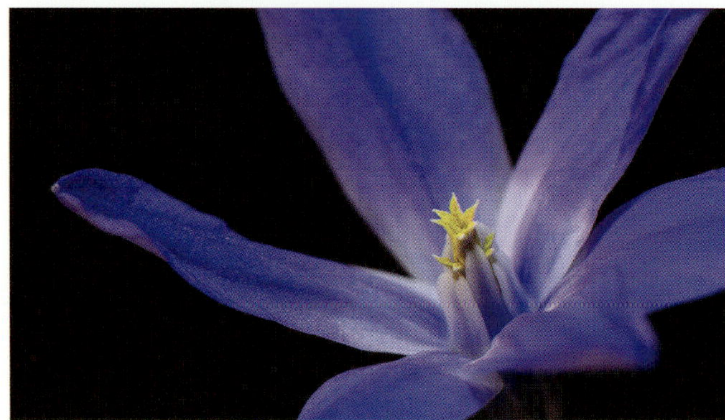

Chionodoxa flower – 1/100 sec at f/11 with a 100mm macro lens, taken indoors.

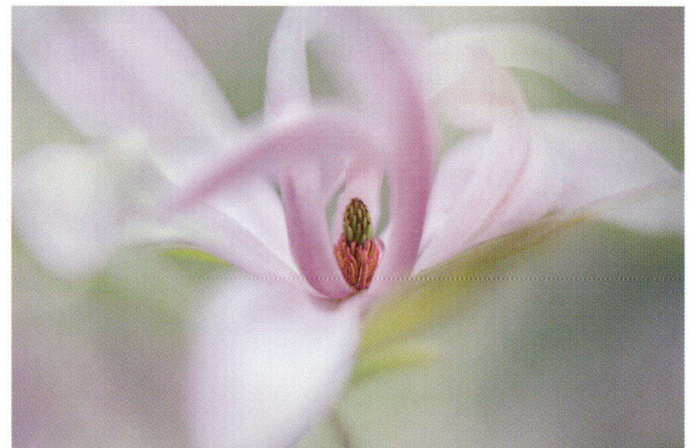

Magnolia flower – 1/500 sec at f/1.8, 55mm with an extension tube.

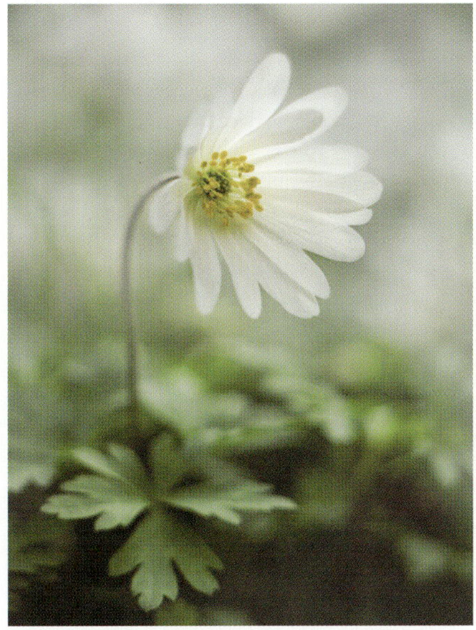

Anemone blanda – 1/500 sec at f/1.7, taken with a vintage lens.

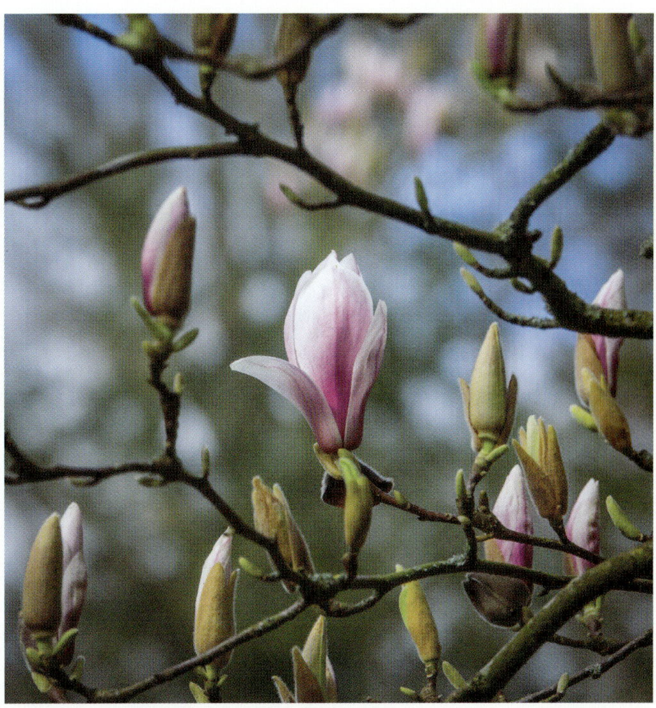

Magnolia buds – 1/640 sec at f/4, 100mm.

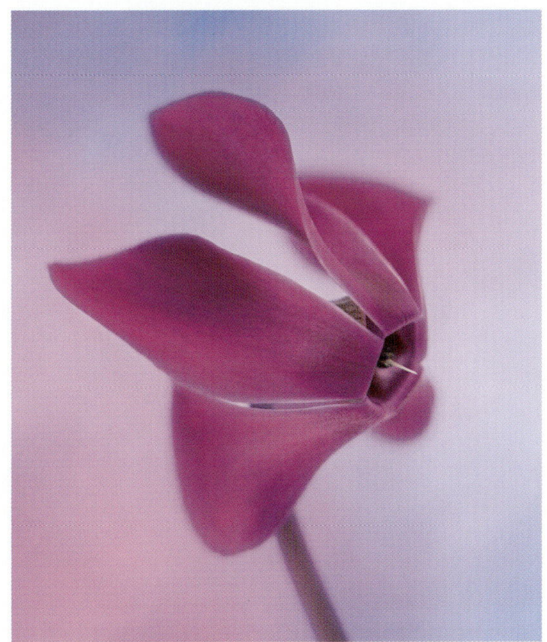

Cyclamen flower – 1/80 sec at f/5, 70mm vintage macro lens. Overlay added in the edit.

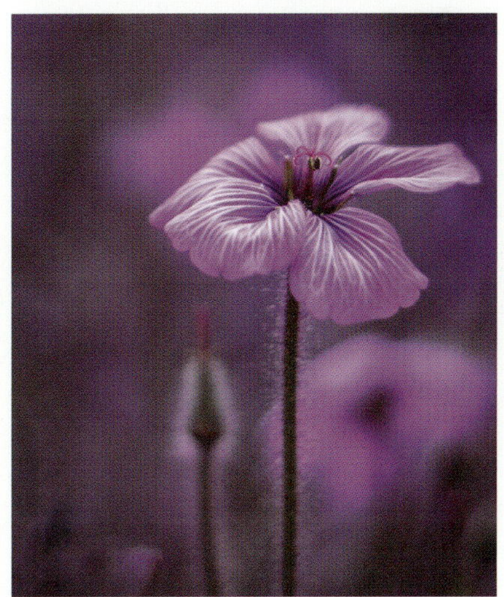

Pelargonium – 1/800 sec at f/2, 50mm vintage macro lens. Photographed in a greenhouse.

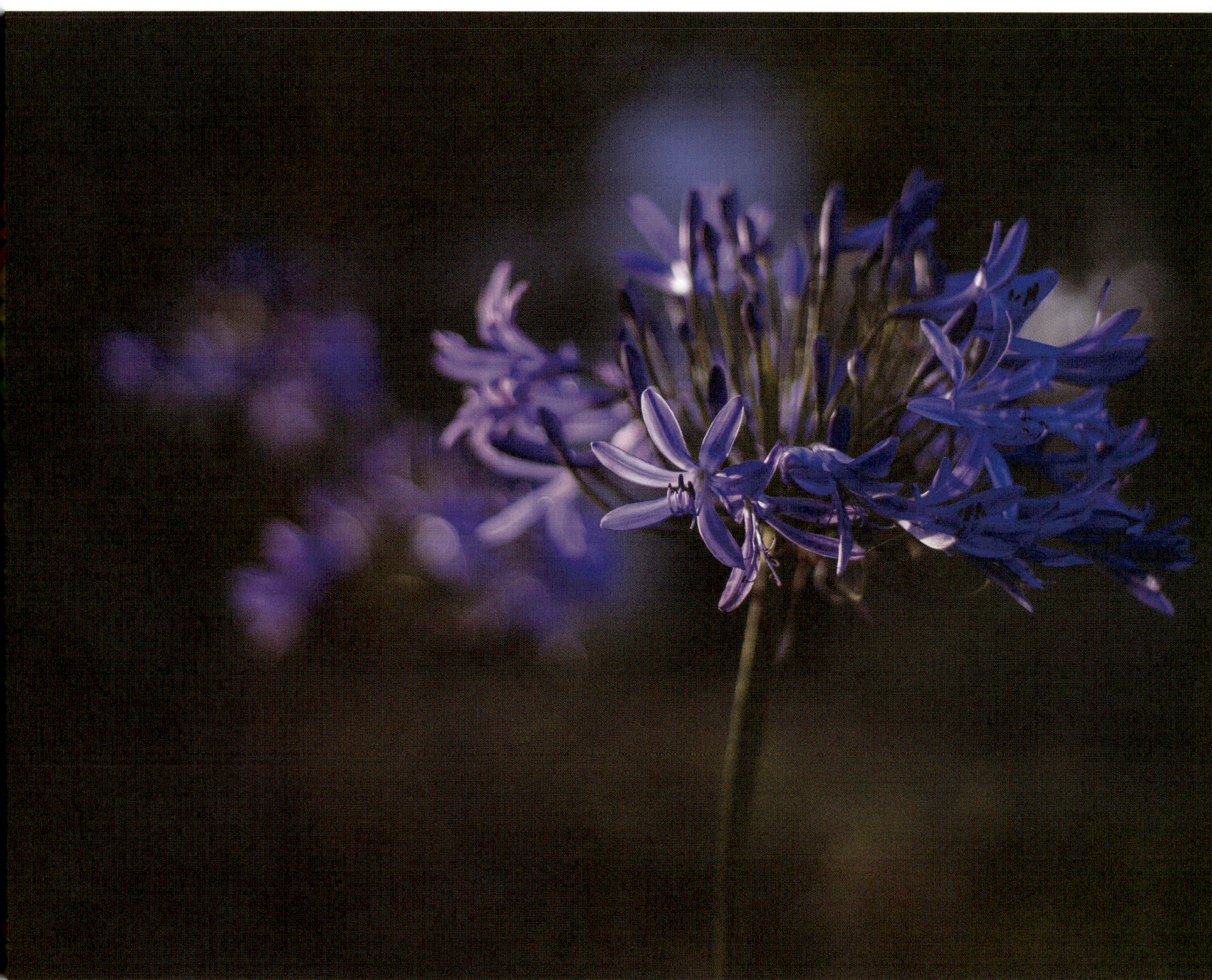

Agapanthuses in evening light.

CHAPTER 4

Background and Bokeh

> Exaggerate the essential, leave the obvious vague.
>
> VINCENT VAN GOGH

The background of your photo is as important as your subject and a good background will transform a photo to a new level. This doesn't mean that it needs to stand out – on the contrary, good backgrounds will often do exactly as the name suggests; stay in the background. As I mentioned in the second chapter, backgrounds that are cluttered, messy or have distracting elements draw the eye away from the subject which makes for a less pleasing result overall.

When photographing your flower or plant always check your background before you press the shutter and ask yourself if it is distracting. Stray leaves from other plants, grasses and other plant-life poking into the frame won't give a clean background which, most of the time, makes for a better composition. One way of achieving a clean background is to simply photograph a flower or plant that has nothing behind it – five metres of empty space with no other plants before the nearest hedge or wall will usually mean a smooth background.

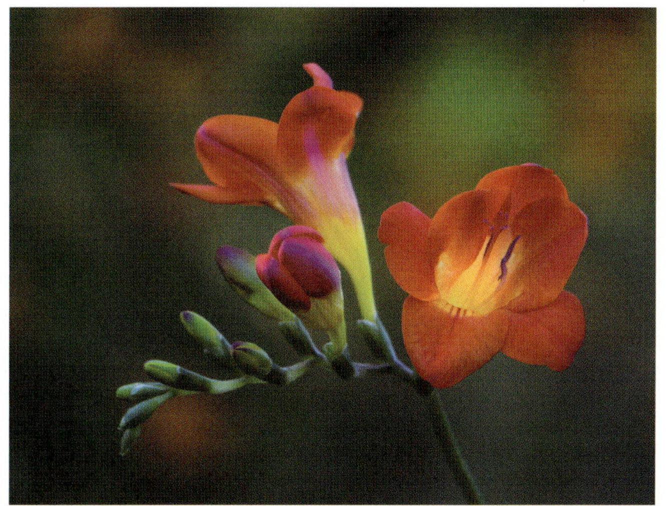

A freesia flower with a smooth background, the subtle orange blobs are out-of-focus flowers some way behind it.

The easiest way however to achieve a background that isn't distracting is to use a lens that opens very wide – preferably under f/2 (f/1.7 or f/1.8 are ideal). Set the camera on its A or AV (aperture priority) setting and dial the lens aperture down as far as it goes as your starting point. It is very likely that some

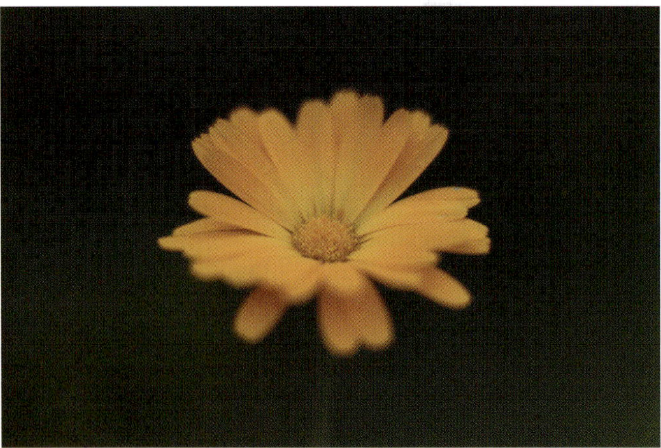

A calendula flower photographed in my garden with a 50mm lens at f/1.8 plus a 10mm extension tube. Notice how whilst the centre is mostly sharp, the petals are slightly blurry and the background is a smooth green.

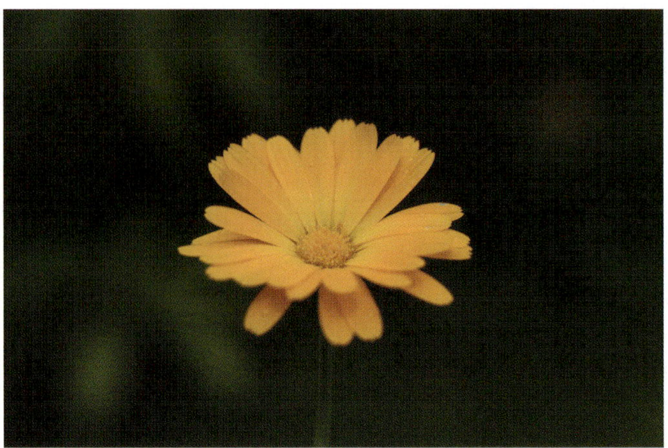

The same set-up, but with the aperture changed to f/5.6. The blurred outlines of some leaves are now visible in the background, which gives nice context and we can see raindrops on the petals. About half the flower is now in focus.

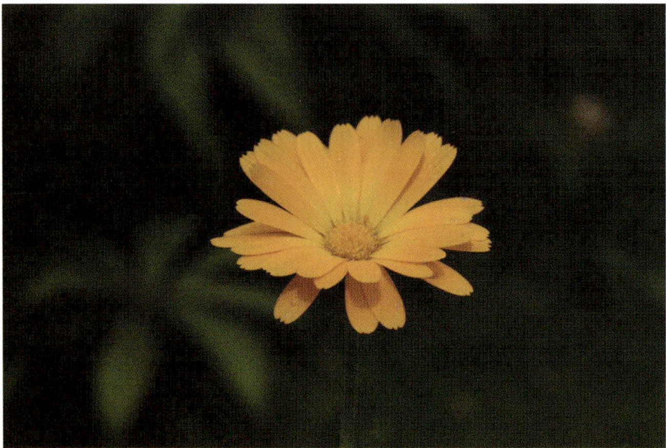

The same set-up, but with the aperture changed to f/11. The flower is almost completely in focus and the shapes of leaves are clearer in the background. Some dust spots are now evident as a result of the narrow aperture. I would go on to clone these out when editing the photo.

of the flower will be out of focus if you do this so make sure your focal point is obvious, and try to get it sharp. A long lens is perfect for this but you might need to stand some way away from the flower.

You might discover that you don't actually prefer the result with the widest aperture, as another setting gives a more interesting background or colour, but definitely experiment with this. There is of course no right answer, and the results different apertures give will vary greatly depending on the type of lens.

The downside of using a wide aperture could mean that many parts of the flower are no longer in focus, which you may decide is not effective and then choose to readjust. Often having the focus only sharp on the centre of the flower (or a particular petal) *does* work, as the partially blurred petals take on a dreamy quality. Just make sure that the point that is in sharpest focus is the most important part of the composition, the place to which the eye will naturally travel.

A blurred-out background can really add to single flower compositions as it draws all the viewer's attention to the flower. Some photographers refer to the blurred background as 'bokeh', especially if it has circles of light in it (more on this later). It is harder, however, to keep the majority of the flower in focus (unless you use a very long lens or make your aperture wider), and you might have to decide on a specific area of focus as you shoot.

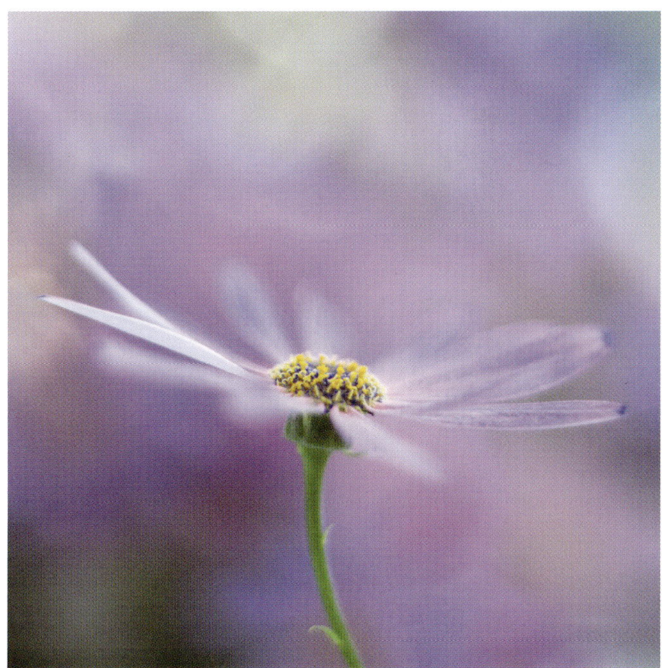

A Senetti flower photographed at 1/400 sec at f/1.7 using a 50mm vintage lens. The other similar flowers behind create the background and only the centre of the flower is sharp.

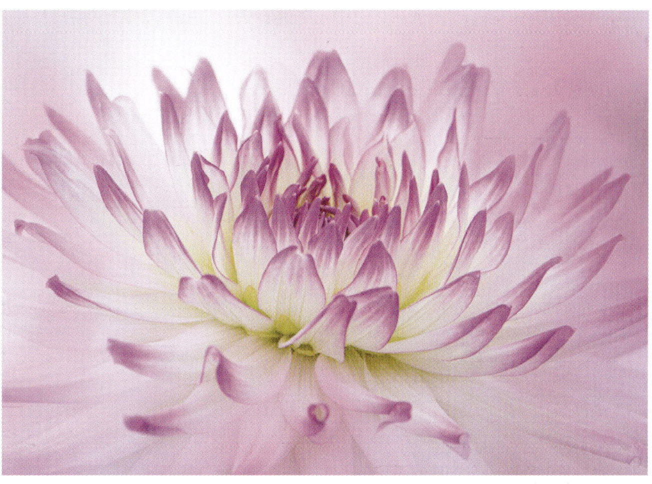

A cactus flower photographed with a long lens at a flower show – the tent the display was in was white and creates the background – I then added a subtle overlay in the edit to make the background more cohesive with the flower.

FINDING GOOD BACKGROUNDS

When you've taken a photo, review it on the rear screen and check the background – if there are grasses or leaves that distract the eye, have another go from a different aspect or position. If the angle from which you take the photo is restricted and you can't move around the flower very easily, you might need to remove unwanted elements in the edit.

Backgrounds can also be changed by elements that you've deliberately placed there, which, if the background is blurred as a result of a wide aperture like f/1.8, will lose their detail and just appear as blurred colour.

I have in the past used the cover of our trampoline, children's toys, wheelbarrows, buckets and washing hanging on the line to create interesting colour, none of which were obvious as they just became blurred blocks of colour in the background. Obviously this becomes harder if you're shooting in a public garden but I have on occasion used a scarf draped over my camera bag, or other visitors walking past (as blurs of colour) to change the background. Position your 'background' as far away as possible and it will take on a more naturalistic feel in the photo. This technique works best with a long lens.

Ultimately, if you are aiming for a 'natural' effect in your garden photography, try for a little more garden 'context', rather than just a flat background (the latter can in itself be beautiful, but not as naturalistic).

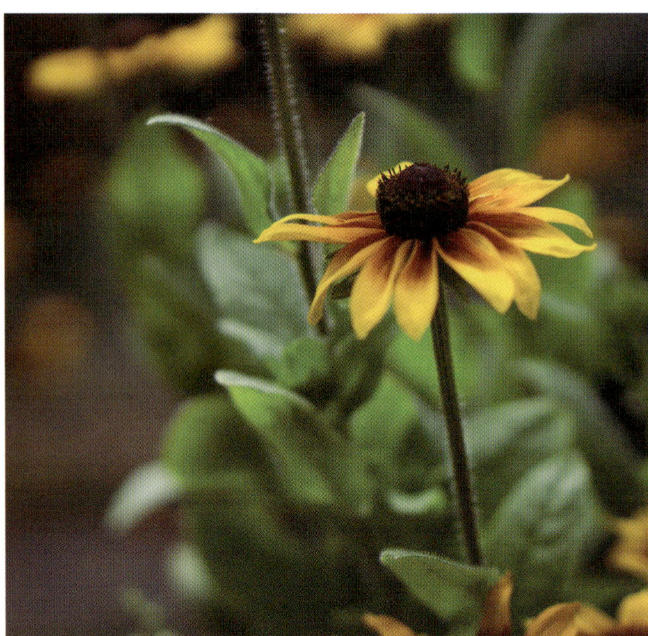

This *Rudbeckia* flower is part of a clump – the stalk of the flower behind intersects the petals and there is distracting foliage. Also the nearest petals are a little too blurry for me in this context.

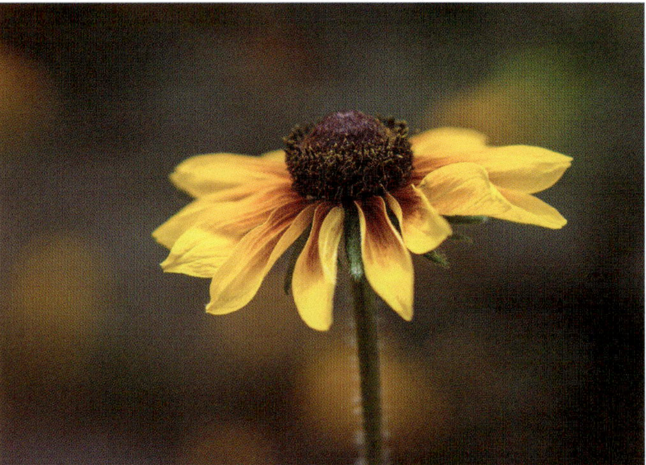

The same *Rudbeckia* flower, but taken from a different angle; because the other flowers and foliage are now further away, they blur into the background and are not a distraction.

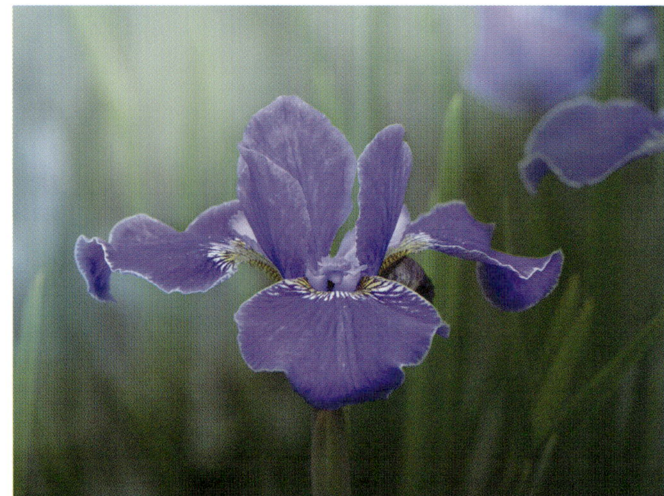

When I photographed these irises I thought that the others in the background were pulling my eye away from the one in the foreground. However I was unable to change my angle as they were growing near water and I couldn't get to the side of them.

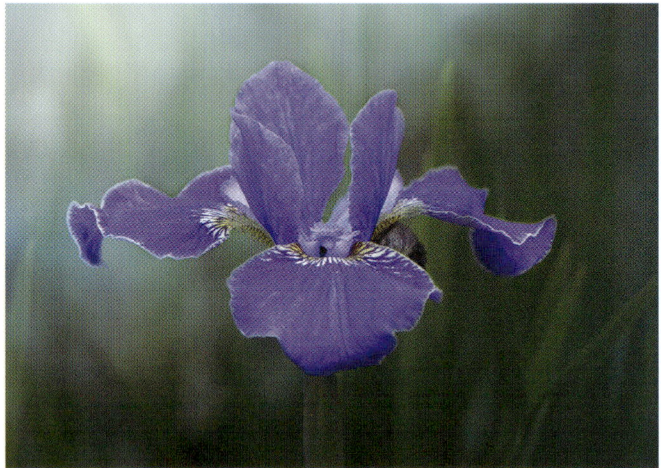

The same photo, but I have removed the background flowers in Photoshop, using the 'content-aware fill'. Had I not had this option I probably would have tried a crop, but if you can, always think about the background at the time of shooting.

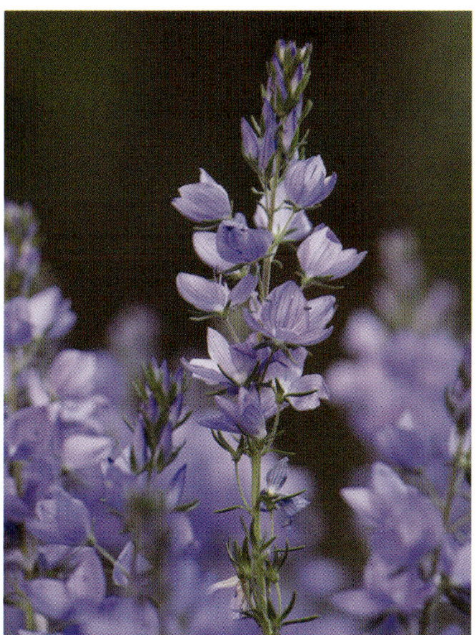

I lay on the ground to photograph these veronica flowers, and their green background was provided by a distant hedge.

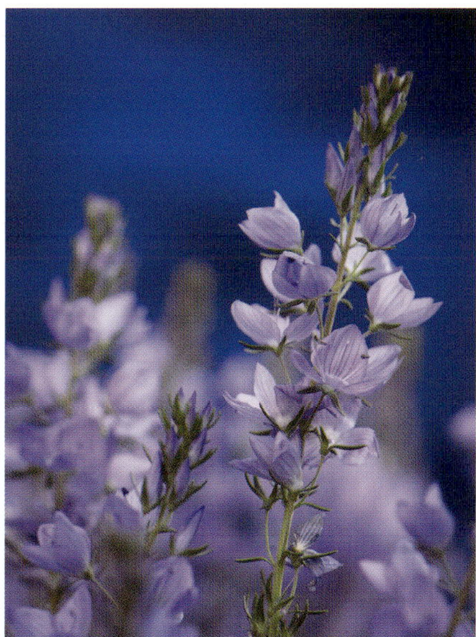

My son then walked past behind the flowers and the background turned blue as he was wearing blue shorts.

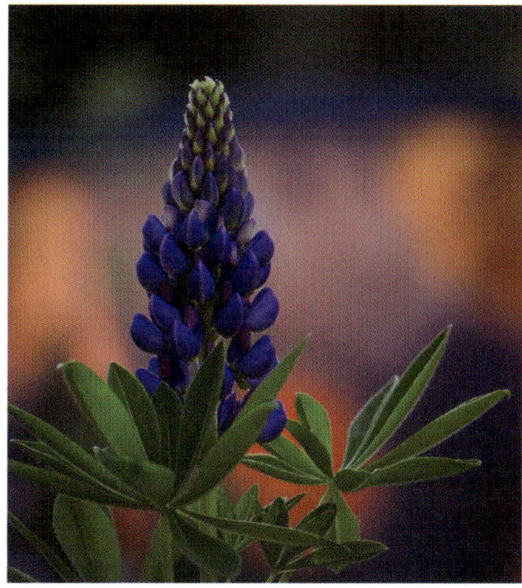

This lupin was photographed in my garden with the background of an orange football goal behind it.

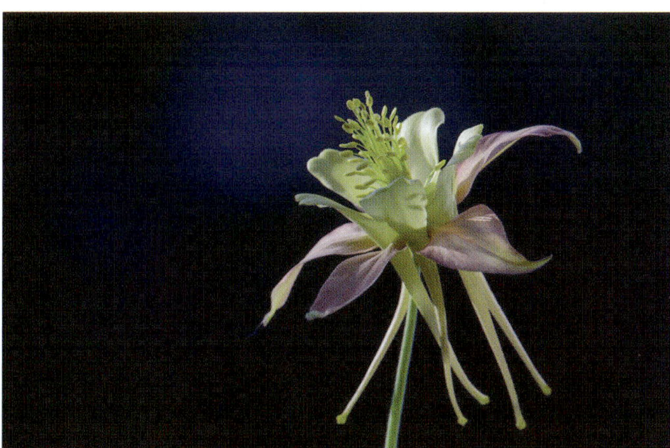

This yellow aquilegia flower has the slightly blue-ish background of my next-door neighbour's blue rotary washing-line.

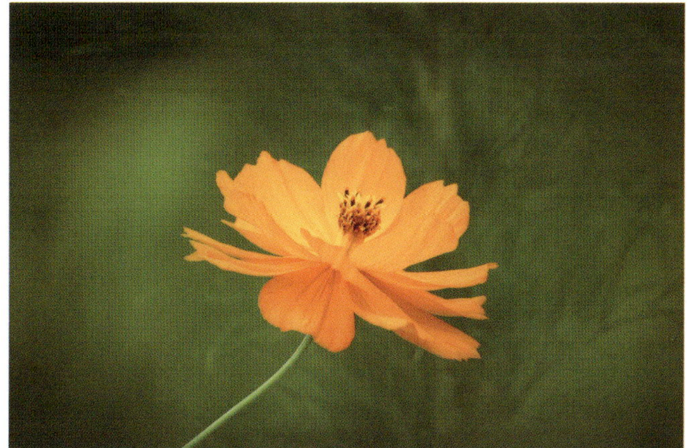

The foliage in the background behind this *Cosmos polidor* flower below gives the photo more depth and context.

Keep it timeless

Try not to have anything man-made in the background of your shot if it is a flower close-up, unless it is very blurred out – brick walls and sheds just don't give the 'timeless' feel that a single colour or natural background does. If the flower is in front of a wall try to take the photo parallel to the wall instead so the wall does not become a feature. Having said this you can often compose a beautiful shot with more 'antique' elements: perhaps a metal watering can or an old door with wisteria growing around it.

Foregrounds

If you're low to the ground, look carefully at the picture in your camera and double check for things that might be making your picture messy and distracting the eye. The obvious contenders for this are leaves and small pieces of debris that draw focus from your subject. If you're able to (and allowed), move any offending items from the composition.

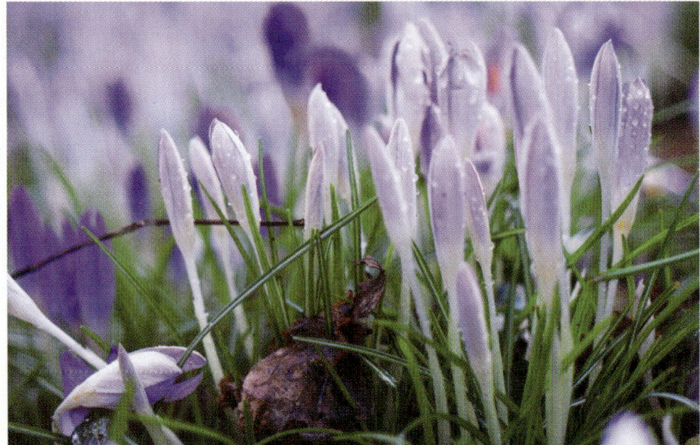

I took this photo of crocuses in a wood about ten years ago and wish that I had removed the brown leaf (and the stick on the left) from the front as it spoils the overall composition.

BOKEH

The word 'bokeh' (pronounced boh-kay) is Japanese in origin and refers to the way that the camera and lens render the out-of-focus light in an image. Some photographers also use it to describe blurred and out-of-focus elements in the background in general.

Many people find the circles and 'blips' of light produced by this effect very appealing, although like many photographic techniques it can be overdone and risks looking a bit artificial. You can even purchase backgrounds on the internet that allow you to overlay bokeh onto your photo but this can often look false if not done well, and to be honest it's much more fun hunting down actual bokeh and interesting background light in real life.

To achieve similar circular bokeh to the above photos you'll usually need a wide aperture lens on its widest aperture, for example f/1.7. The best way to learn how this works is to take a variety of photos from the same position but from slightly different angles, some pointing more to the sky and some less so. You might find that you need to actually lie on the ground in order to capture the light above or around the flower as

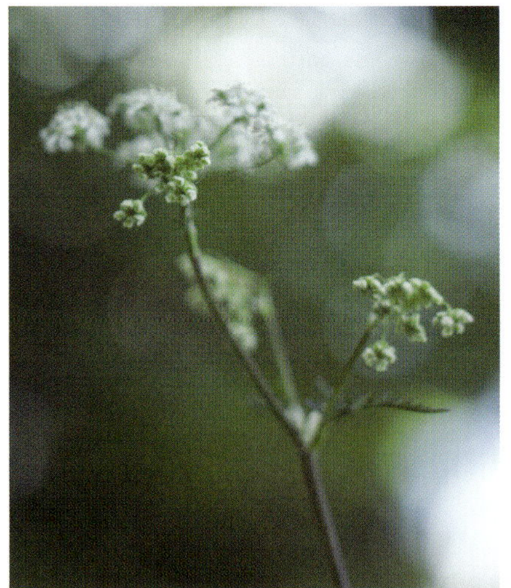

Anthriscus sylvestris (cow parsley) photographed with a wide-open vintage lens with light coming through the hedgerow behind it.

bokeh circles. In general, chinks of light coming through trees or hedges when the sun is low in the sky should work well when the camera is angled towards them with something to focus on in the foreground.

Sometimes the 'circles' of light are hexagonal, and the resulting shape in your photos will depend on how many aperture blades your lens has (lenses with six aperture blades give hexagonal bokeh). Some older lenses have just five or six blades, some will have eleven or even fourteen. Circular bokeh will usually be created by lenses with more aperture blades. Some vintage lenses, such as some Helios versions, are sought after for the bokeh effects they produce.

I sometimes set my camera to manual focus so that I can photograph just the bokeh – this can then be added as a layer on top of a regular photo in Photoshop and I'll explain how to do this in Chapter 11, 'Editing your Photographs'. However I would usually try to get the results I want in-camera if I can, as they usually look more natural.

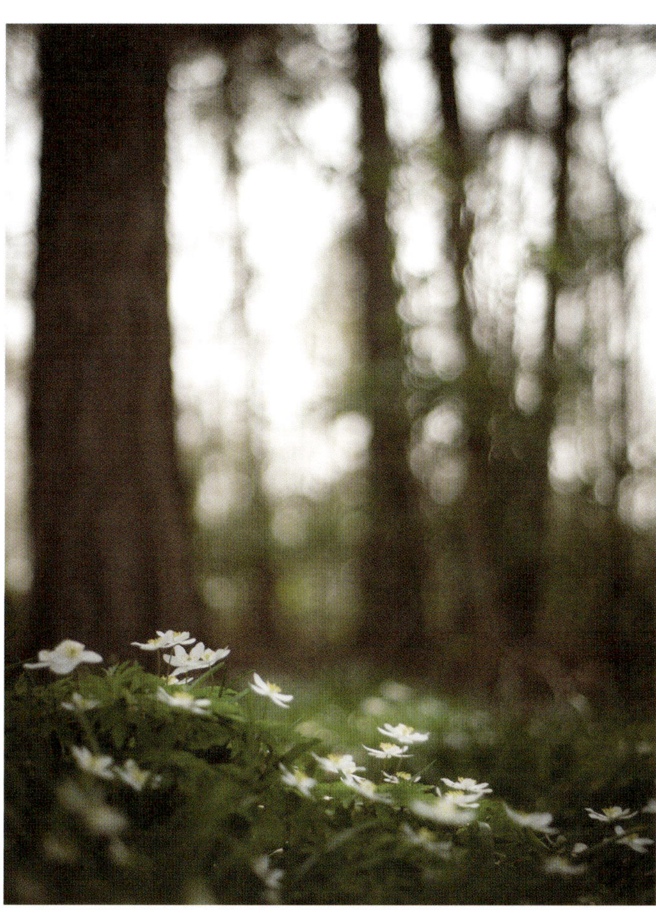

Anemone nemorosa in a forest, with the late afternoon light shining through the trees behind.

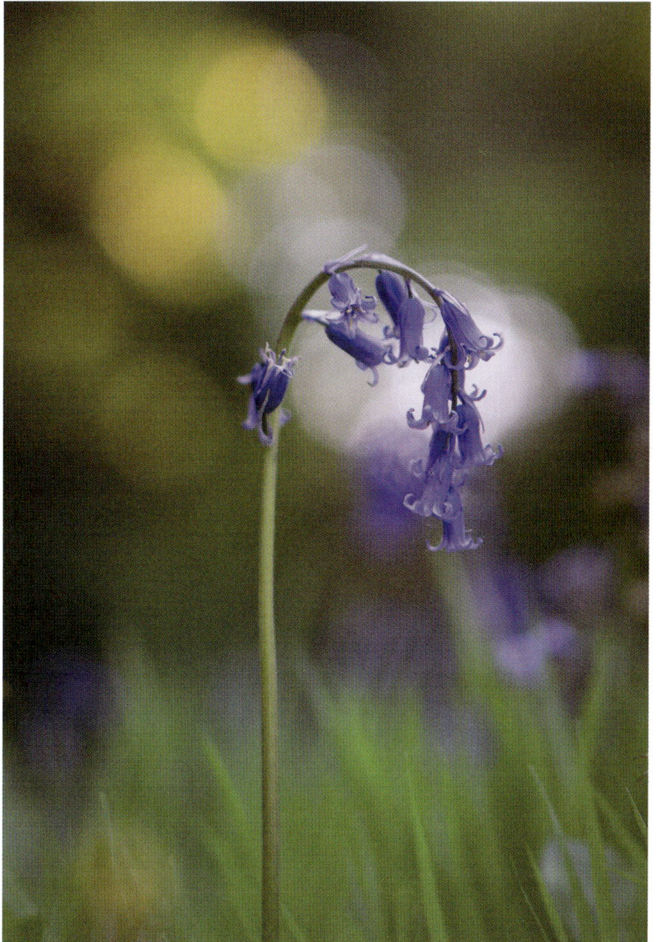

Bluebells, with light from the gaps between far-away trees behind them.

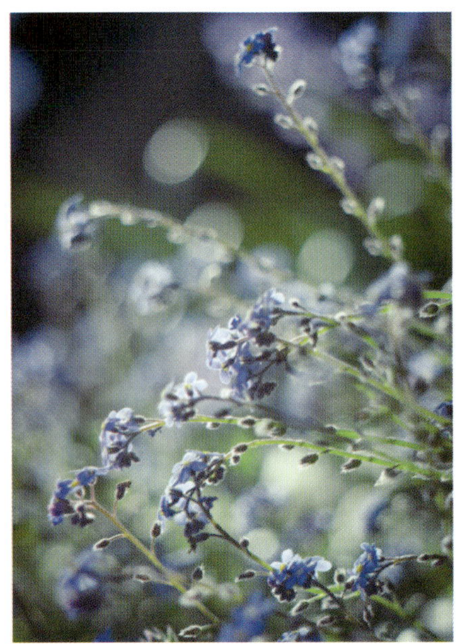

Myosotis (forget-me-nots) after rain – the reflections of raindrops on the flowers further away render as small circles of light.

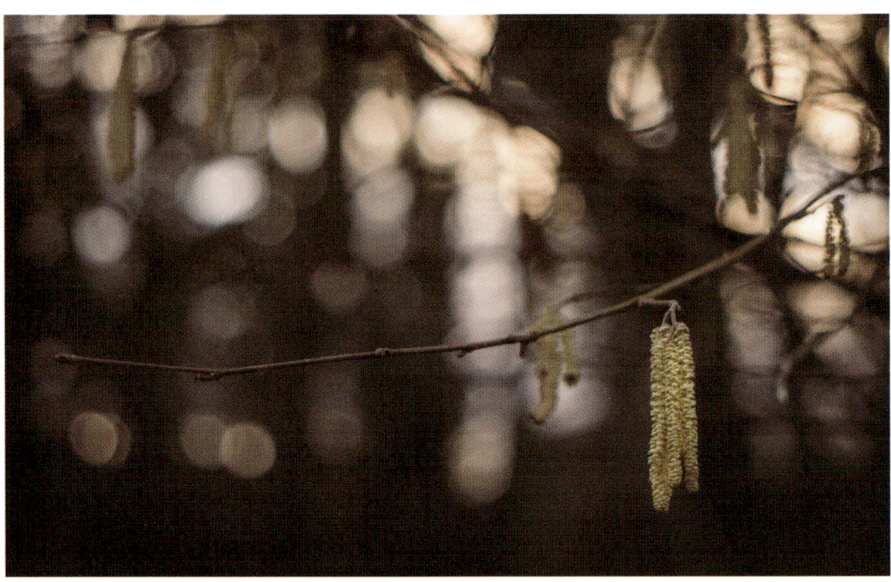

Corylus avellana catkins, with out-of-focus light between trees in the distance.

Bokeh photographed by shooting with manual focus and pointing the camera at light through trees – a long lens or zooming in may help with this.

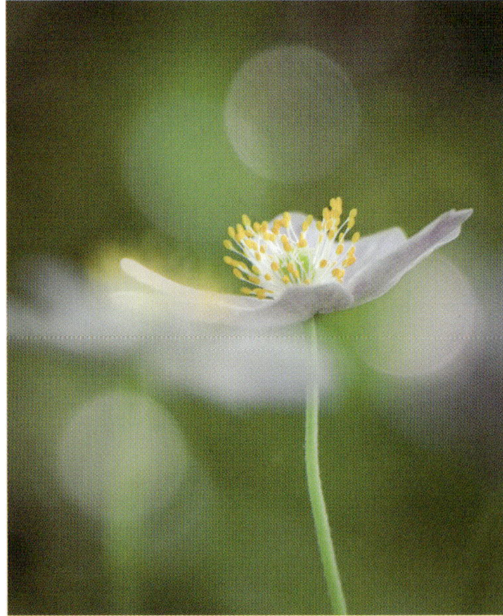

The same bokeh photo, this time added as an overlay on top of a photo of anemone flowers.

Flowers and plants to photograph in April

In April the tulips are at their best and cherry blossom hangs heavy on branches – spring is definitely here!

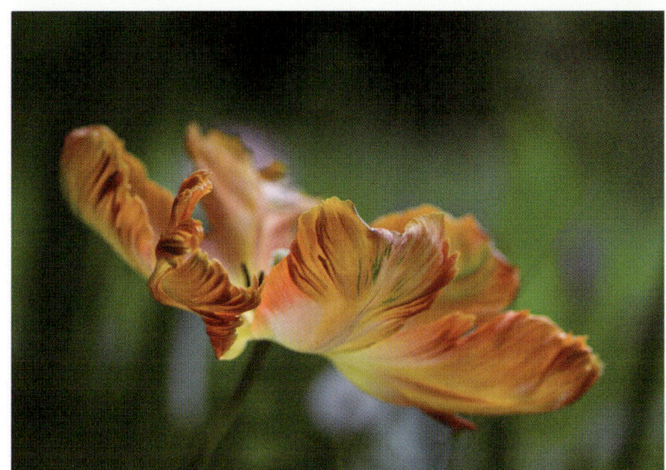

Parrot tulip – 1/640 sec at f/2, 50mm vintage lens.

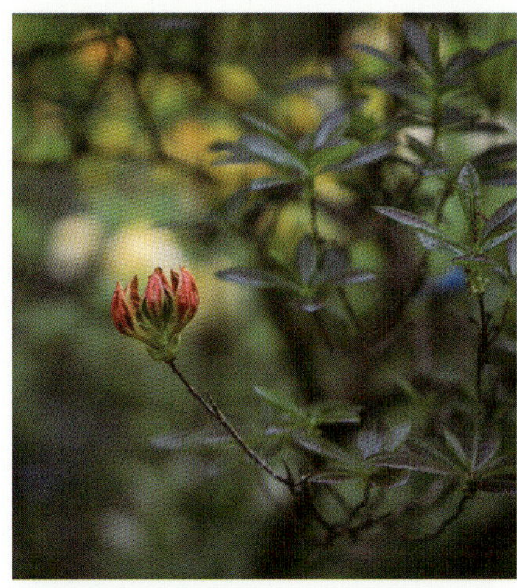

Rhododendron bud – 1/400 sec at f/1.8, 50mm.

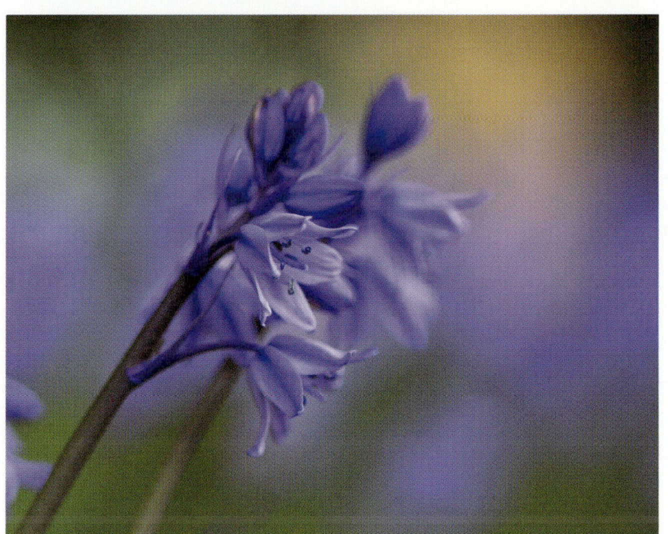

Hyacinthoides hispanica (Spanish bluebells) – 1/250 sec at f/1.7, 50mm vintage lens.

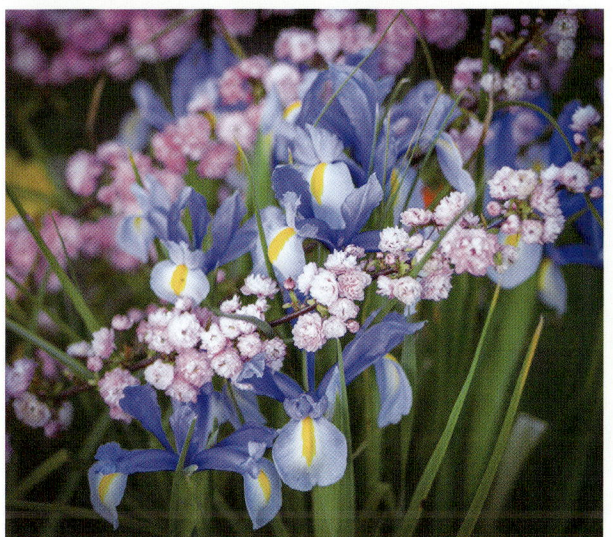

Irises and cherry blossom – 1/125 sec at f/4, 150mm.

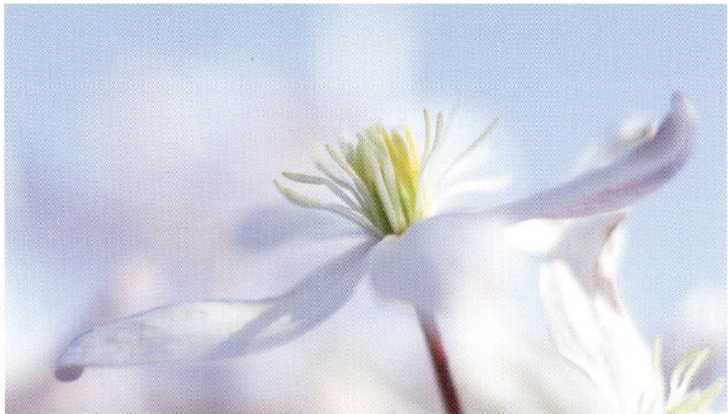

Clematis flower – 1/500 sec at f/1.7, 50mm vintage lens.

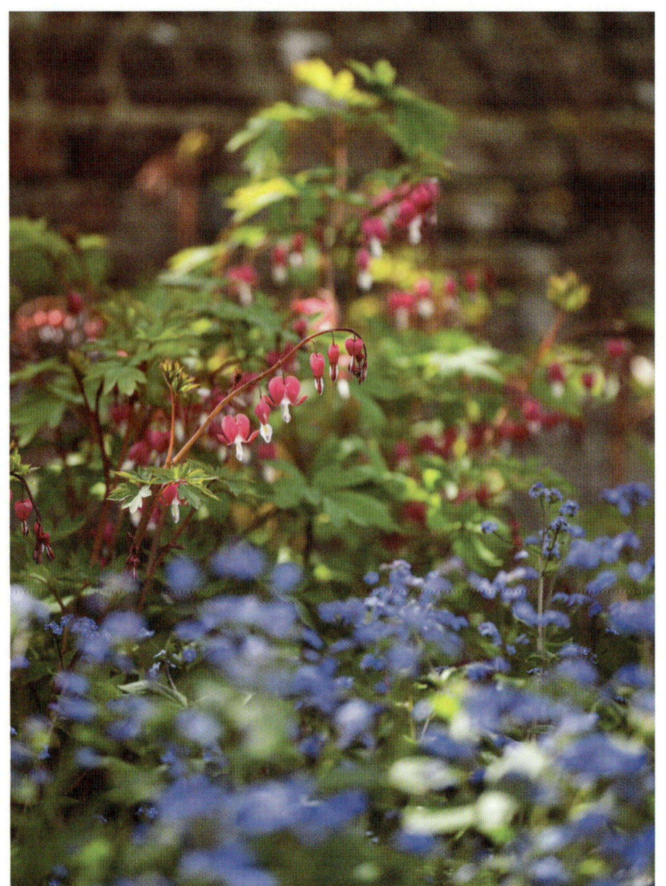

Dicentra spectabilis and Myosotis (bleeding heart and forget-me-nots) – 1/1250 sec at f/2.8, – 105mm macro lens.

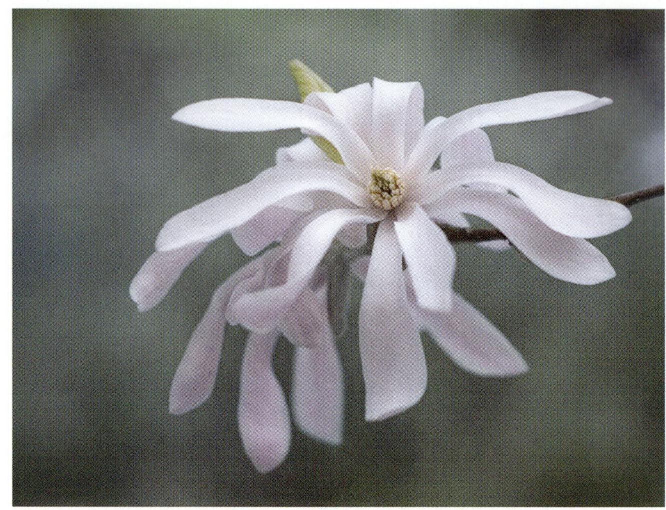

Magnolia flowers – 1/640 sec at f/2, 50mm vintage manual lens.

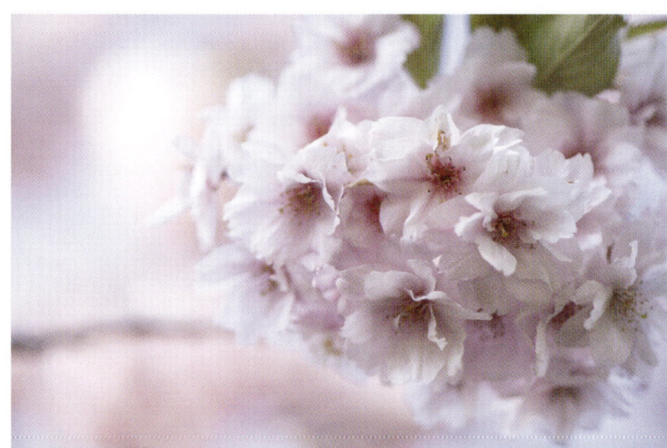

Cherry blossom – 1/640 sec at f/2 – 55mm.

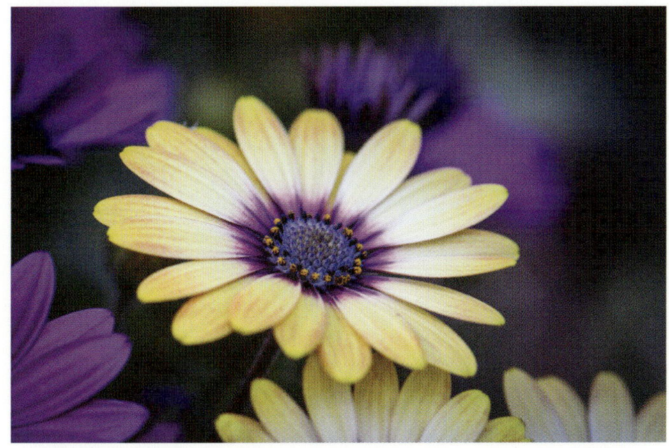

Osteospermum –1/800 sec at f/2, 50mm vintage lens.

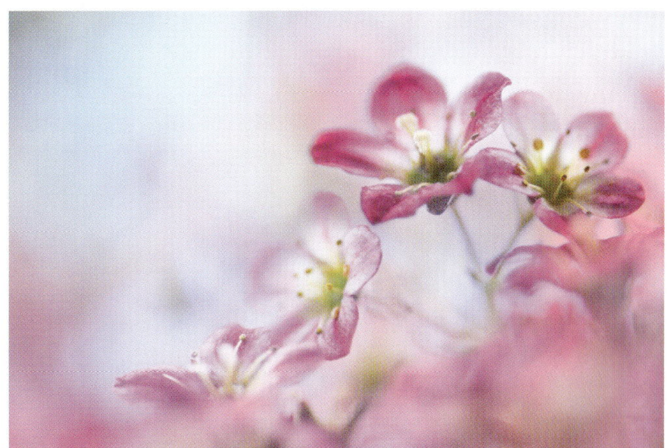

Saxifrage – 1/100 sec at f/1.7, vintage 50mm lens.

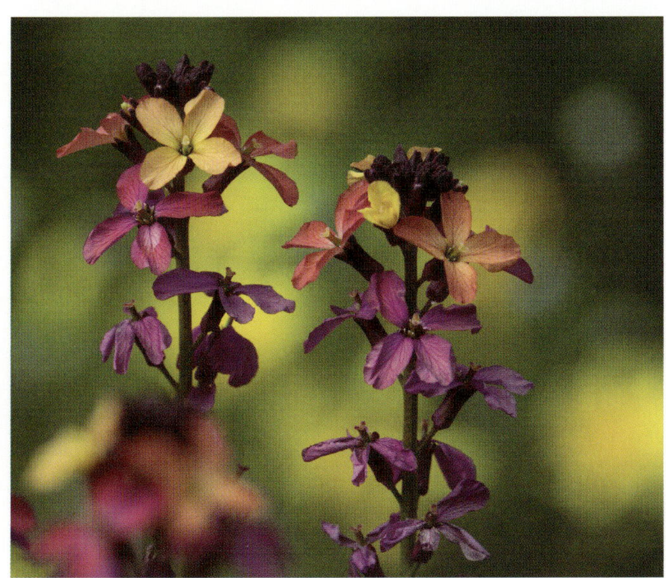

Erysimum (wallflowers) – 1/640 sec at f/4, 160mm.

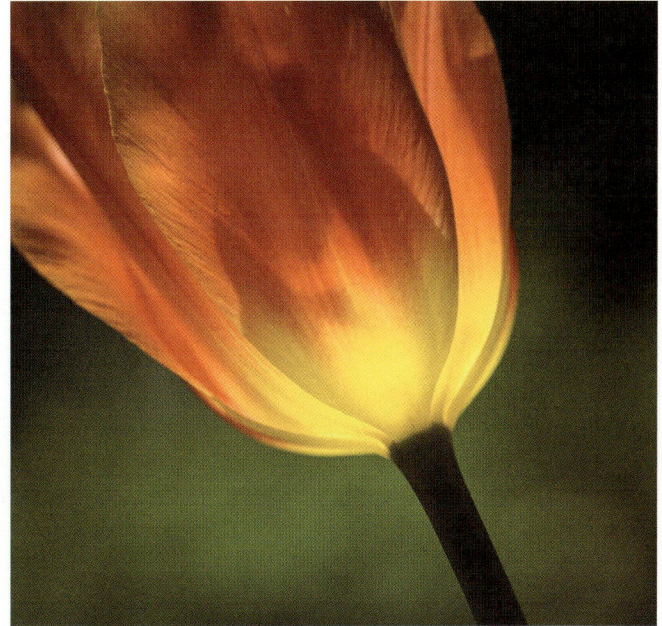

Tulip – 1/5000 sec at f/2.8, 105mm macro lens.

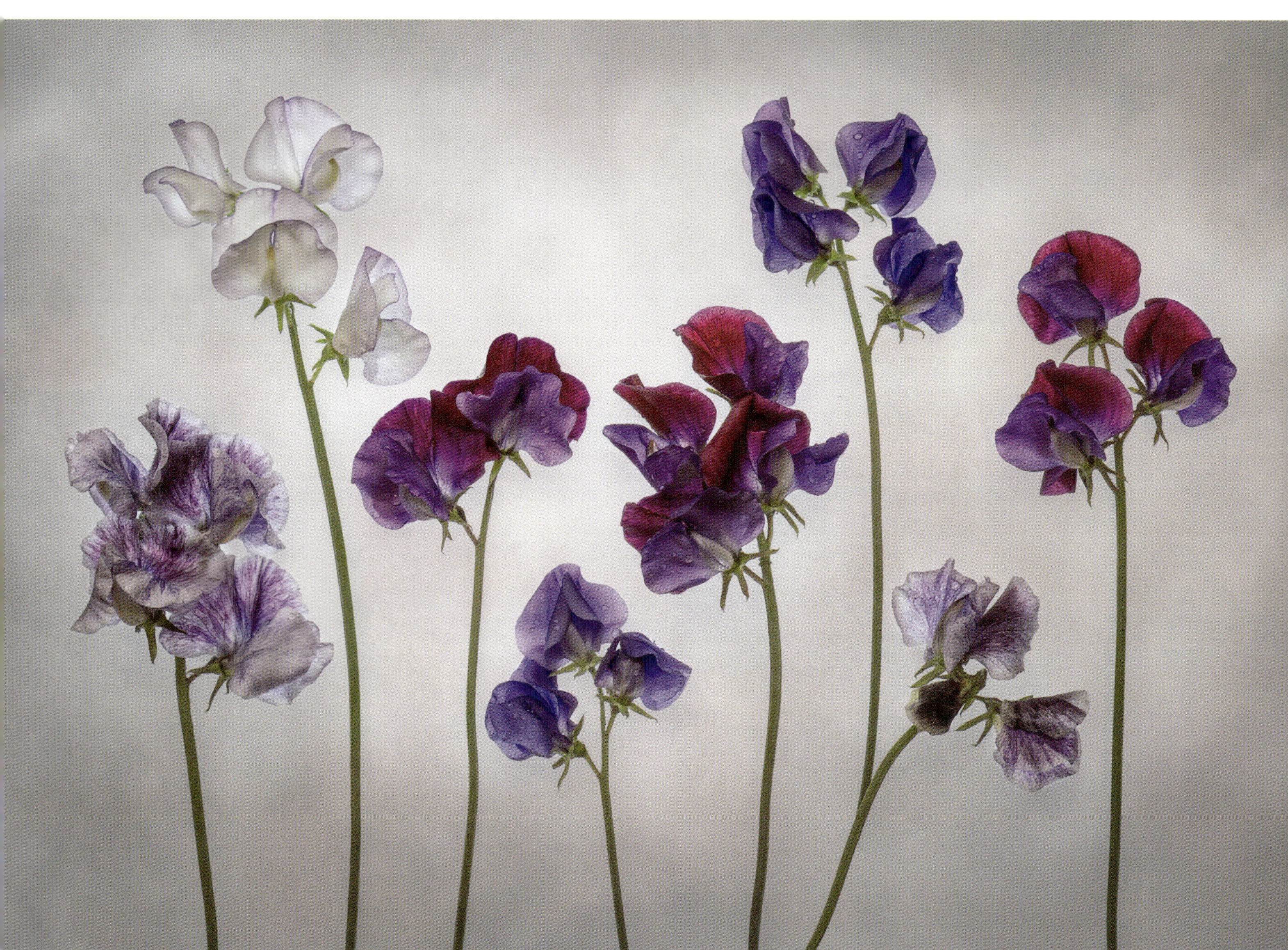

A sweet pea flat lay.

CHAPTER 5

Photographing Indoors

> Don't try to be original. Be simple. Be good technically and if there is something in you it will come out.
>
> HENRI MATISSE

I generally save indoor photography for a rainy day, although it's a great thing to do in winter when the weather isn't giving you great conditions or it's too cold to spend a long time outdoors.

Whilst it can take a while to set up, it is very rewarding as you are free to spend as much time as you need getting the focus and composition exactly right, moving flowers around in a way that you can't do in a garden. Because you are able to slow down and take your time, you actually learn a great deal about how your camera works too as you can try the same shot with a myriad of different settings. Then you can apply what you've learnt on your next garden visit.

Sometimes I photograph flowers from my garden (I love to grow the flowers that I really want to photograph) and sometimes I visit a local florist or garden centre and select blooms or foliage that look particularly promising composition-wise. Always choose the freshest and most perfect flowers and check them over carefully in the shop to avoid disappointment when you get home.

Photography with a macro lens works particularly well indoors as you can fine-tune the focus with the camera on a tripod to get it exactly right.

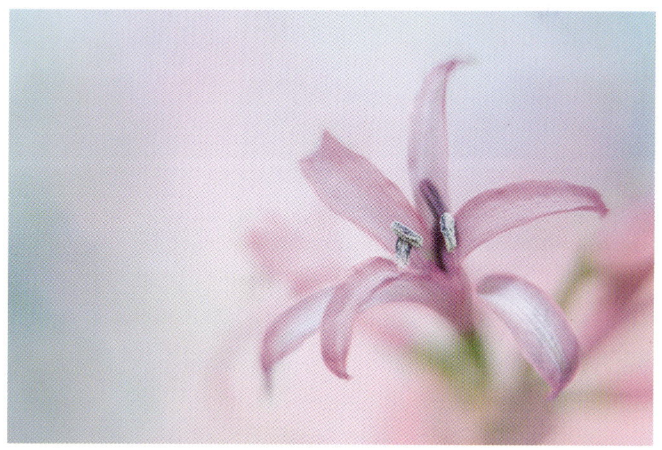

A nerine flower, taken indoors inside a lightbox with a white background and an overlay added in the edit.

I think it's quite important to try a 'natural' set-up when you first start photographing flowers indoors. It can be tempting to buy lots of lights and backdrops but sometimes the more equipment you use, the less natural it feels. Of course 'natural' might not be your aim, which is fine, but try to keep in mind that the beauty of the subject is the most important thing, and extravagant backdrops and lighting can often detract from that.

A BASIC SET-UP

As a first attempt I would recommend sitting with your back to a window in a bright room and having the flower or plant on a table in front of you. Without blocking the light coming in from the window, get down to the level of the flower and shoot it with a wide aperture, like f/1.8. Try changing the background, using different objects and colours (fabric, a chair with something draped over it) but keep the background at least a foot (and preferably more) behind the subject of the photo. You might want to try an extension tube or macro lens if you need to get more of the flower in the frame, or crop in later in the edit.

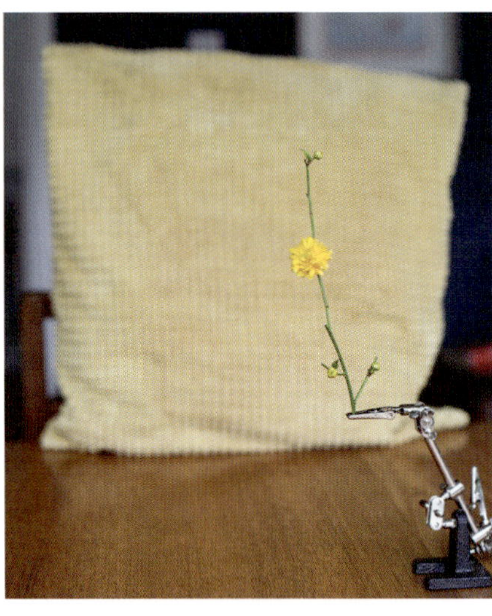

A photo showing my set-up for the *Kerria japonica* flower.

This *Kerria japonica* flower was taken with exactly this set-up, using a yellow cushion leaning against a chair as a background. I was slightly worried that the waffle texture of the cushion might show in the photo but because of the wide aperture and its distance behind the subject, it isn't noticeable. I was sitting with my back to my conservatory window to take the photos. There were no lights on at all in the room and I didn't use any other light source.

It was a cloudy, rainy day so the light wasn't very bright, but if it's a sunny day, as when taking photos outside, try to avoid any actual sunlight falling on the flower. You could use a strip of sunlight on your background to make it more interesting compositionally, but this can be quite difficult to achieve in a small space.

If you are using a camera with white balance settings (cameras are generally set to 'auto white balance' by default), you can try changing these to see what effect it gives and whether you like the colour more. My camera decided it was 'sunny' for the pull-out shot of the *Kerria japonica* set-up (which it most definitely wasn't) but I tried the same shot with different white balances, without editing.

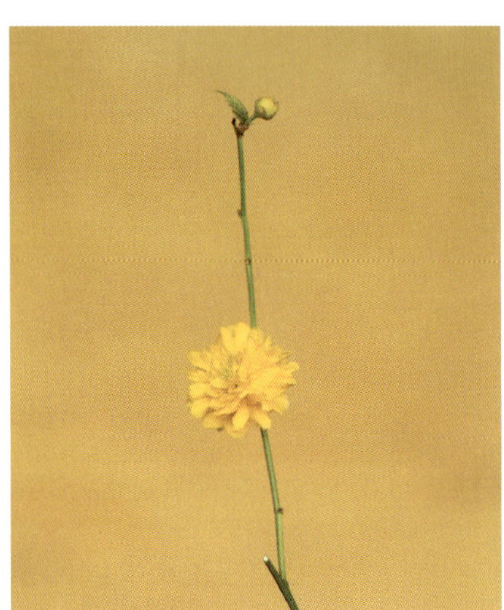

A photo with the white balance set to 'shade'.

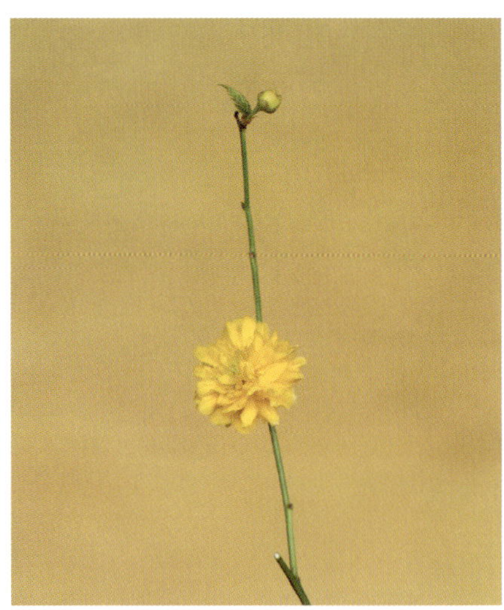

A photo with the white balance set to 'cloudy'.

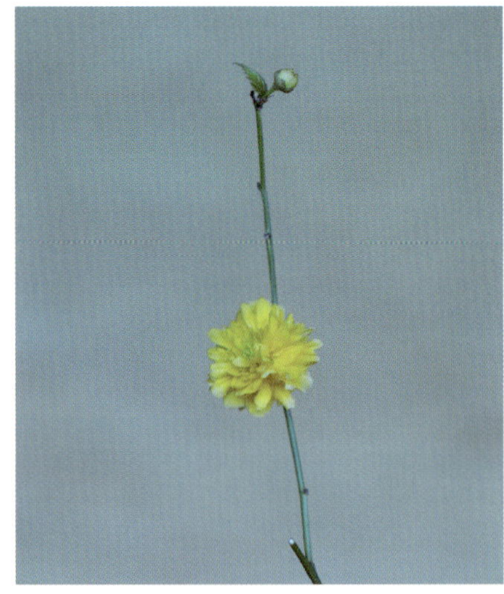

A photo with the white balance set to 'tungsten'.

Looking at the resulting photos, I think I prefer the 'shade' setting as the warmness complements the colour of the flower. The tungsten setting has made the green stem too blue for my taste. Looking at the composition of the flower and stalk I decided that it might work well in landscape rather than portrait so I rotated it in Lightroom (choose the drop down 'photo' menu and then 'rotate right'). I added a graduated filter with the exposure lifted to the top right to give a suggestion of sunshine and to avoid the image being too 'flat' with just one colour behind the subject.

In a similar way I then added a graduated filter from the bottom right with the exposure darkened, to give the idea that the flower is reaching towards the sun – any narrative that you can suggest like this can instantly add interest, but be careful not to overdo it.

The final photo, after editing in Lightroom.

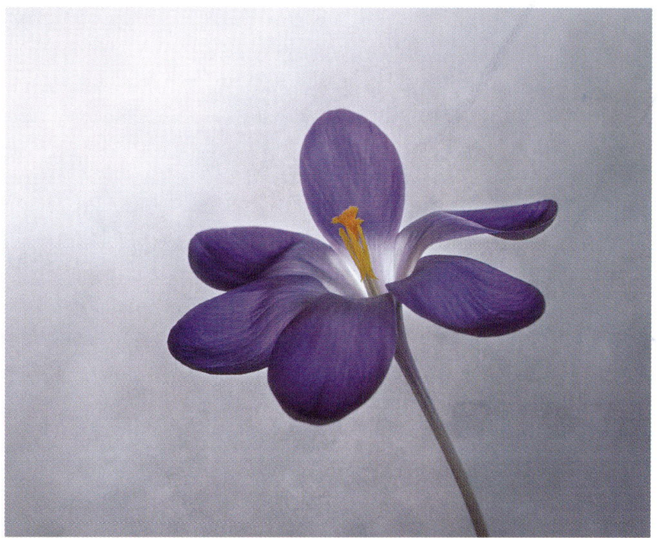

This photo of a crocus flower was taken in exactly the same way.

USING A LIGHTBOX

My usual set-up with a lightbox is to have a flower either in a vase or held by a third hand inside a lightbox, sometimes with an extra LED light positioned as I think best suits the composition. This is usually arrived at by trial and error. Choose a bright room in your house and a sturdy table that won't wobble. My lightbox has seen better days but it's clean and functional and does the job fine. When you buy a lightbox it will often come with backdrops that fold and fit into the back of the box. Mine came with black, white and green. Sometimes, for a white background I will just use the inside of the box without any backdrop at all.

Black backdrops can seem a little on the 'grey' side when you use them but they can be darkened down in post-processing.

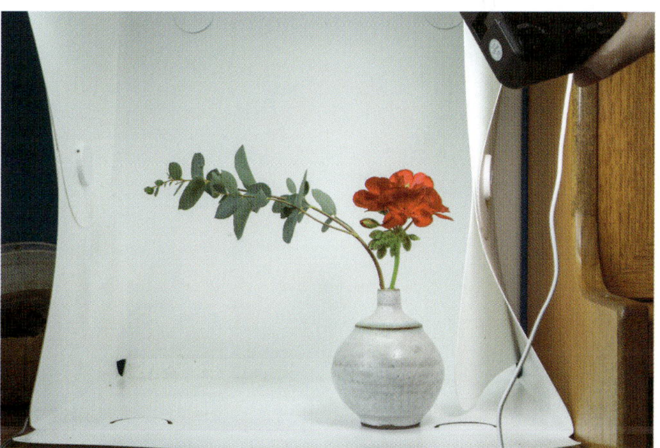

A typical set-up with my lightbox; I'm holding an extra LED light top right to add some additional light from the side.

Of course you can buy or make your own backgrounds. I sometimes use satin scarves or other similar thin fabrics; other materials like velour or velvet are also good as they absorb light and will not give reflections that you would need to clone out later.

Even if your budget is limited, a medium-sized lightbox would be a good investment (they are relatively cheap on the internet) and it will usually come with an LED strip across the top that lights the subject from above. You can supplement this if you wish with additional lighting.

I use a 'third hand' to hold the flower for me and position the flower under the lightbox LED lights, or perhaps a little further back if they are giving off too much shine.

When you've positioned the flower inside the box, turn it around, viewing it from as many different angles as possible before you begin shooting. The composition is crucial and even if your lighting is perfect, you also need to aim for a good composition. Look closely at the shape of the flower, decide where you want your point of focus to be (the stamens are usually a safe bet) and then move the flower at different angles until you find a pleasing arrangement.

Think carefully about aperture – do you want the whole flower to be in focus or just part of it? If the former, you need a small aperture like f/9; if the latter then you can try a wide-open aperture like f/1.8.

You can try the same thing without a lightbox of course – just stand the third hand on a table and use a piece of paper or card behind for the backdrop. You can light the flower from any direction with one or more LEDs if you need extra light, but you might not need to if you're in a room with good daylight.

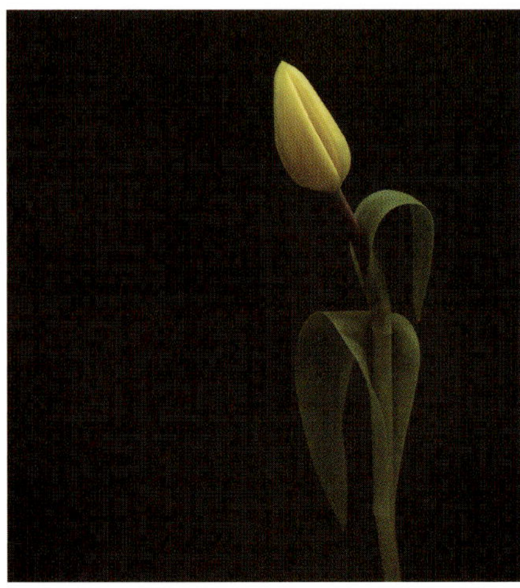

A yellow tulip inside the lightbox, with a dark green background.

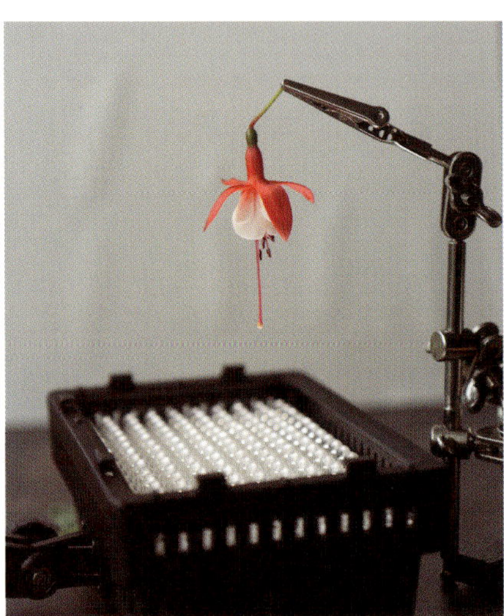

A photo pullback of the set-up I used for a fuschia photo. I put a set of LED lights underneath to uplight the fuchsia flower too, as the dark pink petals would have created too much shadow on the white inner petals otherwise.

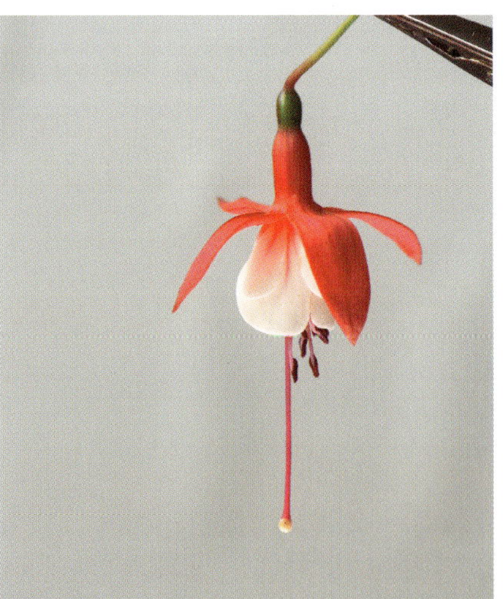

The photo, taken with a 55mm lens and an aperture of f/4; the background is a piece of paper stuck to some card.

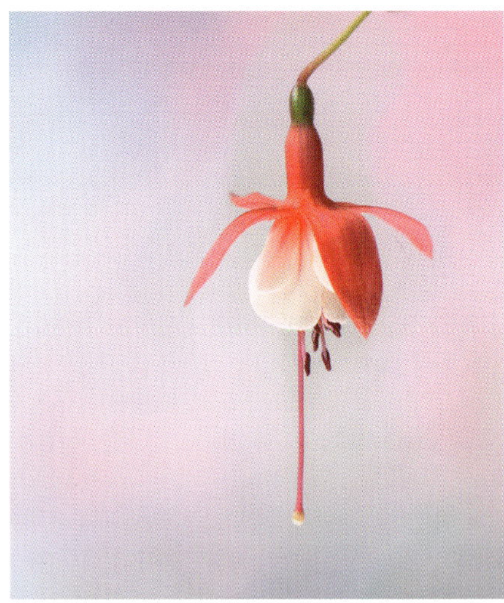

The final edited photo, in which I've cropped out the third hand and added a pink overlay to complement the flower.

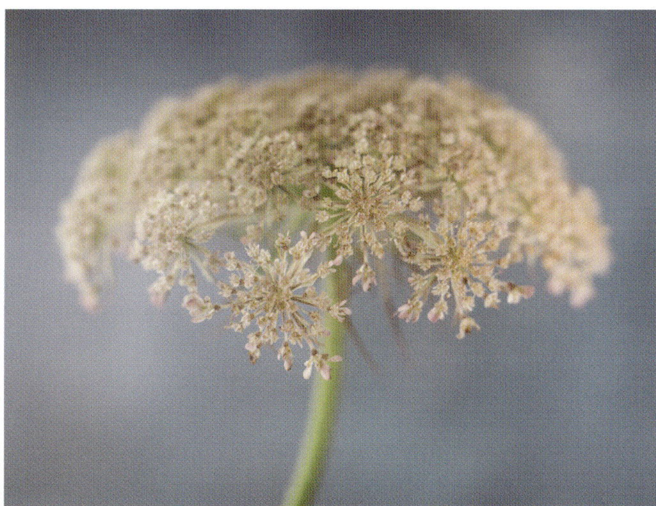

Last summer I picked some *Daucus carota* (wild carrot or Queen Anne's Lace) flowers from the garden and put them in front of a mottled blue background. I didn't use the lightbox on this occasion as there was plenty of light in my conservatory and the flowers were large. This was my first image, which I didn't think was particularly inspiring – the petals closest to the lens have beautiful shapes but the ones that are out of focus behind seemed a bit clumped together.

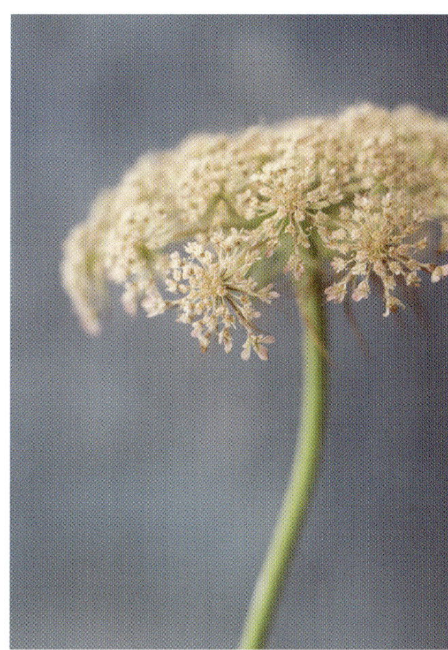

My second attempt was to place the stalk – which had an interesting bend in it – on the right-hand third. For me this worked better as a composition (and I didn't mind that some of the flower had been cropped off on the right) but the rear of the flower still looked rather clumpy.

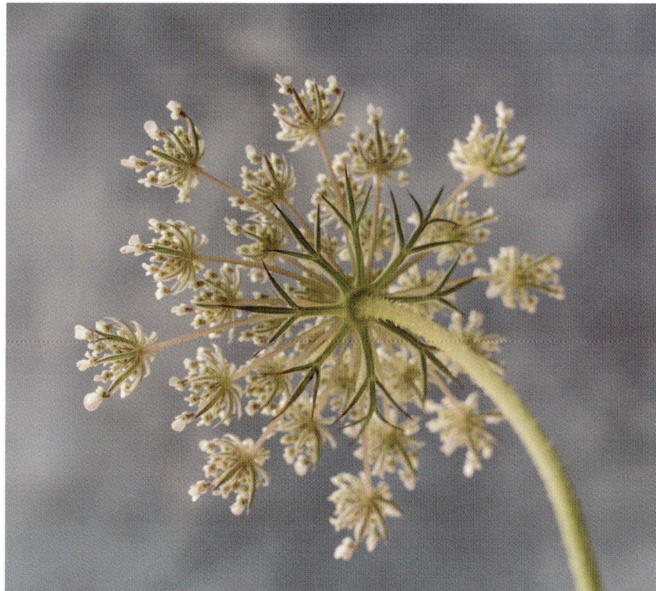

Then I chose another flower from those that I'd picked, one that wasn't quite as 'clumpy', but shot from underneath as I really liked the shape of the sepals, which looked a little like the fractals of a snowflake when viewed from the underside.

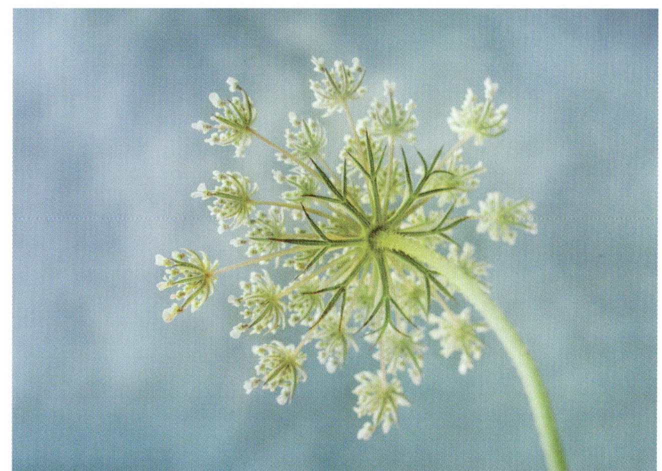

I then lightened the photo in Lightroom and made the background colour more turquoise, as I thought it emphasized its snowflake-like composition. This is the finished image.

PHOTOGRAPH THE WHOLE FLOWER

As you are inside and presumably have as much time as you need, use it to set up as many different angles and shots as possible. Turn the flower around to get different compositions – enjoy the challenge of finding new perspectives. Sometimes the bottom of the flower might be structurally interesting, or the curve of a leaf or petal. Think about the space or gaps in the composition as much as the parts of the flower. Try them overlapping, not overlapping, on the diagonal, on the upright, from above, from below and so on.

When I photograph a flower in this way I might take a hundred photos of it, and then end up with between five and ten that I'm happy with. All these lily photos were taken in the same session and all have the same colour overlay applied in Photoshop afterwards to unite them thematically.

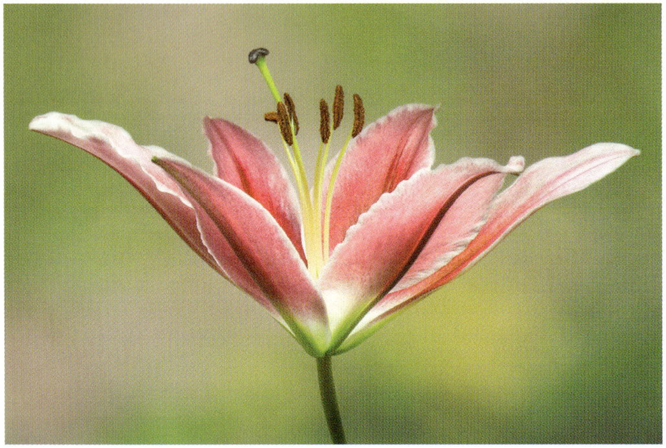

The first of a set of photos I took of an Oriental lily. This captures the whole flower and was taken inside my lightbox. It uses a narrow aperture to get most of the flower in focus.

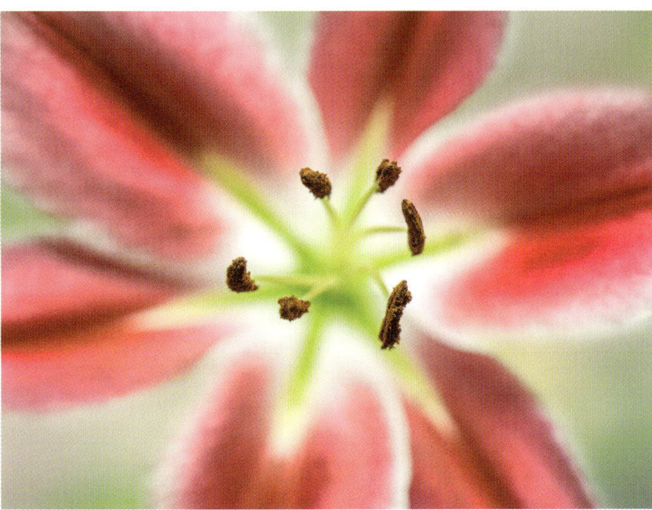

This photo was taken from above and focuses only on the lily anthers with a wider aperture.

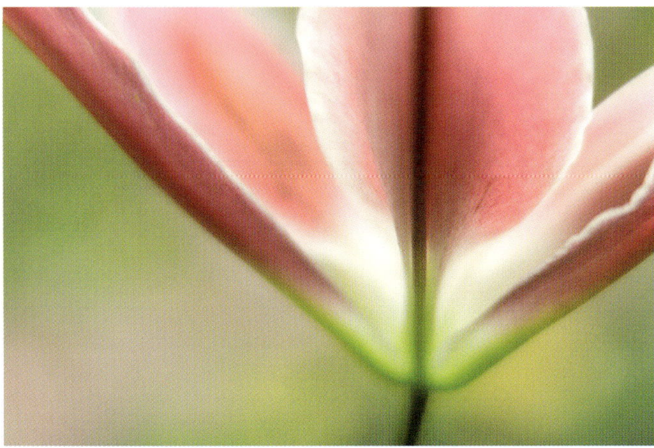

This shot only has a tiny point of focus (towards the bottom of the petal) but I took this with a very wide aperture (f/1.8) and I actually like the impressionistic glow at the base of the flower.

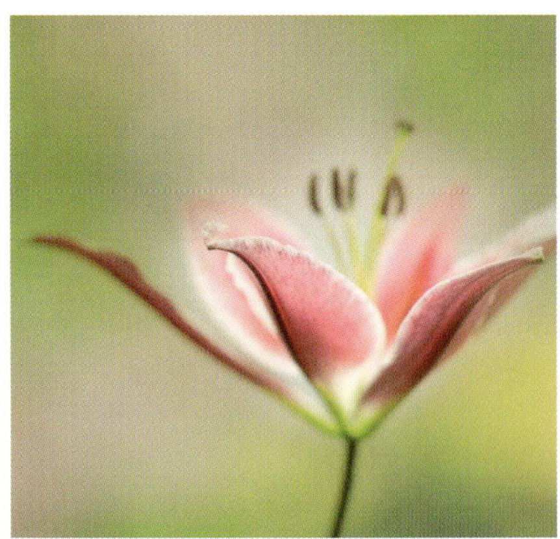

This shot focuses only on one of the petal tips but I like the overall composition and the way that the stamens are present as out-of-focus shapes in the background.

TRY A FLAT LAY

A 'flat lay' photograph is one where objects or items are displayed on a piece of (sometimes themed) background paper or card and photographed directly from above, giving a bird's-eye view. Such projects make great rainy-day challenges and there is always a wide variety of themes you can choose, such as the seasons, months of the year, colours or just flowers you find in your garden at any particular time.

A tip for flat lays is to put your background paper or card on the floor rather than on a table and then stand over it, trying to get directly above it without casting a shadow onto the image.

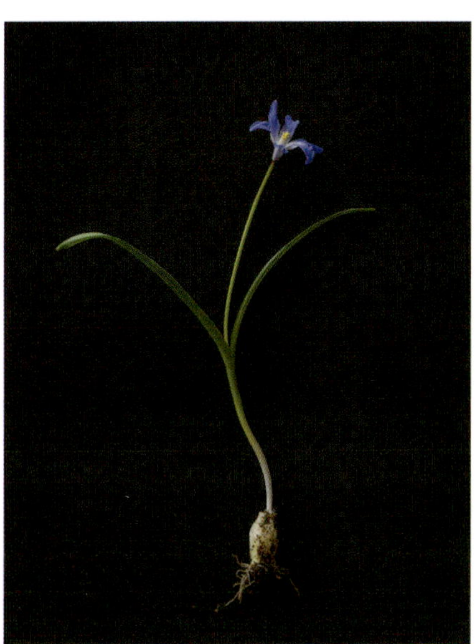

A botanical print inspired this chionodoxa photo – such drawings, popular in Victorian times, show all parts of the flower, or the different elements of the plant in close up. I planted the chionodoxa back in my garden again after I had photographed it.

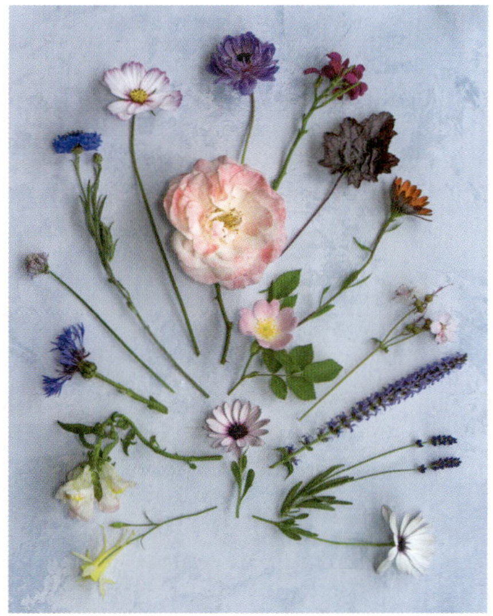

A flat lay such as this must obviously be a home project as you should never pick flowers from public gardens, but it might inspire you to grow more of your own. I picked all these flowers from my garden in the month of June.

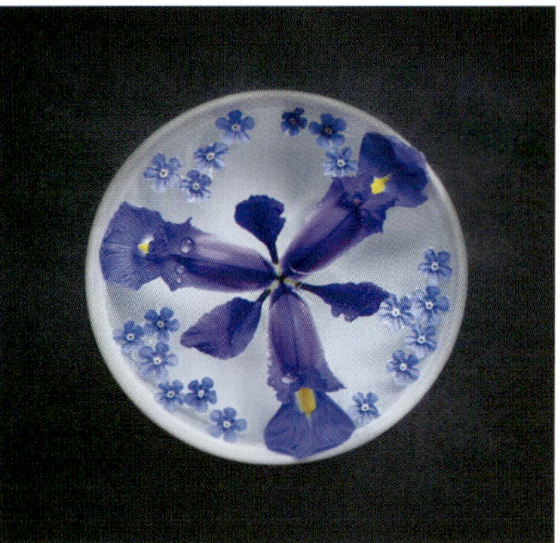

With this image I combined the idea of a flat lay with a still-life photo, shooting the iris and tiny alkanet flowers in the bowl of water from above. I sometimes do flower arrangements like this for the dinner table with seasonal flowers chosen from my garden on the day.

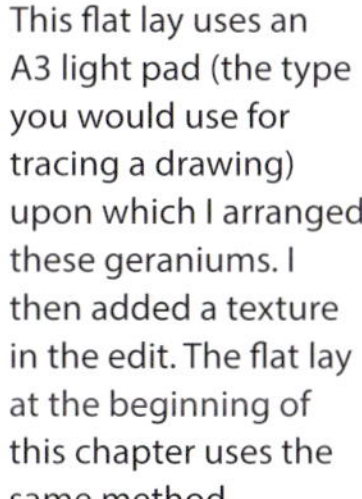

This flat lay uses an A3 light pad (the type you would use for tracing a drawing) upon which I arranged these geraniums. I then added a texture in the edit. The flat lay at the beginning of this chapter uses the same method.

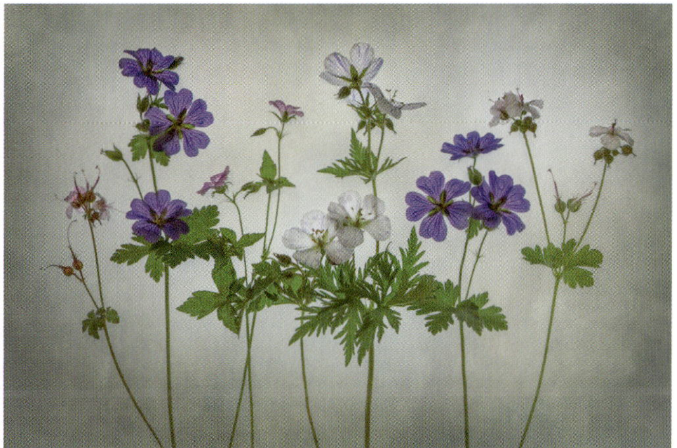

SCAN YOUR FLOWERS

If you have a printer that can also scan, you might like to try this method of photography that doesn't even use a camera. Choose a flat-ish flower with fairly soft petals and lay it face down onto the glass of the scanner. You might need to manually arrange some of the petals, trying to imagine what it will look like from the other side of the glass. Then you'll need some black cloth (I use a black velvet cushion cover) to gently drape over the flower so that it has a black background, and to prevent any light from entering. Then press the scan button and wait for the image to appear on your computer, at which point you can edit it as normal. It will probably take several attempts to get the petals to lie in a way you're happy with, but it's a fascinating process. The better your printer, the more success you'll have with regards to definition and colour but there are photographers who use this method a great deal.

Photographing flowers at the end of their life

If you have cut flowers indoors in a vase, keep a close eye on them; often they take on new shapes and colours as they age. At the point where most people would throw out their flowers, I often begin to photograph their withered beauty, which can give real sculptural interest, making for excellent compositions. You can dry flowers upside down or at angles to enhance the bends and shapes of their stems and petals; muted colours can be enhanced in post-processing. I usually photograph such flowers either on a light pad or in front of a softbox light so that their translucent petals are shown to their full advantage.

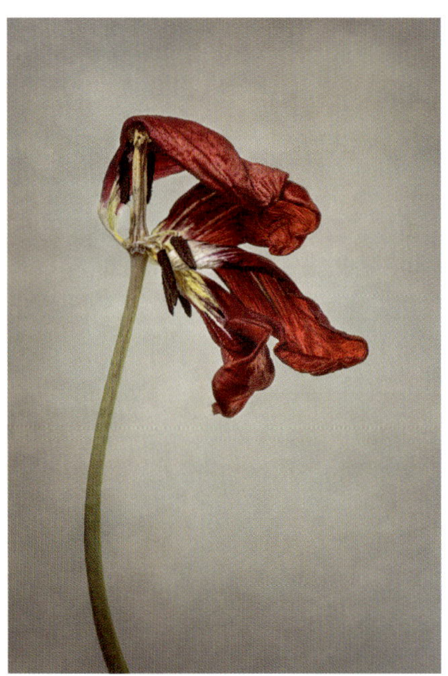

This tulip still has quite vivid colours so I used a darker grey texture in the edit to give more contrast with the subject.

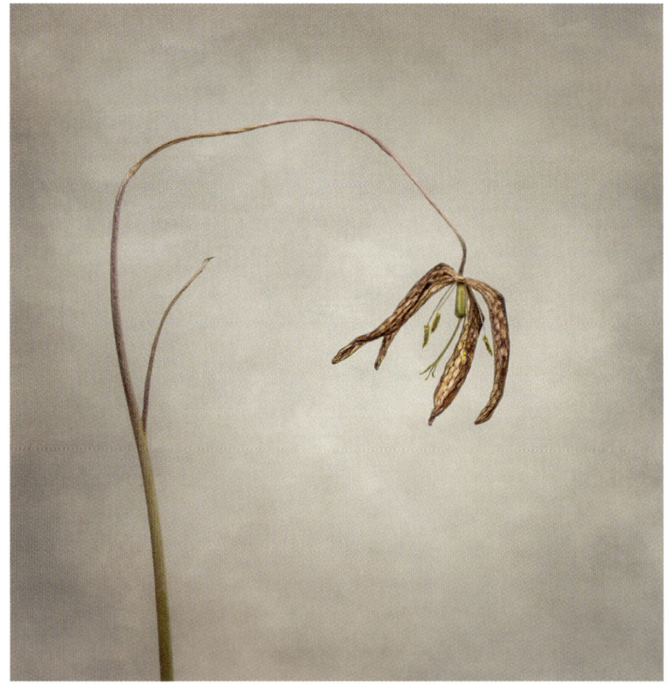

This fritillaria has more subdued colours, and a similar coloured texture in the edit worked well here.

Flowers and plants to photograph in May

May is full of birdsong and the bright colours of alliums, bearded irises and wisteria. Native bluebells appear in woods.

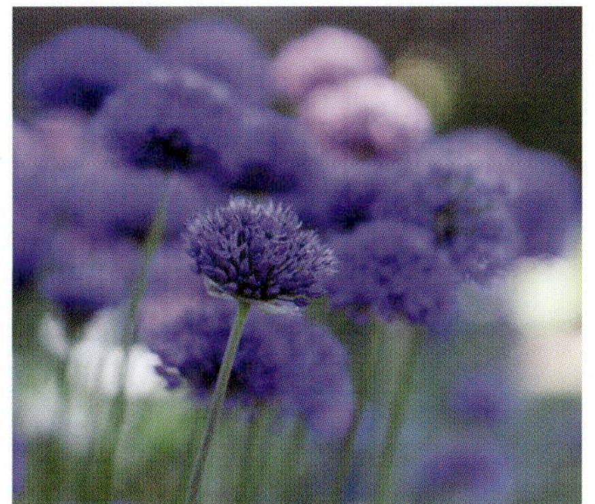

Alliums – 1/1000 sec at f/1.8, 55mm.

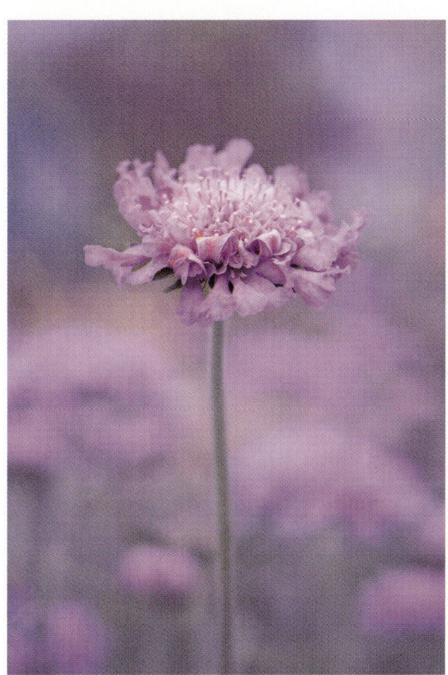

Scabiosa – 1/125 sec at f/4, vintage 50mm lens, overlay added in the edit.

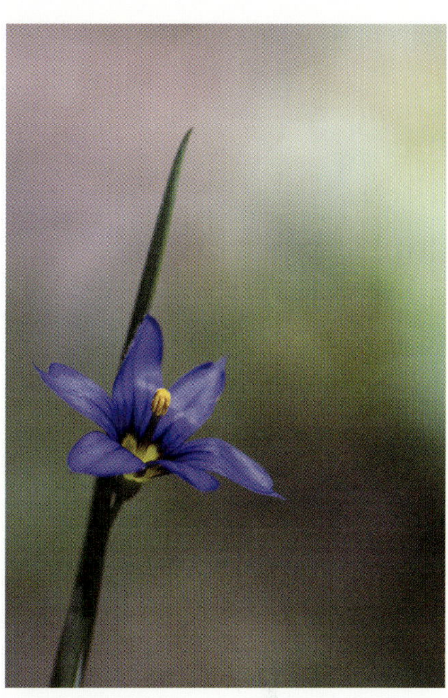

Sisyrinchium angustifolium (blue-eyed grass) – 1/400 sec at f/1.7, vintage 50mm lens, overlay added in the edit.

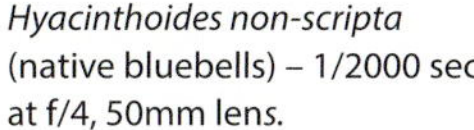

Hyacinthoides non-scripta (native bluebells) – 1/2000 sec at f/4, 50mm lens.

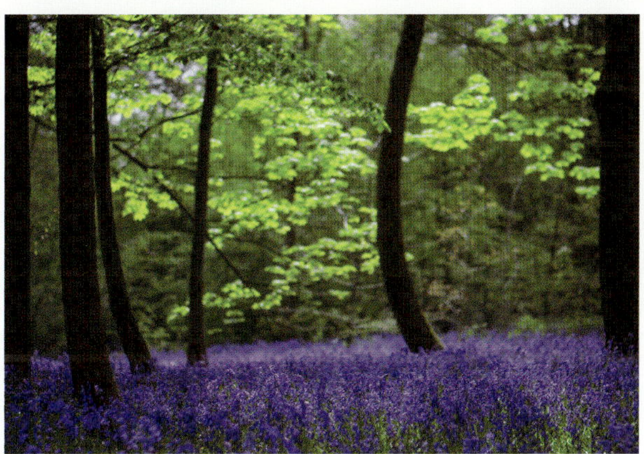

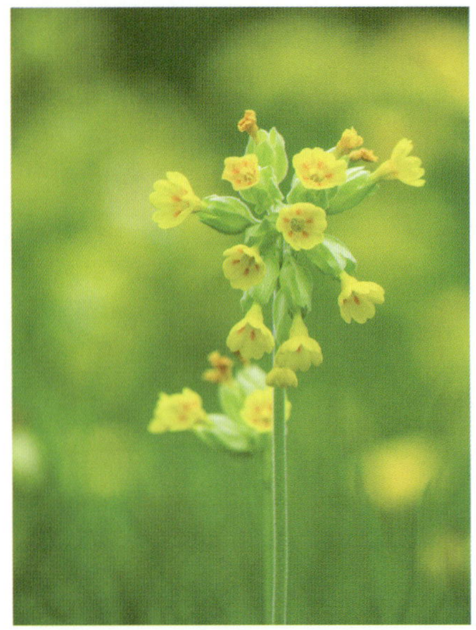

Primula veris (cowslip) – 1/800 sec at f/4, 150mm.

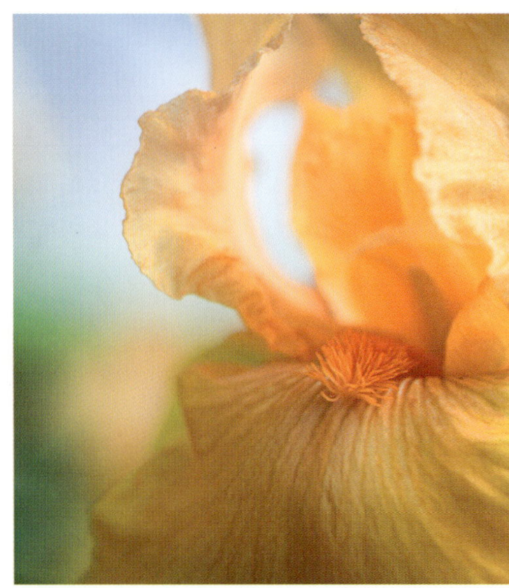

Iris 'Orange Harvest' – 1/320 sec at f/1.7, vintage manual lens.

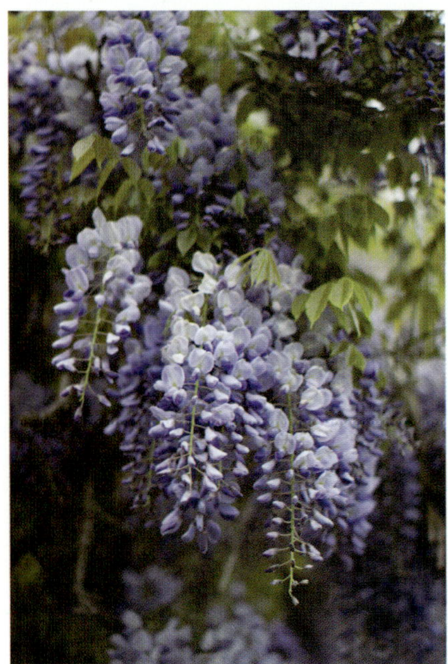

Wisteria – 1/320 sec at f/1.8, 55mm.

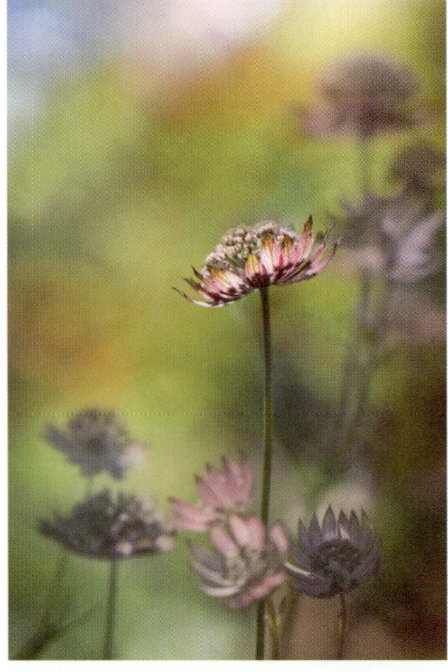

Astrantia – 1/1250 sec at f/1.8, 55mm, overlay added in the edit.

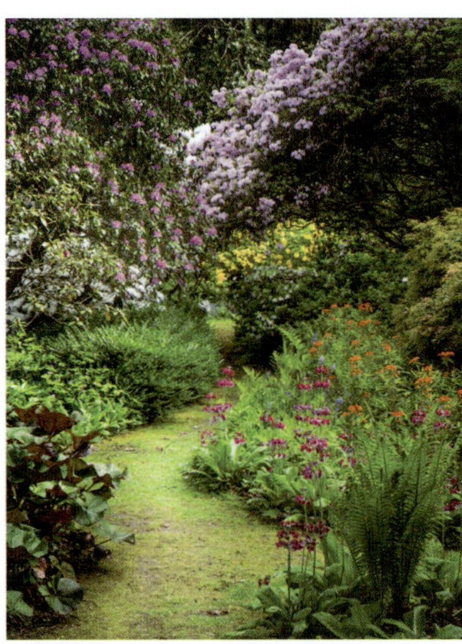

A woodland garden path with rhododendrons, primula candelabra and ferns – 1/100 sec at f/9, 55mm.

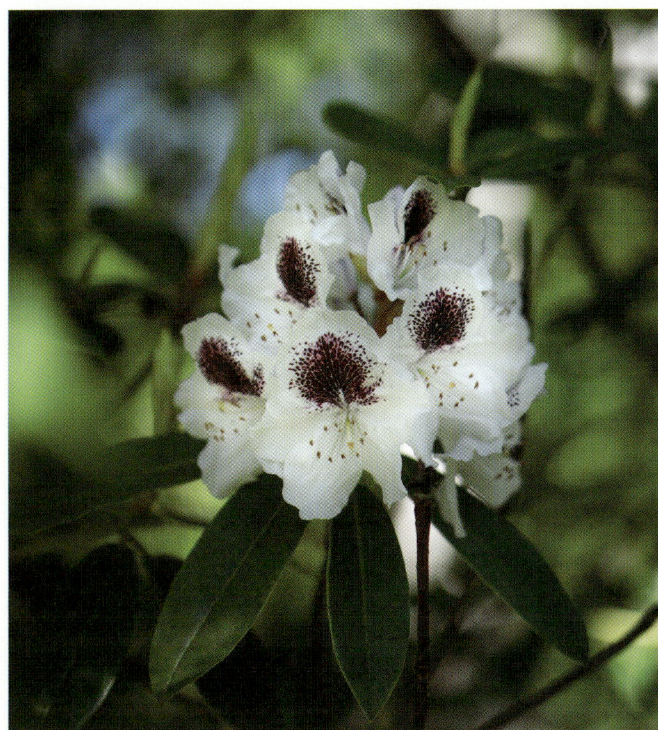

Close-up of rhododendron 'Sappho' flowers – 1/1000 sec at f/8, 55mm.

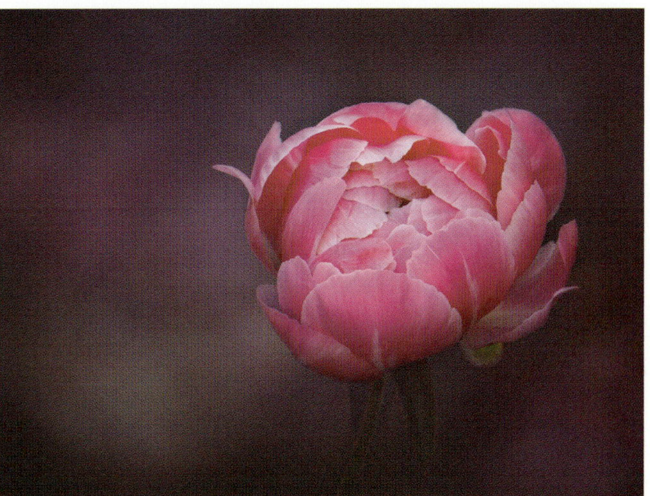

Peony 'Coral Charm' – 1/160 sec at f/4, 160mm. An overlay is added in the edit.

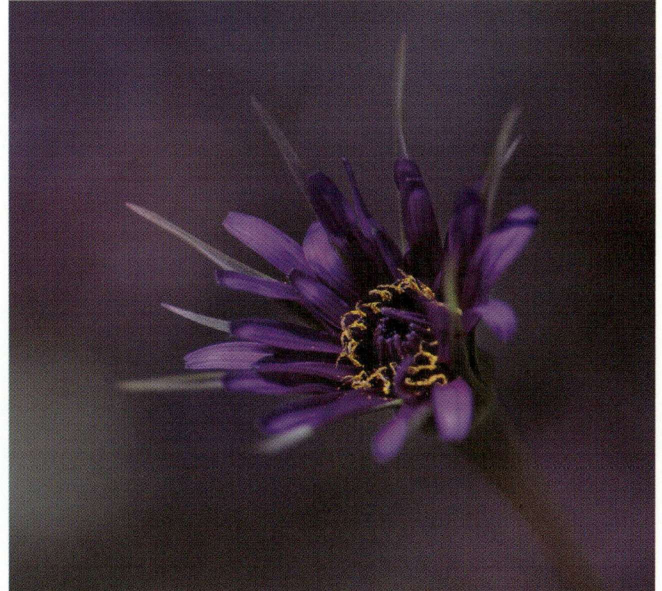

Tragopogon porrifolius (salsify) – 1/1000 sec at f/2, vintage 50mm lens.

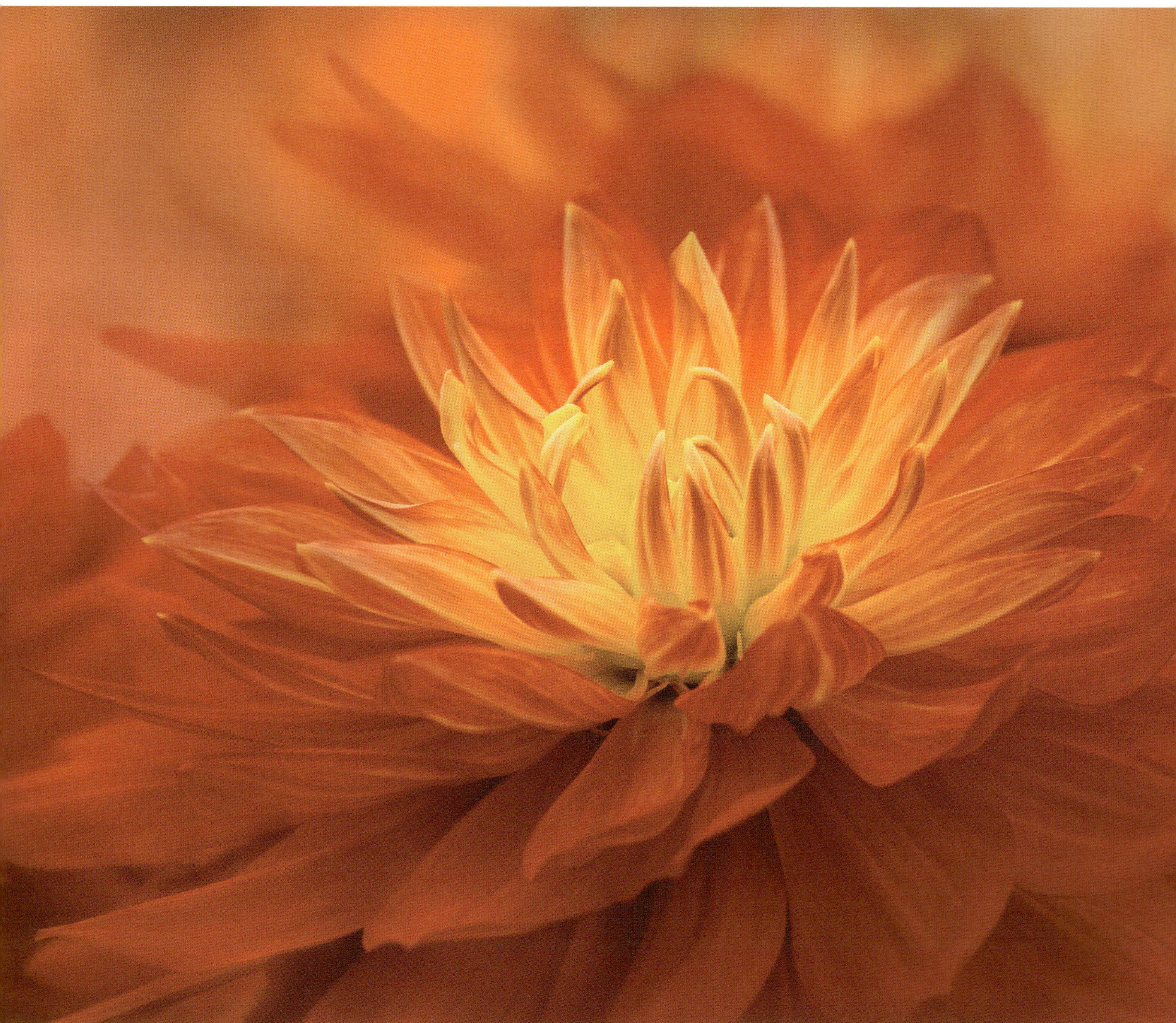

CHAPTER 6

Macro and Close-up

> When you take a flower in your hand and really look at it, it's your world for a moment.
>
> GEORGIA O'KEEFE

Close-up and macro photography is an extremely popular photographic pursuit and is usually considered a genre in its own right. When you get very close to small objects you can unlock miniature worlds that would never normally be observed with the naked eye and this can create magical photo opportunities. Whenever I buy plants from a garden centre or florist I always try to shoot them close-up indoors before I plant them out or put them in a vase.

Extreme close-up photography is known as macro photography, where the camera captures very small subjects and makes them larger than life, or captures small details of larger objects. Lenses for macro photography have become more and more sophisticated and often the subject needs to be very close to the lens, unlike with most regular lenses. True macro lenses are labelled 1:1, which means they can reproduce objects at life-size. 1:2 means that the lens can capture objects at half-size and lenses that can reproduce objects at double life-size will be labelled 2:1. If you're just using a regular lens, such as a 50mm and are unsure about settings or what aperture to choose as a starting point, you might wish to activate the 'close-up' function on your camera, if it has one. This usually looks like an image of a flower on the top dial or screen.

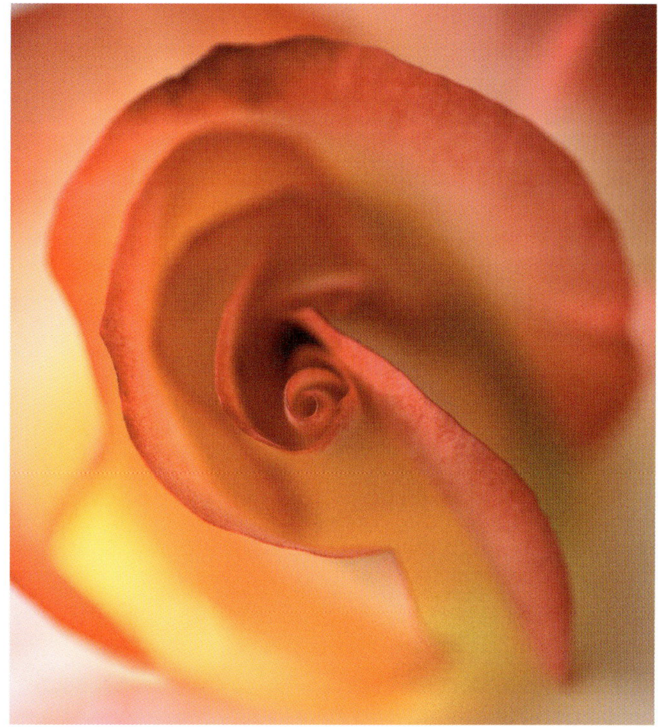

The centre of a rose – only the edges of the petals are in focus because of the very shallow depth of field.

◀ A close-up photo of a red cactus dahlia.

However, there are other ways to achieve the same effect as a macro lens. You can use extension tubes, which you can buy quite cheaply or even second hand and fit to your usual lens. Make sure you get the correct fitting for your particular camera and its lens mount (for example Sony, Nikon or Canon) as the extension tubes fit between the lens and camera. You can also buy macro lenses that fit on the front of a lens like a filter.

Tripods are often used by specialist macro photographers. I would almost always use a tripod with an indoor set-up to avoid camera shake at lower light levels. The reason that a tripod may be needed is because macro lenses have a shallower depth of field than regular lenses and you will have to adjust your aperture to suit this – often to higher 'f' numbers than you would normally. This will mean that less light enters the camera and the image will be very dark. To solve this you'll need to decrease your shutter speed, perhaps to something like 1/30, and slow speeds like this need the camera to be very still to avoid camera shake.

How much of the subject you want in focus in macro photography will vary from flower to flower, and as always experimentation is the key to learning what works best. Sometimes the plane of focus (the area that is sharp) comes down to a matter of millimetres, or in flower terms, a petal edge.

Some public gardens don't like photographers using tripods so I would always check the website or contact them prior to visiting if you're unsure. Whilst I sometimes arrive at gardens with my tripod I often don't need to use it for regular flower photography if the light is good, as I just use a faster shutter speed to avoid hand-shake. If I'm doing very close macro shots in a garden, I would err on the side of using a tripod – it might

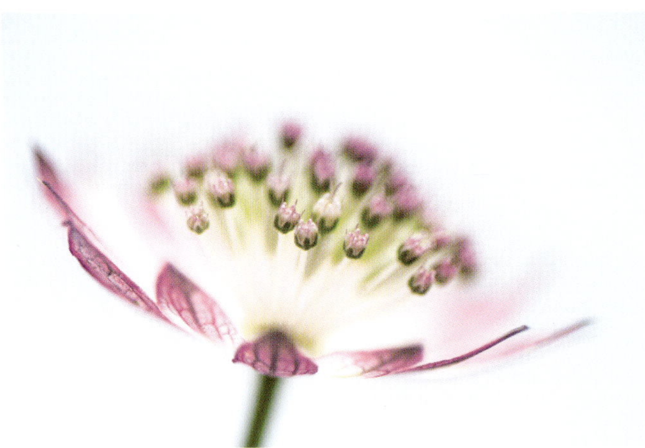

Astrantia bought from a florist, photographed indoors. The flower is about 3cm in diameter.

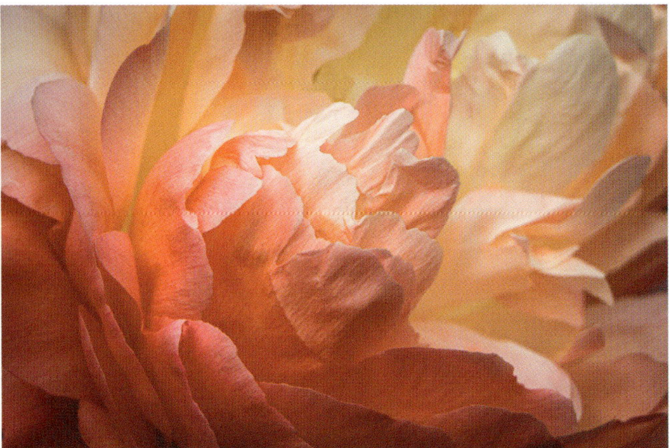

The petals of a peony in close-up. I photographed the flower from the side as it made an interesting flame-like composition and the centre of the peony is not actually visible with this variety.

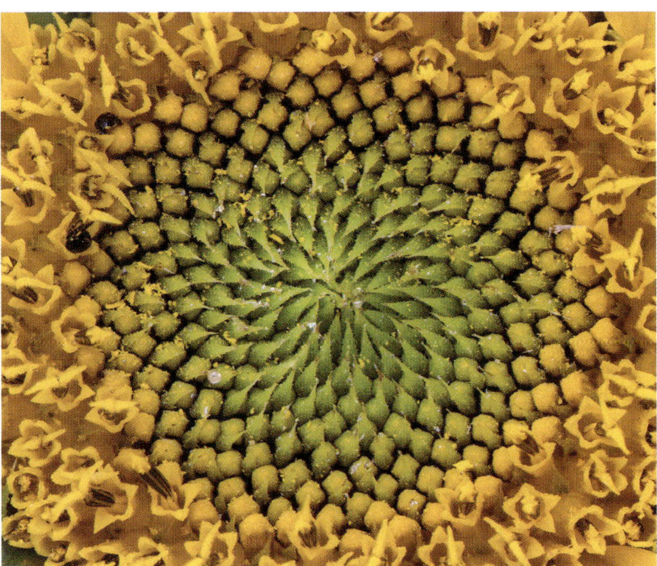

The intricate patterns at the centre of a sunflower, photographed outside.

limit your movement but a much higher percentage of your shots will be sharp – camera shake is almost impossible to avoid when you're shooting very close up (rather than just a flower portrait) and you will probably find a two- or five-second timer helps here too.

Many macro photographers shoot with manual focus so that they can place the point of focus exactly where they want it to be. The camera will often put the object or petal nearest to the camera in focus, rather than the centre of the flower, which you probably *want* to be in focus. Focusing manually takes some practice but once you get the hang of it you'll never look back. Focus magnification is a great tool and most cameras have it – the camera will enlarge the image as you focus and you can see in far more detail on the rear-view screen (or in the EVF) what will be sharp.

OUTDOOR CLOSE-UP PHOTOGRAPHY

Finding something of interest to photograph often takes time, but it's an absorbing activity. Choose a bright day (not necessarily sunny) and stand or sit in an area of a garden, tuning in to your surroundings. If you give yourself a small area of a garden to observe you'll start to notice things that you might have missed otherwise. I might look for small creatures or interesting compositions involving small details of flowers. Observe how and where the light is falling, absorb the different colours and try to look at things from many different points of view. I often sit for far longer than I intended to and it's a really calming experience, especially if you don't have a time limit.

I usually use a long lens (more than 200mm) for outdoor close-up photography as it means that if I want to photograph insects I won't disturb them. I will often also use a macro lens in my own garden but tend to take extension tubes with me to public gardens to keep the weight of my camera bag down. An extension tube or two on your favourite lens would work fine for flower or plant details (again you'll usually need to use manual focus and get very close to your subject).

If you use an extension tube, you'll find that your depth of field is extremely narrow – only a small part of the photo will be in focus. This can really help with composition as it draws attention to only one point. Don't forget you can alter the aperture to try to get more of the subject in focus but you may need to compensate for this with the shutter speed. When you have found a good composition you may need to rock in and out with your camera slightly (if you're using manual focus) to establish the precise point you want to have in focus. When you're focusing on very small things it can be hard to determine from looking at the rear camera screen if the focus is spot on or not, so take lots of (slightly different) shots just in case so you can view them on the computer later and select the best.

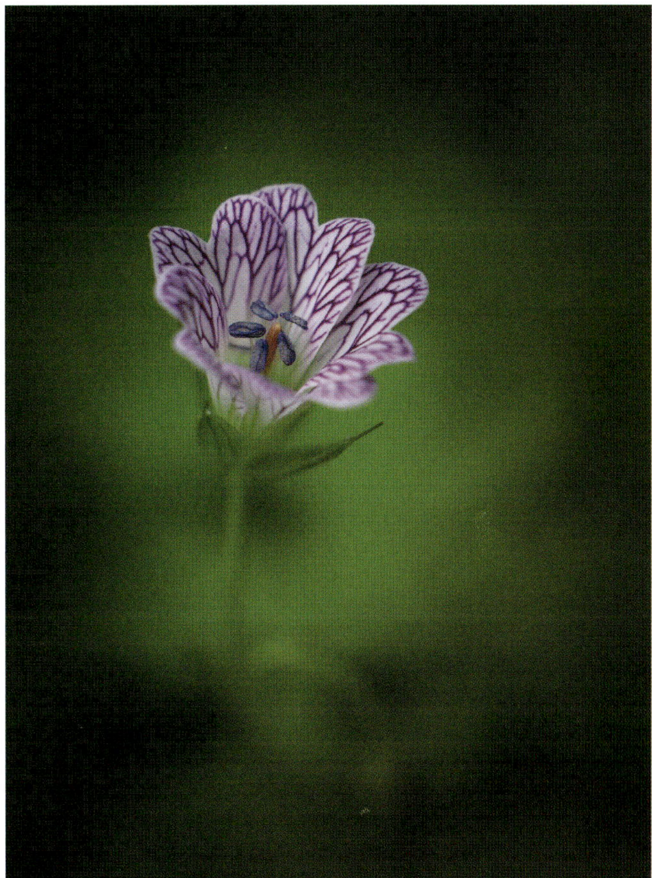

I was sitting on the ground in a garden when I noticed this tiny geranium flower in a shady corner – it was only just over 1cm across but its patterning and anthers were beautiful. This kind of shot would not necessarily be discernible to some as macro, as non-gardeners wouldn't necessarily know how tiny it was.

If you look at the subject you wish to photograph in live-preview or live-view mode (on the screen or through the

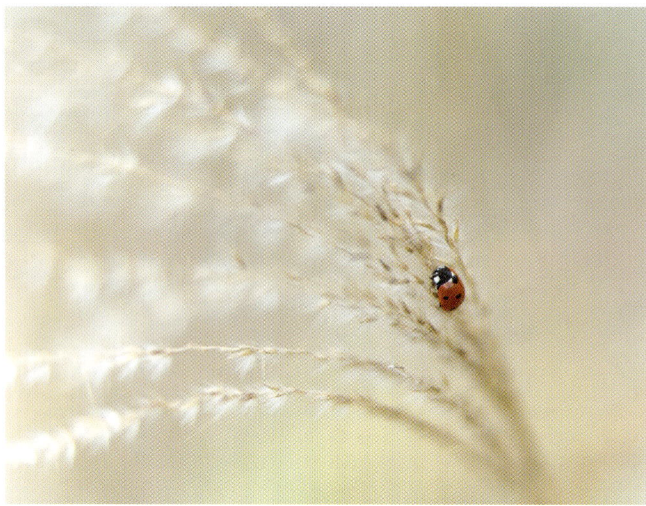

A ladybird on miscanthus grass, taken with an extension tube.

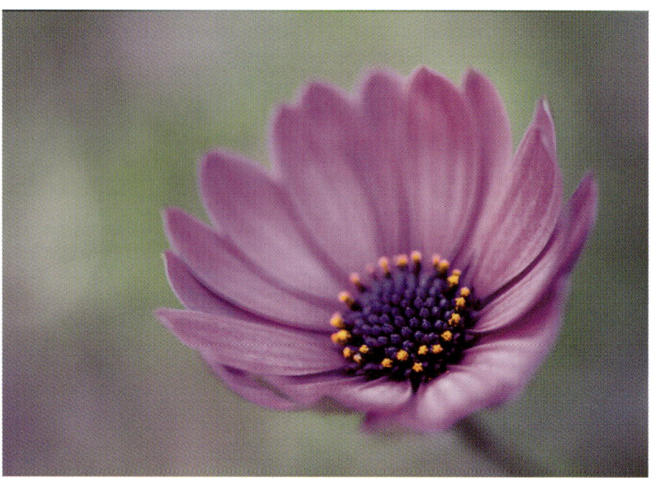

In this osteospermum photo, the depth of field is so narrow that only the front disc flowers/florets of the flower's centre are in focus and the others behind are blurred out. Some people might prefer this, but it's an important thing to consider when you're shooting. If you wanted the whole of the centre of the flower to be in focus, you'd need to use a smaller aperture, such as f/11 or higher when using a macro lens.

electronic viewfinder) you should see white pixels (some cameras will allow you to change from white to another colour) around the sharp points of the image. This is called 'focus-peaking' and can be a much easier way to position your focus really accurately before you press the shutter. If it doesn't come already set up on your camera, you might need to consult your manual (or an online forum) to find out how to activate it.

This ladybird on miscanthus grass image was taken with a generic extension tube of 10mm on a 55mm lens. I love the way that both the grass heads and stalk are blurred out – it enhances the composition of the photo.

As the ladybird is only a small point of focus in the photo, it works; however, had I wanted the ladybird to be larger in the frame I would have had to increase my aperture value; with my macro lens (105mm) I usually photograph ladybirds at about f/9–11.

When you find a good flower or plant, try to take lots of shots from as many different angles as you can: above; underneath; from the side and so on. Make sure you locate the point of focus really carefully on the subject of your image as a starting point.

I discovered some thick-legged beetles and Spanish oil beetles in amongst some yellow marguerite daisies last year and took lots of shots from different angles.

At home later I experimented with cropping my images for more interesting compositions; it helps to have plenty to choose from. Whilst all of these above examples work as compositions, you may prefer one to the others and this is always subjective and depends on experience, taste and so on. Specialist macro photographers would probably say that none of them are technically macro, as they are not close-up enough, but if you are enjoying the photography it doesn't matter; even at competition level there are usually categories to cater for all varieties of close-up and macro. Insects are a very popular macro subject and I'll talk more about photographing them in the chapter on wildlife in the garden.

You don't always have to focus on the centre of the flower; you'll sometimes find that the curve of a leaf or petal can provide an equally beautiful point of interest. When you've taken your first photo, move around slightly and look at what's happening behind the flower; look for backgrounds that will either complement or contrast with your subject.

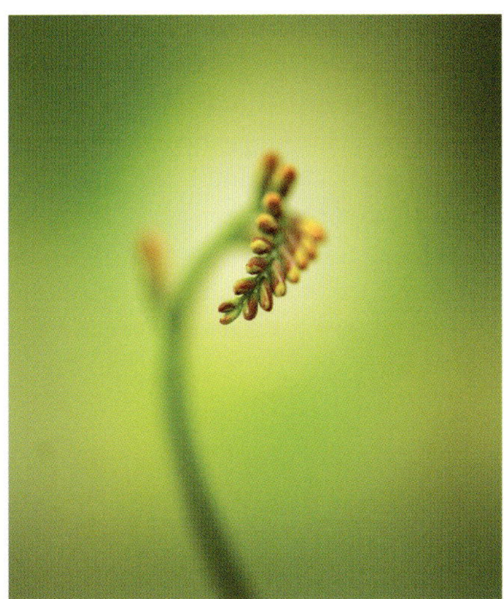

When you're focusing close up, the background is likely to be very blurred, so use any out-of-focus bokeh or 'colour blobs' as part of your composition and consider the effect they will have on your image. Do they distract or complement? I have tried to position this crocosmia bud in front of some white circular bokeh, to act as a spotlight.

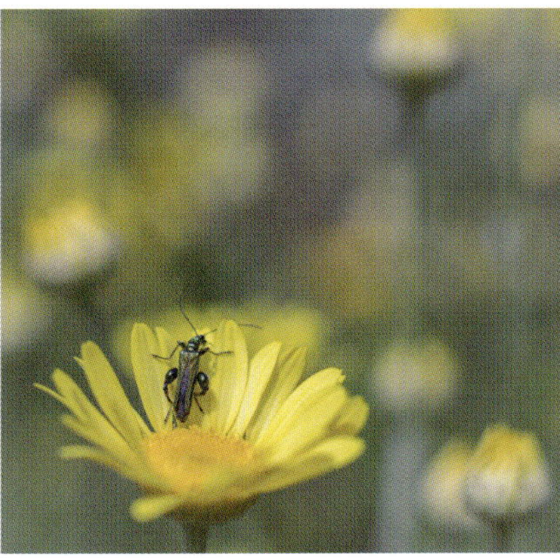

Male thick-legged flower beetle (*Oedemera nobilis*) surveying the view.

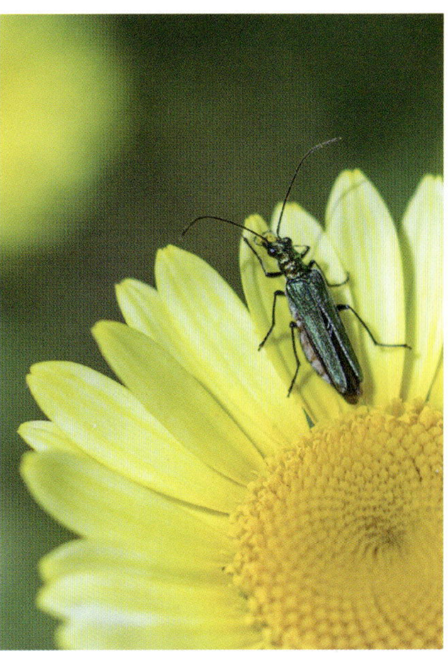

Female thick-legged flower beetle (cropped in the edit).

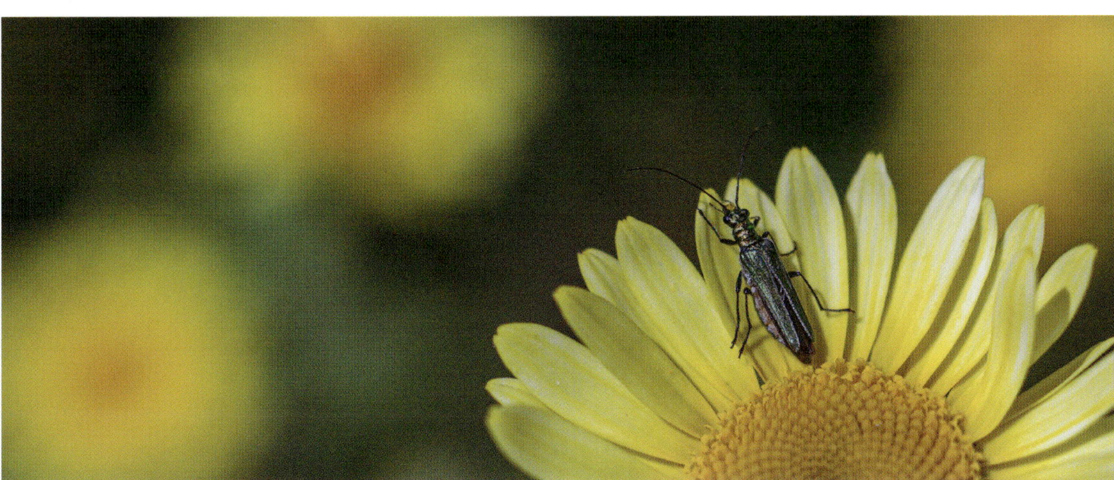

Female thick-legged flower beetle (cropped differently in the edit).

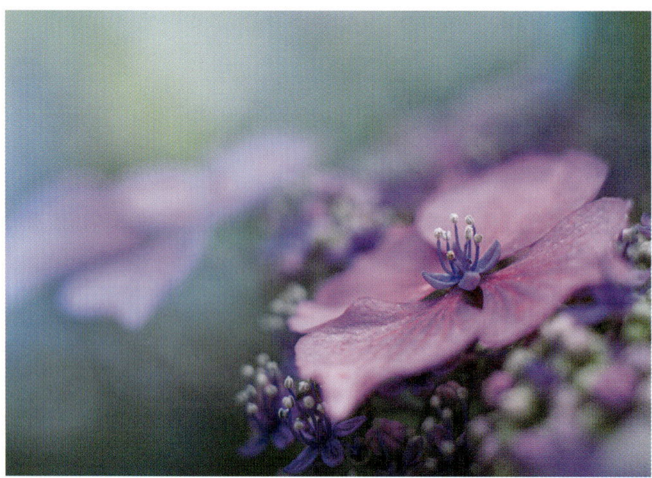

A hydrangea, shot outdoors using an extension tube. This flower is about 2cm across.

If I have small flowers growing in my own garden that I want to photograph close up I'll often take one of my photo backdrops outside and clip it to a bush or tree behind the subject. I'll clip any distracting foliage out of the way so that the flower I want is in focus and clean.

Sometimes this can look unnatural, but experiment with different backgrounds – perhaps there's a group of flowers at a distance that will be as effective a background – and you'll find something you like. For a natural look you can't beat shooting macro outside, and whilst you can 'fake' it digitally with an indoor set-up, it's usually never quite the same. I love photographing with my indoor set-up, but for me it's never quite as fun as being outside in nature.

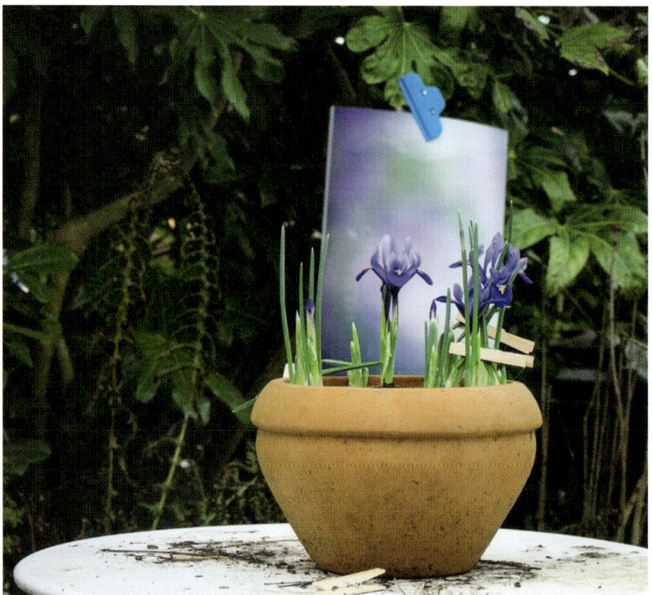

A pull-back shot of small irises in a pot that I wanted to photograph. I chose the backdrop image (made from a deliberately out-of-focus photo of flowers of a similar colour) as I thought the colours complemented the flowers themselves. I also clipped some of the stems aside with clothes pegs to avoid them being part of the picture.

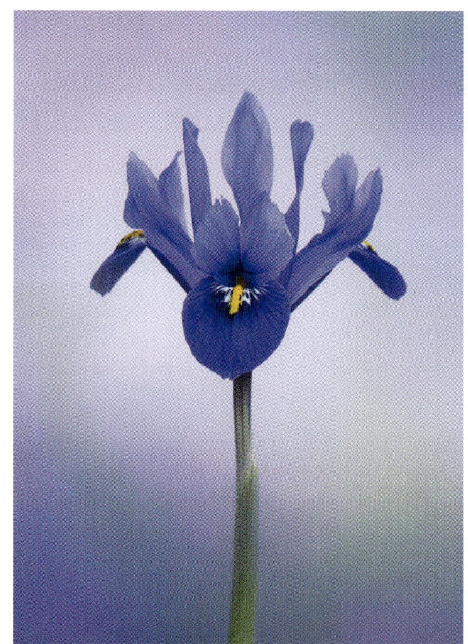

The finished photo. I used a long lens with an aperture of f/5.6 on this occasion as I wanted a substantial section of the flower to be in focus, even though these *Iris reticulata* flowers are very small (only just over an inch high).

INDOOR CLOSE-UP PHOTOGRAPHY

Most of my indoor close-up photography is done with my chosen flowers inside a lightbox as it gives bright lighting conditions that are similar to daylight (*see* Chapter 5, 'Photographing Indoors'). In addition to black, white and coloured cloth backgrounds I also use deliberately out-of-focus photos of parts of my garden (choosing the colour I want) or of material or fabric and have them printed (or print at home) at A4 or A3 size, and then clip this to the rear of the box. I have many of these in shades of green for a more natural look, but also in richer colours to give more impact. If I'm using a white background I will often add an overlay when I edit the photo and I explain how to do this in Chapter 11, 'Editing your Photographs'.

Using a printout of a typical garden background will prove useful for rainy days when you want to cut just one flower and photograph it indoors. If you're shooting close-up or macro, the background will barely be noticeable and when it is, it will be extremely blurred.

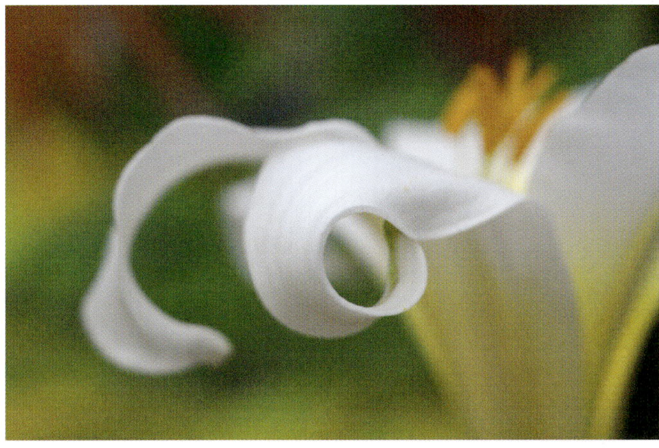

In this photo of a white lily above, the focus is on the curled petal rather than the centre. I actually used one of my children's paintings that they'd brought home from primary school as the backdrop.

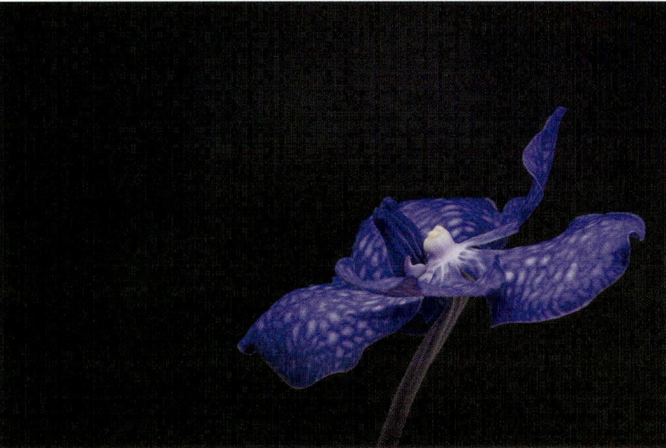

This orchid image uses a dark purple out-of-focus photo in this way and for me, it makes the scene a little more natural as there is a hint of colour and more depth.

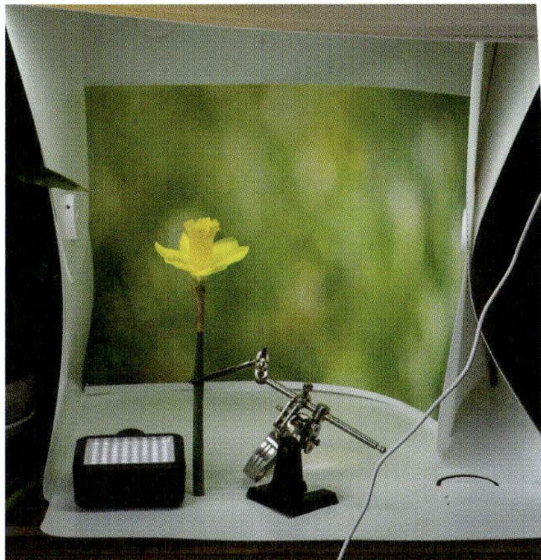

A pull-back photo of an indoor set to photograph a daffodil – I'm using a print-out of an A3 out-of-focus photo as a backdrop.

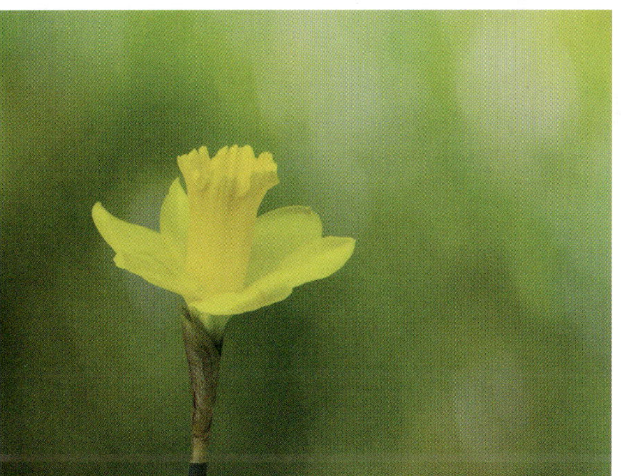

The resulting photo. This is taken with a 55mm non-macro lens.

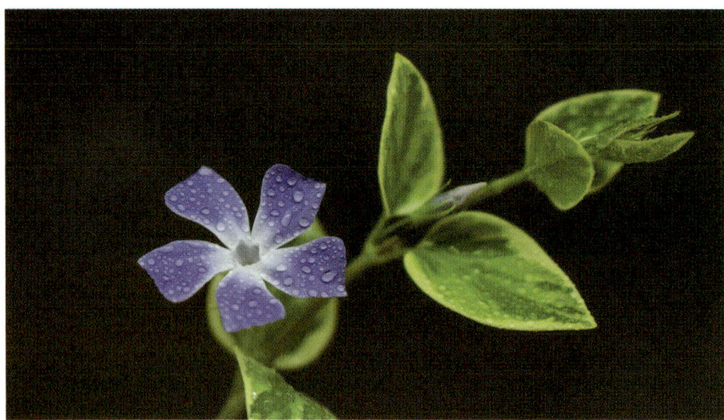

I shot this periwinkle flower with a darker photo print-out, using a 55mm non-macro lens. Be careful to make sure that your aperture is narrow enough to capture all the details that you need in focus in a photo like this. For this photo I used an aperture of f/1.8, and not all of the water droplets are in focus, which feels odd. One of the leaf tips has begun to go out of focus too.

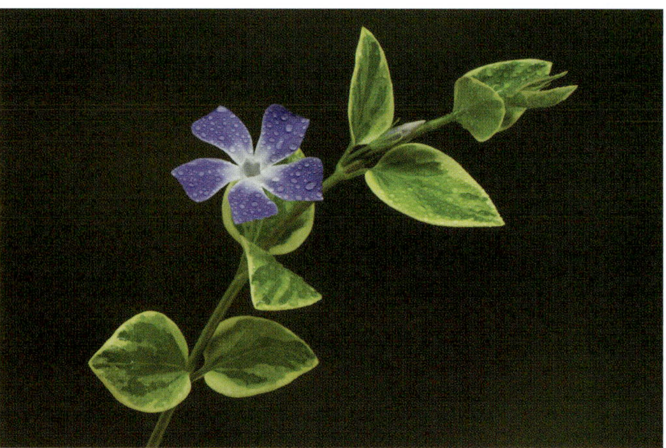

I took another photo using the same set-up but this time with an aperture of f/8, which means that all the water droplets are sharp. I feel that this crop is more successful as the image has a better composition; starting on the bottom-left third and finishing on the top-right third.

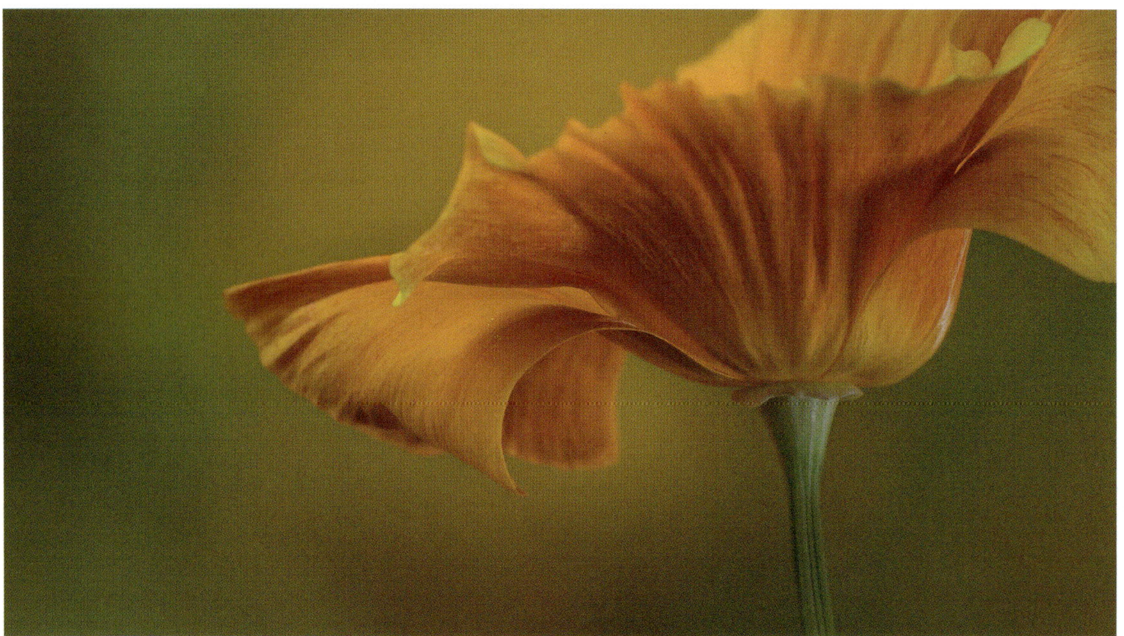

This Californian poppy was photographed in front of a photo background in my lightbox indoors using my 105mm macro lens. I found that even at small apertures many parts of the flower were out of focus, which on this occasion I didn't feel suited the flower. So I chose to focus on the base of the stem and the petal edges instead, which draws attention to this flower's sculptural quality.

You might find it tricky to get enough light into the camera if you're shooting at f/8 or higher indoors (especially with a dark background) and this is where the tripod comes in. The general rule of thumb is that you'll start to need a tripod if your shutter speed number is less than (or longer) than that of the length of your lens, for example 1/50 for a 50mm lens, or 1/300 for a 300mm lens. Using a tripod, as I explained earlier, means that you can use longer shutter speeds and not have to crank up the ISO, which may result in noise.

Sharpness (in at least one point of the photo) is usually crucial in macro and close-up photography. In playback mode, where you can view the photos previously taken on your camera, you can often zoom in and preview the sharpness of the details that you want to be in focus. I will often take many similar images, as sometimes it's just not possible to see the sharpness of small details of an image until you open it up on your computer. I'll also usually set a two- or five-second timer when using a tripod to make sure that the camera is absolutely still when the shutter is released.

I often use my 55mm (non-macro) lens for close-up photography when I'm indoors as it's my sharpest and most reliable lens. If I need the flower to be bigger in the frame (and more close up) I will crop in when I edit the photo. Macro lenses are fantastic for focusing on a single petal or really blurring out lots of the flower for a dreamy ethereal look, but if you want quite a lot of a flower in focus it will be hard to achieve this (especially if the flower is quite large) with a macro lens without using 'focus stacking'. Focus stacking involves taking lots of photos using a tripod with a different point of focus each time and then blending them together with computer software afterwards. Some macro photographers use a focus rail or slider on top of their tripod to make this process even easier. However if your subject is very small, like a daisy or a ladybird, then macro lenses should work very well indeed.

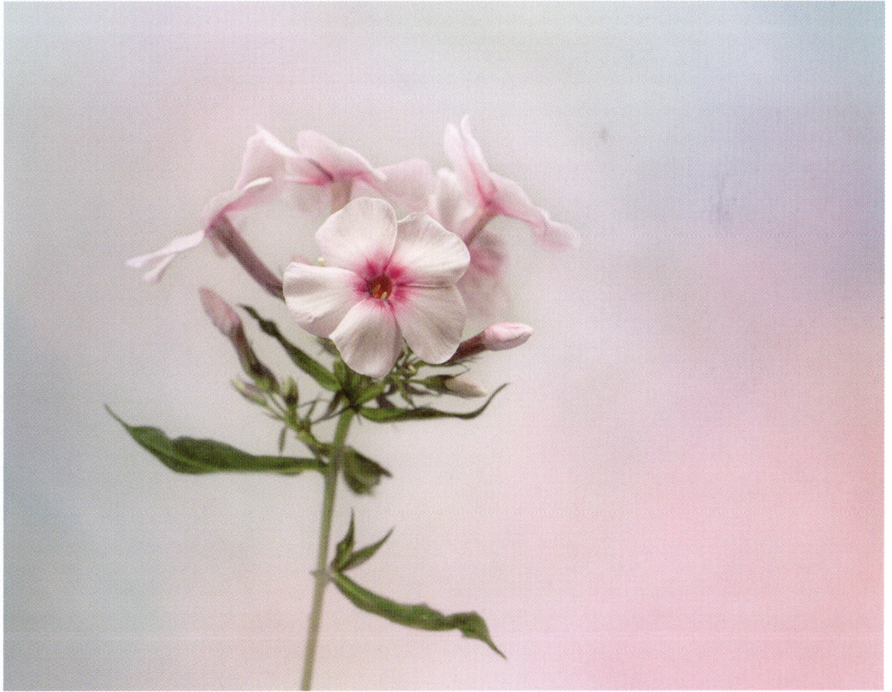

These stocks just had the white inside of my lightbox as a backdrop. I added a pinky-blue overlay on top in the edit.

Flowers and plants to photograph in June

The roses are here! Lupins, delphiniums and foxgloves reach for the sky in a myriad of colours.

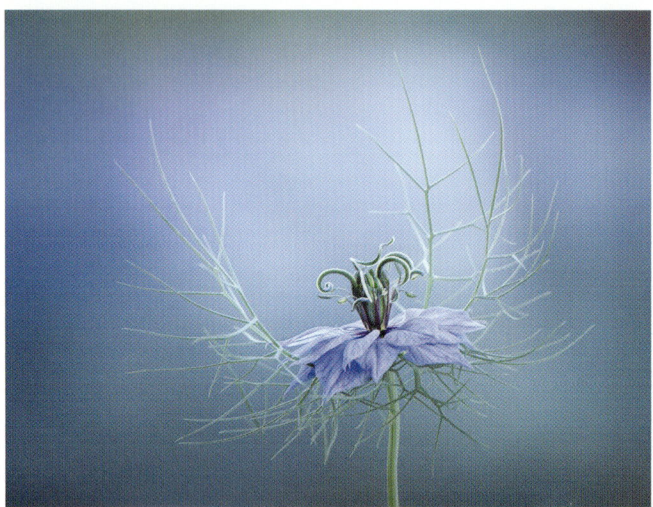

Nigella damascena (Love-in-a-mist) – 1/160 sec at f/5, 160mm.

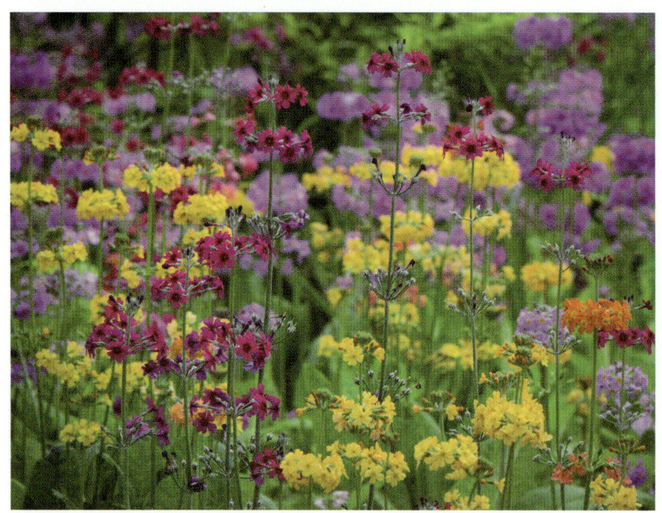

Primula prolifera (candelabra primulas) – 1/250 sec at f/4, 100mm.

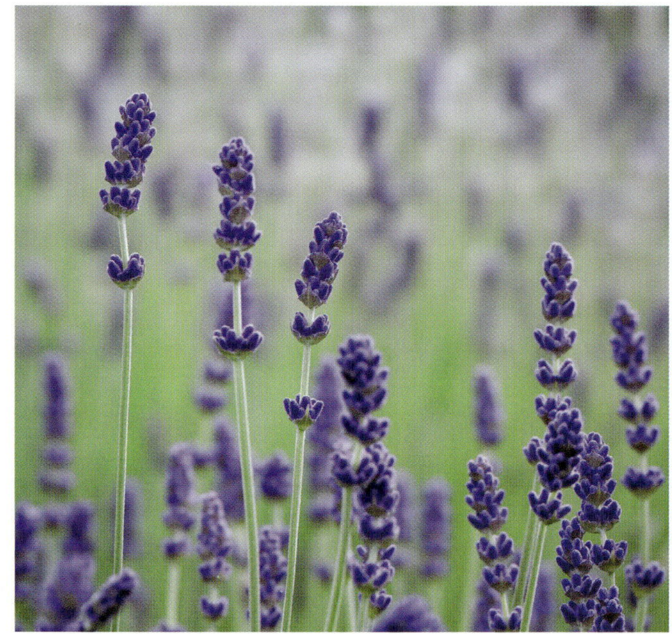

Lavender – 1/800 sec at f/4, 90mm.

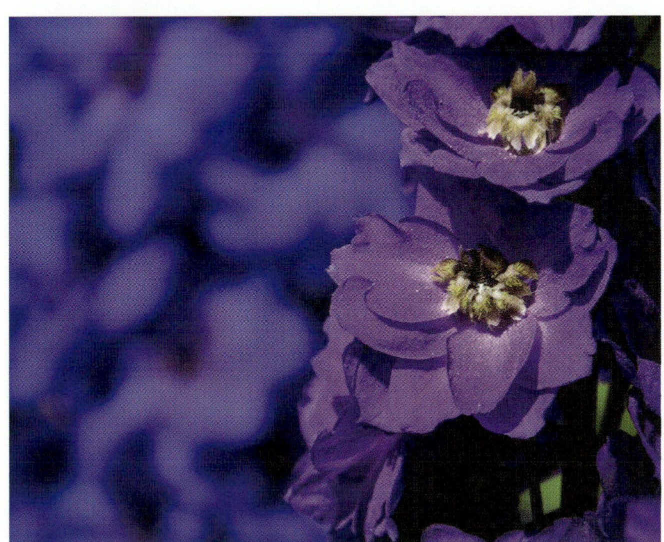

Delphiniums – 1/500 sec at f/4, 220mm.

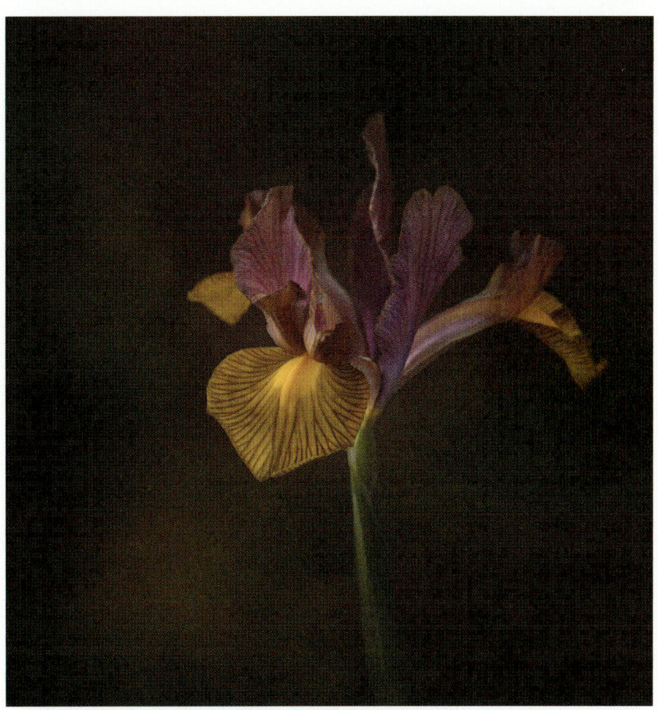

Iris – 1/640 sec at f/7.1, 55mm. Overlay added in the edit.

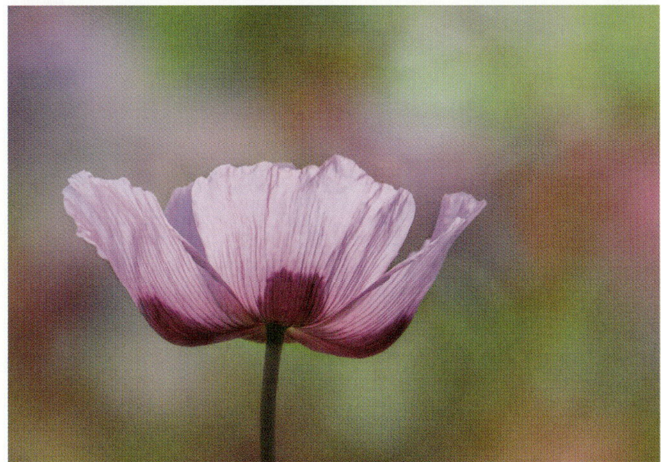

Papaver orientale (Oriental poppy) – 1/640 sec at f/4, 170mm.

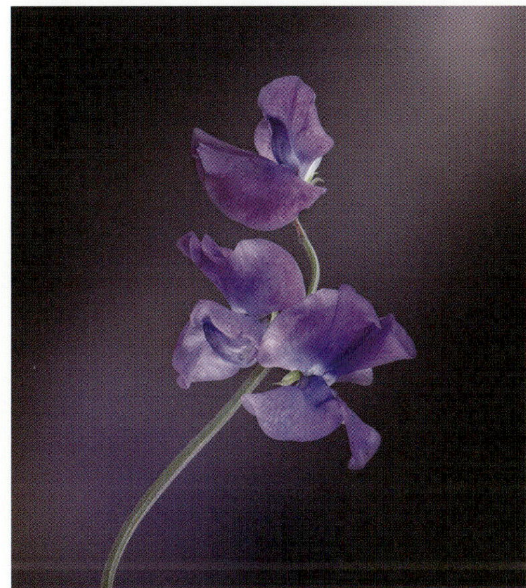

Lathyrus odoratus (sweet pea) – 1/80 sec at f/7, 55mm.

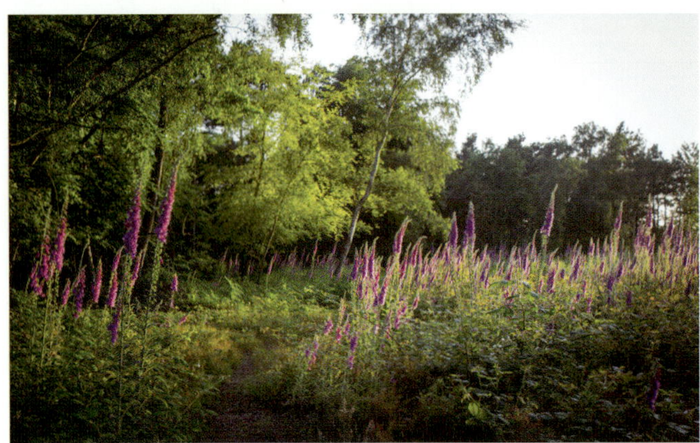

Field of wild *Digitalis* (foxgloves) – 1/30 sec at f/5.6, 28mm.

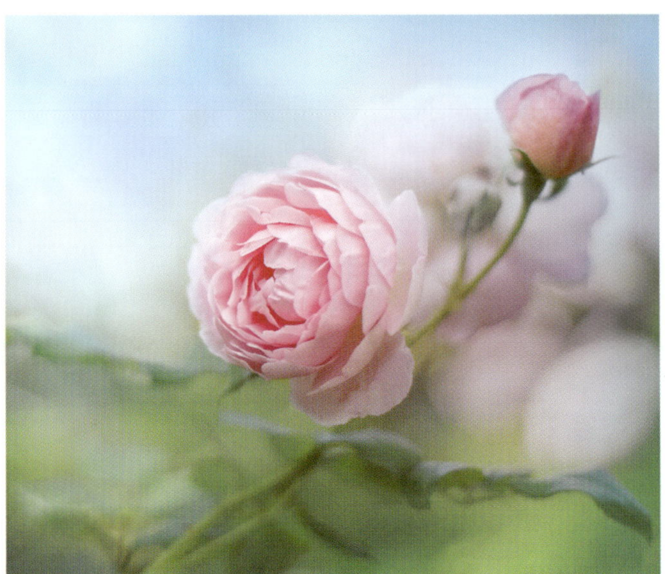

Rosa 'Sceptr'd Isle' – 1/1250 sec at f/1.7, 50mm vintage lens.

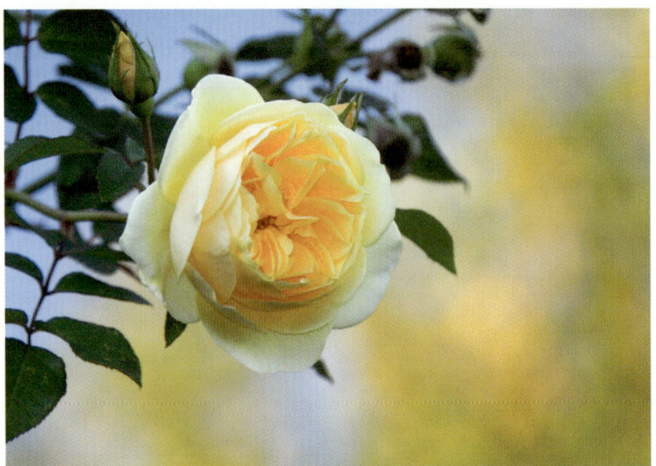

Rosa 'Charles Darwin' – 1/400 sec at f/4, 180mm.

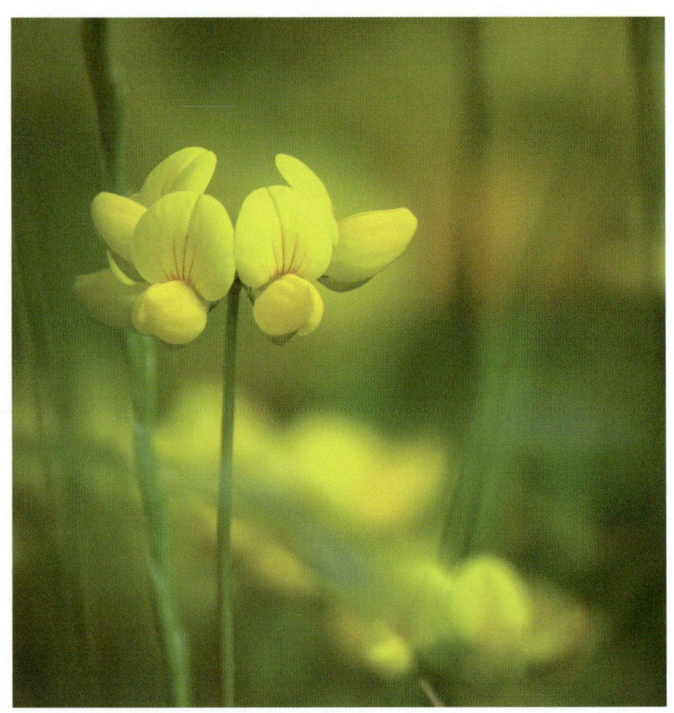

Lotus corniculatus (Bird's-foot trefoil) – 1/400 sec at f/4, 210mm.

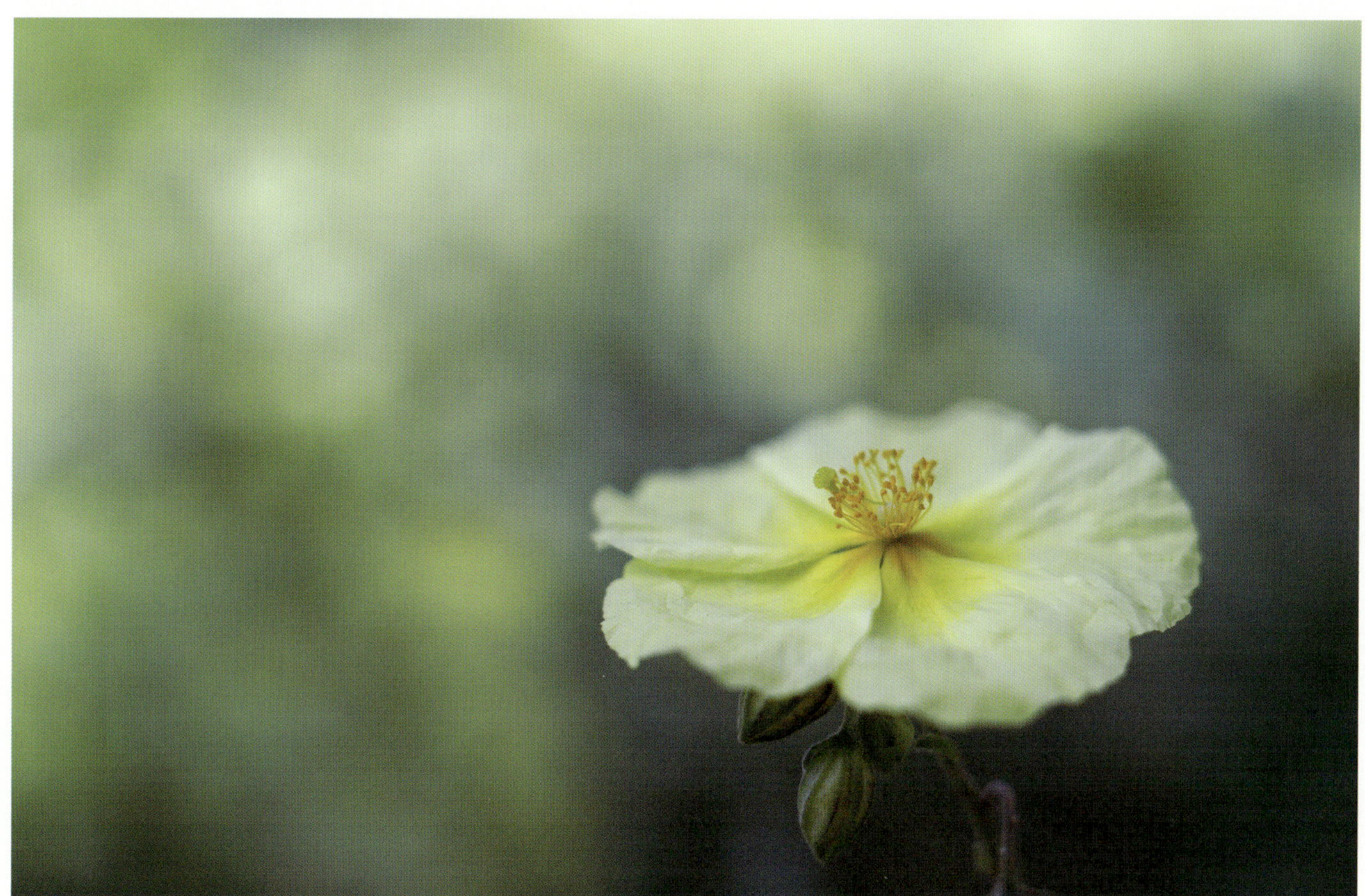

Helianthemum – 1/640 sec at f/1.7, 50mm vintage lens.

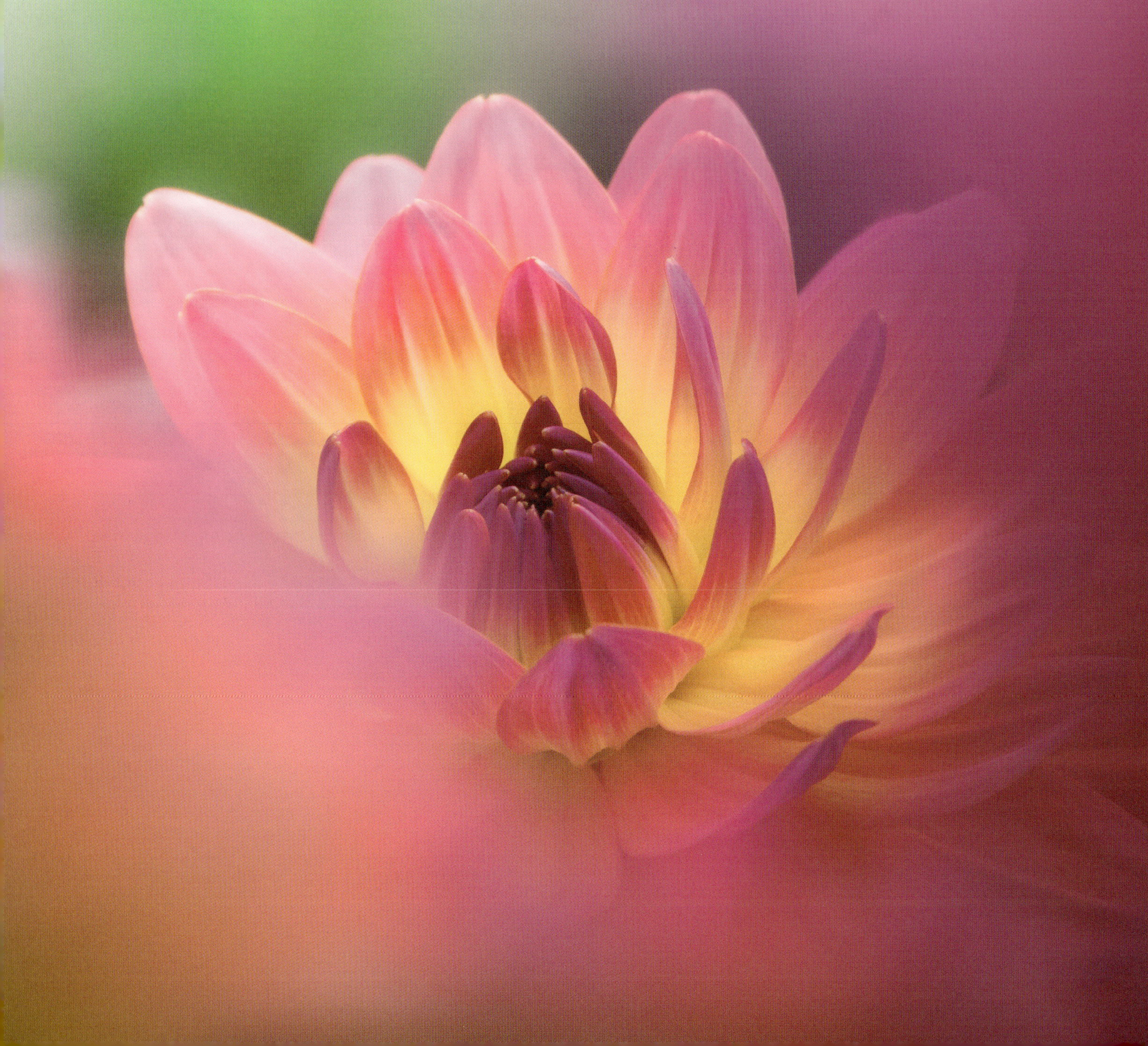

CHAPTER 7

Shooting Through

> Learn the rules like a pro – so you can break them like an artist.
>
> PABLO PICASSO

'Shooting through' is a technique that gives a very Impressionistic effect as it blurs the colour around the subject that you are focusing on. Similar in fact to the blurred backgrounds I've discussed earlier in this book, except that in this case the blurred colour is in the foreground rather than the background.

When you have selected the flower/s to be the subject of your photo, you then need to look around for other flowers that you can use to create the shooting through effect. If you have a longer lens (and this technique usually does work better with long lenses) the foreground flower/s can actually be a little way away. Then you need to actually position your lens so that your foreground flower is slightly to the side but a little in front of the main subject, possibly almost touching the glass of the lens. It will then appear as an out-of-focus coloured blur in your photo.

You may need to set your camera to manual focus; on autofocus it may keep trying to focus on the foreground flower rather than the one you have selected as your focal point. If you are in your own garden you could actually pick a flower or leaf and hold it in front of your lens to create the blurred colour.

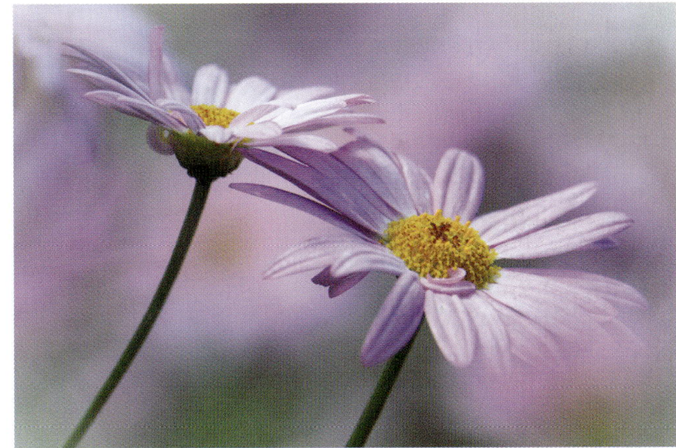

Two *Argyranthemum frutescens* with other similar flowers providing an out-of-focus blur around them.

◀ Dahlia 'Ken's Rarity'.

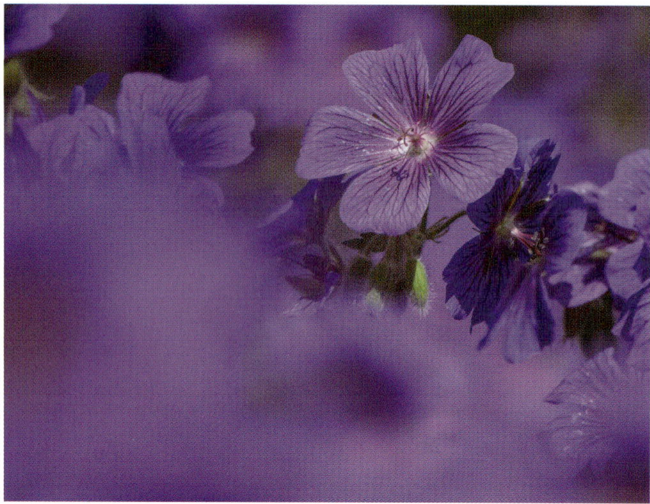

The main geranium flower in this photo is positioned on the top-left third, looking into the photo. Other similar flowers create the purple out-of-focus blur in the foreground.

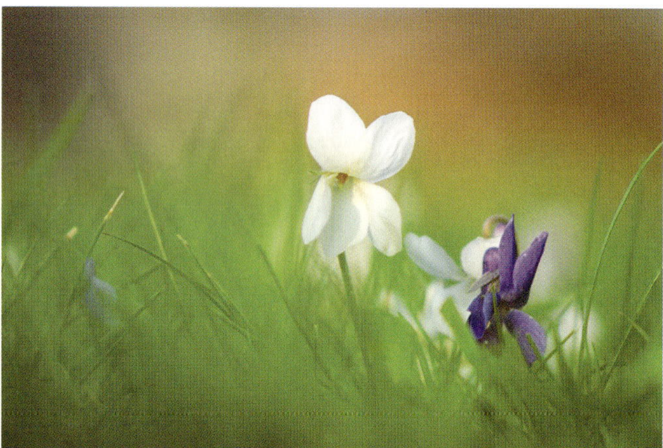

Here the out-of-focus green patch in front of the *Viola odorata* (violets) is created by grass in the foreground, which gives a more subtle effect.

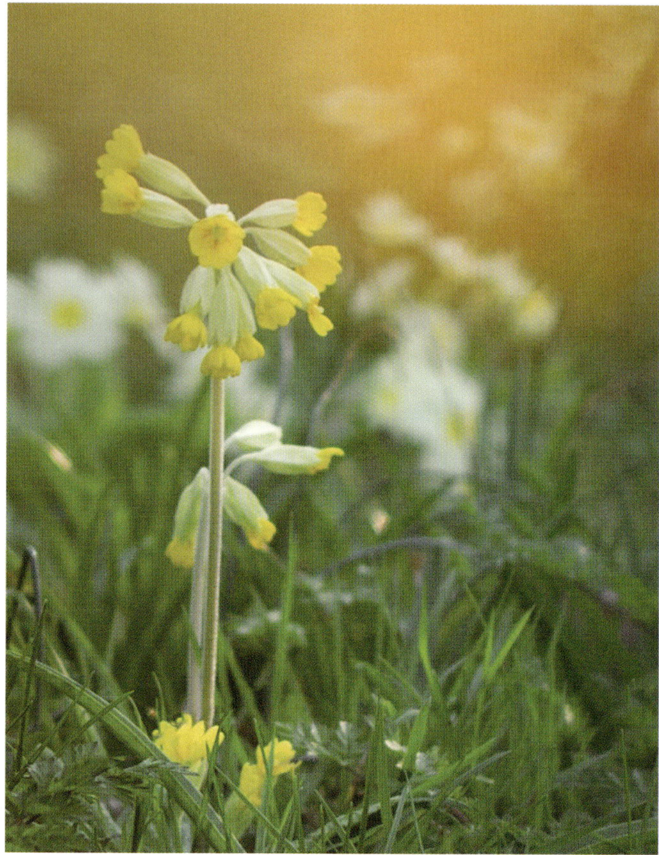

In this photo, the orange blur at the top right is made by another primula flower just in front of the lens.

Grass, long or short, can create very ethereal effects in the foreground if you are lying on the floor and shooting through it to your subject. Groups of small flowers can be just as effective with the shooting through technique as single ones. You might even be able to use the blur of what you are shooting through to hide distracting background elements in the image.

I love to use this technique in woodland gardens where dappled light and foliage can create all kinds of magical effects. I sit on the floor and look for a composition with foreground leaves and plants creating a frame around a flower or flowers further away.

I shot these bluebells from about four metres away at full zoom (220mm) through grass with my bridge camera. There is hardly any editing involved, just a crop and a little vibrancy added.

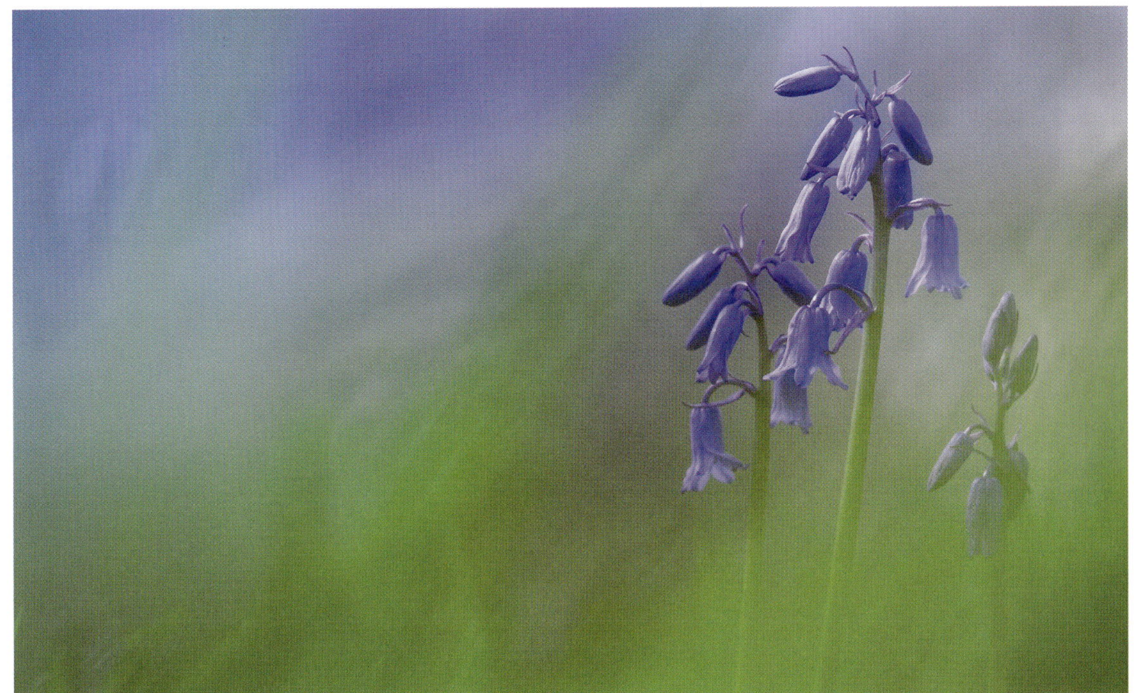

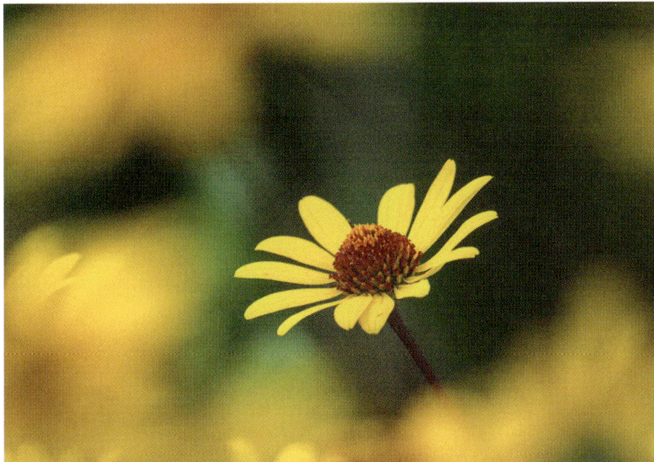

Here I've tried to surround the central yellow dahlia with a halo of out-of-focus foreground flowers. I looked for some time to find a distant flower that could be seen through a 'window' of flowers nearer to me.

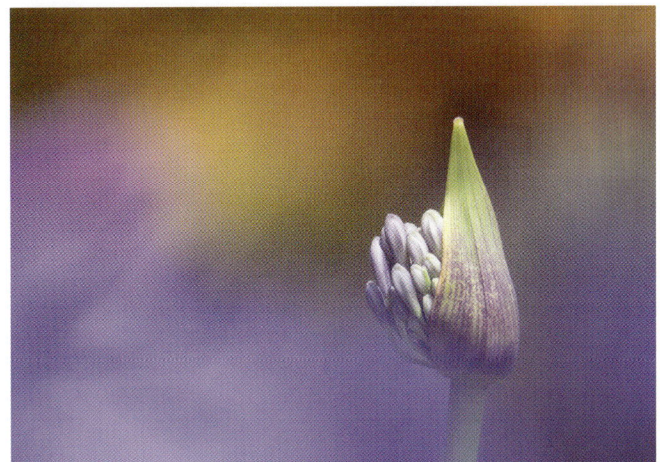

The purple in the foreground of this photo is agapanthus flowers that were already flowering. They make a nice contrast to the bud of the emerging agapanthus, which is the subject of the picture. Negative space works well here for this reason.

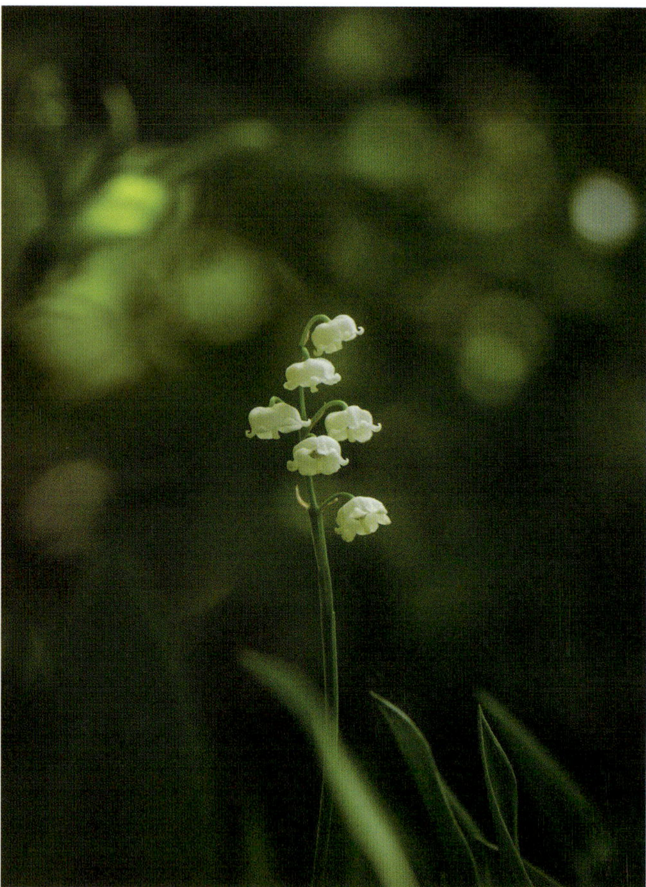

This *Convallaria majalis* (lily-of-the-valley) image is a little different as the out-of-focus foreground leaves are mostly very dark, which gives a more subtle, vignette-like effect.

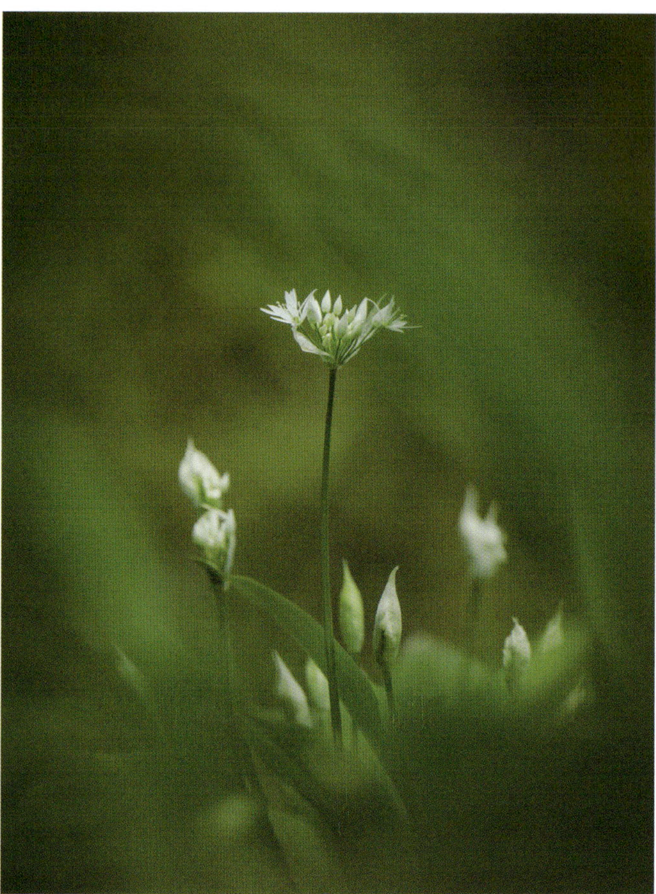

Wild garlic in a woodland garden, shot through other garlic leaves.

One of the more interesting shoot-throughs I did recently was with a spiky phormium plant, which had long, red, spear-like leaves. I focused on a far leaf that was covered in rain drops and had the out-of-focus leaves on either side. I placed the leaf in focus on the right-hand third and chose quite an elongated crop, which seemed to suit the composition.

CREATING THE SHOOTING THROUGH TECHNIQUE ARTIFICIALLY

A fun thing to try is to use something other than foliage or flowers to create the blur next to your lens – my go-to for this is tissue paper in different colours. Normally I would use a shade similar to that of the flower that I'm photographing, but experiment and see what works well for you. You could carry tissue paper with you in your camera bag on a garden visit or just try it at home in an indoor set-up.

Raindrops on a *Phormium* leaf.

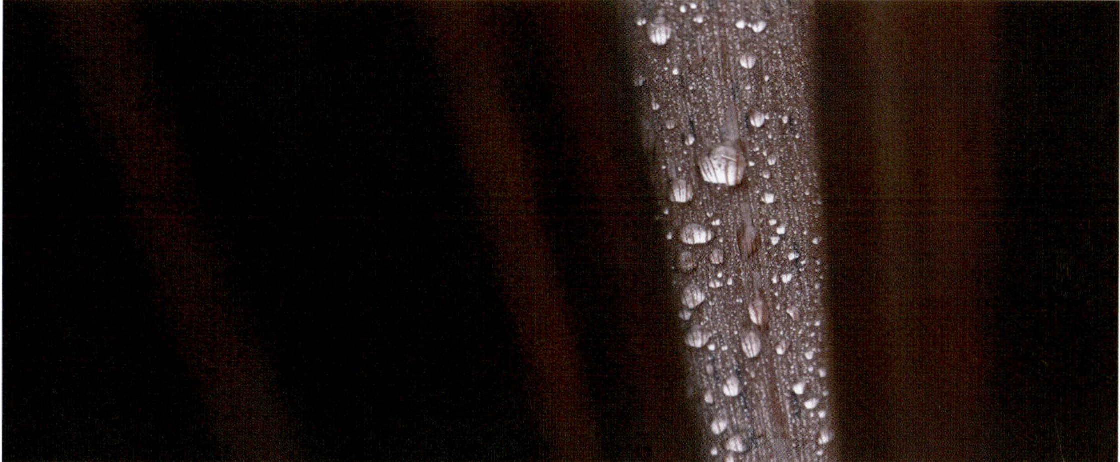

The set-up, including purple tissue-paper around the lens and third hand holding a crocus flower from my garden behind.

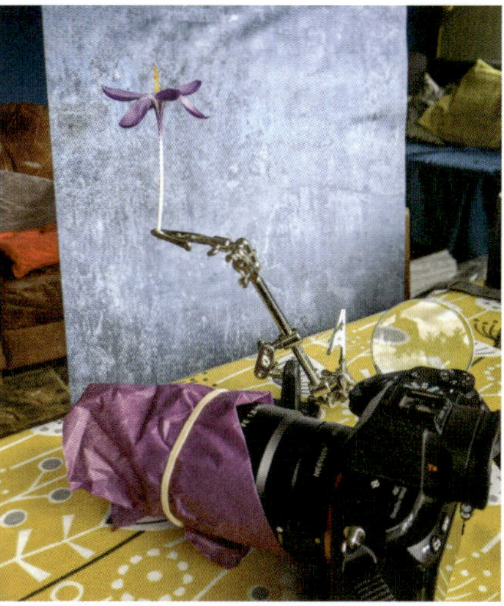

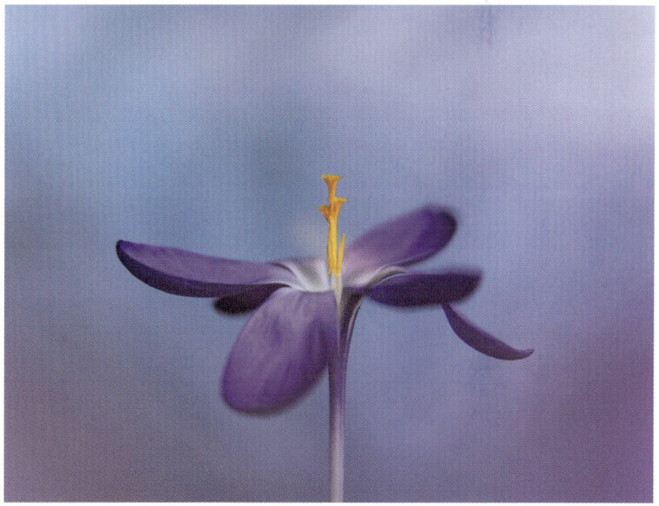

The finished photo, taken with a normal 55mm lens fitted with an extension tube.

Tear a piece from a single sheet of tissue paper and wrap it around the front of your lens, securing it with a rubber band. Push just a little of the tissue paper up from the bottom until, looking through the viewfinder, you can see a colour blur come onto the picture. You could use a cardboard or photo background for this or just a coloured wall two or three feet behind. Alternatively you could take the tissue paper and camera outside for more natural backgrounds.

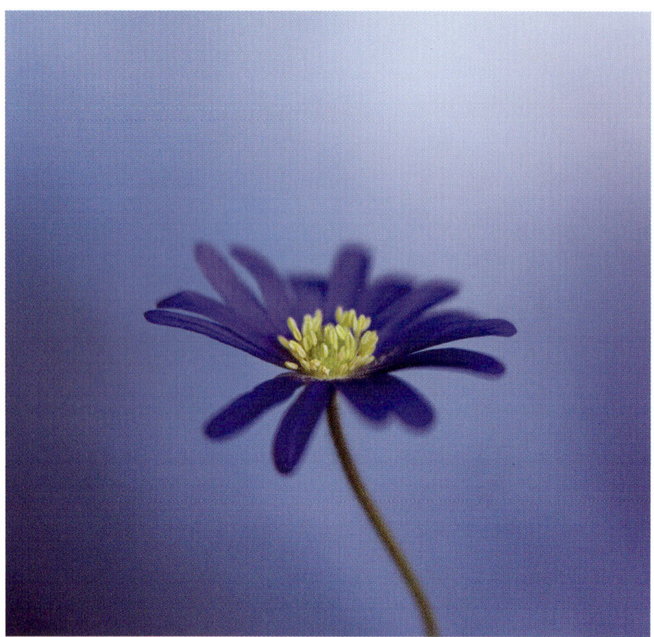

Blue *Anemone blanda* flower, shot with blue tissue paper around the lens.

Depending on how much of the tissue paper you use the effect can be subtle or more bold, and as ever, experiment and see what works for you and what doesn't.

You could also try thin fabric, such as voile, for this technique. The possible combinations of colours and flowers are almost limitless – it's a good project for a cold day when you'd rather be indoors!

Another way of using this technique is to bring the outside inside – if you have a pot with some greenery or flowers in you can bring it indoors (or even use a houseplant) and use this in a similar way to the set-up above.

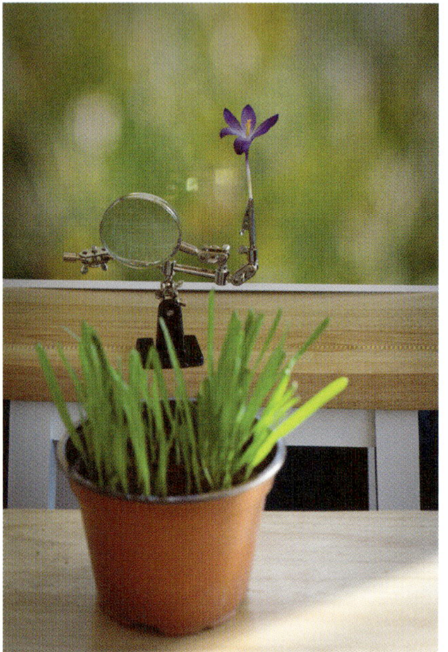

This set-up uses a pot of cat-grass positioned about two feet in front of the subject, another crocus. I am using a stool for the third hand and crocus with a photo backdrop behind, and another stool nearer me for the potted grass. With a 50mm lens I positioned myself at the level of the grass so that the crocus flower fitted into a gap in the grass stalks.

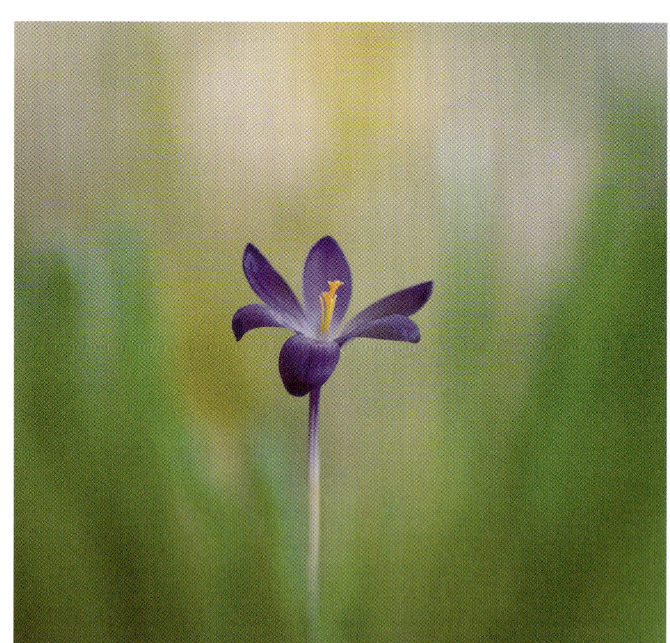

The finished photo, which has been cropped.

Flowers and plants to photograph in July

July is midsummer and lilies, penstemon and summer-flowering clematis create a riot of colour.

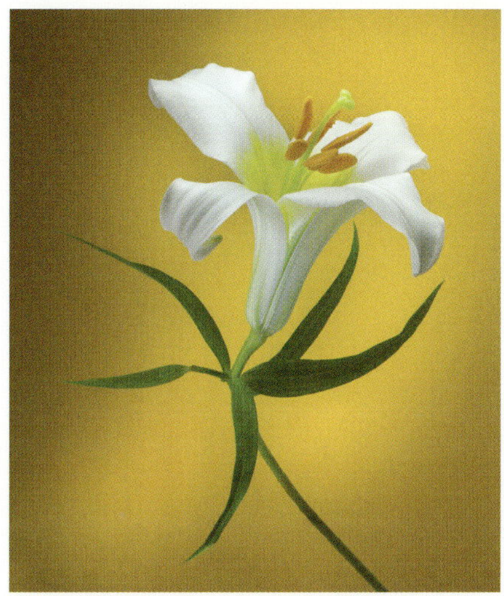

Lilium orientalis (Oriental lily) – 1/25 sec at f/16, 55mm (with tripod). The yellow background was one of my son's school exercise books that I took outside with me.

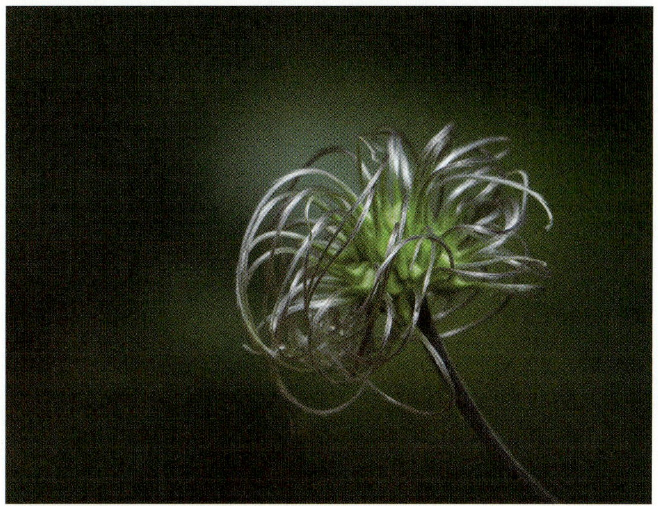

Clematis seed head – 1/1000 sec at f/4, 140mm.

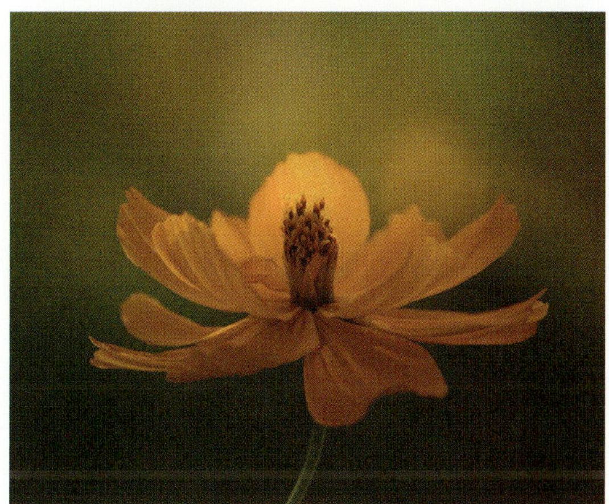

Cosmos polidor – 1/600 sec at f/6.3, 100mm.

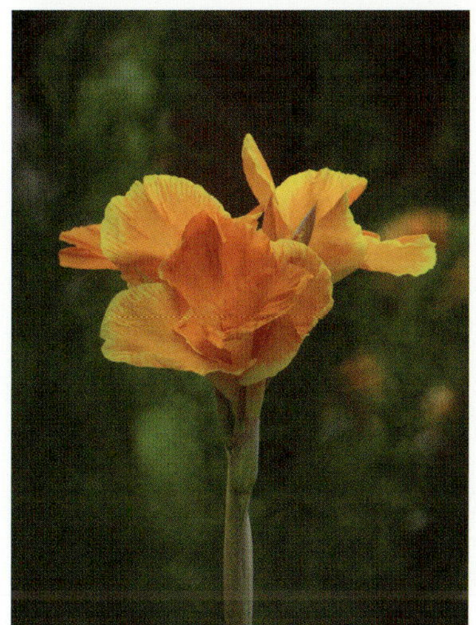

Canna lily – 1/500 sec at f/4, 100mm.

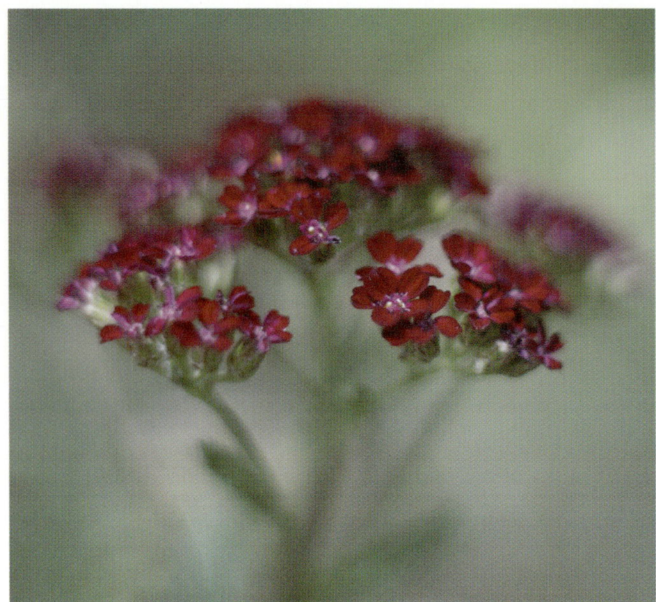

Achillea – 1/2500 sec at f/2, 55mm with extension tube.

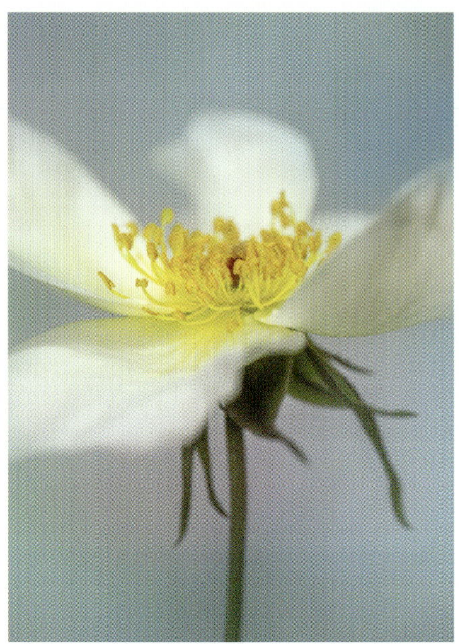

Rose – 1/125 sec at f/5.6, 105mm macro lens.

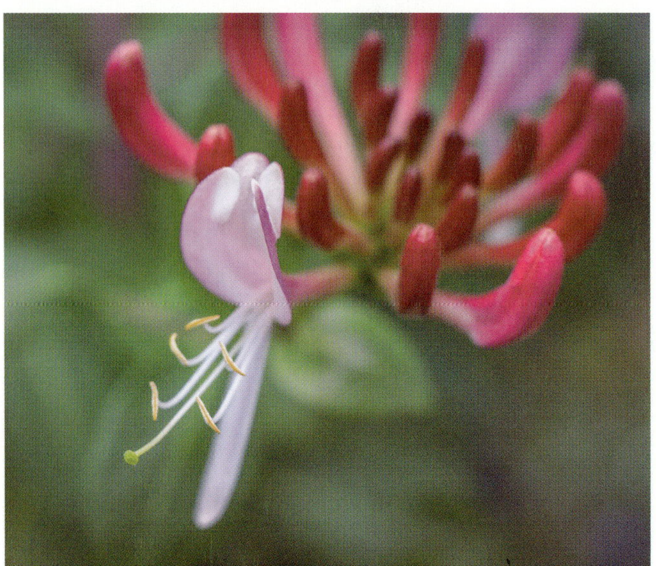

Lonicera (honeysuckle) – 1/200 sec at f/1.7, 50mm vintage macro lens, overlay added in the edit.

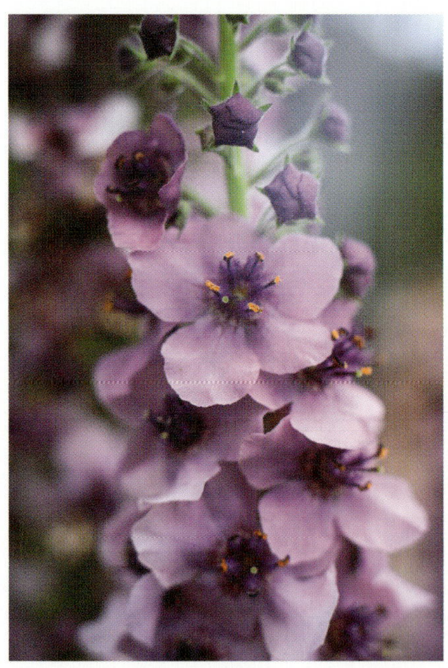

Verbascum phoeniceum – 1/320 sec at f/2, 55mm lens with an extension tube.

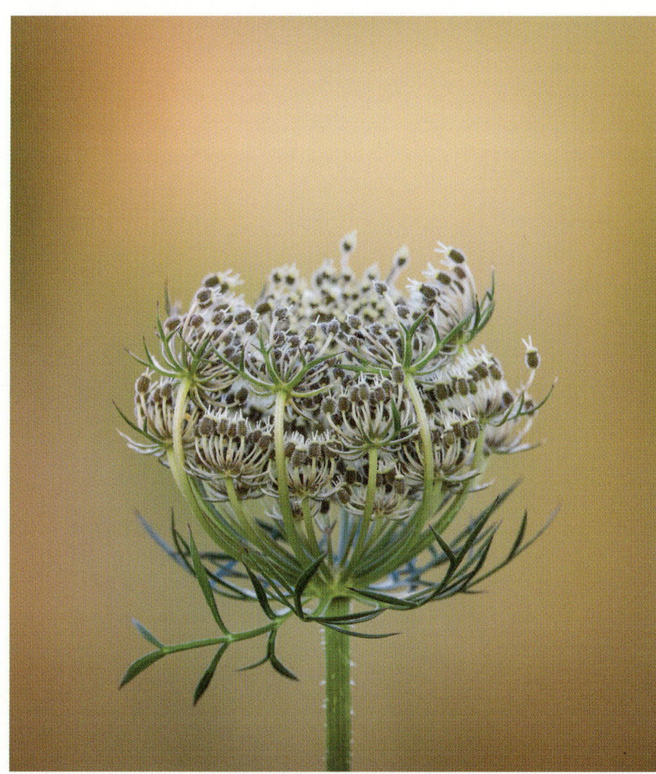

Daucus carota (wild carrot flower) – 1/400 sec at f/4, 180mm.

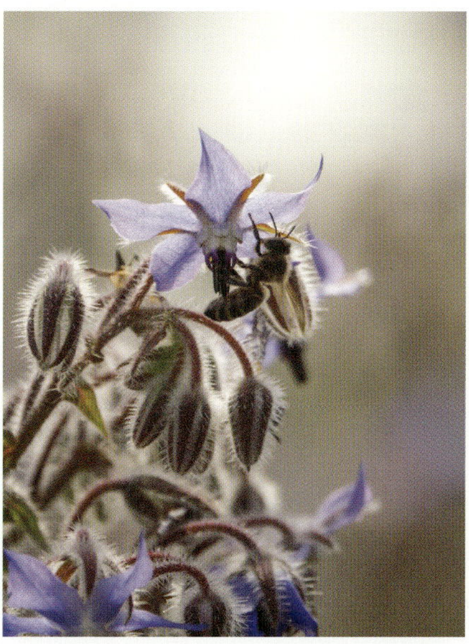

Honey bee on *Borago officinalis* (borage) – 1/2500 sec at f/4, 210mm.

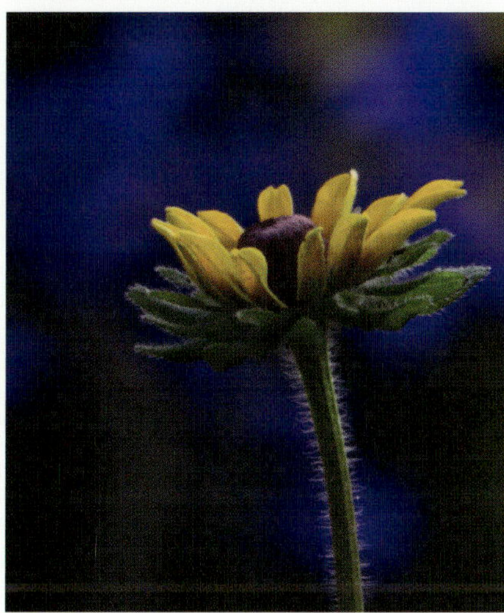

Emerging *Rudbeckia* flower with purple delphiniums behind.

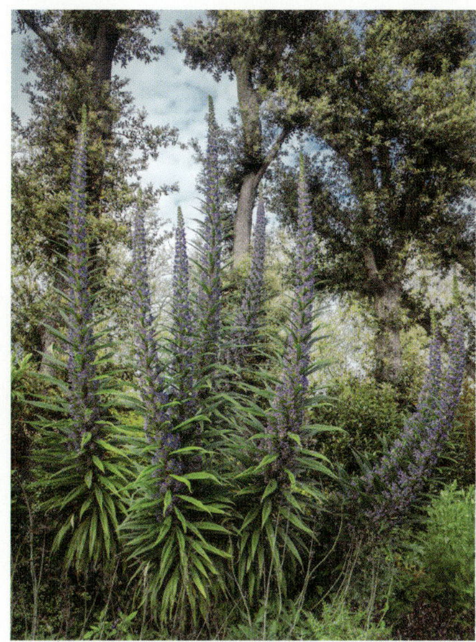

Tall *Echium pininana* with trees behind – 1/800 sec at f/2.5, 20mm.

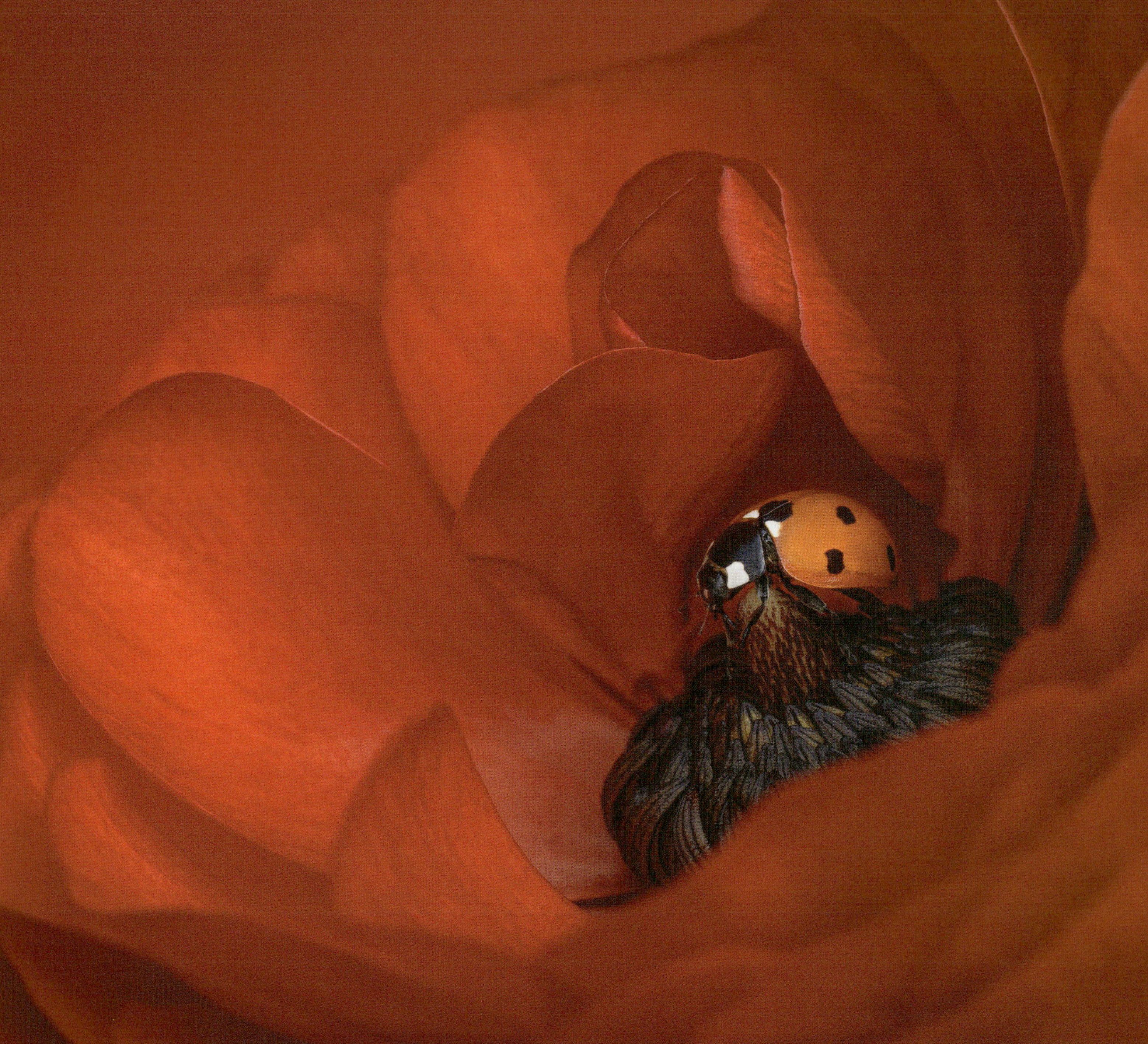

CHAPTER 8

Wildlife in the Garden

> Look deep into nature and then you will understand things better.
>
> ALBERT EINSTEIN

For me, a garden doesn't feel complete without wildlife in it. Many gardeners (and farmers) are now embracing various rewilding/wilding schemes to try to bring back species of British wildlife whose numbers have dropped alarmingly over the last fifty years.

I have always enjoyed feeding my garden birds and watching them in the garden gives my family great pleasure. More recently I have tried to bring more insects into the garden, and during lockdown I tried to attract wildlife into my garden by adding pollinator-friendly plants, most of which I grew myself from seed. I am now seeing, and photographing, the results. With the help of books, websites and apps, a little research can help you to grow flowers and plants to attract wildlife, even if you only have a small outside space. More and more public gardens are doing the same and many now have entire areas planted to encourage wildlife, such as meadows or prairie areas. Photographing wildlife in places such as this can be as enjoyable as taking photos of the garden itself.

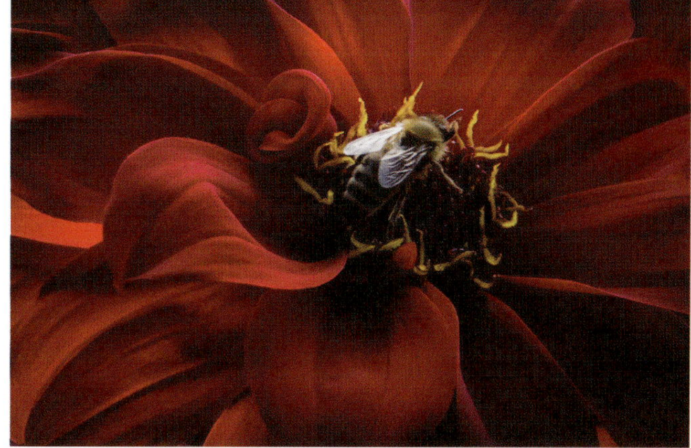

A honey bee in the centre of a dahlia. I took this photo in St James' Park in the middle of London as I was walking through it one day.

◀ Ladybird on red ranunculus flower.

INSECTS

If you've been photographing plants, photographing insects may seem tricky by comparison – they move, and often fast! This is not going to be an instructional piece about photographing insects very close up, as often you would use a specialist lens and software for this (investigate 'focus stacking' if you're interested). I am more concerned with how to use wildlife as part of your flower and garden photography compositions, to show 'life' or provide a narrative.

I would usually recommend the use of a tripod with garden insects and preferably a lens with a long reach or zoom. This means that you can zoom in on the insect without disturbing it. When you are zoomed in a great deal it is very hard to keep the camera steady and photos will often be blurry without a tripod. If you have no tripod with you, try sitting on the floor and resting the camera on your knees in front of you. Alternatively, set a fast shutter speed to capture insects that move quickly. Sometimes I just use a 50mm lens, knowing that the subject won't be that large in the frame but with the aim of forming a composition with the wider area around the insect visible to give a sense of context. If I need to get in closer for more stationary insects like beetles or crickets, I can use an extension tube or two which will then give me more magnification.

If you're shooting insects that move quickly and have a camera with a 'continuous' or 'tracking' autofocus setting I would definitely recommend using that, so that when the insect moves, your camera will keep it in focus as you follow it. Many insect photographers will use flash or a speedlight behind a diffuser, which will give the extra light that is often needed to bring out the insect's colours and allow you to narrow your aperture to get all of the insect in focus. I more often use a small LED light (which has its own white plastic diffuser in front of the LED bulbs) mounted to the hot shoe of my camera.

Whilst it's not always possible to move the creature you're photographing (I would never lift or move wildlife in the garden except perhaps snails) it is often possible to move *yourself*, to get a better angle for the photograph.

Insects usually have 'faces', and just as in human portraiture their features usually need to be at least partially visible, otherwise it's a bit like making a portrait of the back of someone's head. There are exceptions of course (such as butterflies) but in general 'from behind' shots don't look as good, although they can sometimes add comedy value!

Rhagonycha fulva (common red soldier beetle) surveying the garden from the edge of a blue eryngium flower.

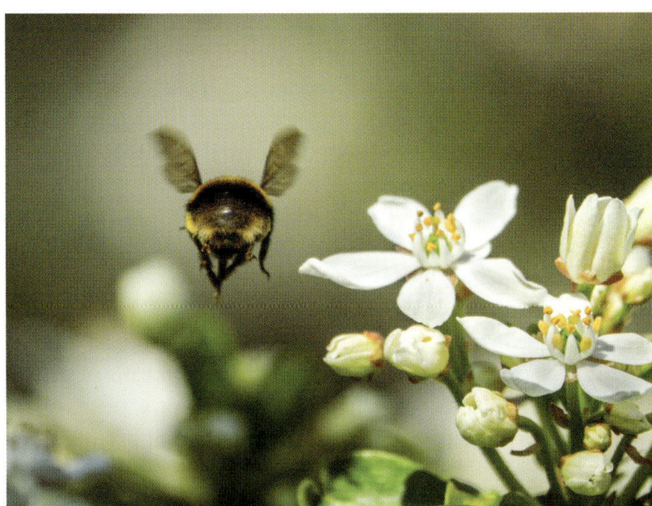

The rear of a bumblebee as it flies away from *Choisya* flowers.

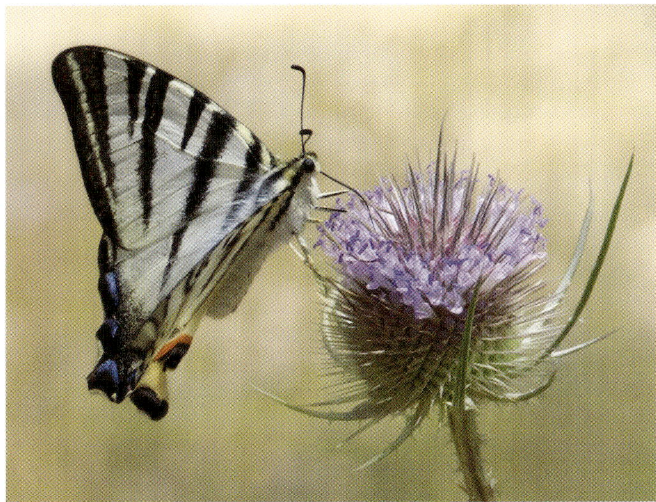

Papilio machaon (swallowtail butterfly) on a teasel – I took this photo in France whilst on holiday, but some can be found in the east of the UK now.

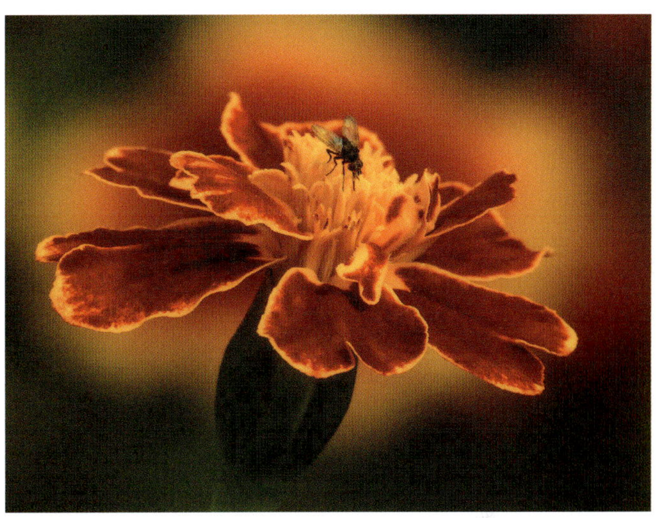

A fly on a calendula flower. I lined the main flower up with a larger one behind it to give a halo of colour.

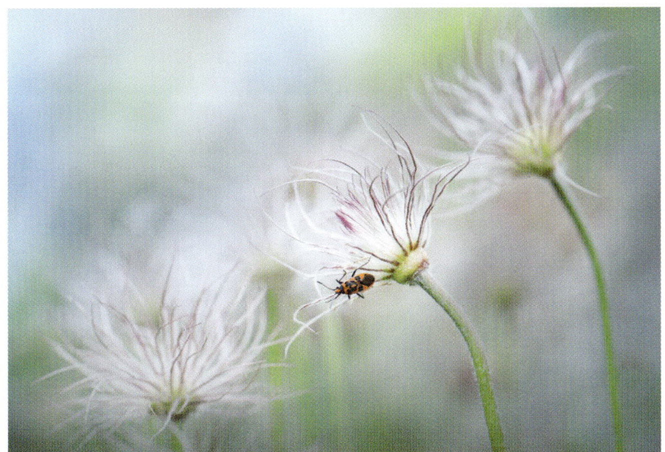

Corizus hyoscyami (cinnamon bug) on the seedheads of pasque flowers – I liked that the flower heads seem to grow in size from the bottom-left third of the photo to the top right.

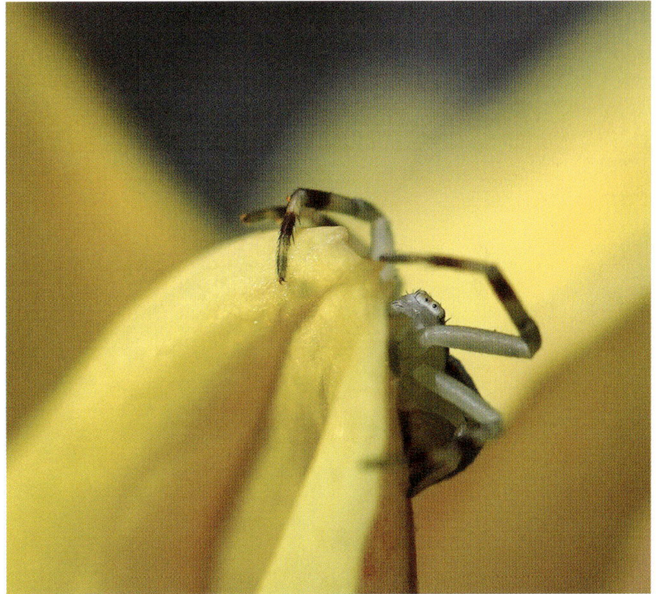

This spider clings to the edge of a yellow dahlia petal, which will give you some idea as to how tiny it is. Not all of the limbs are in focus but I was very surprised to be able to see its eyes and hairy face so clearly. This photo was taken with a regular 55mm lens and then cropped in on the computer afterwards, which is another option, although of course then the overall image size will be smaller, which may make printing at a reasonable size difficult.

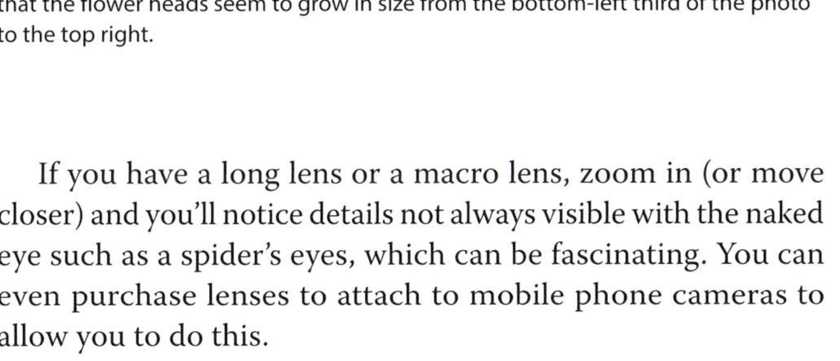

If you have a long lens or a macro lens, zoom in (or move closer) and you'll notice details not always visible with the naked eye such as a spider's eyes, which can be fascinating. You can even purchase lenses to attach to mobile phone cameras to allow you to do this.

Ladybirds and beetles

Ladybirds and beetles are a good starting point for insect photography as you can often find them resting. Move around them until you find a composition that works for you. Don't forget to try all possible angles and take lots of shots in case some aren't quite sharp – you may only notice this when viewing on a computer later. Many beetles such as ladybirds have striking colours and it is a nice challenge to find a background that contrasts or complements the beetle's colour for good impact.

Whilst ladybirds will always be very popular and photogenic subjects, there are many other colourful beetles to be found, such as the red soldier beetle and green shield bugs. Often these are hard to find until you just sit (or stand) and quietly watch for a while, and again researching the flowers or plants that different insects like to frequent will help. I have learnt over the years which parts of local gardens (aside from my own) particular insects are to be found in and this experience helps greatly with the hunt.

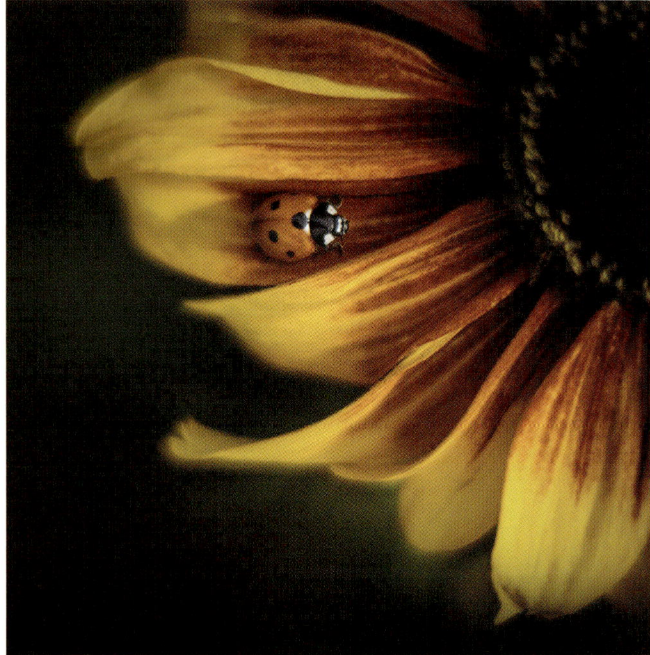

Even though I took this photo in my own garden, I couldn't get to the angle I wanted to photograph the ladybird's face. So I changed tack and shot from above – the bird's-eye view and hard crop give an interesting composition and the *Rudbeckia* flower still gives good context.

Dragonflies and damselflies

Dragonflies and damselflies are fiendishly difficult to capture mid-flight but I've had some success with ones that are resting. They are almost impossible to get 'sharp' from nose to tail (unless you focus-stack) so you might have to decide which part should be in focus. The eyes are usually most important but try to make the wings sharp too if you can; you might need a narrower aperture or a longer lens to do this. If you are able to photograph them in profile (from the side) you should be able to get most parts sharp, or you could photograph them from the front and get the eyes sharp and let the rest of the body blur into the distance, which can be quite attractive. A common 'problem' with photographing damselflies in particular is that they tend to rest on tall grass or reeds and it can be hard to capture them with a clean background that isn't cluttered with out-of-focus lines made from chaotic grass stalks behind. Move around them and try to find either a clean background or one where the background grasses or plants add something to the composition.

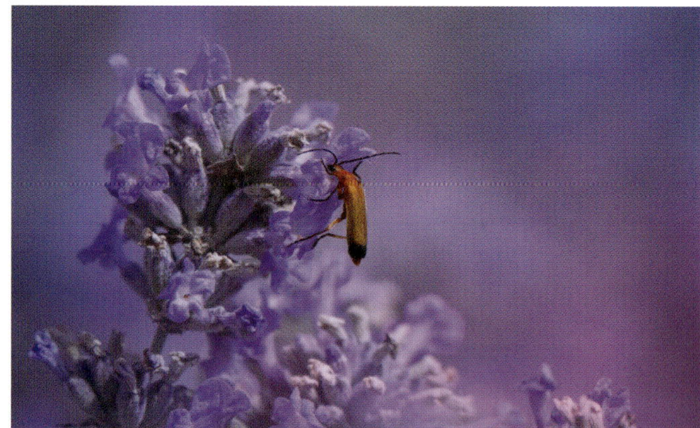

I watched this red soldier beetle climbing to the top of a lavender flower and photographed its progress. I have added a similarly coloured overlay in the edit to remove distracting elements from the background and throw the attention on to the beetle.

Enallagma cyathigerum (common blue damselfly) clinging to a grass stalk. I used a very long lens for this photo as damselflies scare very easily, often before you've even lifted up your camera!

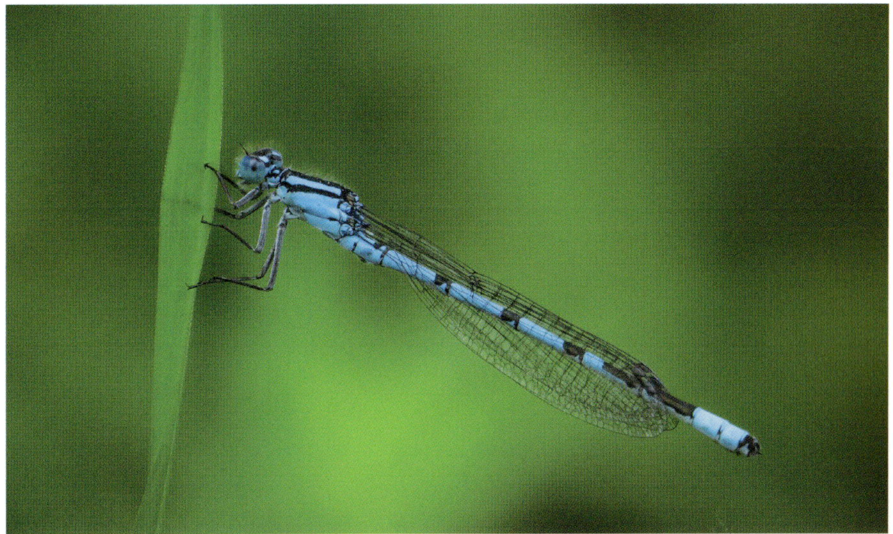

A *Sympetrum striolatum* (common darter) dragonfly rests on a bamboo stick in a local garden. The colour behind was a shrub with yellow leaves and I thought they complemented the dragonfly's colour well.

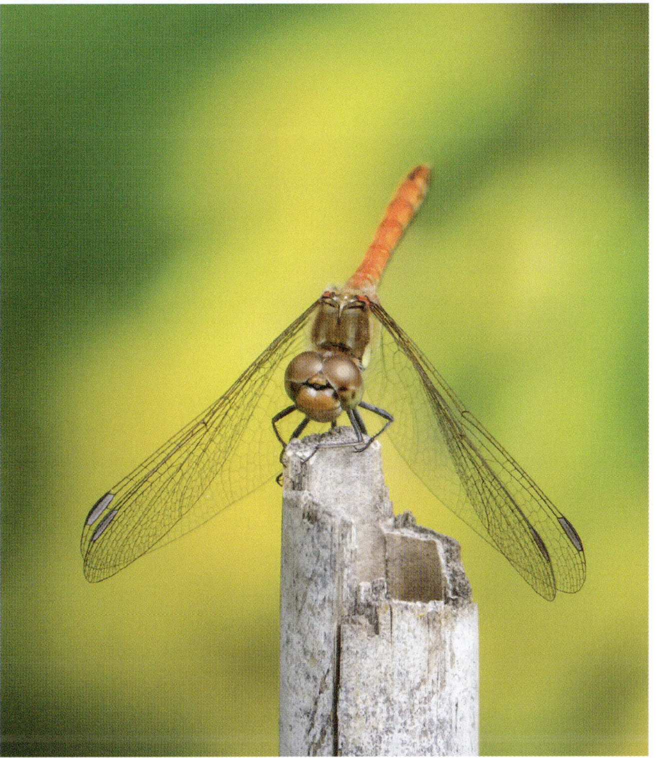

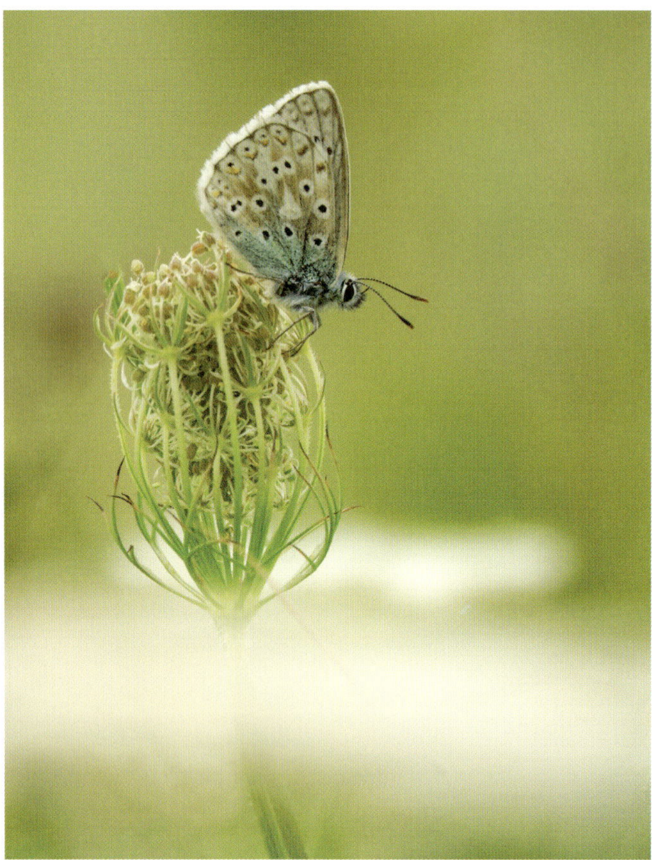

This *Polyommatus coridon* (Chalkhill blue) butterfly was resting on a wild carrot flower when I photographed it. Its wings are a beautiful blue on the inside but I actually liked the composition of it in profile here as the out-of-focus carrot flowers in the foreground make it seem like it's above the clouds.

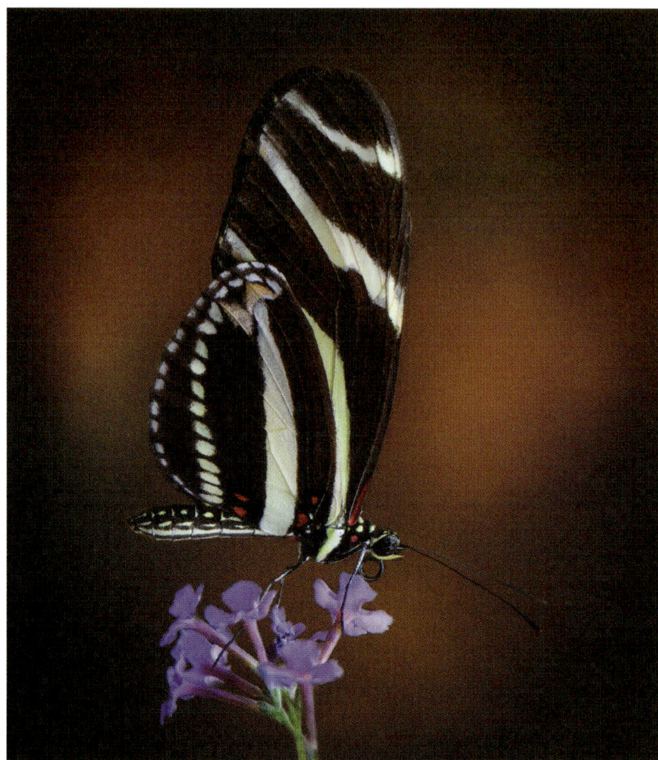

Many larger gardens and zoos have temporary or permanent butterfly houses that will give you the opportunity to see and photograph many species that you would not normally find in your garden at home. This *Heliconius charithonia* (zebra longwing) butterfly was taken in such a glasshouse, resting on the flower so beloved by butterflies; buddleia.

Butterflies and moths

Butterflies and moths are probably the most photographed of all garden insects and are often more decorative than the flowers they are visiting. They are often at their most still and photogenic at dawn or dusk and the low light at these times can be really used to your advantage too. Whilst I mainly discuss butterflies here, moths can be just as beautiful and are often to be found just after sunset, or during the day if the vegetation they are resting in is disturbed; as you walk through long grass for example. If you join Butterfly Conservation (UK) you can take part in organized walks to look for rarer butterfly and moth species and this can also be a great way to find areas local to you where you can photograph them, aside from learning more about them.

If the butterfly or moth is moving quite quickly over flowers, try using the 'continuous focus' setting so that your camera continually resets the focus point as you follow your subject. Whilst they can look beautiful in profile, often their colour is best with their wings open so it might be worth watching and following the butterfly for a while to decide how to capture it. If the butterfly has good colour on the tops of its wings, shooting from slightly above rather than on the butterfly's level can work well.

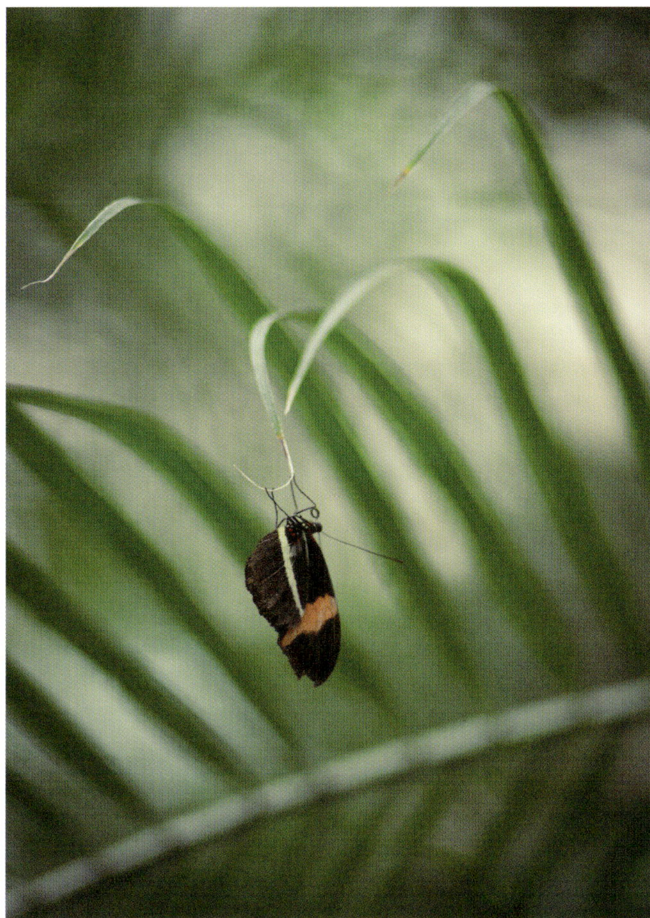

Don't forget that good surroundings will often make a more interesting composition – this is one occasion where stepping back might give you better results.

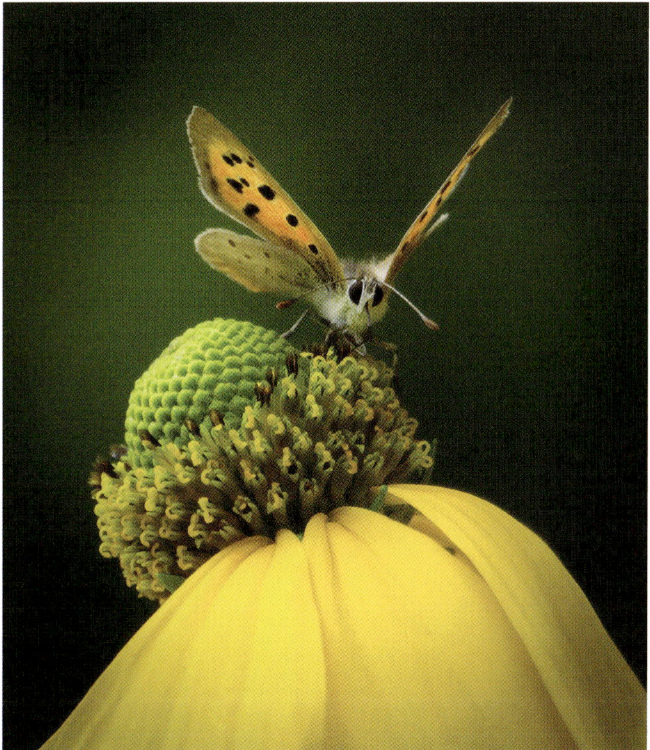

A *Lycaena phlaeas* (small copper) butterfly rests on a rudbeckia flower. This butterfly is about the size of a fingernail and I had to crop in quite heavily when editing it, as I wanted to capture its features.

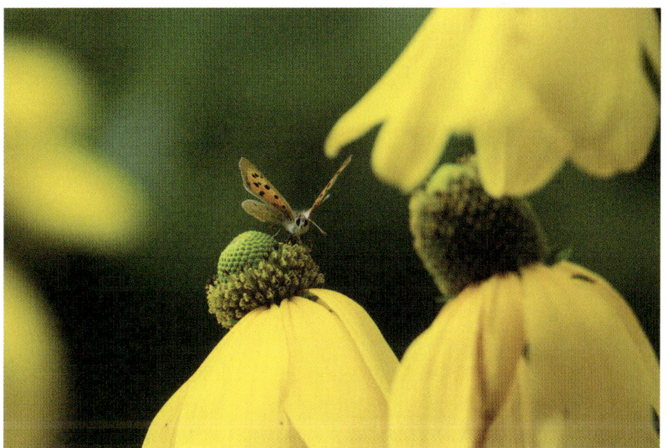

The original photo of the small copper, before cropping. As you can see I also cloned out some of the yellow petals that were near the butterfly. Heavy editing such as this (or adding overlays) is not allowed in some competitions as the insect's environment is no longer as it was in real life, but from a fine art perspective it can be good to try and can often result in a more simple and pleasing composition.

Burst mode

If you have a burst mode or 'continuous shooting' setting on your camera (you'll usually find it next to the timer setting) do try it out with butterflies and bees as they tend to turn and move quickly once on the flower. Both my cameras are also set to have a silent shutter so that the noise doesn't scare what I'm photographing, and this is particularly relevant with burst mode. Mobile phones often have a burst mode feature too. Take a practice shot with the settings as you want them first, so that you know you won't need to adjust much in the edit. Try not to get carried away and shoot hundreds though as you'll need to look through them all afterwards to find the best one. I've made this mistake on several occasions and once ended up with over 400 photos of the same butterfly!

Portrait or square crops often work well with butterflies if their wing shapes are quite elongated when viewed in profile. Look for interesting light (butterflies in silhouette can be very beautiful) and shapes in the background to create good compositions.

To capture a butterfly's features you may need to crop in when you edit the photo; this will also let you find a more successful composition if the surrounding plants or foliage are quite busy.

Bees

Bees make good subjects too and often spend some time on the same flower, giving you a chance to set your tripod and compose your shot. Again, try to have them in profile or facing you – I often wait for them to crawl over the whole flower before I finally get a composition I like. It's always nice to see their eyes: try to make sure that these are sharp.

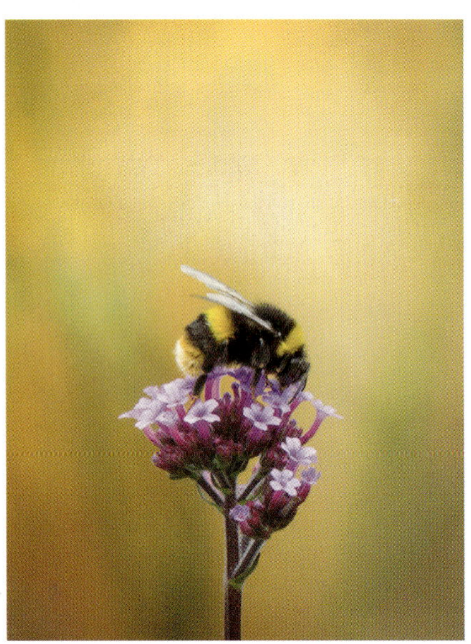

Bumblebee on *Verbena bonariensis* at sunset. A portrait crop echoes the shape of the flower and stalk.

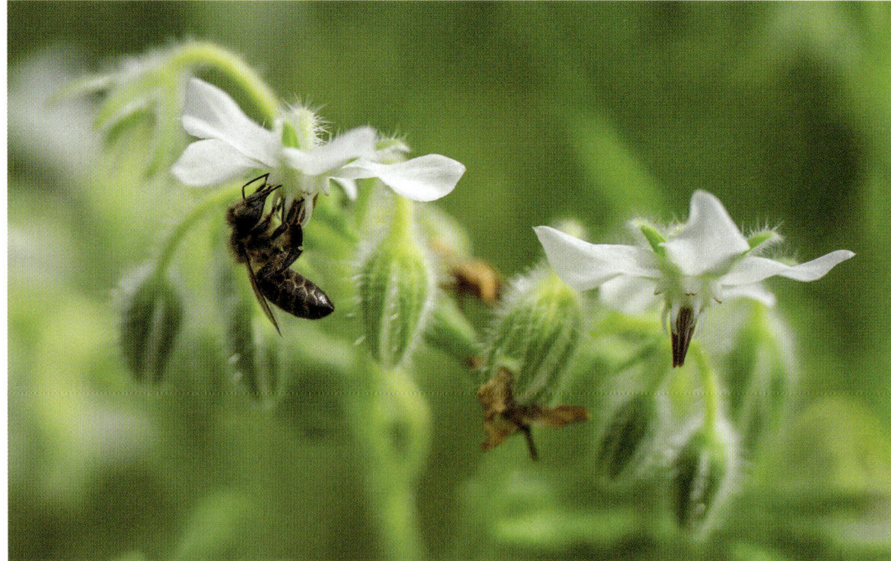

Honey bee on borage – there wasn't much of interest above the flower so I cropped in to allow the viewer to see the bee's eyes. There is an even closer crop of this photo at the start of the book which allows us to see far more of the bee's detail.

'Freezing' bees and other insects in mid-flight

Bees are the best insects to try this method on, as it's a bit easier to predict where they might be going next. You'll need to put your camera on shutter priority (or manual) and set the shutter speed to at least 1/1000th or 1/2000th of a second. The camera should adjust the other settings to make this possible, but you might need to set your ISO to auto, or increase it until the image in the viewer is light enough. To freeze the wings of a bee completely you might need to go further than 1/4000th of a second, but some cameras do not have shutters that operate this fast. However I always think that a bit of blur on bee wings actually looks good, conveying a sense of their movement through the air. Often bees carry pollen sacs that are brightly coloured (depending on the flower they've been visiting), so choose an angle that makes these clearly visible if you can.

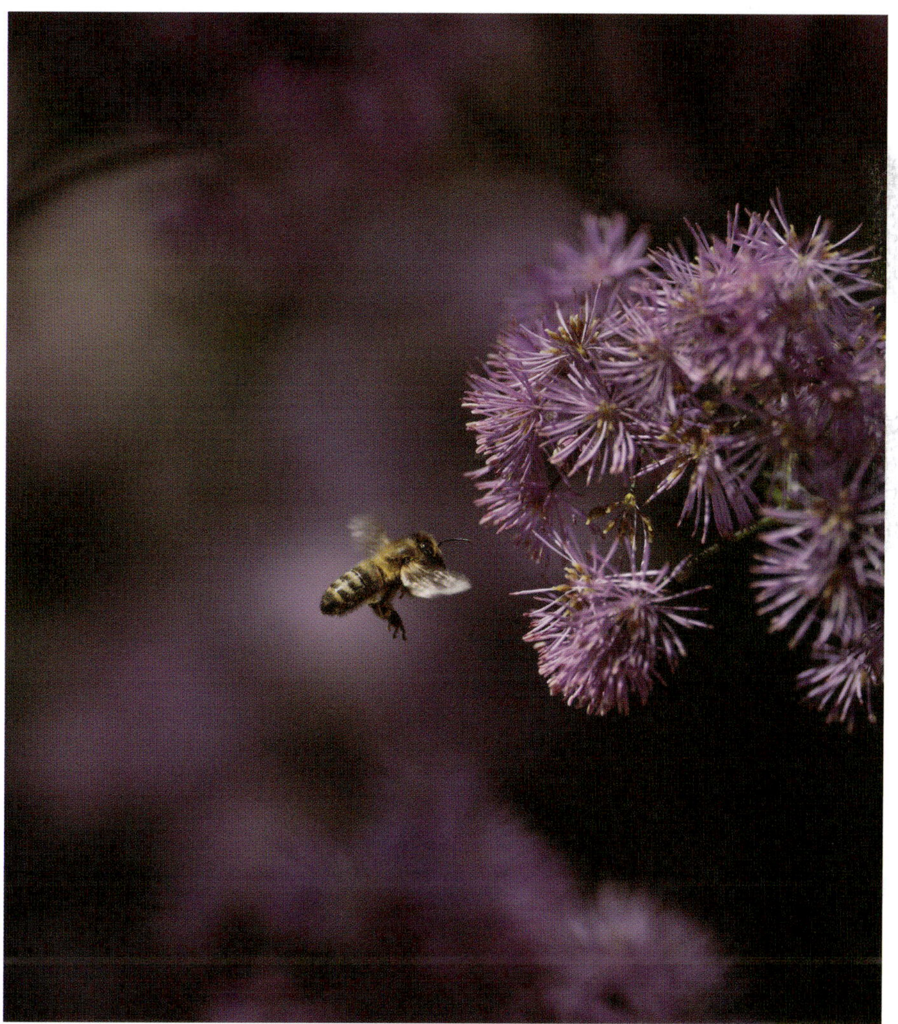

A honey bee hovers in front of the thalictrum flowers he's about to land on. I lined him up with a patch of sunlight in the background.

BIRDS

Birds make ideal garden subjects, especially in the winter when they frequent gardens more often due to the lack of wild food. Long lenses are really required for birds as their 'people-radars' are very sensitive and you can rarely get close (although some birds such as robins are sometimes willing to come closer to take food). If you're planning to photograph your garden birds regularly it might be worth constructing some 'stick' perches near your bird feeder as natural wood always has a more timeless quality to it than a metal bird feeder.

Many bird photographers construct hides in their garden to watch and photograph the visiting birds but I'm happy on a cold day to sit inside the house and look out – if your windows are clean you can often take photos through them as long as you put the lens right up against the glass, which was what I did to photograph this robin. You can also buy anti-glass lens hoods made of silicon if you plan to do this regularly; they prevent reflections appearing in your photographs when shooting through glass.

Bird photographers will often use a lens of 400mm upwards and such lenses can be very expensive (and heavy). You might find just using your longest lens and then cropping in later gives good results. These bird photos were taken with my bridge camera, which has a very long zoom but is not as heavy to carry around.

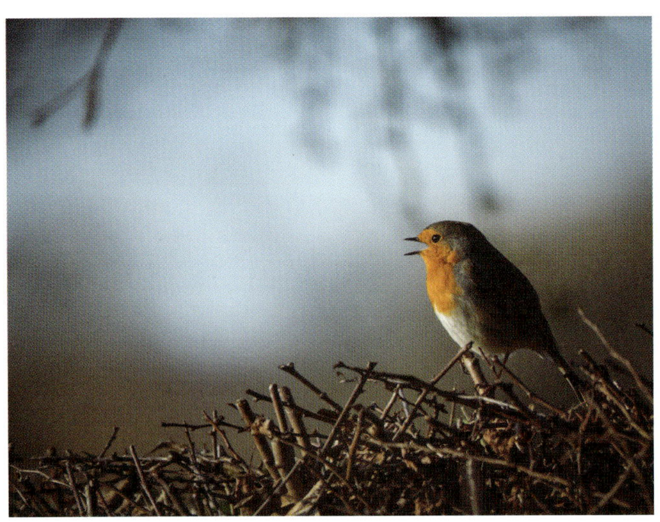

A robin sings in the early morning light. This was taken through a window using a long lens.

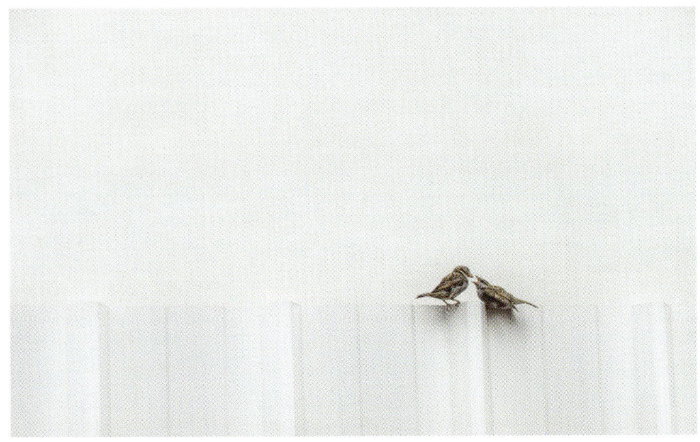

This mother sparrow feeding her baby is more of an urban shot but I was drawn to the simplicity of the composition; I liked the minimalist effect. 1/600 sec at f/5.6, 100mm.

Flowers and plants to photograph in August

August is late summer and brings the arrival of dahlias and rich-hued summer bulbs like agapanthus and canna lilies.

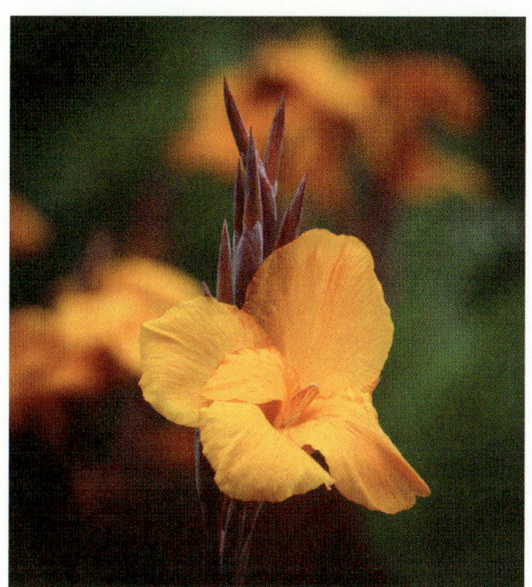

Canna lily – 1/500 sec at f/4, 100mm.

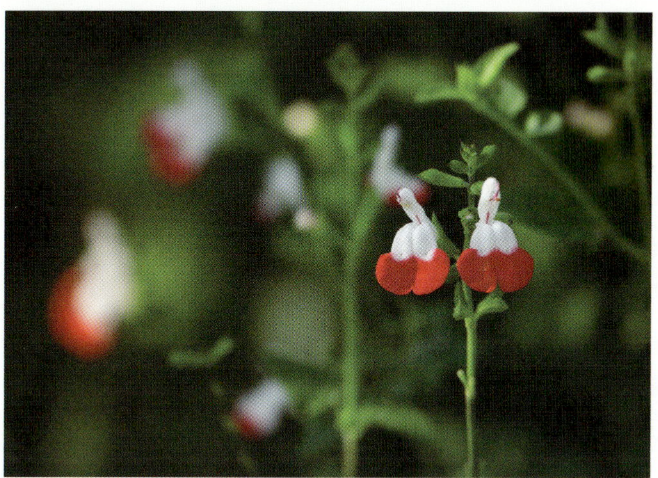

Salvia 'Hot Lips' – 1/320 sec at f/4, 220mm.

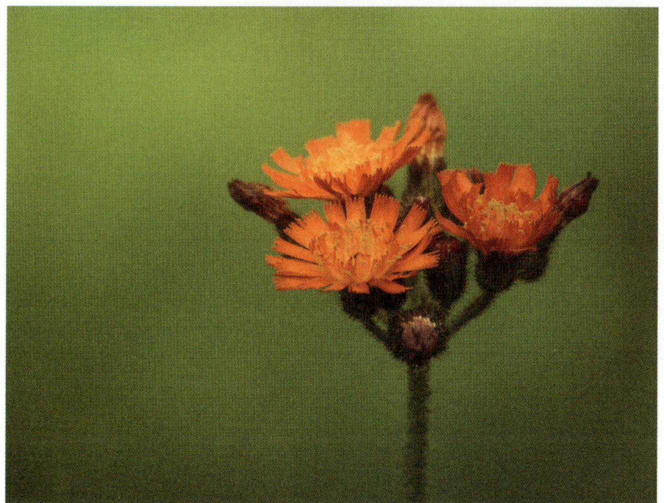

Pilosella aurantiaca (orange hawkweed) – 1/1600 sec at f/4, 200mm.

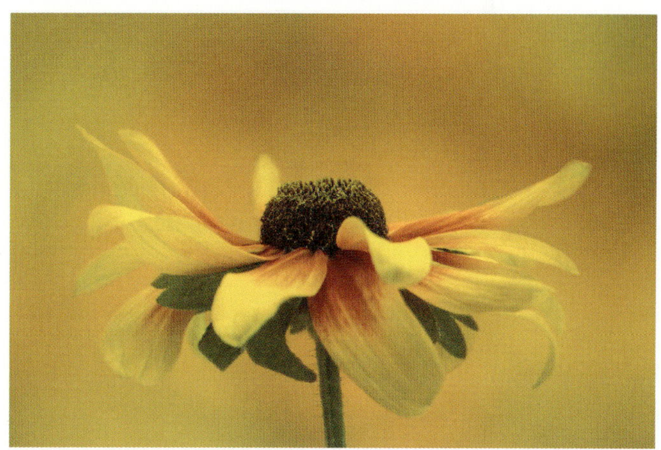

Rudbeckia – 1/640 sec at f/4, 220mm.

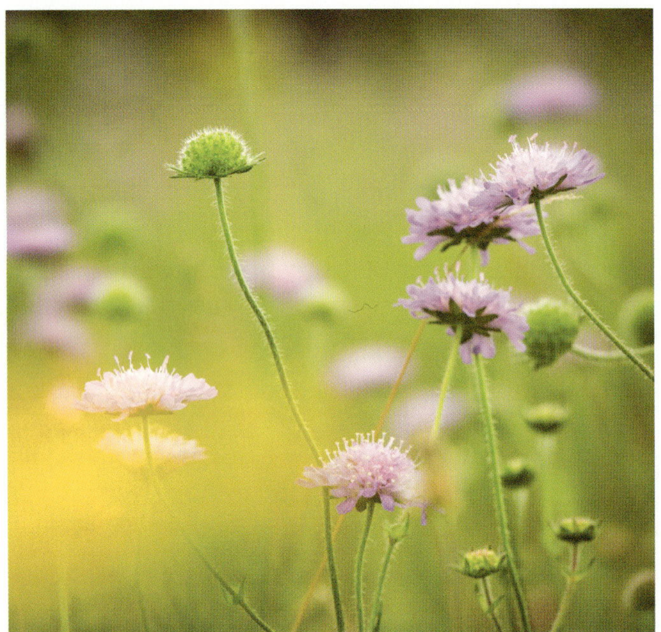

Knautia arvensis (field scabious) – 1/640 sec at f/4, 140mm.

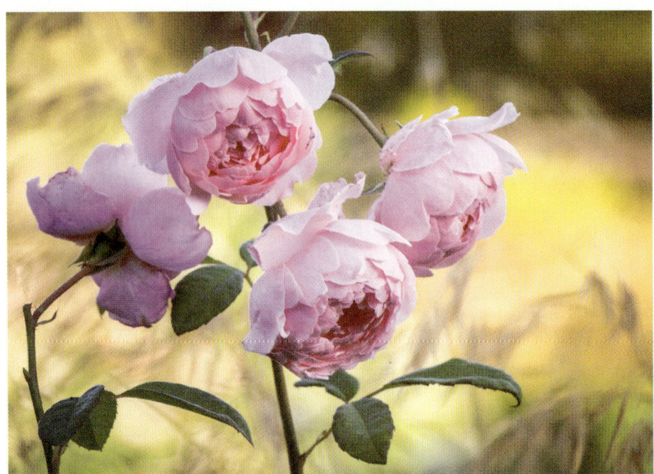

Roses – 1/125 sec at f/6, 150mm.

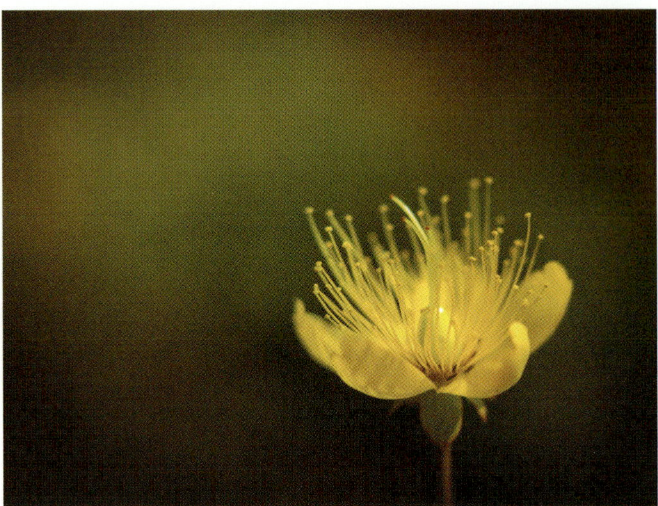

Hypericum – 1/2500 sec at f/2.8, 55mm lens (cropped in the edit).

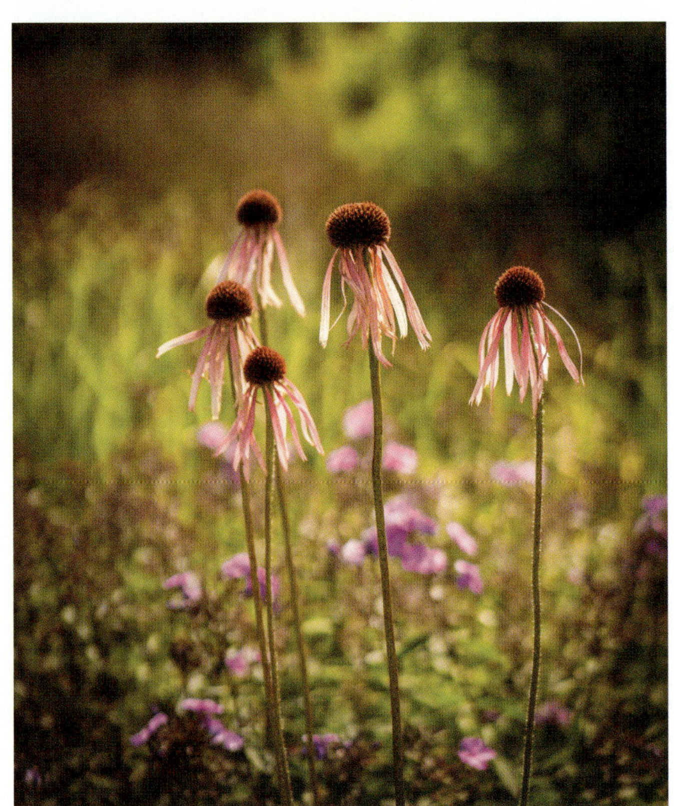

Echinacea pallida – 1/5000 sec at f/2.2, 55mm.

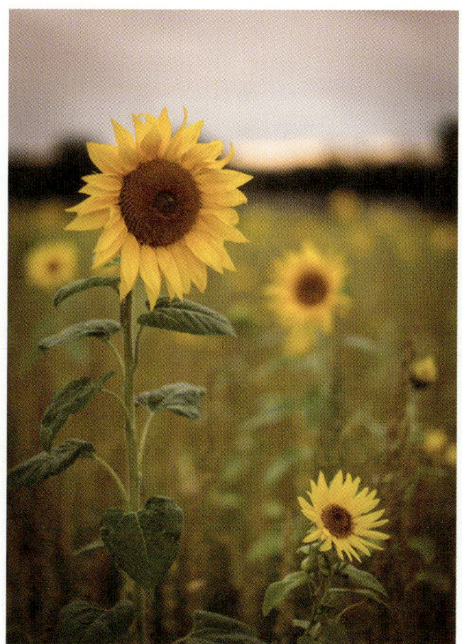

Sunflower field – 1/400 sec at f/1.8, 55mm.

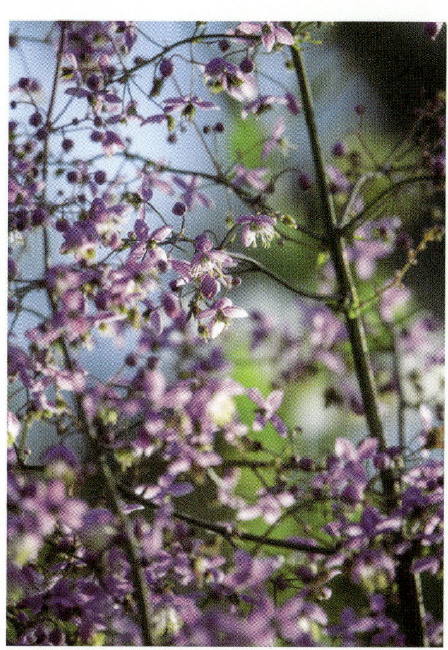

Thalictrum delavayi – 1/640 sec at f/4, 140mm.

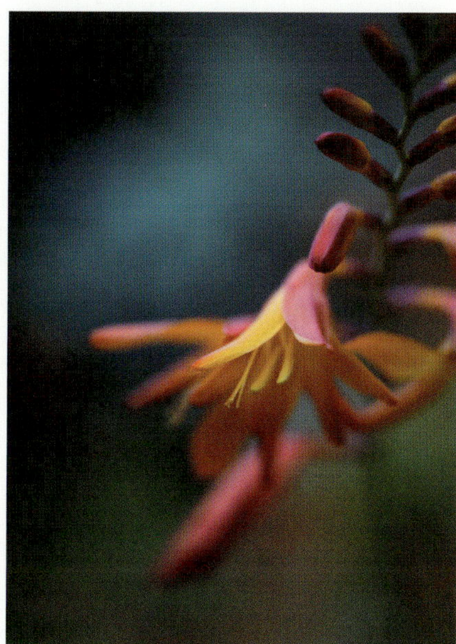

Crocosmia – 1/400 sec at f/1.7, 50mm vintage manual lens.

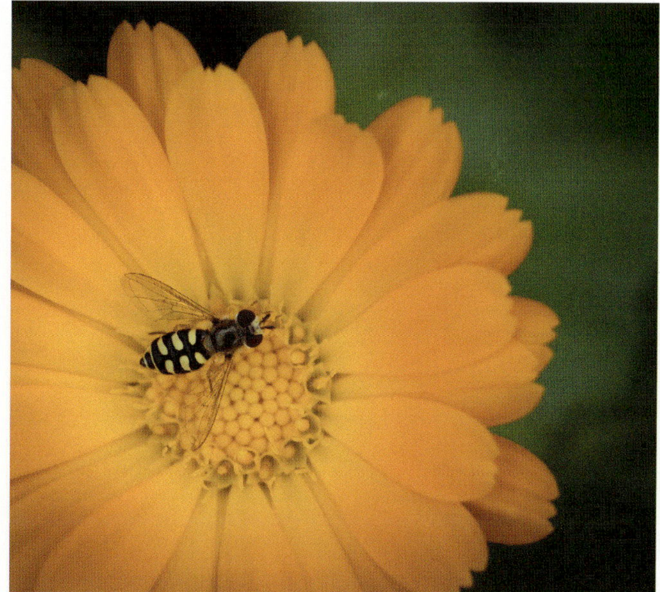

Hoverfly on calendula – 1/160 sec at f/7.1, 105mm.

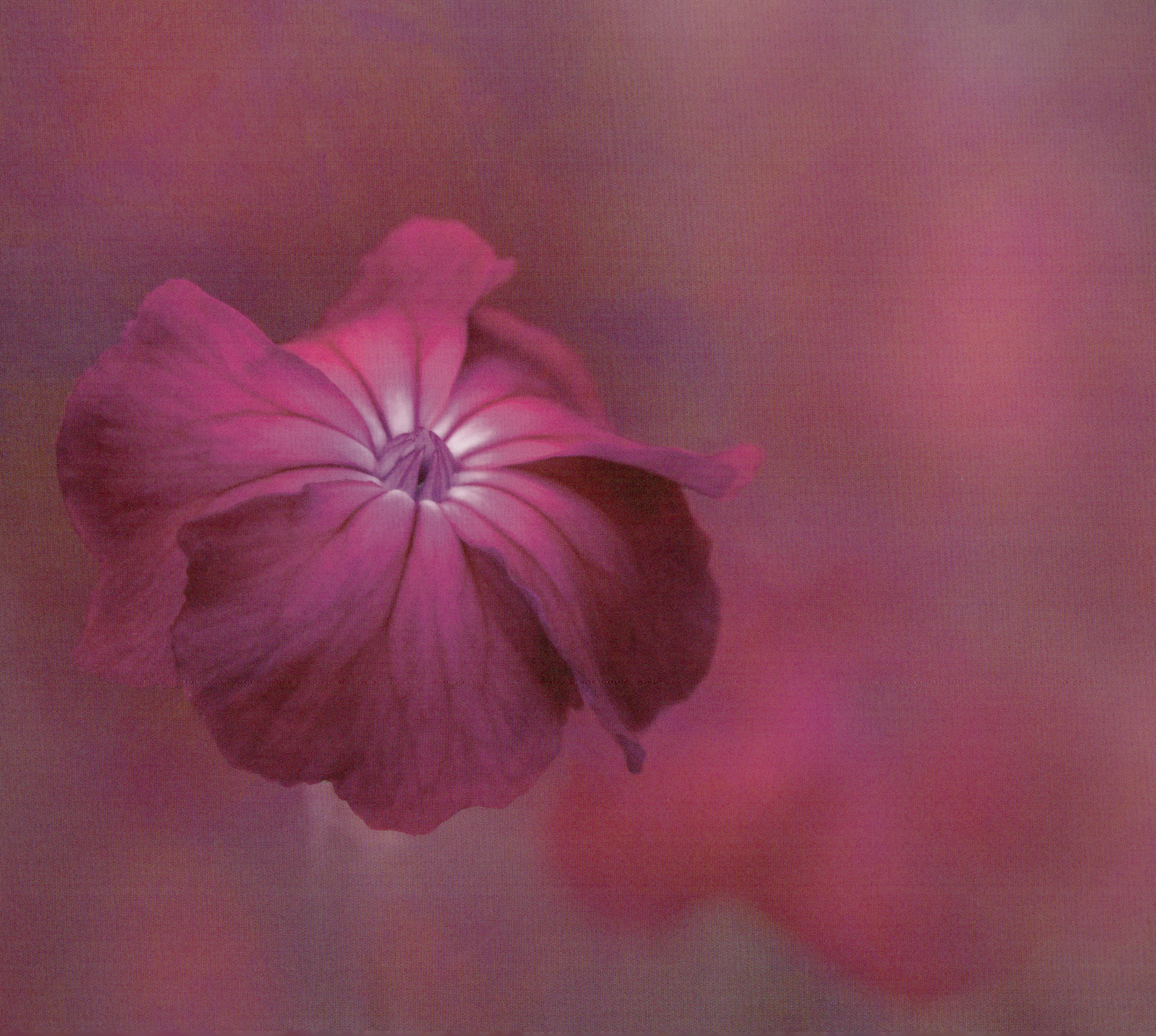

CHAPTER 9

Colour and Pattern

> Colour! What a deep and mysterious language, the language of dreams.
>
> PAUL GAUGUIN

Have you ever tried to decide what your favourite colour is, or what your favourite *flower* colour is? We will always have our preferences and this is often to do with childhood memories or other 'connections' that we may have with nature.

I have always loved the colour green, as it seems to speak most of nature and gardens in general and of spring, which I sometimes feel is my favourite season. So often we feel that our photos should be full of vivid colour to make them striking, but this is not always the case. Many gardeners are now choosing plants whose main interest lies in their structure and sculptural form, where pattern and texture is deliberately emphasized at the expense of colour. This type of garden gives year-round interest with a myriad of greens as well as sculptural form.

It can be fun to challenge yourself to focus in on the textures and shapes of leaves and plants, and try to take an 'all-green' photo with other colours playing just a subsidiary part. This should help you to develop your eye for composition and texture, looking more closely at the non-colour elements in any chosen subject.

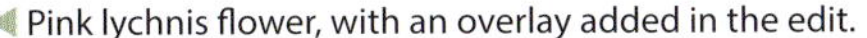
Pink lychnis flower, with an overlay added in the edit.

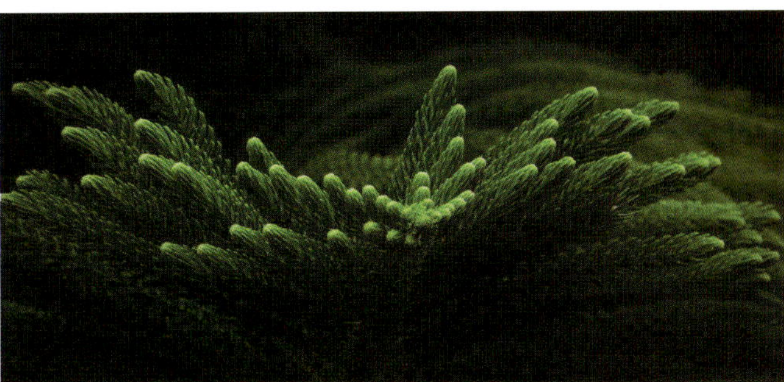
This fir tree was in a large glasshouse; I liked the way that light fell on the tips of its twigs.

I was at a garden a few years ago when it started raining. It was only a shower and I took shelter photographing some ferns in a nearby greenhouse. When I came out the garden was fresh from the rain and I photographed a hosta – I loved its velvety texture and the raindrops like jewels that sat in the indentations in the leaves, like rungs on a ladder. For me, one of the real challenges of photography is to take something usual, like a leaf, and present it in a different way that elevates the subject – it's much harder than photographing a beautiful

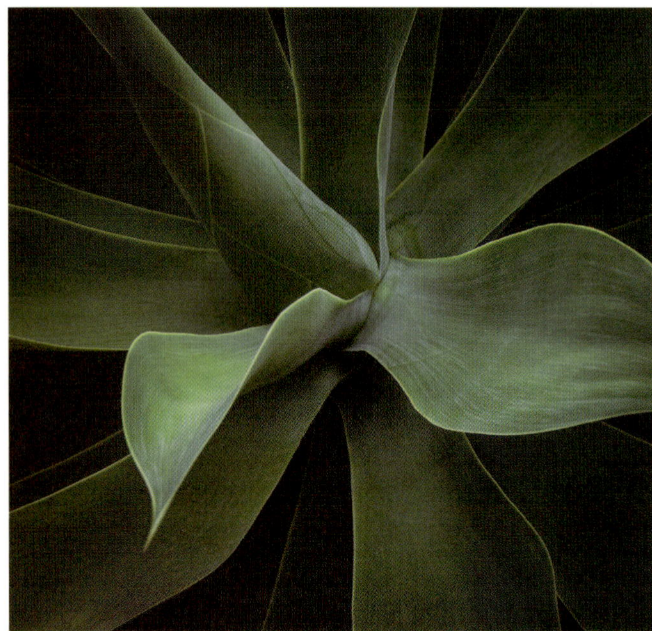

This agave was extremely large and I couldn't get it all in shot, so I cropped in, observing the lines and structure of this sculptural plant.

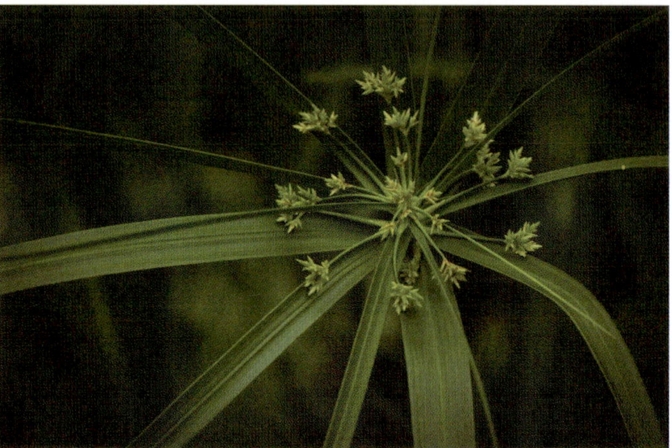

This grass has a 'crown' of central seed heads and the leaves explode outwards from this, giving a firework effect. I kept the background muted to draw attention to the shapes of the grass.

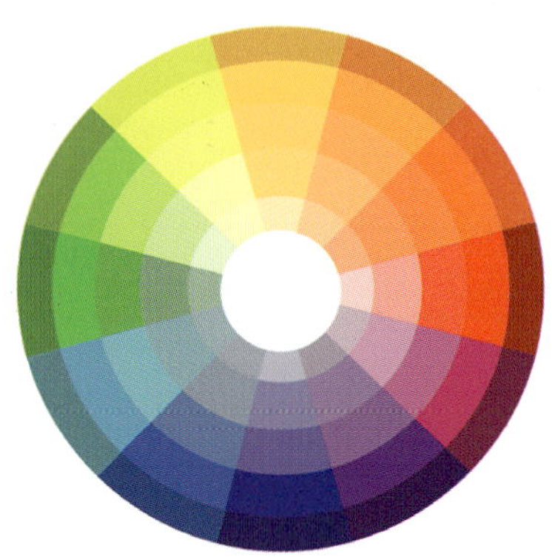

The colour wheel.

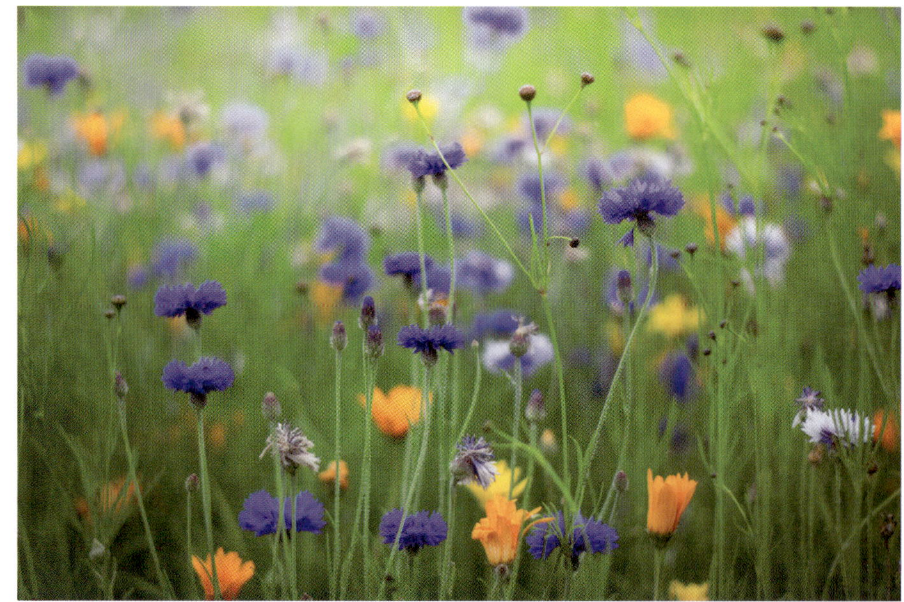

A wildflower meadow featuring the contrasting or 'opposite' colours of orange calendulas and blue cornflowers.

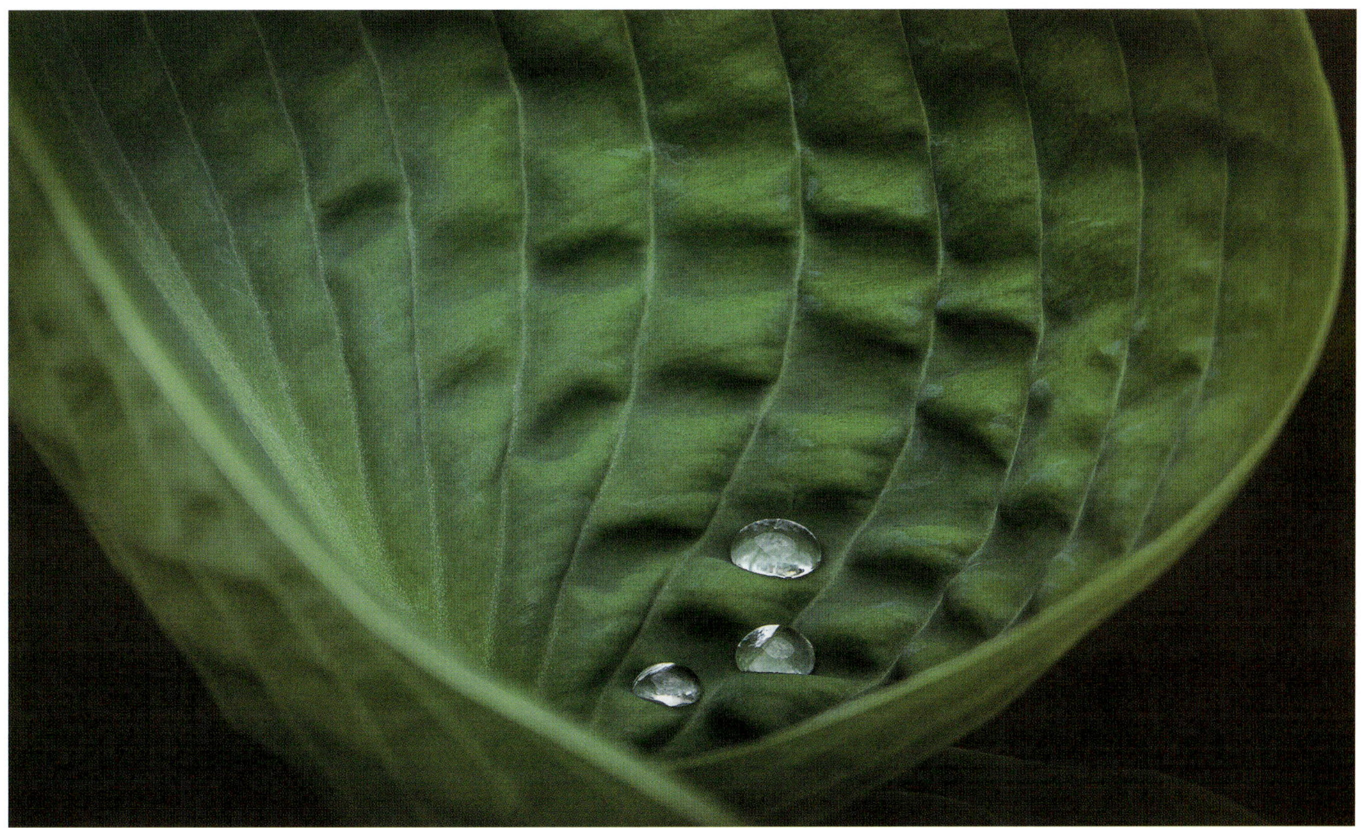

A hosta leaf after rain. I added a dark green overlay behind the leaf in the edit to throw the attention on the leaf even more.

flower and encourages you to look for the unusual in the usual as you look around gardens.

If you study fashion, art, interior design or photography, you may be taught about the 'colour wheel' – a system based on primary, secondary and tertiary colours arranged by their tone.

Put simply, the colours both adjacent to and opposite from each other on the wheel complement each other and it can be fun to play with different colours whilst photographing in gardens.

More often than not, the gardener will have done the work for you, creating extraordinary colour schemes that are either complementary, deliberately clashing or muted single tones, such as the Sissinghurst 'White Garden' in Kent. Having said this, I do feel that nature rarely gives us colours that don't work well together and even colour combinations that historically are considered to *not* work well sometimes do. Even if I think the colours in a photo won't work together, I still take the photo and review it later on the computer just to see.

When you're in the garden look for colour and particularly colours that could work well in the background, behind your main subject. As I mentioned in Chapter 3, 'Light', shooting in the golden hour is particularly good as it makes colours richer.

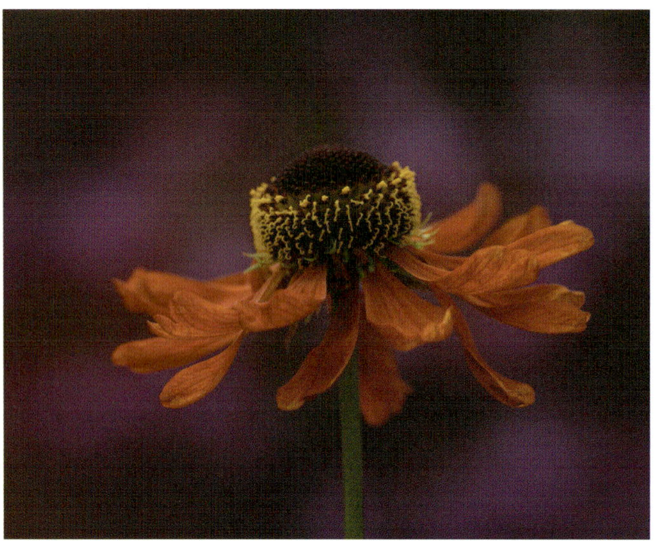

Red helenium with purple flowers behind. I didn't think this colour combination would work when I took the photo but actually I really like it!

TRUE COLOURS

Some photos I come across on the internet and Instagram deliberately alter the main colours of the flower, or overlay a texture or colour, perhaps for a more artistic effect. Sometimes this works very effectively but when the colour of the scene ceases to look real or natural, for me this is a step too far.

OVER-VIVID COLOURS

Many cameras have difficulty rendering bright red and magenta colours, and the image will seem as if it's been over-saturated when viewed afterwards. If you are photographing brightly coloured flowers in bright conditions it might be worth turning the exposure compensation dial on your camera so that it is one or two stops under, which will balance this somewhat, and you

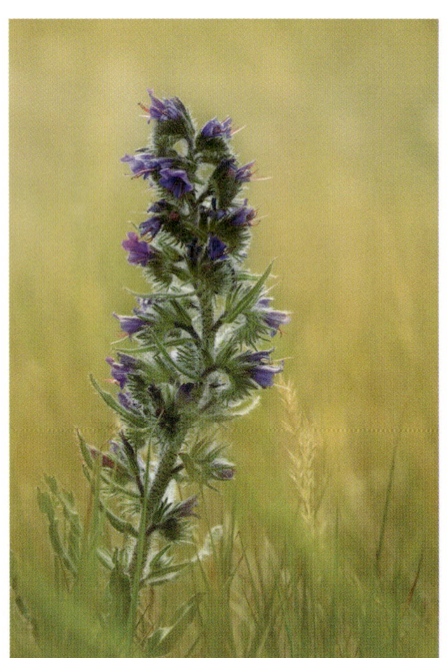

A photo of a wild echium flower in afternoon sunshine. The colours are original and have not been altered.

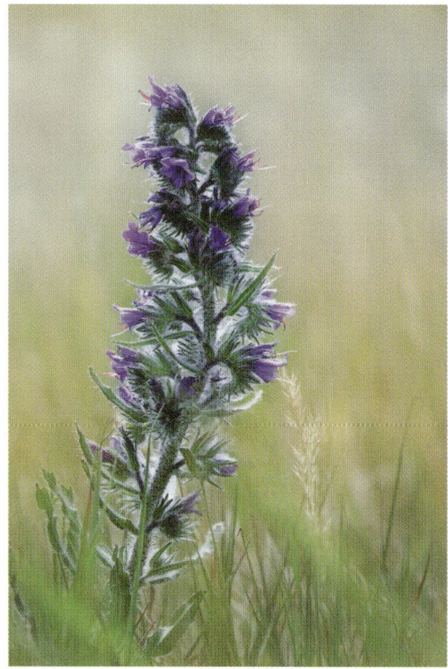

This photo uses a Lightroom colour preset, which I think works because the purple of the flowers and the yellow/green background is preserved.

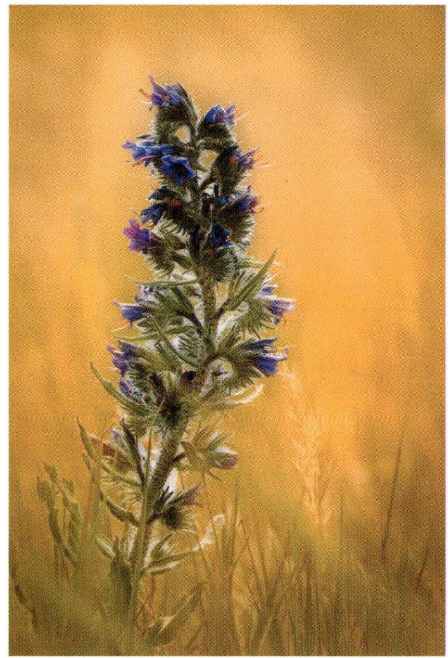

Another preset, chosen deliberately to show colours that are, in my opinion, a step too far. It feels unnatural and 'over-cooked'.

can always then lighten the exposure a little in post-processing if the photo feels too dark. Perhaps also try using a diffuser between the flower and the sun.

Alternatively, when you edit the photo, find the individual colour sliders in the right-hand 'HSL/Color' editing panel in Lightroom and lower the saturation or luminance (try both and see what works best) of the colour that is too powerful.

These sliders are also useful to increase particular colours in your photo, for example in a garden landscape where you want to bring out particular flowers amongst a green scene.

Single-colour frames

Something that can be particularly effective in such a colourful genre as garden photography is a single-colour frame, where the whole image consists of tones or hues of the same colour. It can make for real impact, and particularly strong colours can be very striking.

A poppy flower (unedited) where the red colour feels over-saturated – this is sometimes caused by sunshine on red flowers and is referred to by some as 'red blow-out'. If lowering the exposure (either in-camera or in the edit) doesn't work, I would bring down the saturation of the red channel in either Lightroom or use the 'camera raw filter' and then 'colour mixer' in Photoshop.

Long lenses or wide apertures are best for creating this kind of photo (or a macro lens/regular lens with extension tubes) as you can focus in on one single flower or leaf and position other flowers/leaves of the same hue around the flower. Move around your subject when composing the shot so that you can position as much of the same colour as possible around the flower. If the other flowers are slightly further away the blurred effect should give an even better result. I will often use an overlay of the same flower out of focus to make the colour even richer, something that can work well, but you need to remember to take the out-of-focus photo at the time you photograph the flower.

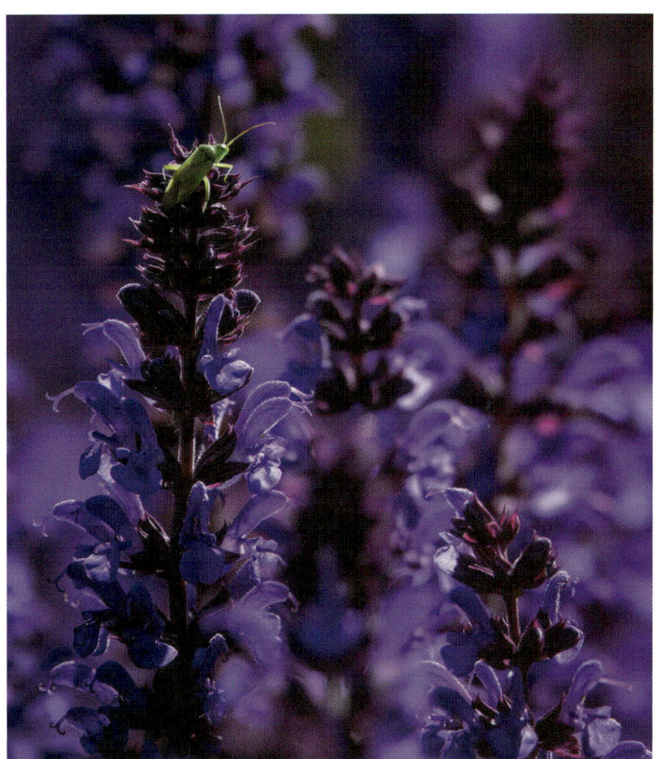

A grasshopper surveys the view from the top of rich-coloured salvia flowers. Late afternoon sun has increased the colour depth and I have not altered it at all in the edit.

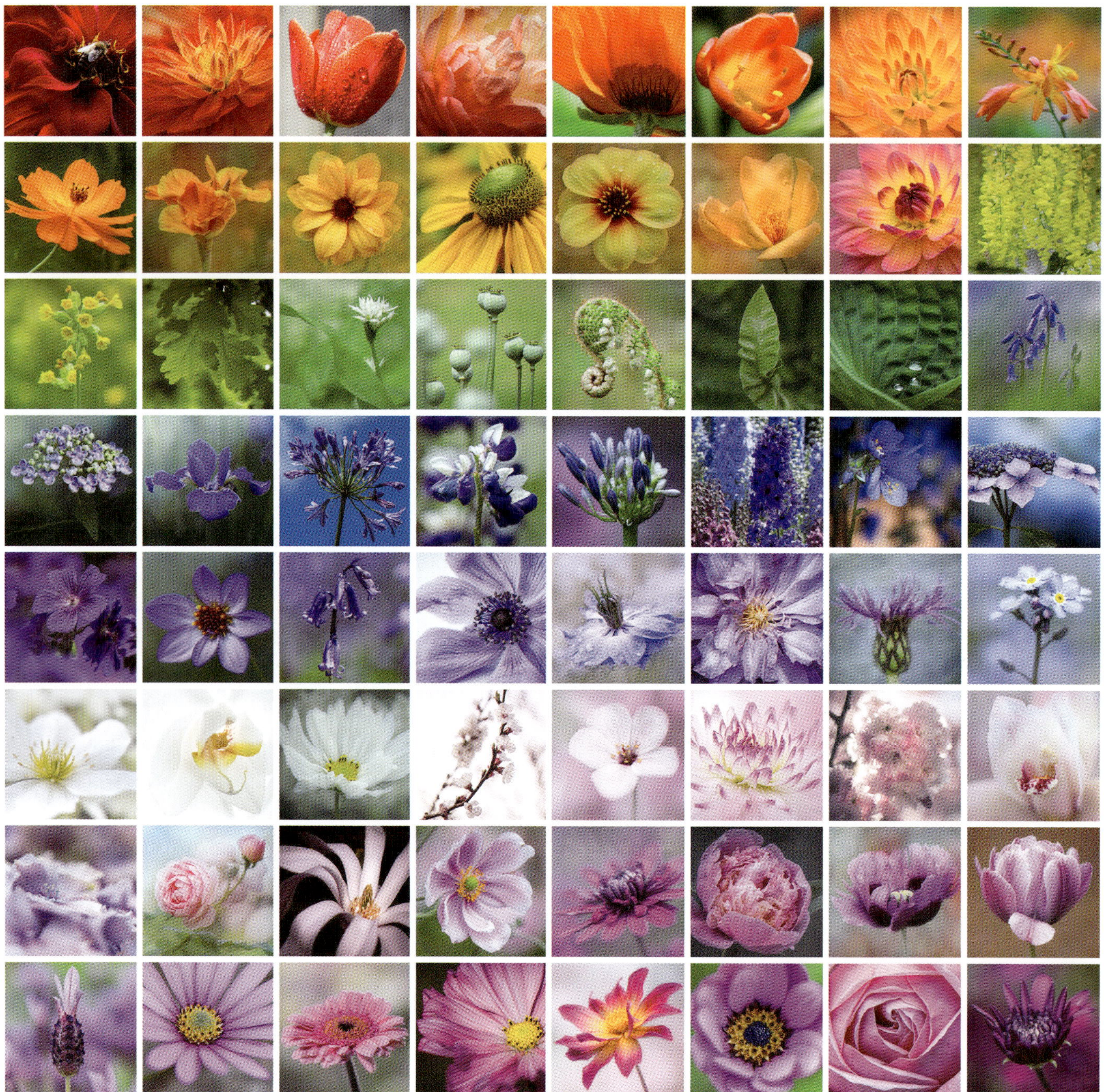

A rainbow collage of flowers.

TRY A SINGLE COLOUR COLLAGE

It can be really satisfying to group flowers of the same colour into a montage or collage – something like this will always have great impact. I use the software called Adobe Spark (free with the Adobe photography cloud package that includes Lightroom and Photoshop). There are many other free collage-producing software programmes to be found on the internet.

I once made a rainbow collage with flowers I had photographed in a single year and it was a really fun project; you could also make collages inspired by a particular season. A collage is also a lovely way of collecting photos together that you're proud of, and if you have it printed it will remind you to keep going if there are ever times when you've lost your mojo (which happens to us all).

BLACK AND WHITE PHOTOGRAPHY

Black and white photography works brilliantly for some subject areas (landscapes with clouds, winter scenes and documentary-style street photography for example). It focuses the attention on tone, form and texture without the 'distraction' of colour. However, given that flowers and gardens are usually so colourful it might seem rather perverse to convert them into black and white!

For me, black and white can work well in a flower photo when there is lots of tonal contrast in the picture, rather than lots of medium tones, which when converted to black and white often give dull, muddy-looking effects. So don't just convert to black and white for the sake of it; actively seek out flowers and plants which have a clear structure and make interesting abstract patterns. To demonstrate this point, here's a regular flower photo converted to black and white. It demonstrates that if the range of contrast isn't there it won't make a strong image.

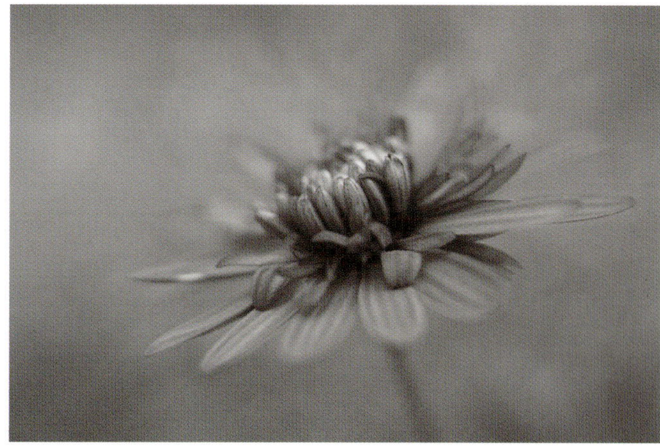

A photo converted to black and white in Lightroom (by clicking on 'black and white' at the top of the 'Basic' editing panel) – for me this doesn't work as there is little contrast in the image and as a result we see lots of greys, rather than literally black and white.

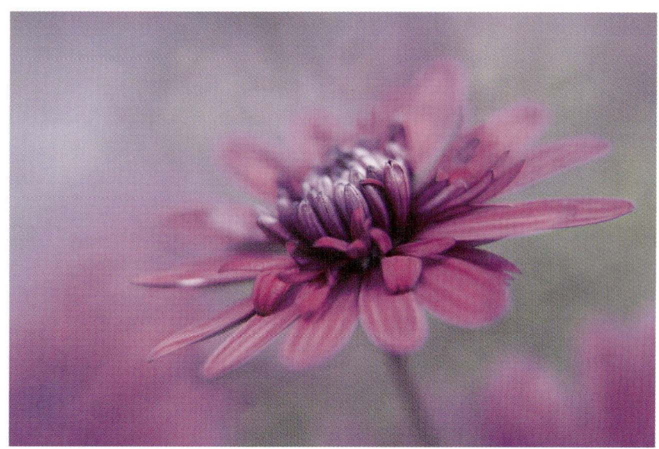

The original works far better, and the colour is so glorious that it seems crazy to get rid of it.

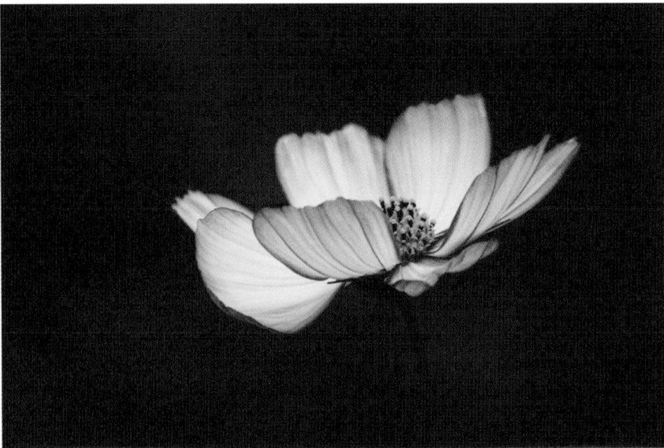

A brightly lit white cosmos flower with a dark background. This was taken in a garden in a shady corner and the obvious contrast of light and dark in the scene makes it a good choice for a conversion to black and white.

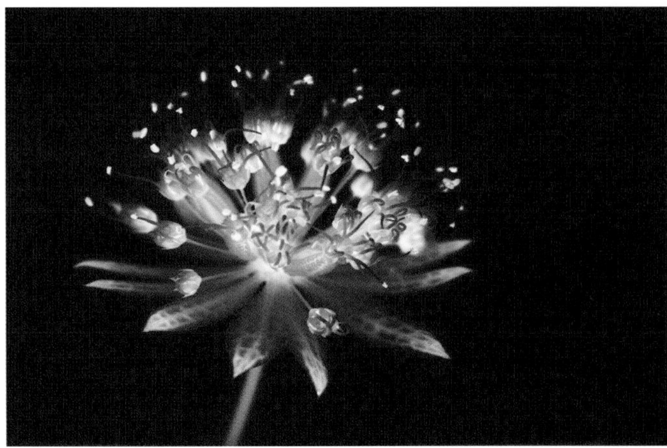

An Astrantia flower that I photographed in my lightbox in front of a white background, before converting it to black and white. I then turned it into a 'negative' image which of course switches black to white and white to black. To do this, lift the bottom left point of the 'Tone Curve' line in Lightroom to the top, and then move the top right point to the bottom.

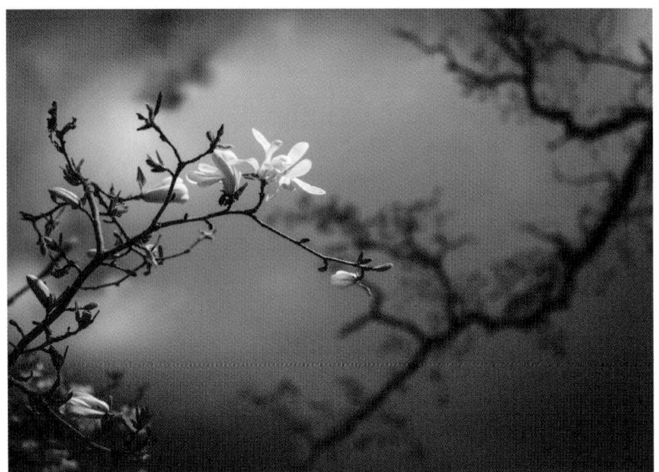

Don't forget to look out for vistas in gardens with high-contrast elements. I was definitely in the right place at the right time when visiting a local garden where a storm blew up in the distance as I was looking at magnolia trees. The white petals contrast with the stormy sky and the distant tree on the right reaches into the frame to meet the one on the left. I'd like to say that I was inspired by Michaelangelo's *Creation of Adam* when I photographed this scene, but like many things it was a happy accident that I didn't notice at the time!

For a good place to start, white flowers with a dark background can work well, as the colour contrast is strong; this will be preserved in black and white.

If you're really brave, have a go when you're 'in the field' as it were, by switching your camera to its black and white or monochrome setting. You'll soon get a feel for what works after a little experimentation.

You can also convert black and white images to achieve a 'negative' effect in Lightroom; this can sometimes give interesting results, especially if good contrast and structure is there to start with.

FLOWERS AND PATTERN

Single flowers will almost always have some kind of natural symmetry in their structure but unless you look closely it can be easy to miss. Being aware of these underlying patterns can be helpful when you are trying to arrive at a composition or crop that most reflects the character and shape of the flower.

Numbers are often odd in nature and flowers will regularly (but not always) have odd numbers of petals. If you put flowers in a vase, three or five petals will always give a better arrangement than two or four, as the shapes they make are more interesting. The Pythagorean mathematicians were fascinated by the presence of numbers in the natural world and this is definitely a topic worth reading more about. I find it fascinating to explore numbers in everything I photograph – a row of five birch trees seems to make more compositional sense than four for example, possibly because the eye is led into the photo to a central tree, in the same way that it would with three.

Circles

As you can imagine, it's really very rare for flowers to have only one 'petal', and far more often it will be a group of petals masquerading as one. Some flowers have so many petals that they take on an almost perfect circular shape, like daisies and sunflowers, and it can be easy to see how these are 'targets' for bees and other flying insects.

Of course, most berries (and many fruits) are spherical, many of them advertising their presence to birds and mammals by way of their shape and colour. When photographing a 'one' flower, make sure it has plenty of space around it, particularly at the side towards which it is facing. If the flower has a circular shape it should work well if photographed directly from above, and you could also try cropping right in so that the frame is filled with the flower and there is no background at all.

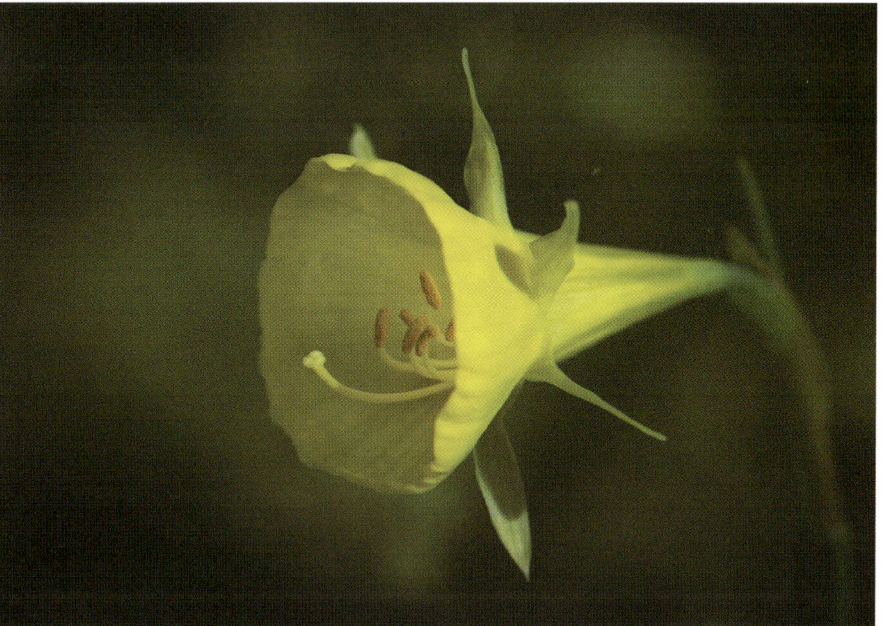

This *Narcissus bulbocodium* has an elongated corona or 'trumpet' and seemingly no petals. However if you look closely you can see that they are very small and further back in the manner of sepals.

Patterns of three

'Threes' are more common in flowers, with irises and snowdrops being perhaps the most well known, and also trilliums and tiger flowers (*Tigridia*). Flowers that have three petals form a very pleasing symmetry.

Throughout history the number three has always been regarded as especially significant. The ancient Greek philosophers considered three to be the most perfect number, the number of harmony, wisdom and understanding. In Christianity it was the divine number as it signified the Holy Trinity.

Triangles have been used throughout the history of art to give the subjects of paintings a solid foundation that then tapers to a point at the top, which in religious art can suggest that the subject is ascending to the heavens. The triangle is also used in art to give a strong compositional structure; I have used a design based on a triangle in this sunflower still life.

The base of the triangle, even if we are only vaguely aware of the stalk on the right, gives stability to the composition. There are also other triangles that are probably just as obvious in the composition.

If I were to use this set-up again I would try a larger vase or smaller flowers, as the composition seems a bit top-heavy.

When you're photographing plants and flowers, see if you can find triangles within the frame to give structure to your image.

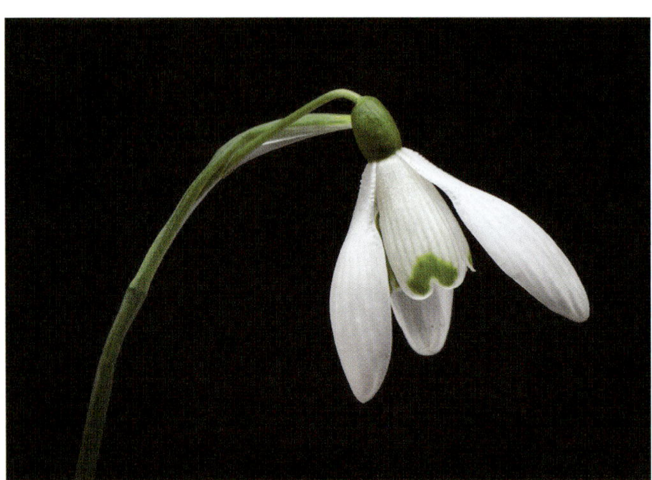

A snowdrop, photographed in my lightbox against a black background for contrast. I usually try to make sure that all three petals can be seen when I photograph snowdrops.

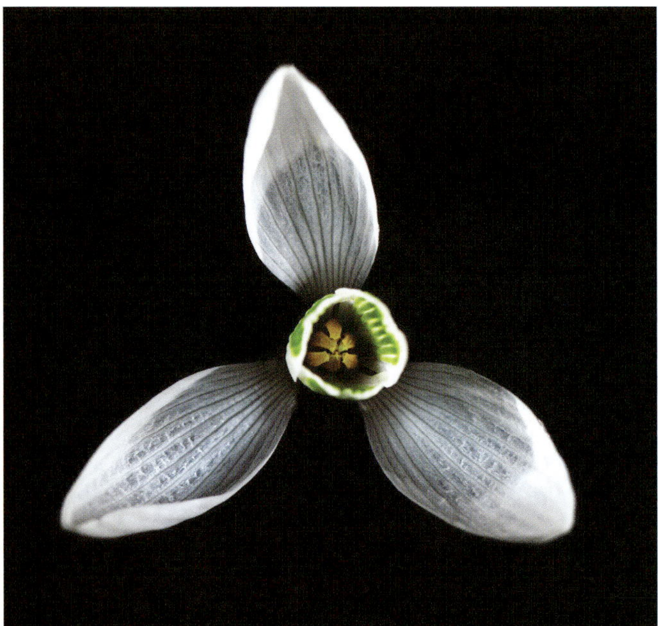

To get this underside view of a snowdrop I floated it upside down in a black saucepan, and then cloned out the reflections from the LED light I lit it with.

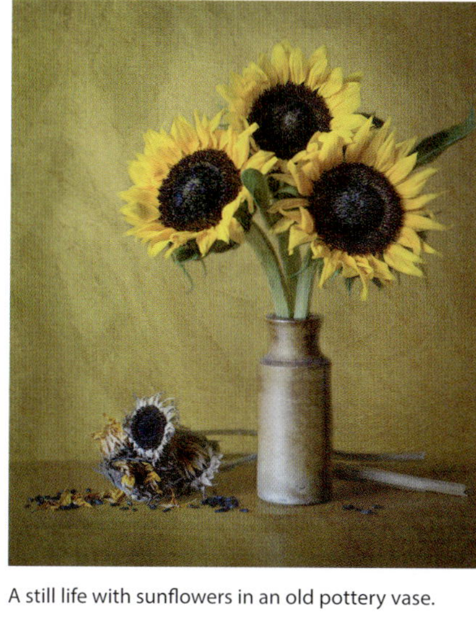

A still life with sunflowers in an old pottery vase.

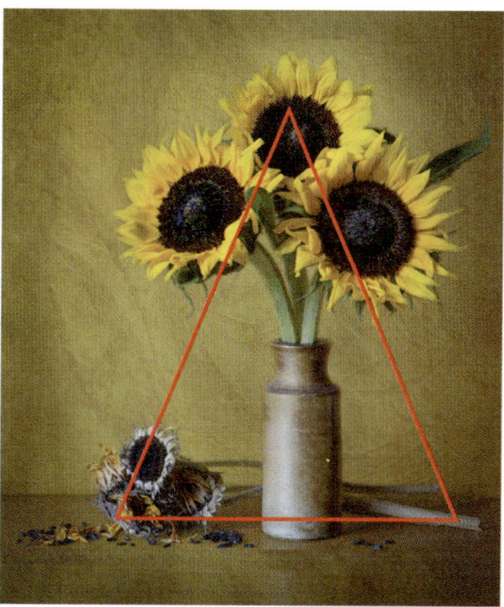

A triangle in the composition made by the outer elements of the subjects.

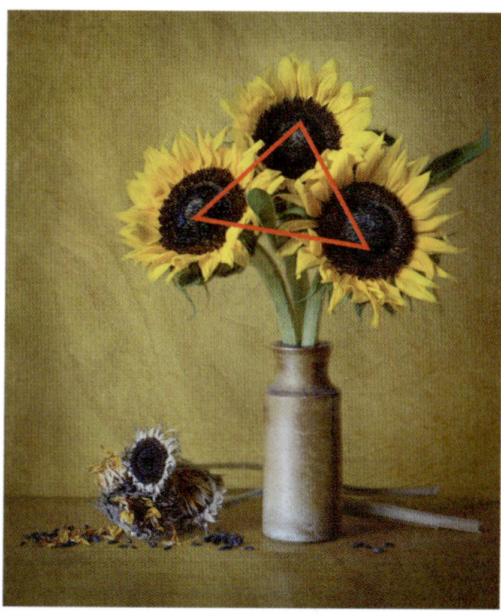

A triangle formed by the position of the three sunflower heads.

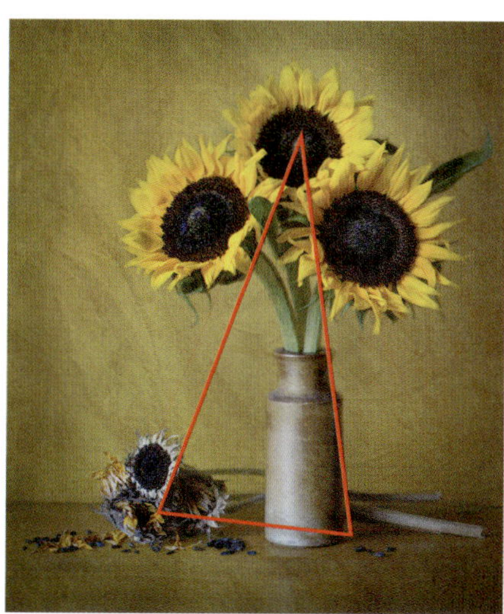

A triangle formed by the three largest structural elements.

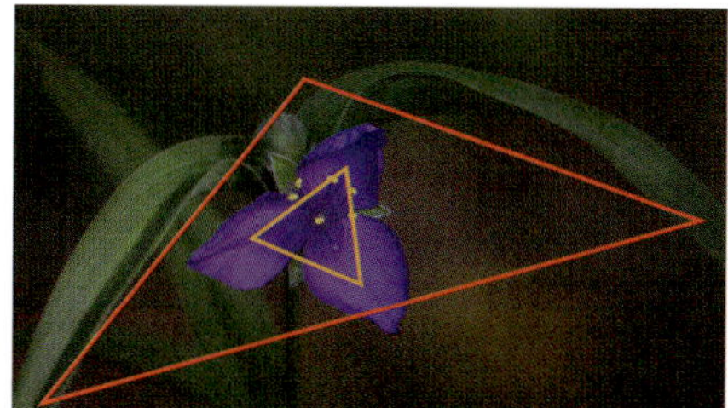

This photo of a *Tradescantia Virginiana* has two observable triangles. I have cropped the image to reflect the scalene triangle shape of the larger one.

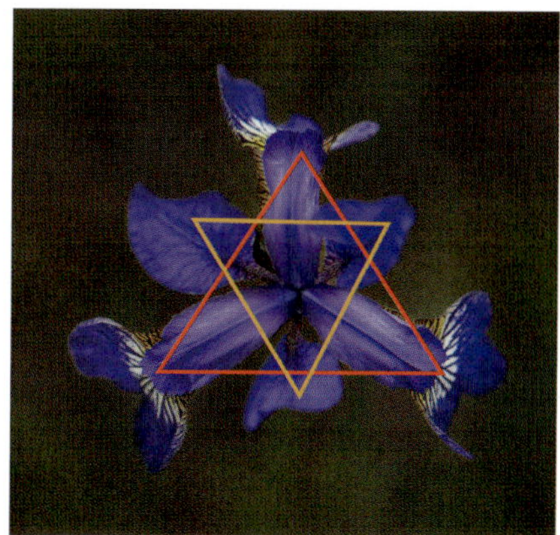

This iris has two interlocking triangles when viewed from above. A square crop works well as the triangles are equilateral ones.

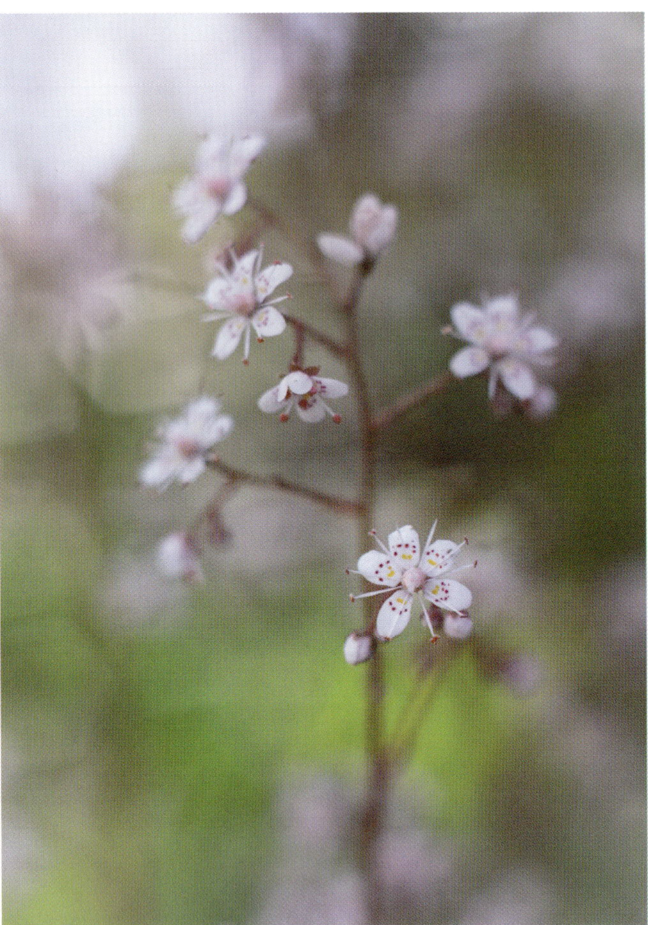

Heucheras are normally sought after for their foliage, but their tiny flowers are like stars.

Other petal numbers

Five-petal flowers are quite common, especially in spring, interestingly. Almond and cherry blossom trees often have five-petalled flowers, as do *Helianthemum* shrubs. Experiment with different angles and see what gives the most pleasing results; they often feel quite 'star-like' to me and I like to try to have all five petals clearly visible.

Narcissi (daffodils) commonly have six petals and can be very hard to photograph close up if the centre protrudes out a long way. Use a narrow aperture such as f/11 to make sure the whole flower is in focus if you want to capture both the corolla (trumpet) and the petals.

Other spring flowers such as crocuses also have six petals, and when brought inside into the warm, the latter will often open right up displaying their stamens, which can make for a more unusual photograph. Tulips (the standard varieties) appear to have six petals but actually have three petals and three sepals, the sepals being the same colour as the petals.

There are many, many flowers with seven petals and more. As the number of petals begins to increase the petals often fan out in a circular shape, meaning that you can photograph them nicely from most angles, including from directly above (*see* Chapter 2, 'Composition').

Of course, there are no rules regarding photographing flower patterns but pausing for a moment's thought before you press the shutter could pay off in terms of a good finished result. Look for symmetry and see if you can exploit it to make a more balanced composition. My general rule of photography is to try everything and over time you'll develop a sense of what works compositionally and what doesn't.

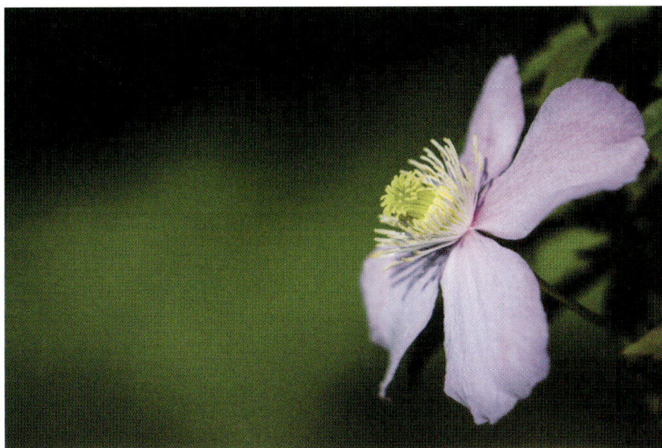

A Clematis flower photographed in a shady corner with plenty of negative space for it to look into. I tried to angle my shot so that all four petals are visible.

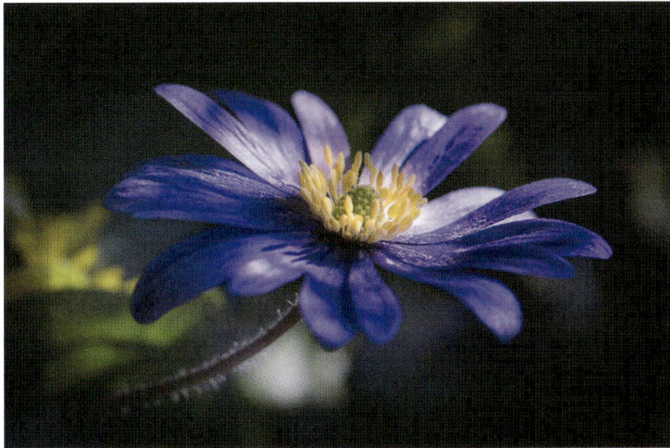

The springtime *Anemone blanda* has many more petals than its late summer cousin (the *japonica*) and a profile shot such as this at the same level as the flower will capture their graceful and delicate shapes.

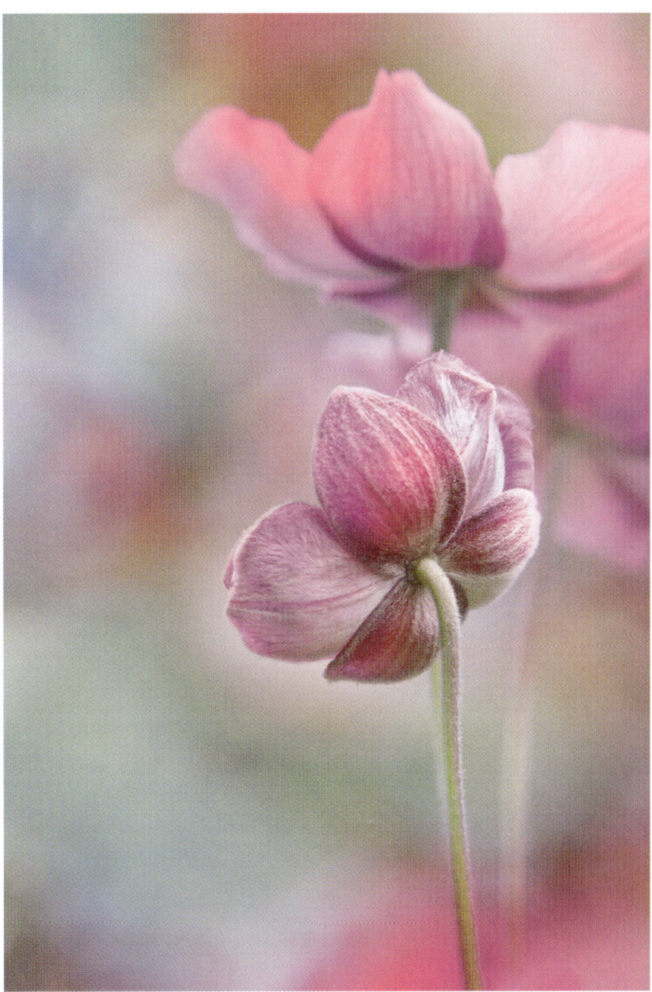

The six interlocking petals of the *Anemone japonica* can be seen clearly from behind, and whilst I wouldn't normally photograph flowers in this manner I loved the curve of their petals and pattern seen from this angle.

Flowers and plants to photograph in September

Dahlias are now everywhere and the salvias, sedums and nerines also come into their own. We feel the first chill of autumn.

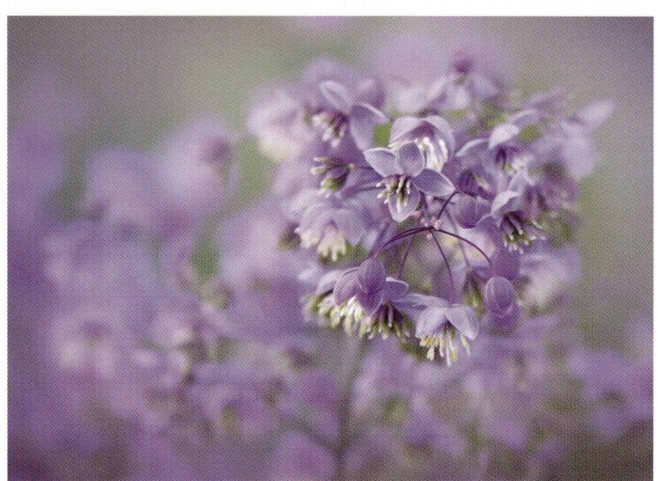

Thalictrum delavayi – 1/500 sec at f/4, 220mm. Overlay added in the edit.

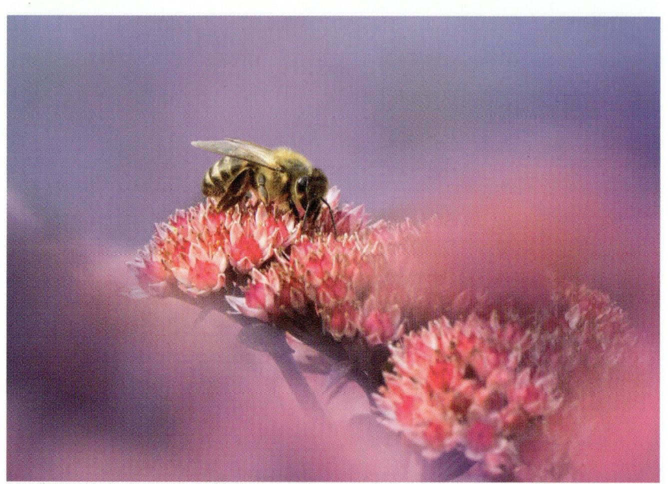

Honey bee on sedum – 1/1000 sec at f/4, 200mm. Overlay added in the edit.

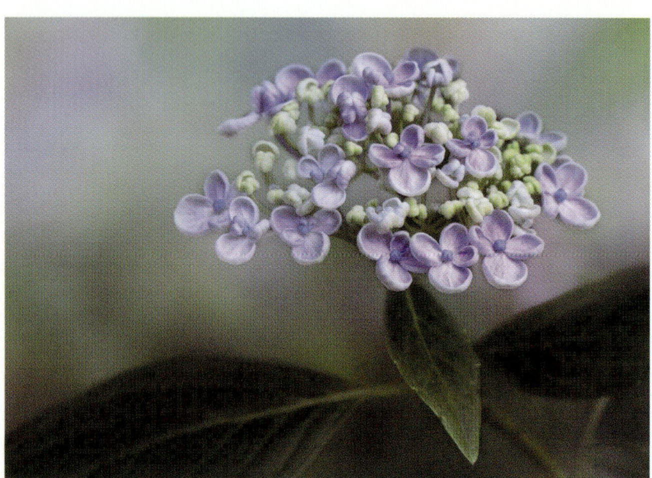

Hydrangea macrophylla 'Ayesha' – 1/100 sec at f/4, 130mm.

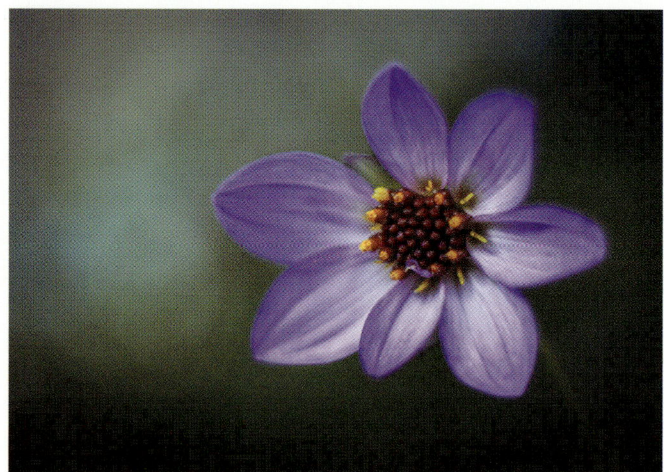

Single dahlia – 1/200 sec at f/1.7, 50mm vintage lens. Overlay added in the edit.

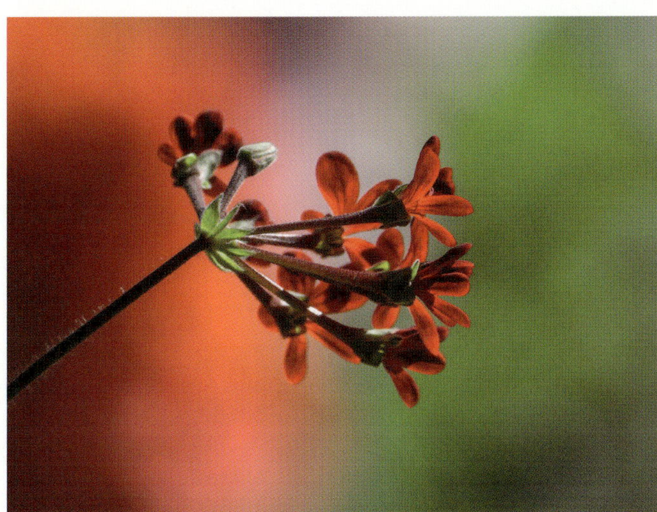

Pelargonium x ardens – 1/640 sec at f/4, 220mm.

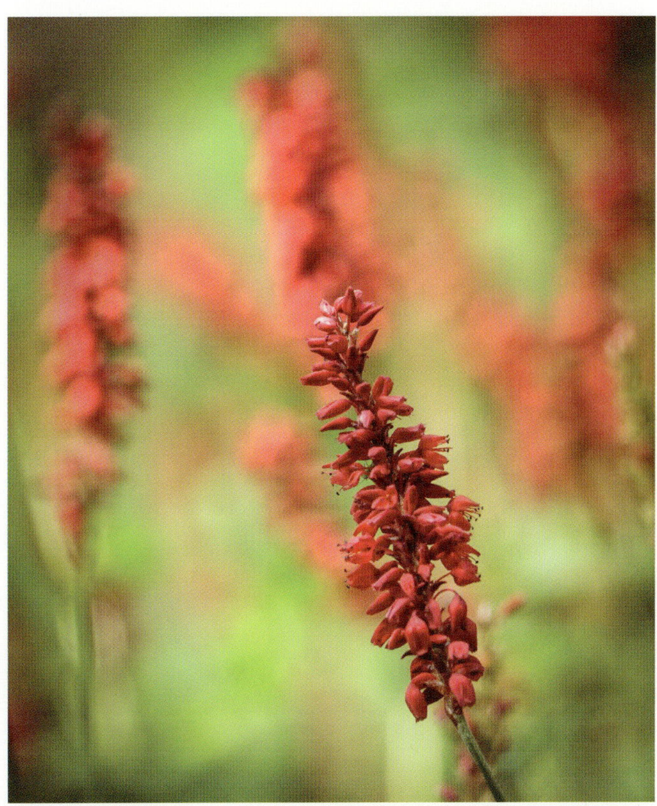

Persicaria amplexicaulis – 1/200 sec at f/4, 150mm.

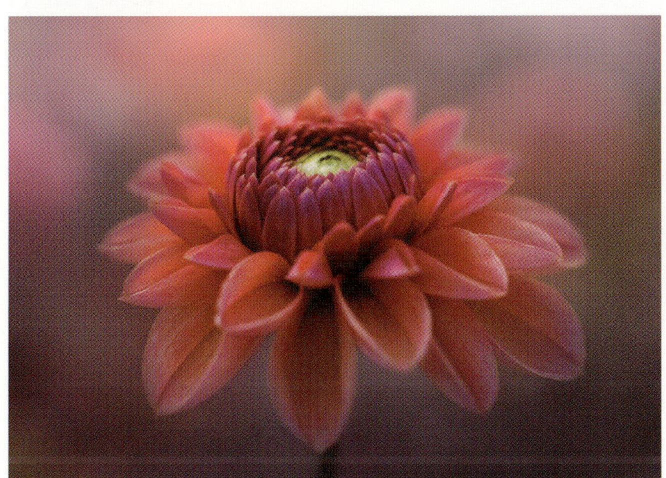

Dahlia – 1/250 sec at f/1.7, 50mm vintage lens. Overlay added in the edit.

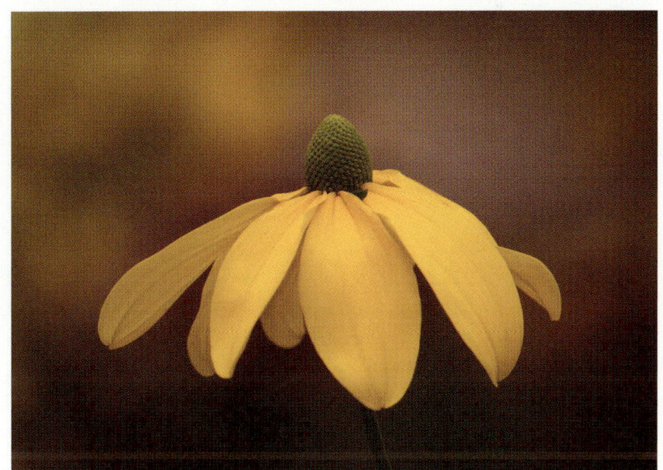

Rudbeckia laciniata – 1/2000 sec at f/4, 180mm.

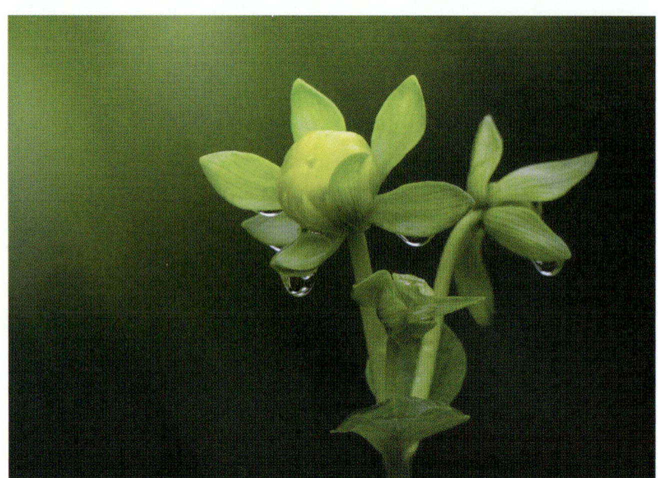

Dahlia bud after rain – 1/500 sec at f/5, 220mm.

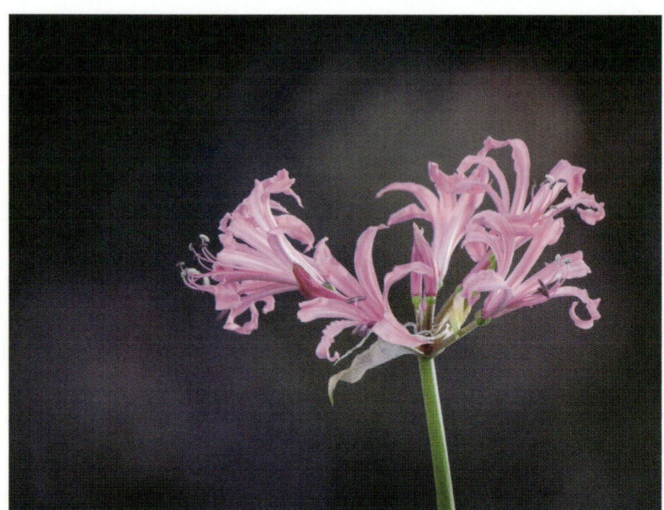

Nerines – 1/100 sec at f/4, 140mm.

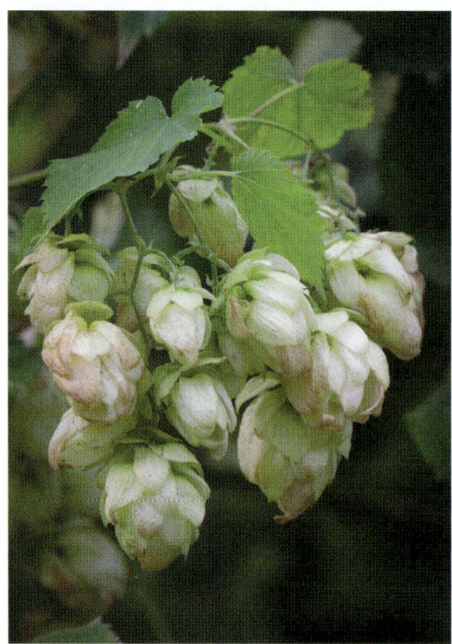

Humulus lupulus (hops) – 1/100 sec at f/5.6, 220mm.

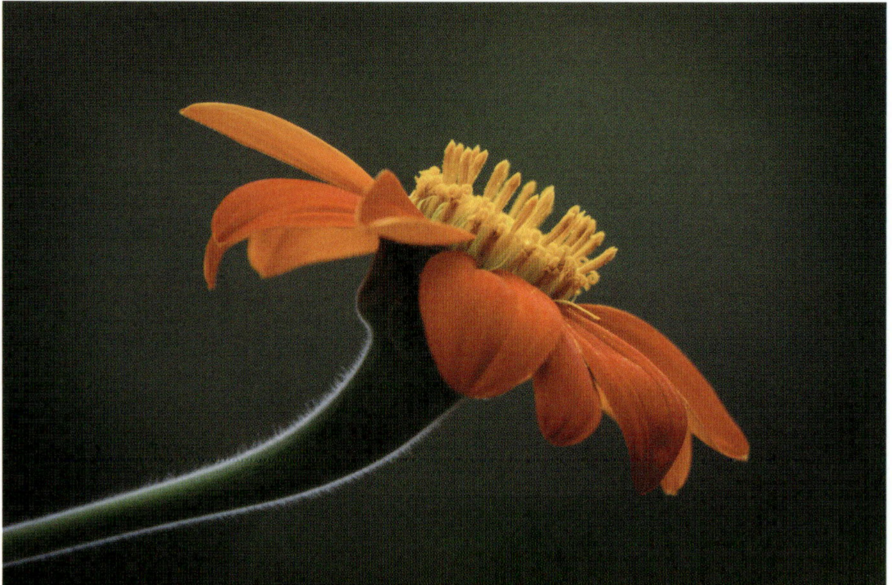

Tithonia (Mexican sunflower) – 1/200 at f/4, 210mm.

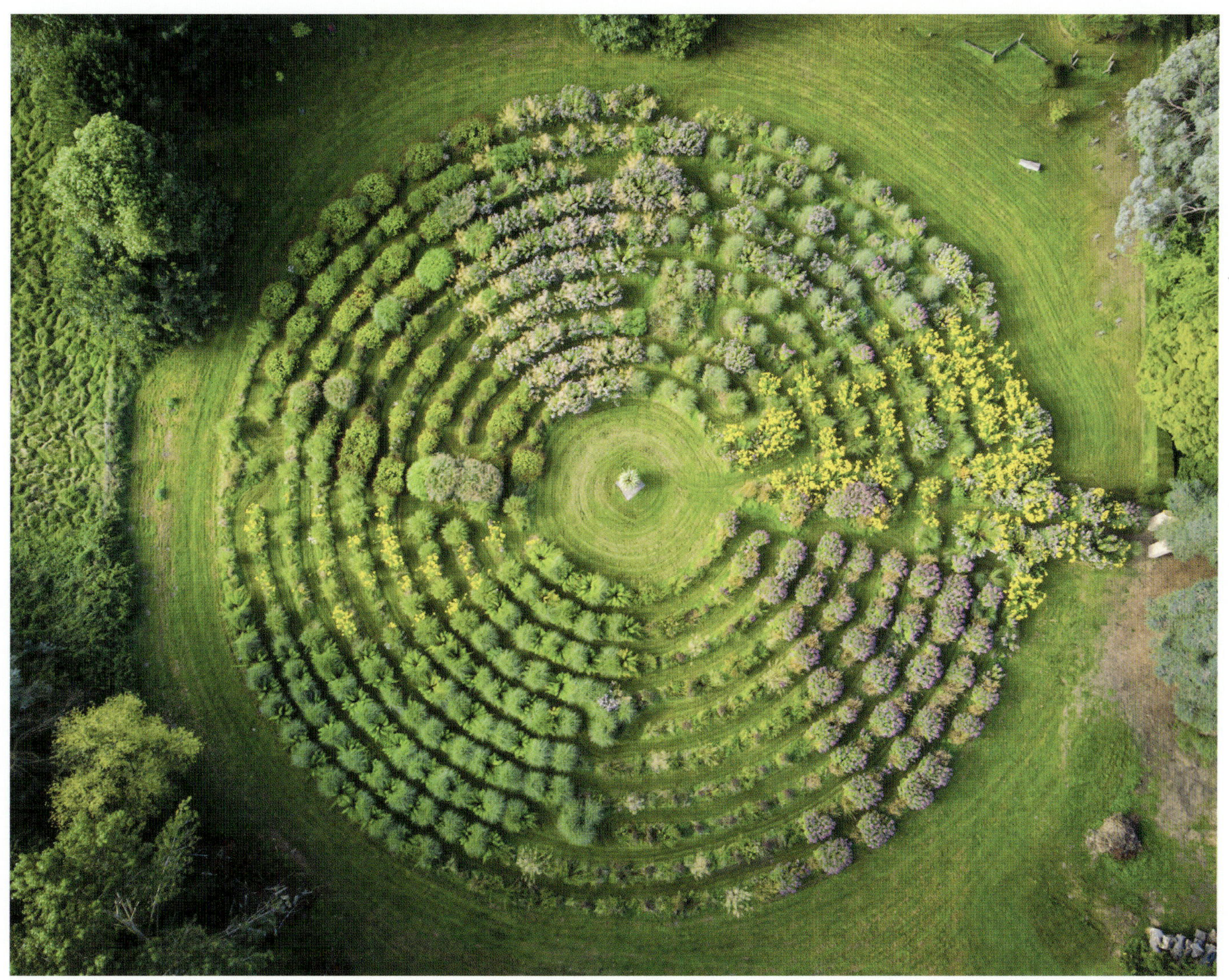

An overhead 'birds-eye' shot of a garden maze taken with a drone camera. 1/80 at f/2.8, 10mm lens.

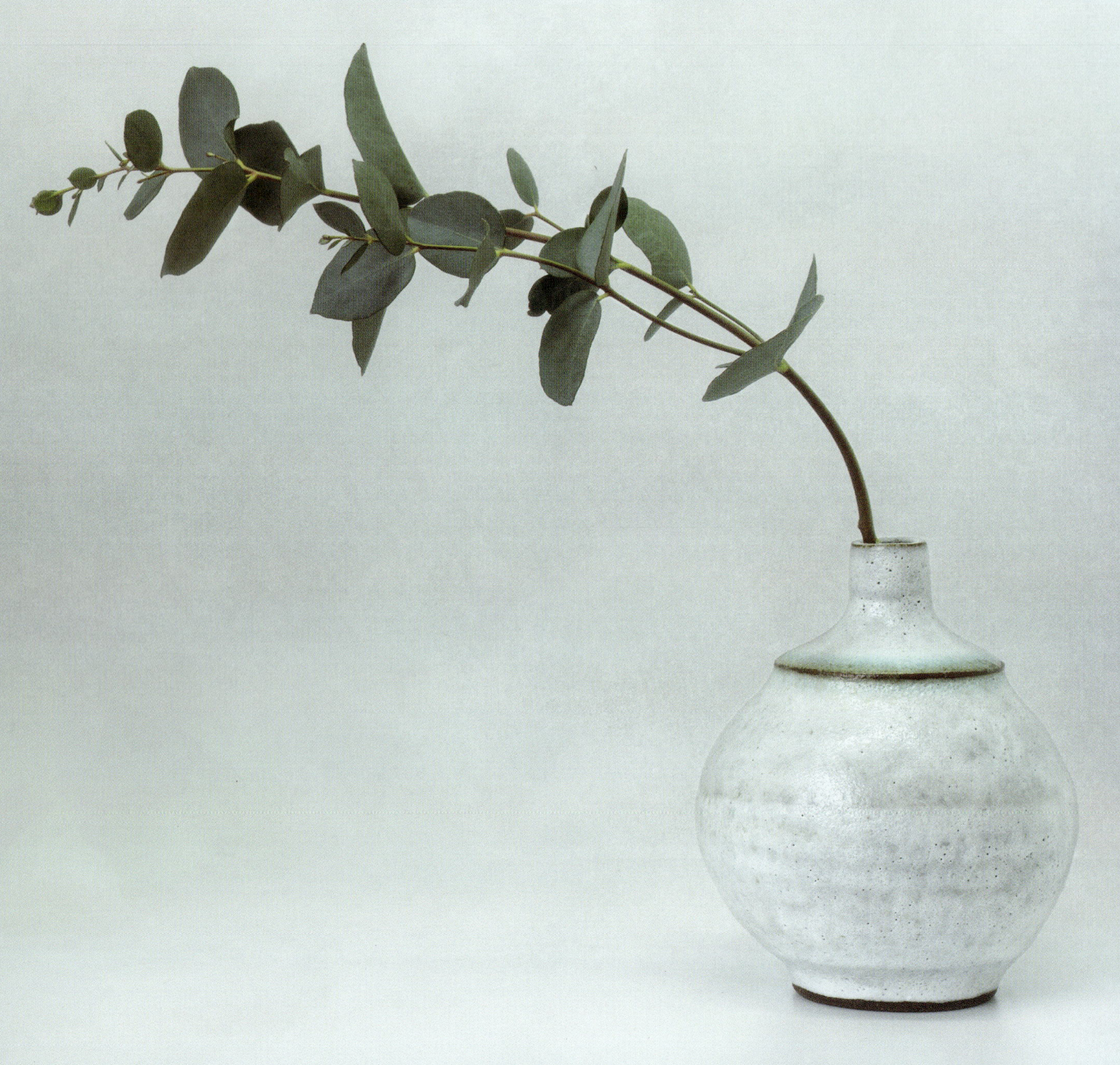

CHAPTER 10

Still Life

> Choose only one master – Nature.
>
> REMBRANDT

Still life can be another great project for a rainy day but some pre-planning is required, as you'll possibly need things other than flowers to feature in the photo. Perhaps the best 'planning' however is to research other still-life work by artists and photographers, as this will give you inspiration and ideas. I am particularly fascinated by *'Ikebana'* or *kadō*, which is the Japanese art of flower arranging; trying to find new life and beauty when removing things from the natural world and placing them in a different environment.

My first still-life photo was not actually something I set up myself; I was looking around a church whilst on holiday and came across a basket of fruit in an alcove, which was part of a Harvest Festival display. The church interior was fairly dark but a patch of sunlight had fallen on some of the fruit and I loved the effect it gave. The use of chiaroscuro (the interplay of light and shadow) was something that artists such as Rembrandt and Caravaggio used to good effect. Besides churches, many stately homes often have beautiful flower arrangements indoors that you're allowed to photograph, so keep an eye out and do ask if you're unsure about whether photography is allowed.

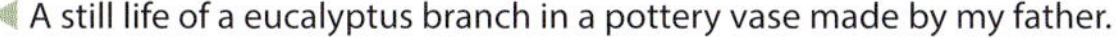

◀ A still life of a eucalyptus branch in a pottery vase made by my father.

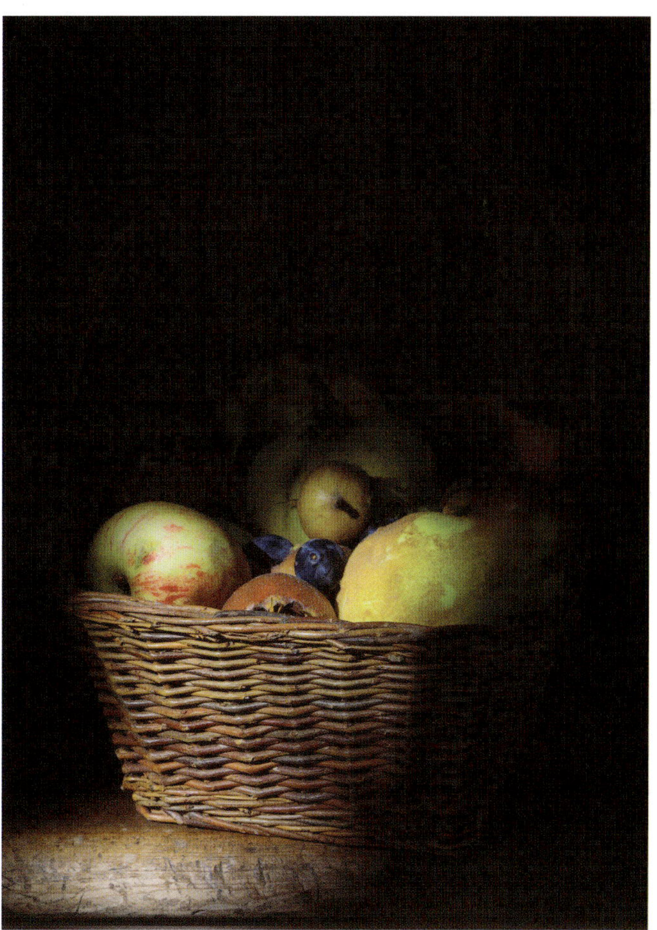

A photo of a harvest fruit basket – I didn't want the shadows to be completely black as I still wanted a suggestion of the basket and wood behind. I also lowered the highlights a little in the edit (I was shooting in raw) as the sunlight patch was originally very bright and definition was lost on some of the fruits.

In terms of props, vases are the most obvious choice and I've built up a small collection from charity shops and car boot sales. Other things traditionally used in still life are fruit (grapes, lemons, oranges with their leaves), cloths and tablecloths, baskets, bowls and glasses or goblets; you can look for specific items on the internet second hand. Ornamental vegetables like gourds or small pumpkins can also work well – especially if you're working with a theme like 'harvest'. If you want a more 'classical' still life, try to avoid items that are made from plastic and search out things that have a more timeless feel to them.

BACKGROUND

Choosing a sympathetic background for still-life subjects can be hard as you'll usually need a fairly plain background, but probably not a plain white or light-coloured wall, unless you are planning to use a texture or colour overlay at a later point in post-processing, or are going for a minimalist or black and white approach.

Bear in mind that if your still-life set-up is too close to the wall or backdrop behind it, it may cause shadows (depending on the lighting) so if you can't bring your table away from the wall then a patterned background will help reduce the impact of shadows. In addition, the more space there is between the main object and

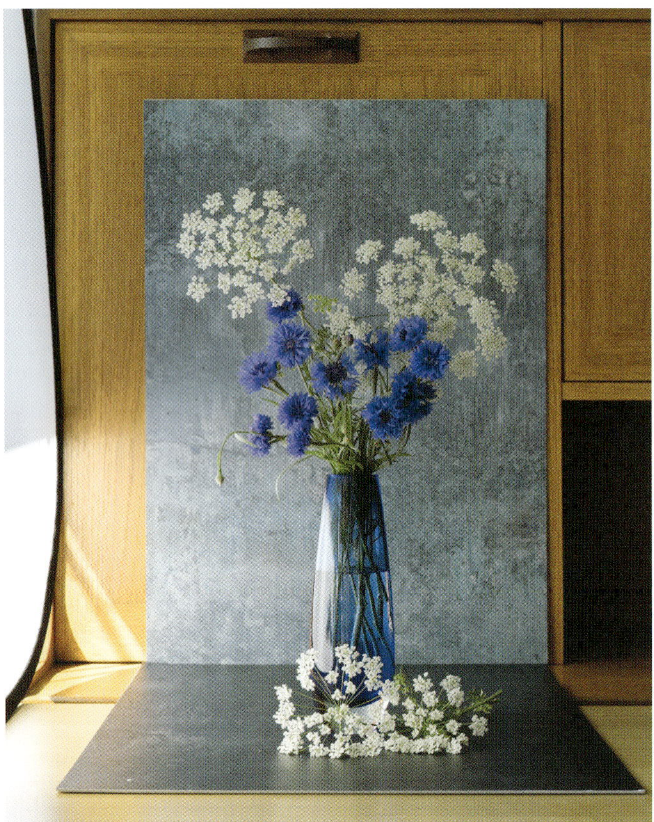

The set-up of a still life with blue centaurea and white ammi flowers. You can see I'm using a large diffuser on the left to subdue the strong sunlight coming through the window. There are two backdrops; the one behind the flowers and the one they are standing on.

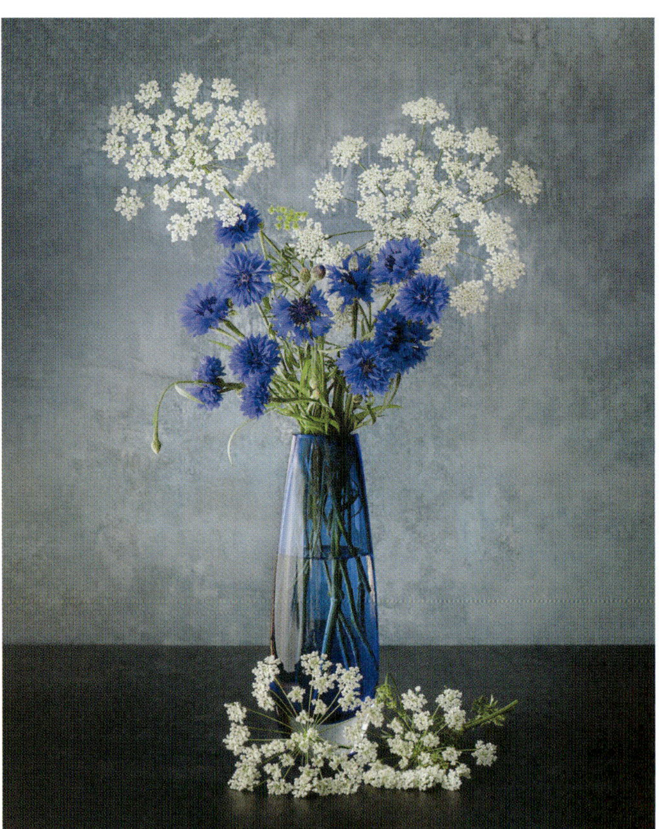

The finished photo.

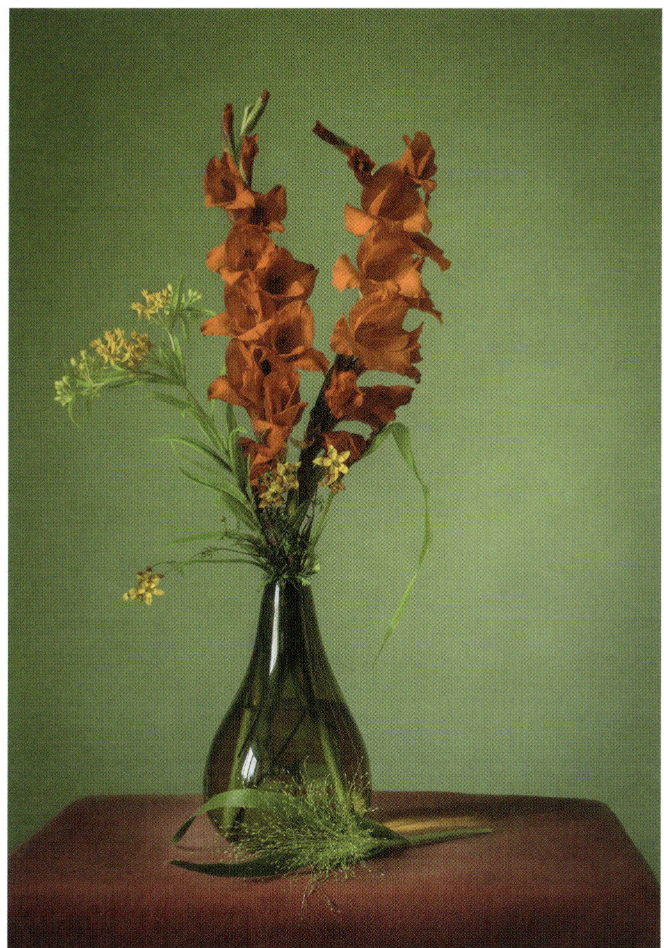

This gladioli still life was photographed in my bathroom as I thought that the wall colour there would complement the vase colour. I had to take out tiny spots of toothpaste on the wall in the edit that I didn't even realize were there! The only light in the set-up was natural and coming from a window on the left.

the background, the more depth the photo will have. However, some photographers such as Robert Mapplethorpe actually use shadows as part of the composition and this can be very effective.

There is quite a trend currently for using 'rustic' buildings (such as a shed interior) as a background and some still-life shots, particularly those involving fruits and vegetables, are often set up to look like a potting bench in the shed. Some photographers prefer patterned backgrounds, such as Arts

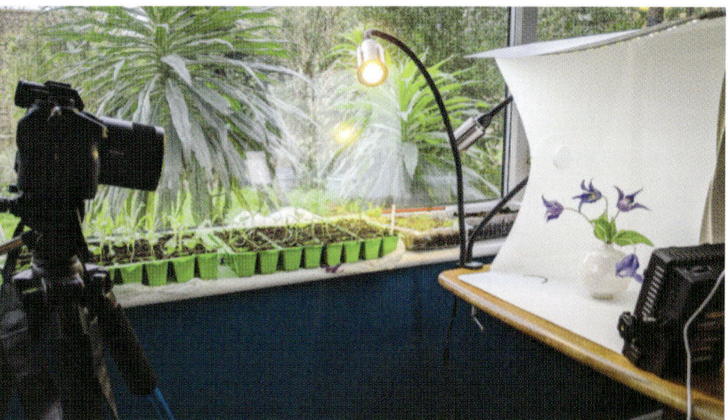

The set-up for a clematis still life I photographed last year. I used a lightbox with strip LEDs at the top, a portable LED light on the right and additional daylight lamps on the left (though they are not being used in this particular shot as it was quite a bright day). The daylight lamps are chiefly for my seedlings but I do sometimes use them in my indoor photography, pointed at the ceiling to get 'bounced' light onto the scene.

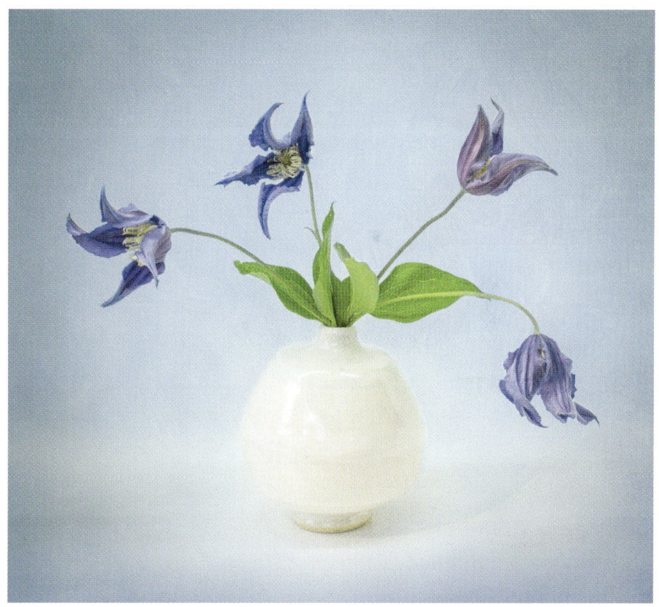

The finished photo, with a digital texture (added in the edit) I made by taking a photo of a sheet of plywood painted with blue acrylic paint. The shutter speed was a slow 1/10 sec (for which I needed a tripod) and the aperture was f/14.

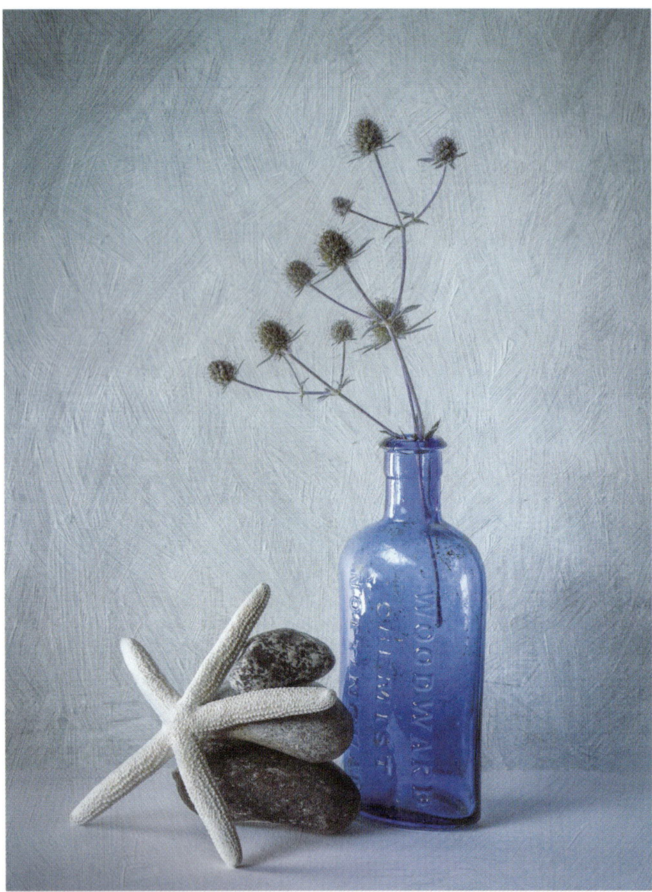

This *Eryngium* (sea holly) still life was photographed with a 55mm lens (on a tripod). The vase and items were placed on a white piece of paper with a board behind painted light blue; you can see the brush strokes as I wanted an 'oil-painting' effect. I then photographed this separately to create a texture I could use in the future if I needed to, and in fact the same texture is used digitally in the previous clematis still life.

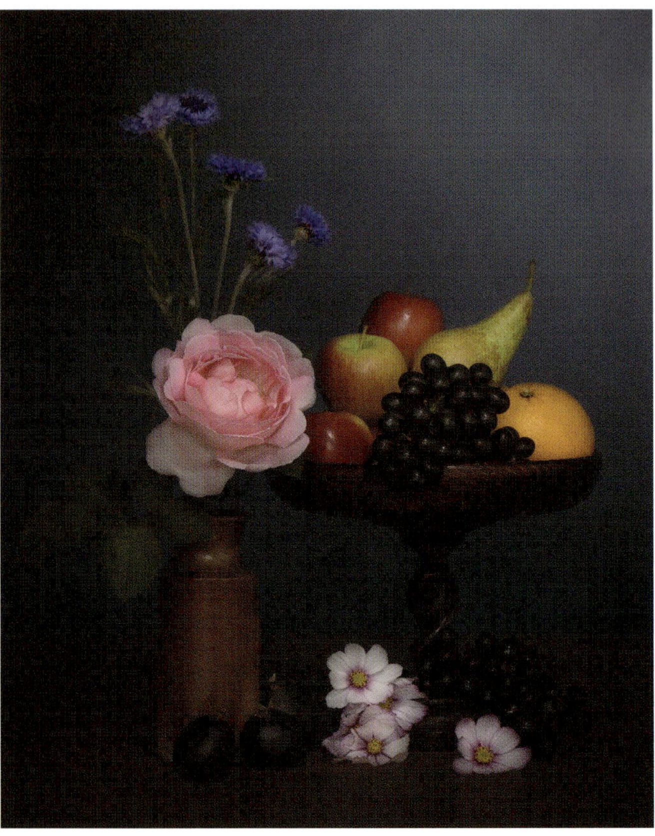

This fruit and flowers still life was photographed on a table in front of a bold blue wall in my house. The light is mostly natural daylight, entering the room from behind me; there is a slightly darkened texture on the finished result to make it look a bit like a classical oil painting.

and Crafts-style wallpapers, but be careful that these don't overpower your subjects.

In terms of bought backdrops you can buy a range of designs on the internet pre-made that are printed on heavy paper – you can tape these to a wall, or glue them to large sheets of cardboard which is generally what I do. They are usually A2 or A1 in size. You could also photograph some natural wood or rough stone and have it printed very large with a 'matt' finish by a photographic printer – you might find that this is too reflective though and you'll need to be careful with your lighting if this is the case.

I also keep a sheet of plywood in my conservatory that I can paint in the colour I need for any particular shot, and sometimes I simply set up my still-life subjects in front of some of the darker-painted walls in my house.

If the background of the still life is light-coloured, I will often add a texture or overlay in post-processing (*see* Chapter 11, 'Editing your Photographs'). Sometimes if the flowers I am using

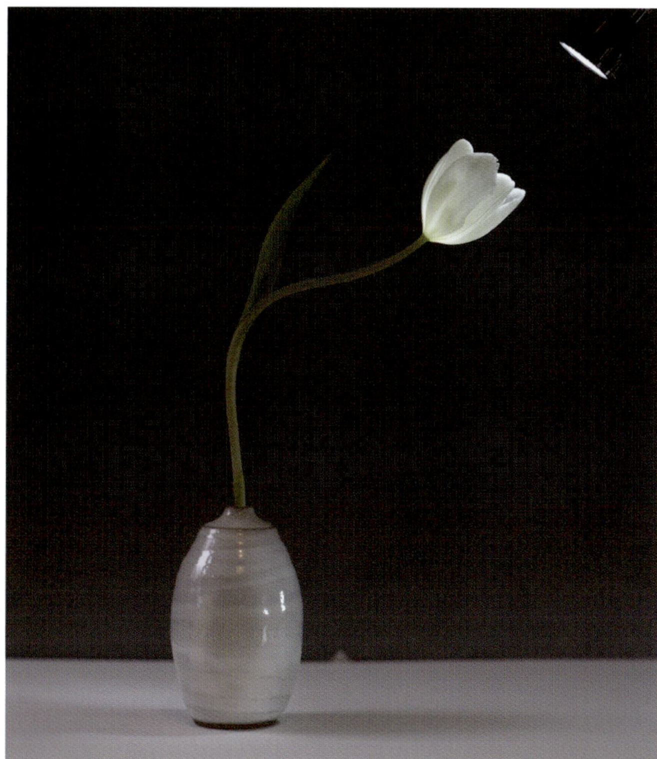

The unedited photo – you can see the torch in the top right that I cloned out afterwards.

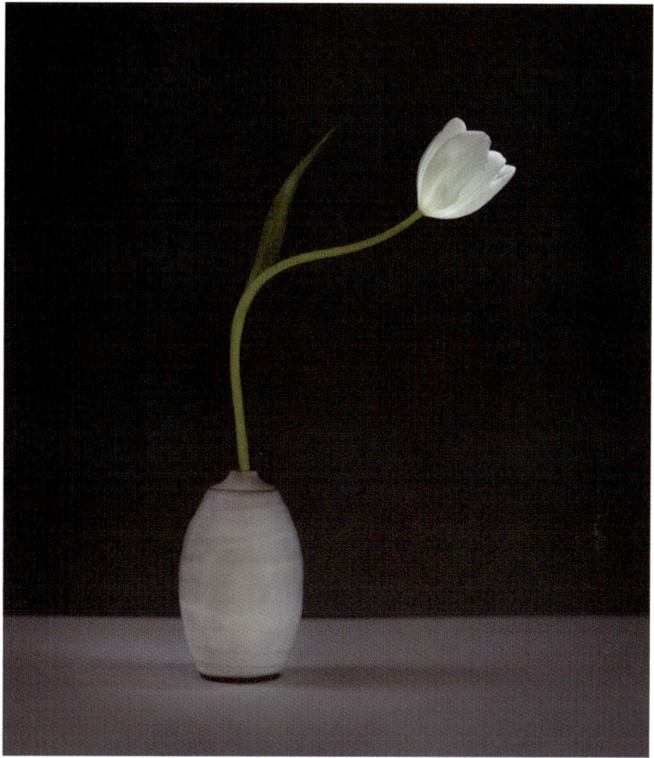

The finished photo.

are quite small I will use my lightbox to get an even white (or black) background and then overlay one of my own textures in post-processing.

A tripod is essential for still-life photography, as you will need a narrow aperture (probably from between f/9–f/14) to get all of the plant and vase/items in focus and therefore the shutter speed might have to be quite slow.

Whatever flowers or other objects you are photographing, it's really important to spend some time getting the arrangement right *before* you start taking photographs. Choose a vase that balances your flowers in terms of colour and size and try to create a composition with some sense of symmetry or shape. Remember that odd numbers usually work better than even ones (my clematis photo was an exception but suited the curved stalks) and sometimes simplicity is best.

Having said this, some of the most beautiful classical still-life paintings show large vases crammed with an abundance of different flowers, perhaps to show the wealth of the patron or the abundance of their garden; these are visual feasts. As with so many things, it comes down to experimenting with different subjects and lighting and getting a feel for what works well. Many still-life photos use very strong lighting from one side (perhaps to imitate the effect of window-light) and this is something else to try if you already have lights for portraiture.

I experimented with light in one still-life photo I took last year, as I wanted the overall image to be fairly subdued but with a bright white tulip flower as a point of focus. The tulip had a bend in its stem that I thought would make an excellent composition. It stands on white paper (on a table) in front of a blue wall in my conservatory.

I put the camera on a tripod and set the timer so that I could point a small torch into the flower head to light it up a little. Other than the torch, the only other light is natural daylight, coming into the room from behind me. In the edit I added a dark grey/blue colour overlay to make the tulip stand out a bit more. I also had to take out the small blip on the board at the back and for this particular picture I chose to remove the reflections on the vase in Photoshop to enhance the simplicity of the composition. Finally I added a little more foreground in Photoshop by cropping outwards at the bottom of the frame.

I love seeing the raw version of a photo (or a set-up shot), then the end result after it has been edited and I think it's a terrific way of learning how to do things in photography.

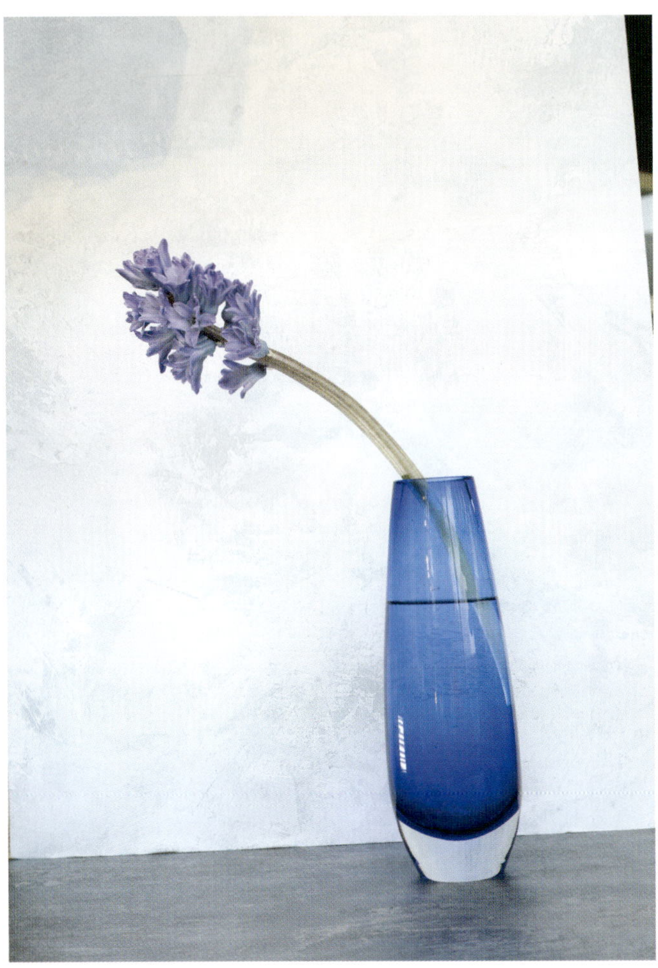

I shot this hyacinth still life on a table in my conservatory with two backdrops – one underneath the vase and one behind it. As you can see, I wasn't very straight with my original, so had to straighten it in Lightroom and then crop in to lose the shadow of the LED light in the top left (the only other light is natural daylight from the window behind me). I removed the reflections from the glass as they're rather distracting and added a subtle blue texture to connect all the blue elements of the scene.

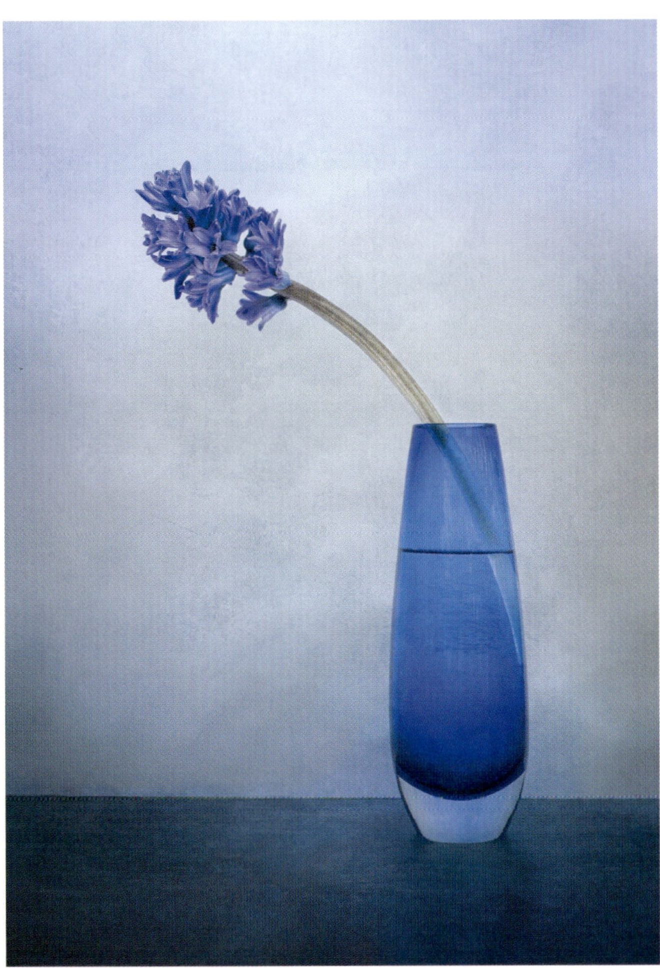

The finished photo. The editing here probably took about forty-five minutes but I'm happy with the end result so consider it time well spent.

Flowers and plants to photograph in October

Rain returns with a vengeance so try to use it to make your flowers sparkle. October is the best month for great autumn colour so visit a local garden or forest to make the most of it.

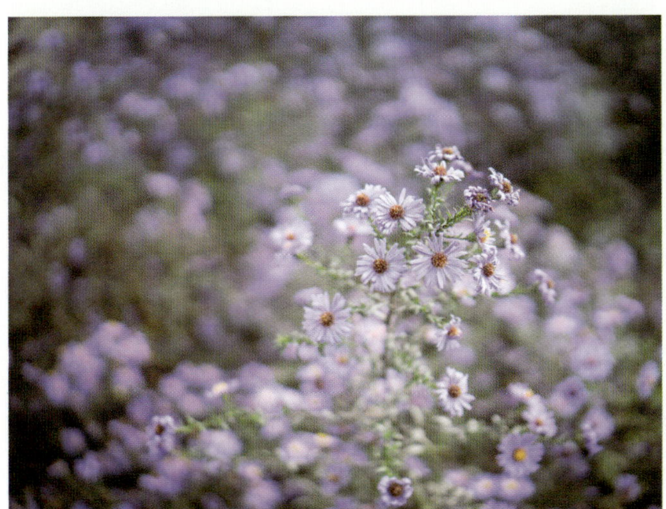

Asters – 1/400 sec at f/1.8, 55mm.

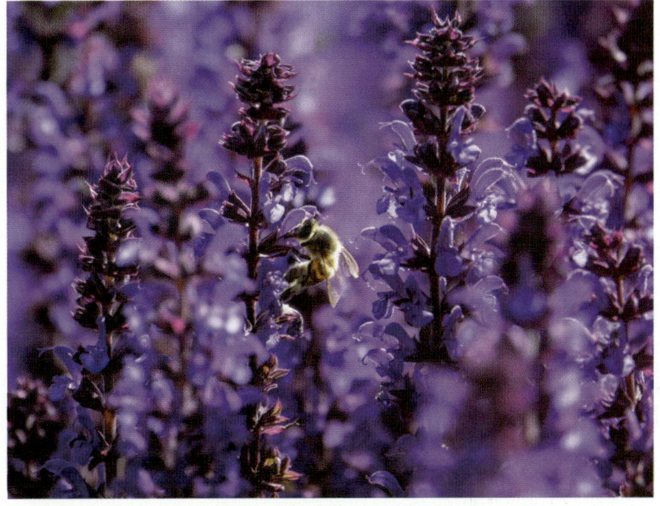

Honey bee on *Salvia* – 1/800 sec at f/4, 210mm.

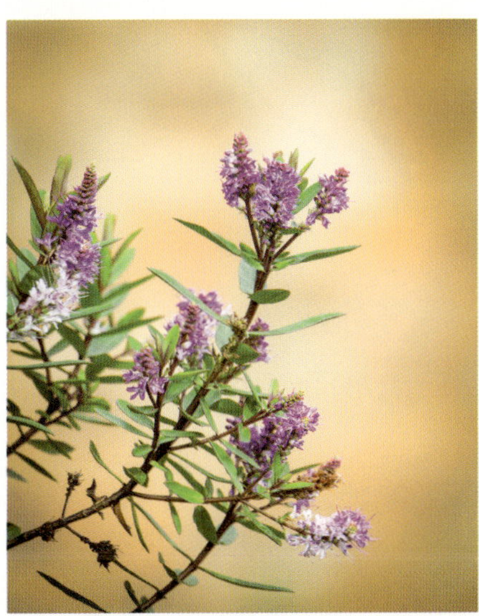

Hebe – 1/400 sec at f/4, 220mm.

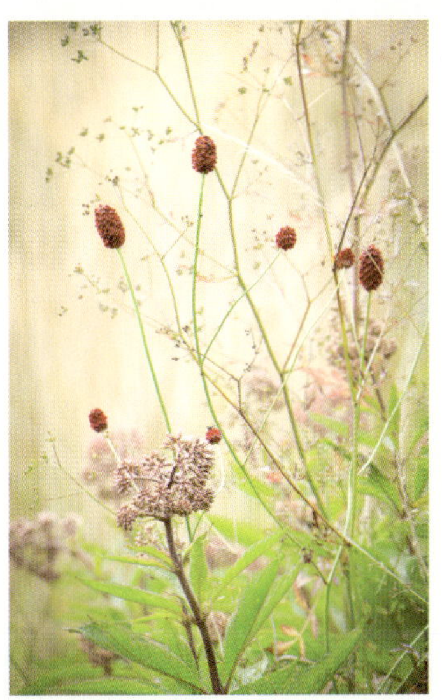

Sanguisorba, *Eupatorium* and grasses – 1/125 sec at f/4, 90mm.

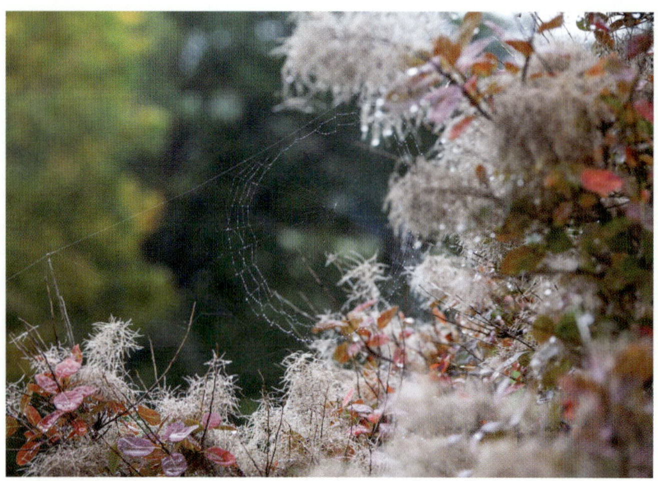

Cotinus coggygria (smoke bush) and spiderweb – 1/125 sec at f/4, 80mm.

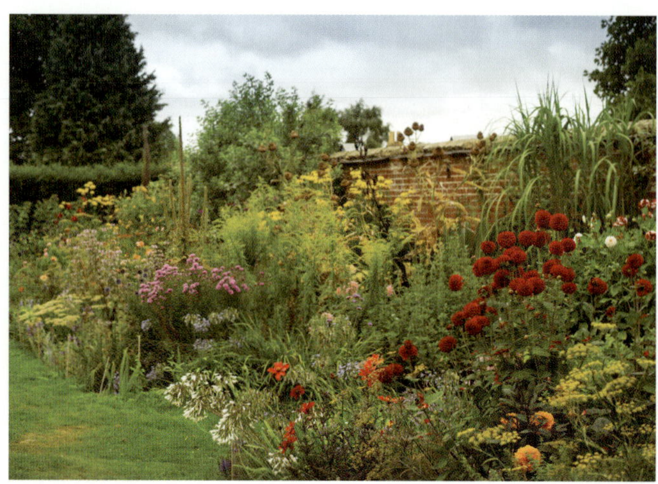

Autumn border – 1/640 sec at f/4, 55mm.

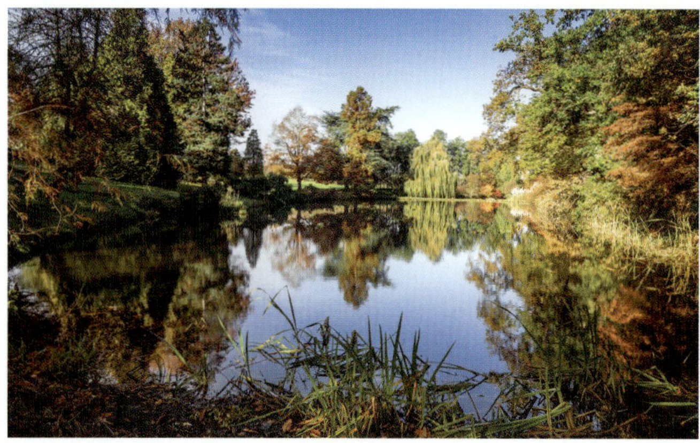

Lake with autumn colour – 1/100 sec at f/9, 24mm.

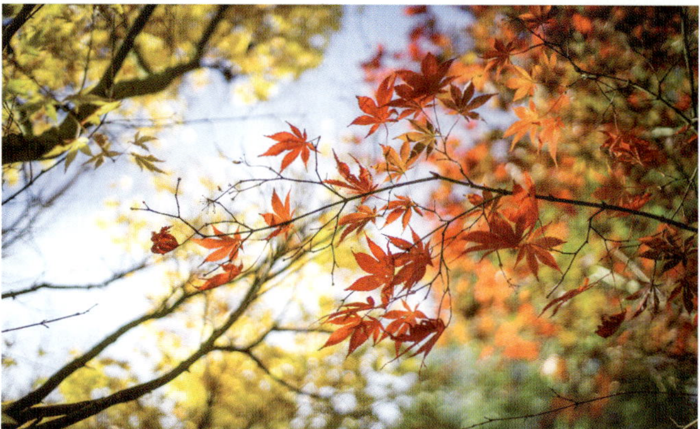

Acer palmatum (Japanese maple leaves) – 1/2500 sec at f/2, 50mm vintage lens.

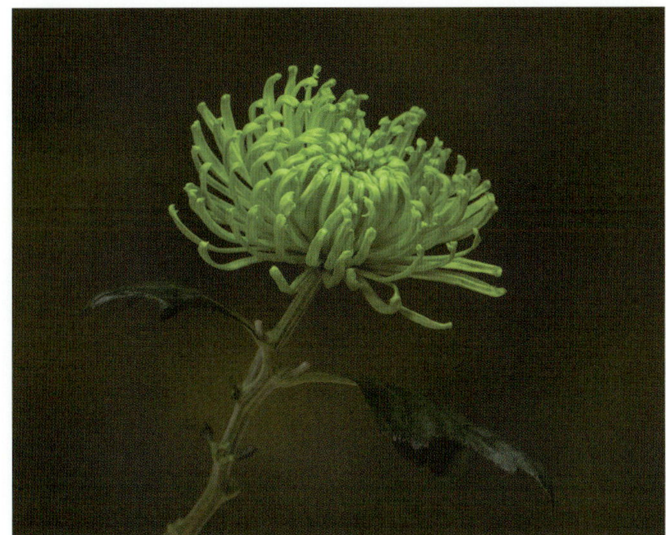

Chrysanthemum – 1/125 sec at f/9, 55mm, photographed indoors in a lightbox.

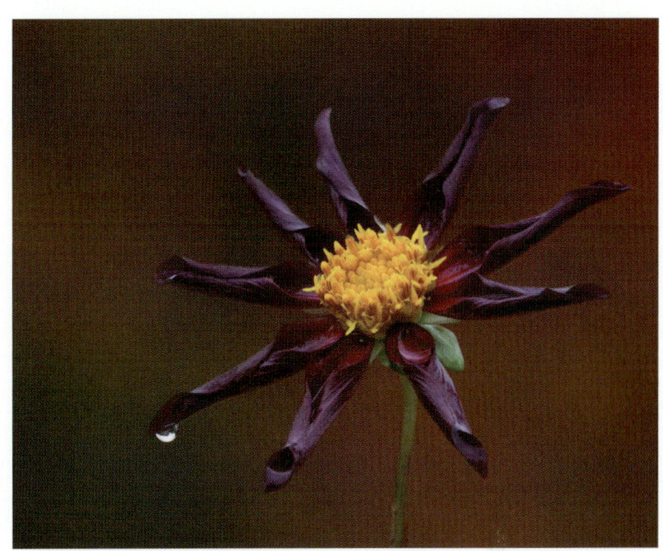

Dahlia – 1/250 sec at f/6.3, 220mm.

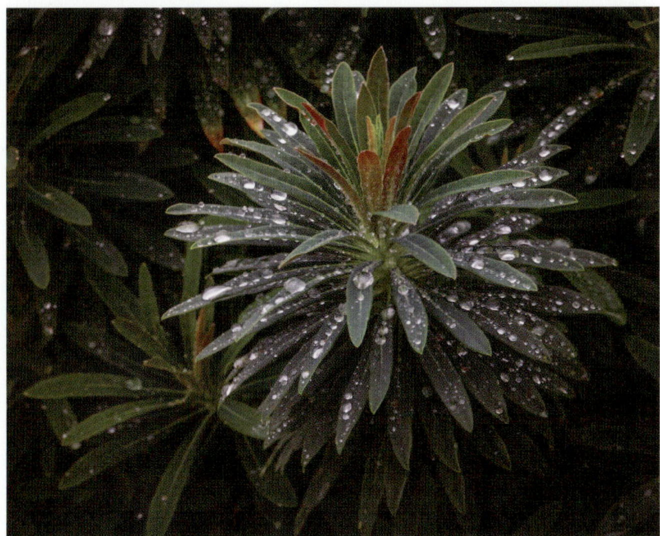

Euphorbia – 1/320 sec at f/5, 80mm.

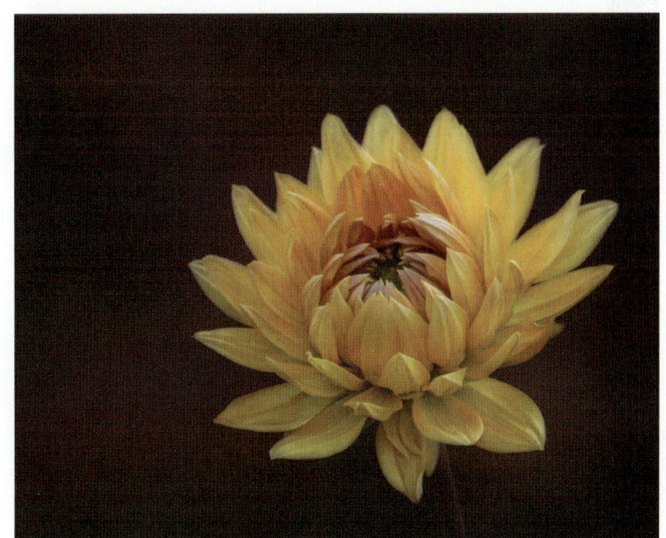

Dahlia – 1/250 sec at f/4, 220mm.

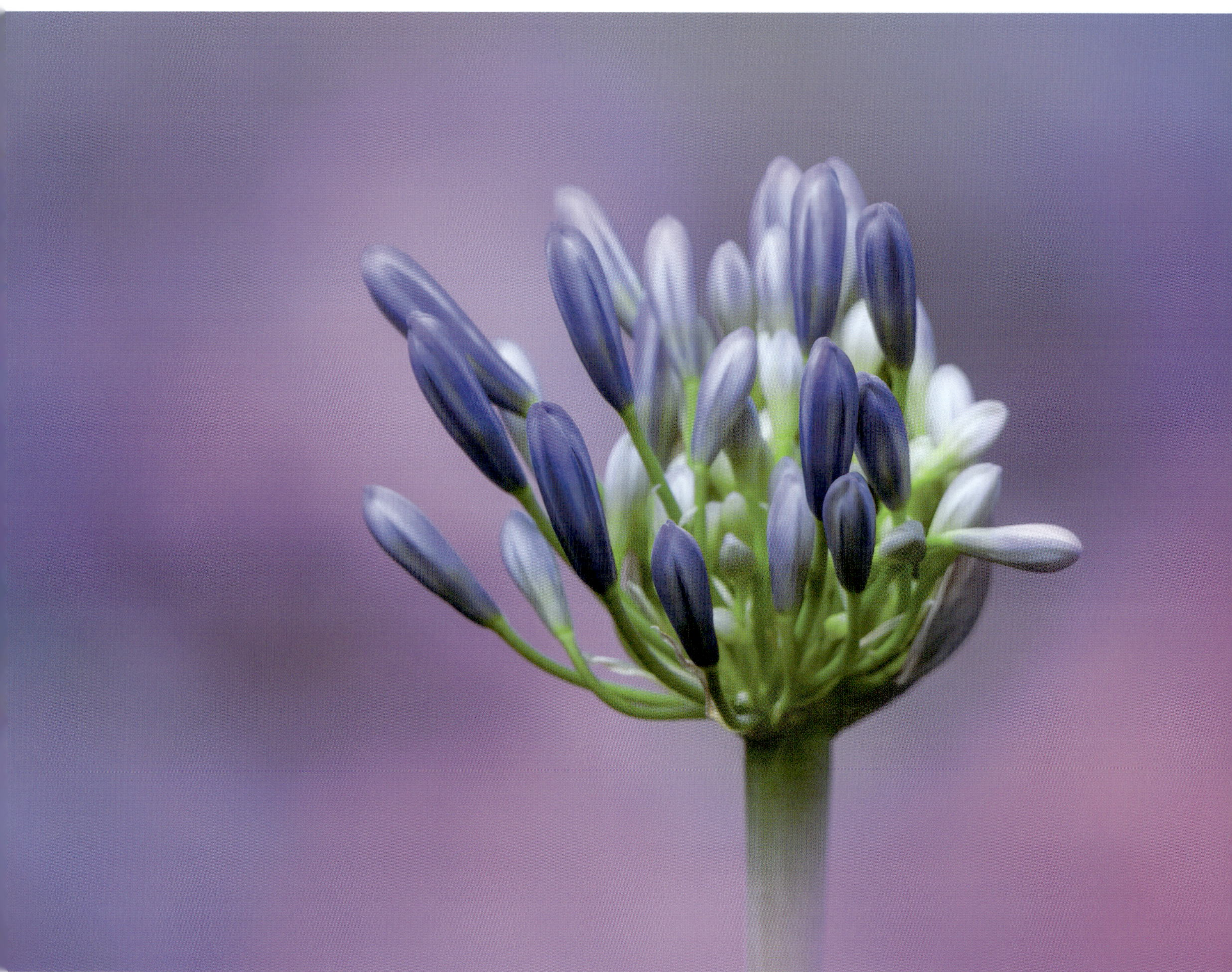

Agapanthus bud. Overlay added in the edit.

CHAPTER 11

Editing your Photographs

> Art does not reproduce the visible; rather, it makes visible.
>
> PAUL KLEE

The term 'post-processing' is used by the majority of photographers to refer to the editing done (usually on a computer) after the photo has been taken. It takes most photographers a long time to learn the finer points of this process, and many (myself included) would say that they are still learning, even after many years of practice.

In digital photography, post-processing extends the creative range of a photograph just as darkroom manipulation did in the past. Take this part of your journey slowly; there is so much information and advice out there it can be overwhelming. Most photographers would say that when sensitively used, some post-processing or editing can turn a good image into a much better one.

There are still those that argue against too much editing, as it makes the final image too 'artificial' or 'unnatural' but it all comes down to a matter of taste really, and tastes are continually changing. It's also good to bear in mind that in the days before digital cameras, photographers spent hours in the darkroom 'finessing' their pictures by making thoughtful and (usually) subtle adjustments to contrast, composition and many other variables.

RAW OR JPEG?

Before you even take the pictures that you will be editing, you need to make a decision between shooting with a raw or JPEG file format, provided that both of these are available to you on your camera.

In a nutshell, when you take a picture, the camera captures data and creates a digital image. There are many different types of file formats in which this image can be saved as and the following are the most common ones (all acronyms excepting 'raw', which is just a noun and shouldn't really be capitalized, although it often is).

- JPEG – Joint Photographic Experts Group
- TIFF – Tagged Image File Format (a high quality uncompressed file, often used in the photography industry)
- PNG – Portable Network Graphics
- DNG – Digital Negative (a type of raw file)
- Raw

Raw and JPEG are the best-known and most common image file formats used by photographers. There are many opinions on why you should choose one over the other. With a JPEG file format, the camera does a certain amount of editing for you in-camera, so the image you see has usually been brightened and has had a little colour (saturation) added to it, amongst other things. JPEGs are also a compressed format, which means that the image will take up less space (measured in megapixels) on the camera or computer.

A raw file contains unprocessed, uncompressed picture data from a digital camera's image sensor and will almost certainly then need to be edited to achieve a 'finished' result.

Many professionals will shoot in raw because it allows greater freedom in the editing process (although they will often convert the image to a JPEG when they have finished editing it). If for example you have over-bright highlights in a photo, a raw file will usually allow you to pull them back and recover lost detail; a JPEG file may not, or render the highlights a muddy grey. There are disadvantages however. A raw file takes up much more space on your camera card/computer than a JPEG, and the thought of having to close-edit every single photo puts many people off. I know several excellent photographers who will choose to shoot JPEG, confident that they can get things as good as possible *in* the camera and not have many issues to address in post-processing.

Ultimately it's your choice. I started with JPEG and then moved to raw, which I now shoot most of the time. Incidentally, mobile phones can often also shoot in raw these days and apps like Snapseed can edit raw files as well as JPEGs.

USING ADOBE PHOTOSHOP, LIGHTROOM AND OTHER EDITING SOFTWARE

Firstly, I should say that I am on a continual quest to get my photos as perfect as I can in-camera, and to minimize (or even cut out completely) the editing that I have to do afterwards. Many people will choose to take photos for the pleasure of just taking photos, and not wish to include any editing as part of the process; this is absolutely fine. Sometimes I'll shoot in JPEG as a challenge to see if I can get everything right in-camera and then not need to edit much, or at all. You may however want to start editing your photos if you feel you'd like to take your photography to the next level, or enter competitions.

There are many brands of photography editing software that all do similar things, but the industry standards are Adobe Lightroom and Photoshop, which come as a pair in a cloud-based photography editing package. These are the ones I use. Even if you use another programme you should find most of my suggestions will work with your particular piece of software, but you may have to look up the equivalent methodology.

Lightroom

The best thing about Lightroom is that it organizes your photos into a 'workflow' that you can then sort and store on your computer.

Importing

I import my images straight into Lightroom (using the 'Library' module at the top of the screen) although I know some photographers put them into a folder on their computer first and then import them into Lightroom. When importing photos from a card onto my computer I am very careful about labelling; if you're taking lots of photos you need to be able to find them easily at a later date. I always put a date of some kind as part of the import folder name too, such as *2018Junepoppies* or *2019Oct3rdGardenmacro*.

Organizing and deleting

Once I have imported my photos into Lightroom I navigate to the 'Develop' module at the top and look at every photo in turn, rating them with a number between 1 and 5 (5 is outstanding, 1 is out of focus and unusable). I often check fine details while viewing the image at 100 per cent so this can take some time, but will save you so much time later. If you turn on the caps lock then Lightroom will automatically move on to the next photo after you've rated it. When I've finished rating I then go to the 'Library' module, and select 'view' then 'sort by' and then 'rating'. This ranks them all in order from five down to one, and using the shift key to select the first and last photo I will then delete every photo that has a rating of two or one. This can be as many as half the photos I've taken on a bad day or only a quarter if I'm lucky. It does depend on your choice of photography subject though; as I work with macro on a manual focus setting quite a bit I often can't see on my camera rear-view screen if the photo is totally in focus (even when I zoom in) and so I will often have lots of 'almost but not quite' shots.

Once I'm left with the good and reasonable shots (in case you're wondering, there are only usually a handful of '5s'!) I set about editing the first photo. Sometimes I'll edit all the 5s first and then the 4s, and sometimes I'll re-sort them chronologically and edit them that way.

Using the 'Basic' editing panel I'll begin to move the sliders to achieve my desired look – a useful tip to reset these is to double-click 'WB', 'Tone' and 'Presence' at the top of each of the three sections of this panel; they will all return to zero.

Sync settings

A really good feature of Lightroom to use if you're editing similar types of photos (for example all macro or all garden landscape) is the 'sync settings' feature, which is found in the drop-down 'settings' menu at the very top of the screen (when you are in the 'Develop' module).

If you spend time editing the first photo of your imported batch carefully until you're completely happy with it, you can then apply the settings you've used for this photo to all the others. With the first, edited photo still selected (highlighted), select all the other photos using the shift key and clicking on the last photo in the batch. Then click 'settings' and then 'sync settings' at the top and tick the edit features you would like Lightroom to apply to all the other photos in the batch (the default option will usually be fine here). This should save you a lot of editing time! You will still need to edit your favourites in detail, but this should be much quicker now.

After applying the 'sync settings' feature I then start to close-edit, starting with the 5s and finishing with the 4s. I usually don't edit the 3s as they are just there as a back-up option.

If I were to show you my typical starting point settings in the 'Basic' editing panel, the sliders would look something like this, although this of course will vary greatly according to what I'm photographing, the light available on the day and so on.

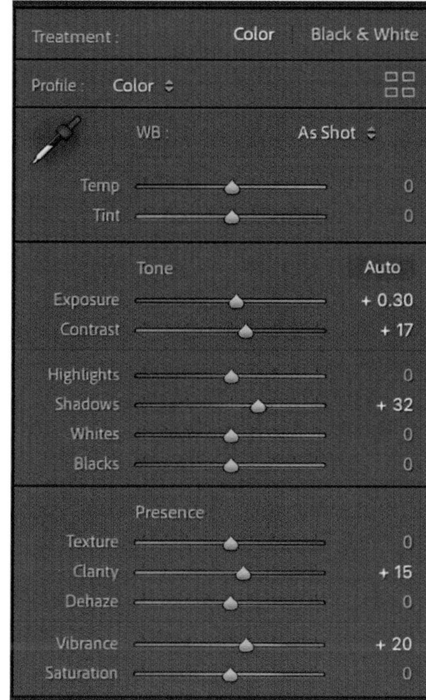

Close-editing

My close-editing workflow usually proceeds as follows:

- Decide where the point of focus is and make sure it is sharp. Crop the image so that the eye is drawn to this part of the frame.
- Adjust the following, to taste: exposure, shadows, highlights (making sure that parts of the image aren't too bright – blown – or too dark), vibrance and clarity. I might use other sliders here, such as texture or blacks but I rarely use the 'saturation' slider – vibrancy should really be enough.
- I then scroll down and make sure the image has been sharpened a little and de-noised.
- I might then add a slight vignette, found on the left-hand side under 'presets'.

Some typical settings for sharpening and de-noising in Lightroom; again these are highly dependent on the photo you're editing. Do read more about this on the internet and experiment to find what works best for your photography.

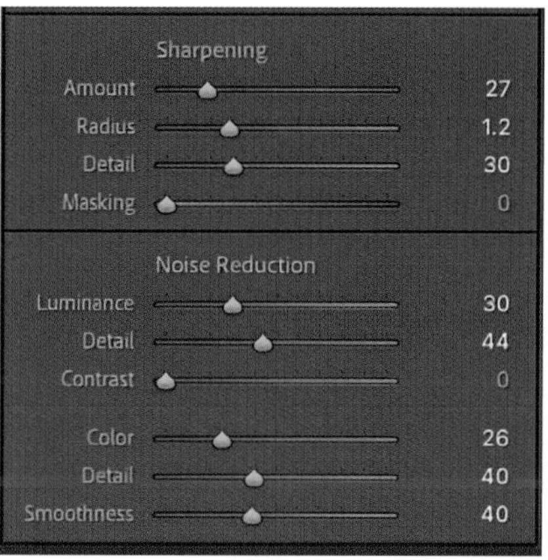

I think there is nothing more off-putting than a heavy vignette in flower photography, except perhaps if it is a more stylized black and white image. Vignettes are used to subtly pull the eye towards the subject of the photo, but if the vignette is noticeable then it can have the opposite effect. I sometimes then return to the right-hand editing panel and add a graduated filter if I feel the image requires it (this is at the top to the right of the 'crop' option). This can help lighten or darken skies, and sometimes is used to darken the area below a plant or flower so that the eye is not pulled to it. Again, use this filter sparingly, it should still feel natural.

Select the grad filter and draw down from the top of the image, as far as you want it to go. You can then change the intensity by using the regular sliders, such as exposure, as you would normally.

If I have a horizon in my image, I check that it is straight and if not adjust by using the 'rotate' slider which is further down in the 'Transform' editing panel. At this point, I'm normally finished with my Lightroom edit, and am ready to export and save the edited photo.

To export, I return to the 'Library' module at the top and select 'export' at the bottom left. It is really important that you give your photo a file name that corresponds to what it actually is, and then you'll be able to easily find it in the future with a search. I rarely batch-export; it's quicker but makes it harder then to search for particular photos in the future. You can at this point open the photo (after you've edited it in Lightroom) immediately in Photoshop by pressing 'control e' or 'command e' on the keyboard. This will open it in Photoshop as a TIFF (or PSD) file, rather than opening it as a JPEG by exporting as above and then opening the file within Photoshop. If you think that you may edit it further it is better to save it as a TIFF file, which is an option in the 'file settings' section.

It is a good idea to get in the habit of backing up your photos on a very regular basis, and possibly in more than one place if you can. There are internet storage companies where you can pay to store your photos in the cloud but it's always worth keeping everything you may want in the future on an external hard drive.

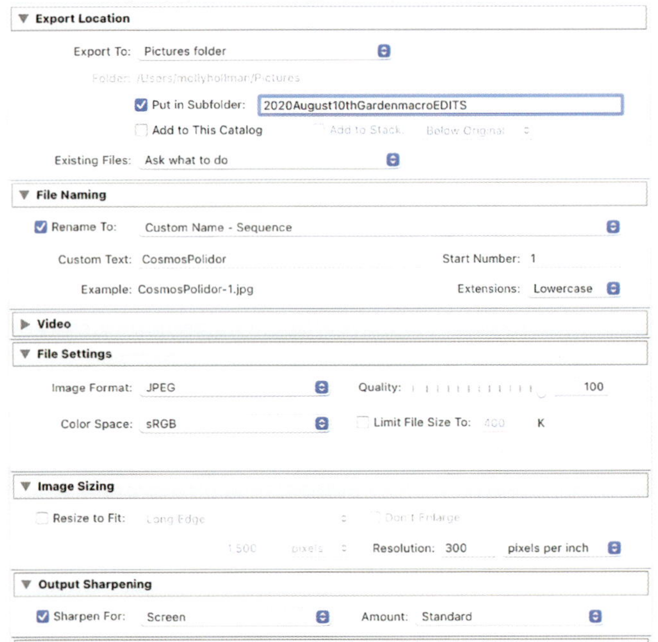

A typical export screenshot with my labelling and settings.

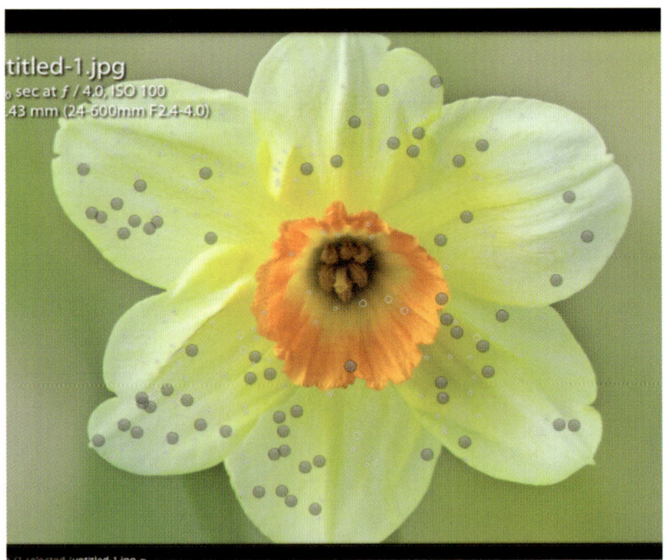

This was a particularly dirty daffodil and as you can see, I had to clone off many, many specks – with hindsight I would have found a better specimen.

Cloning out imperfections and distractions

This can be done in Lightroom using the 'spot removal' tool in the 'Develop' module, but I find it a quicker, more accurate and easier process in Photoshop.

Other than dirt or flower imperfections, the thing I most often clone out is dust spots, which everyone gets from time to time from having a dirty sensor (the problem is much more noticeable when shooting at a narrow aperture like f/11). For a perfect picture you should really scrutinize every inch of your photo at 100 per cent magnification, to spot small imperfections and dust spots. These are always noticed at competition level.

Photoshop

There are two main ways to remove spots and unwanted parts of the picture in Photoshop. The first is the 'spot healing brush tool' on the left, which has an icon like a sticking plaster. Set its size at the top left to cover the dust spot or object that you want to remove. This method works best for small details.

To remove larger blemishes try using the 'content-aware fill' method. Select the lasso tool on the left-hand side and carefully draw around the object, stem, leaf or whatever you want to remove. Then, in the top 'edit' menu, select 'content-aware fill' and colour around the part that you have 'lassoed', then press 'ok' at the bottom right. This should remove the object.

The 'spot healing brush' tool, which is found in the icons on the left-hand side.

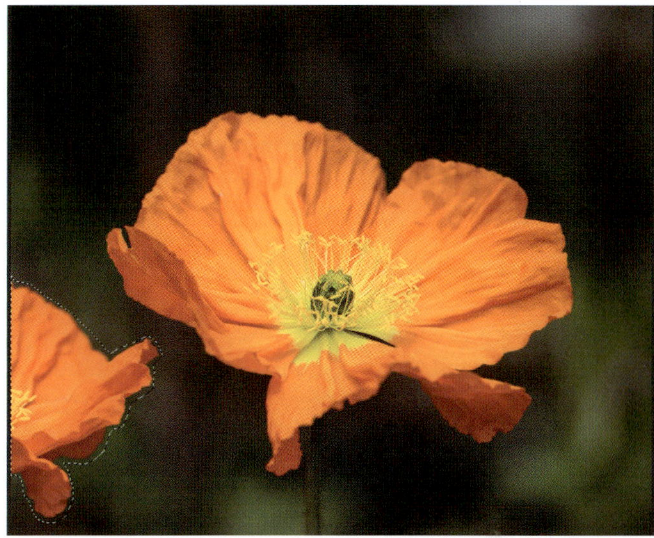

A photo where I have drawn around the flower I want to remove with the lasso tool.

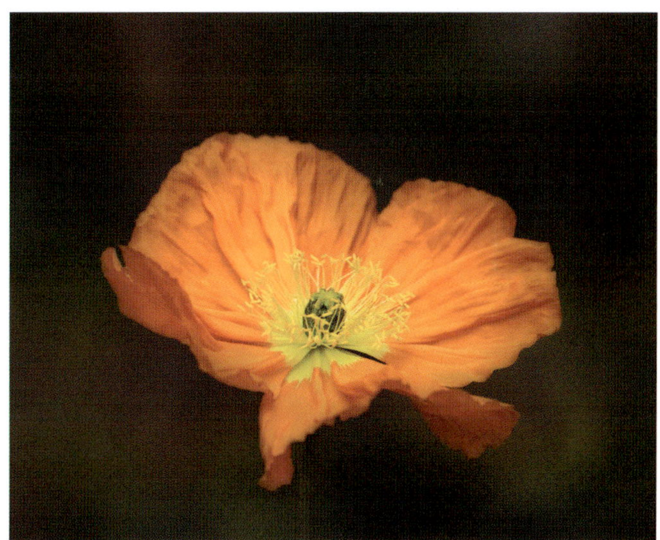

The finished photo.

Overlays and textures

Other than using the above two methods for removing unwanted objects from my photos, the main reason I use Photoshop is to add an overlay or texture. I do this for many different reasons, but mostly because I want to achieve a more 'fine-art' result. The use of a texture or overlay is usually to subdue any real-life background and focus all our attention onto the subject of the photograph, but can also be used creatively to add light, depth or additional colour to a photo.

Still-life photos often work well with artistic textures, where they might just give a hint of brush stroke, grain or other 'texture' to give the kind of effect you would see in a painting. A colour overlay for me differs as it avoids the brush strokes or detail of a texture; it's just a blur of colour. Many photographers would refer to both as textures but I like to differentiate for the sake of clarity.

A texture made from acrylic paint on board.

An overlay made from an out-of-focus photo of flowers.

Making textures and overlays

There are many instructional videos on the internet about this so I won't talk about it in depth, but it's very easy to paint your own textures using a large piece of card and some paint and a happy hour can be spent in a garden with your camera focus set to manual taking some blurred photos to use as overlays. I often take a photo of some out-of-focus flowers each time I visit a garden just so that I don't end up using the same overlays again and again. As I showed in Chapter 5, 'Photographing Indoors', you can also print these and use them as backdrops. That way, both textures and overlays can be used as actual backdrops, or digitally as a layer in Photoshop.

Using textures and overlays digitally

There are several different ways of approaching this but most photographers will use Photoshop to add a texture or overlay.

First, you need to import into Photoshop the photo you wish to edit. I took the photo I'm going to use in my garden, but there were many other similar flowers crowding it and I used a piece of white card behind it for a clean background and gently clipped the other flowers out of the way. I used a small LED light pointed at the cone of the flower to bring out the details, as it is quite dark. It is a good potential choice for a digital overlay background as it's not sharp from front to back, and the softness will help it blend into a digital background later. I edited the photo as I would normally in Lightroom and then imported it into Photoshop.

Now you need to put one of the overlays or textures you have made (or bought) on top of the photo. Choosing which one is often the hardest part as the colour you think will work sometimes doesn't, and vice versa. If you add an overlay, start working on it and then feel it doesn't quite work, it's easy enough to abandon it and start afresh.

To add a texture or overlay, find the one that you want and drag it on top of the photo in Photoshop. I'm choosing an out-of-focus photo of flowers that has some orangey-red in it to hopefully complement the flower colour.

You will need to resize the overlay to cover all of your photo. Drag out the corners to make it fit. You can turn it by 90 or

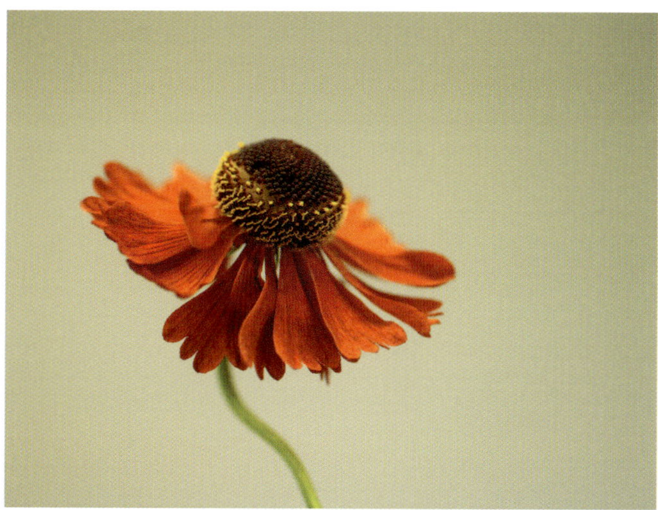

The *Helenium* 'Moerheim Beauty' that I photographed to use with a digital overlay. This image has been edited in Lightroom. It was a cloudy day and the surrounding garden is giving the white backdrop a greenish tinge, but this doesn't matter.

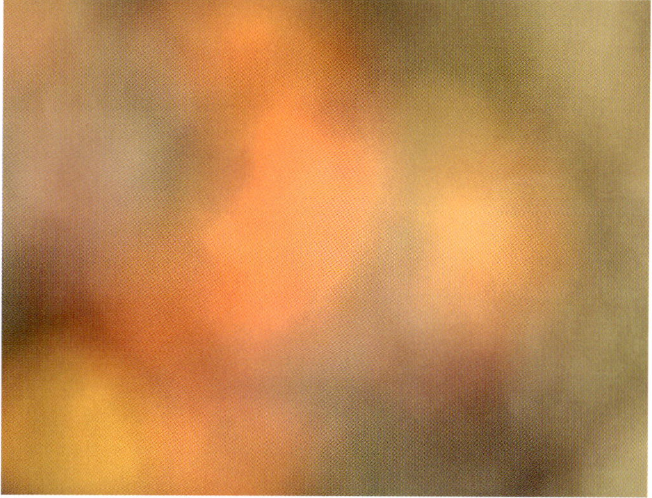

My choice of digital overlay, this was an out-of-focus photo of some orange roses.

180 degrees if you wish. When you're happy with the placement press the enter key.

At this point you need to adjust the opacity so that you can see the flower underneath – use the opacity slider in the 'Layers' panel on the bottom right of the screen. Start by bringing it down to about 40 and see what happens. I usually edit with the opacity set at about 40 but might end up using anything between 20 and 80; you can move the slider at any point. I have used a 60 per cent opacity in this instance as the flower itself has quite a strong colour and a 40 per cent opacity looked too pale against it.

You could actually stop at this point if you wanted an ethereal effect. However, in this case I would choose to remove some of the overlay that is directly over the flower. Click on the 'add layer mask' button; it's the one that looks like a camera on the bottom right.

Then choose the brush icon on the left-hand side of the screen and set the opacity at the top of the screen to about 80 per cent. Further to the left you can also change the size of your brush. With the mouse, paint away at the flower, going almost to the edges of the petals and stalk – but not quite. You'll probably need to change your brush size at different points while doing this.

You'll notice in the photo that I haven't painted the overlay off the stem yet, or the stamens at the top of the flower. To do the stem I usually set the brush opacity much lower, at about 30 per cent – be careful not to go over the edges!

I will then change my brush opacity down to about 40 per cent, zoom right in and set a much smaller brush size to do the edges of the flower and petals. This gives a softer approach and avoids the flower looking like it has been 'stuck on' to the background.

You're pretty much finished! I usually drag the slider back up to 100 per cent briefly to see if I've missed any bits, and then I move the slider up and down to decide the final opacity and what looks best. It's usually about 45–65 per cent but could be higher or lower as I indicated above.

When the image is saved, I might then take it back into Lightroom to add more/less colour or a graduated filter. In this instance I actually added the same texture on top again (still in Photoshop), and rotated it 180 degrees, as I wanted more colour on the right-hand side of the frame. Then I painted off the parts of this second layer that were over the flower. Finally, I opened the image in Lightroom and checked that I was happy with it. In this case I used a radial filter to add a little more colour to the background and then added a slight vignette.

The opacity slider in the 'Layers' panel in the bottom-right, of the Photoshop window. The slider is set to 60 per cent.

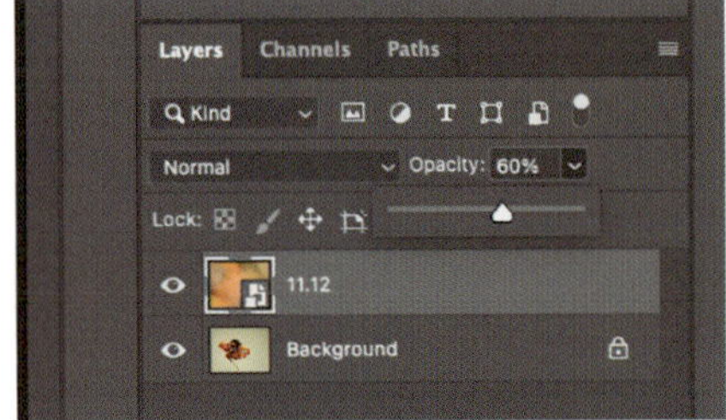

A screenshot showing the 'add layer mask' icon.

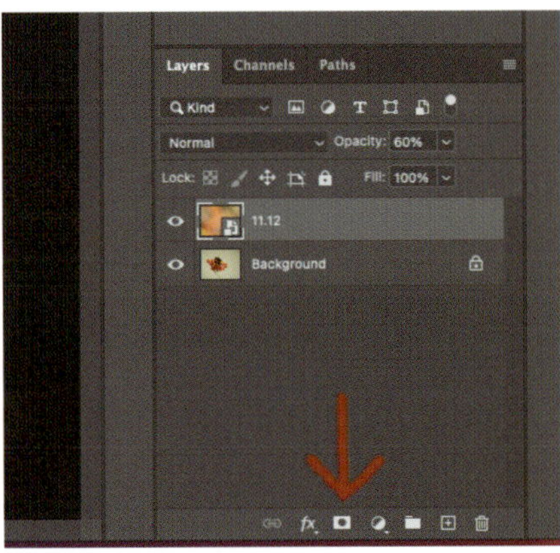

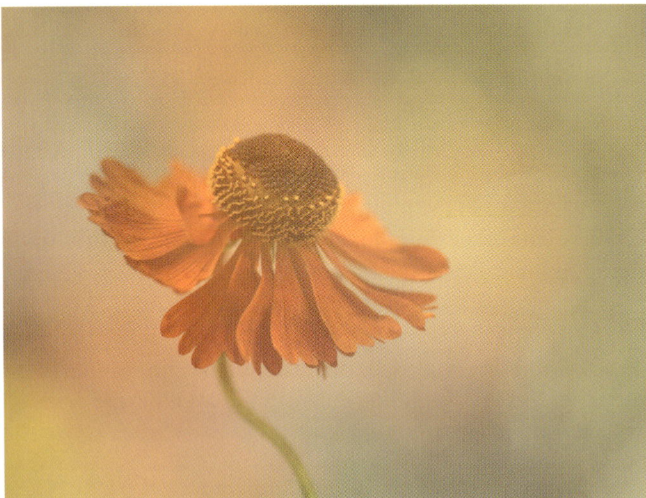

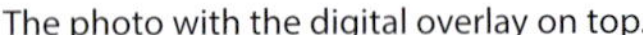

The photo with the digital overlay on top.

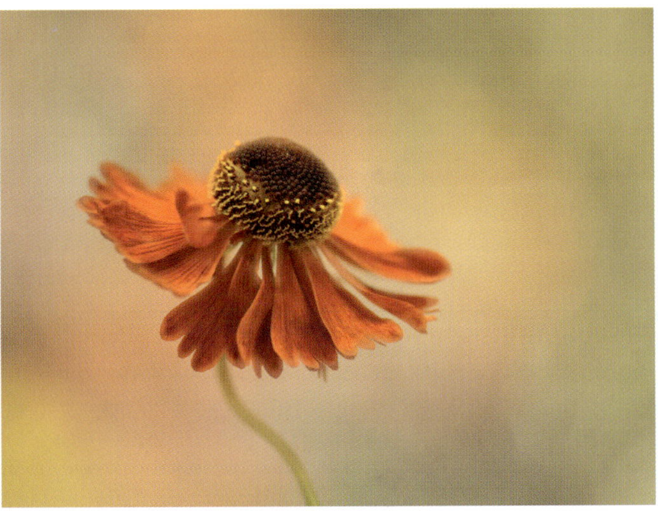

A half-completed version of the image where I have removed most of the layer on top of the flower, but have not yet taken the texture off the edges of the petals.

If you are using a texture, the final result might not be as close to nature as an overlay, which is why I usually save my textures for still-life photos: I like a more natural look on my flowers. But it's your prerogative and everything should be experimented with, to find styles and effects that suit you. Sometimes it's good to try something really bold with a texture or overlay; you may discover something that has real impact.

For me, the most important thing is to remember that a texture or overlay can't make a flower or plant that isn't interesting any better; its job is merely to enhance what is already there.

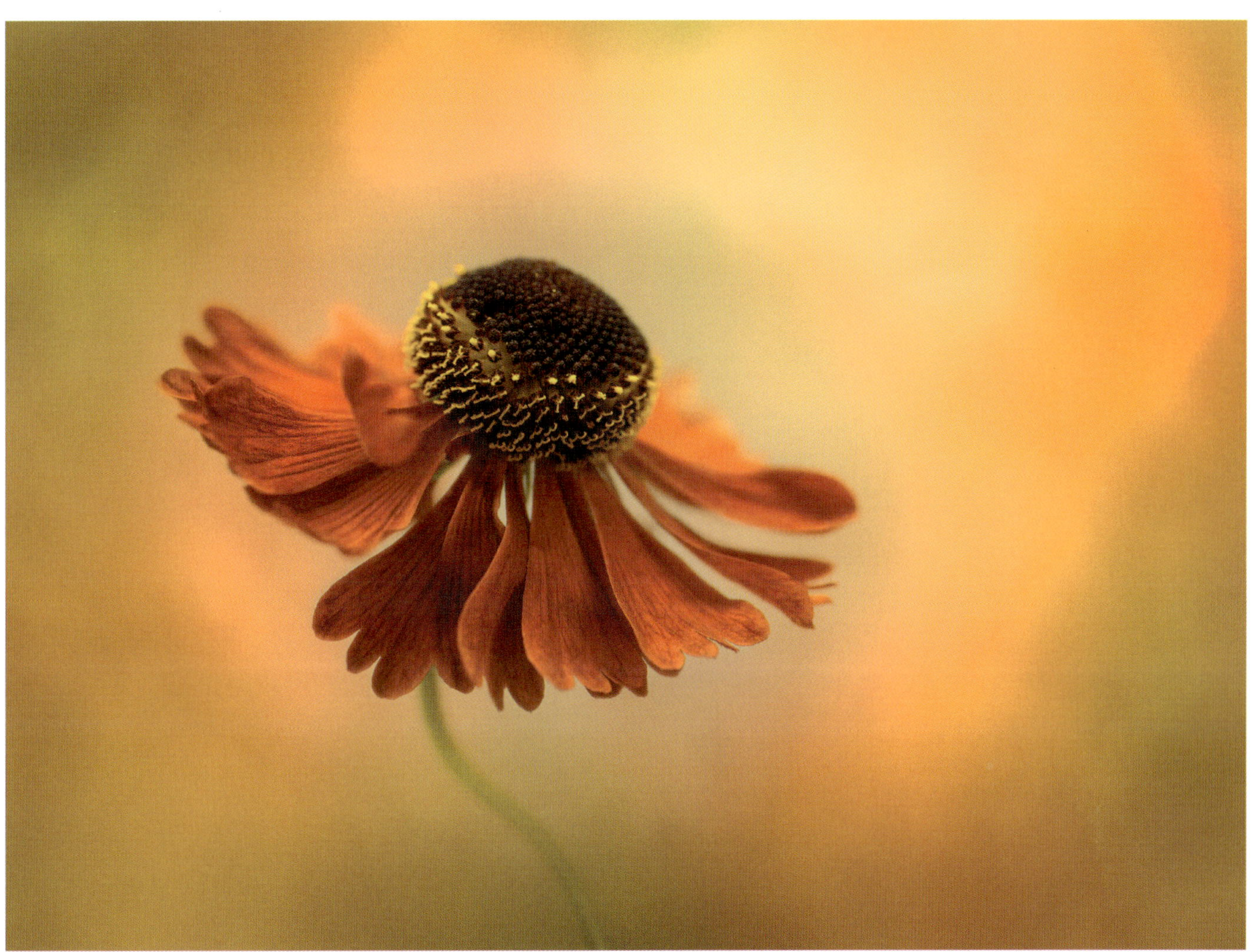

The finished image.

Flowers and plants to photograph in November

Insects begin to look for hibernation spots and the first frosts arrive. Berries give splashes of colour to the garden.

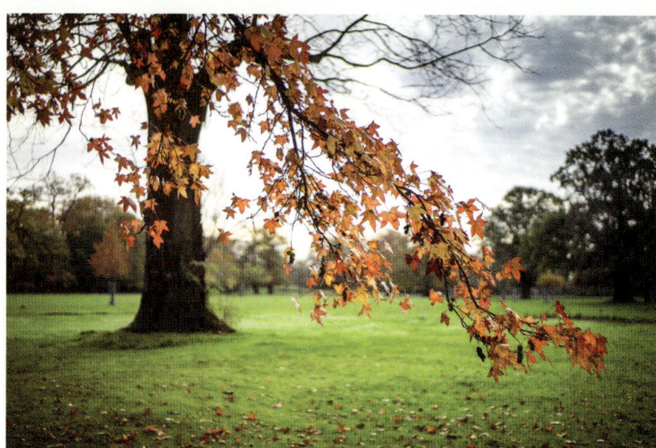

A low-hanging branch of a *Liquidambar styraciflua* tree. 1/4000 sec at f/2, 50mm vintage manual lens.

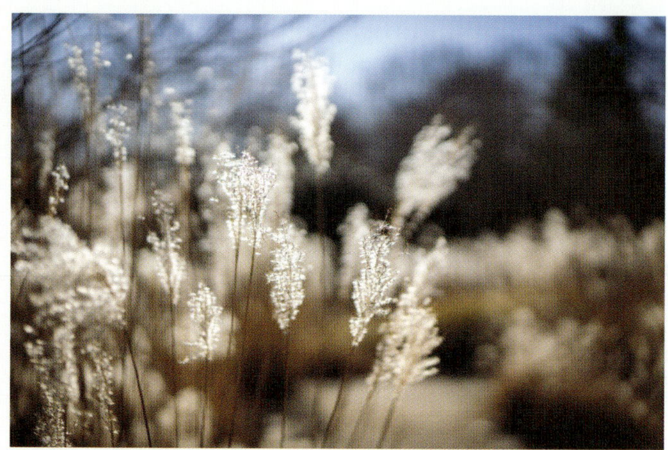

Backlit *Miscanthus* grass – 1/4000 sec at f/1.8, 55mm.

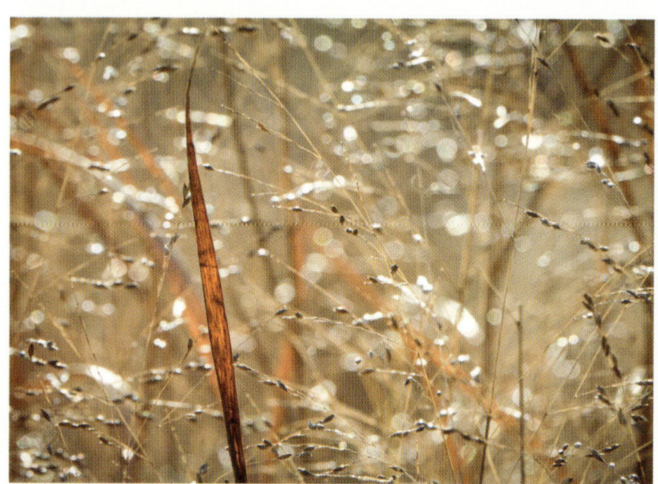

Backlit grasses – 1/320 sec at f/6.3, 220mm.

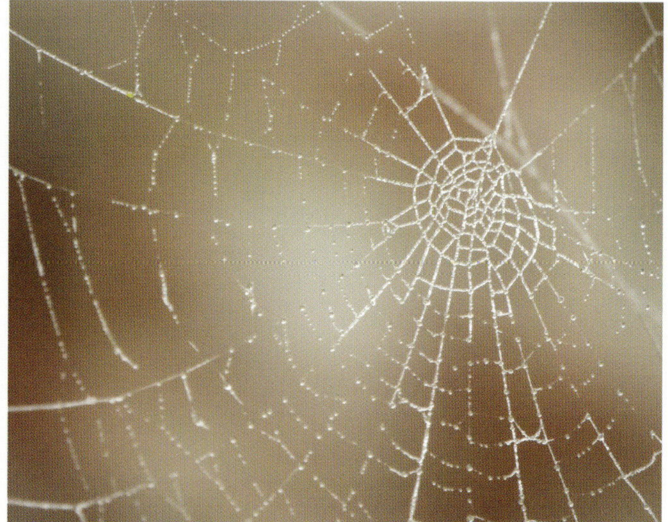

Spider web with dew – 1/250 sec at f/4, 210mm.

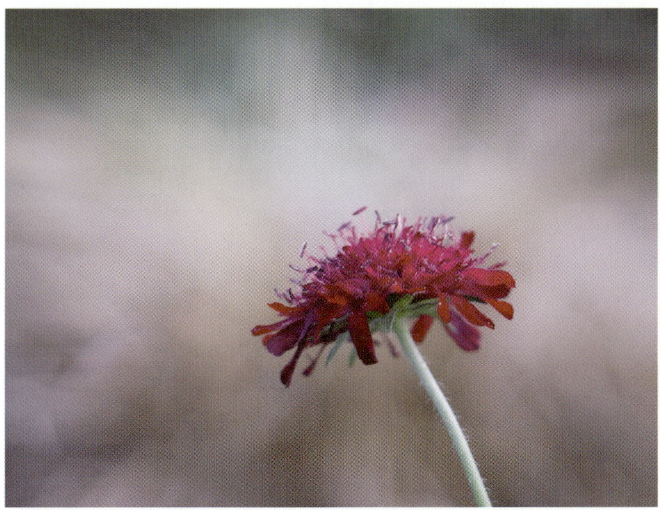

Knautia macedonica – 1/640 sec at f/2, 50mm vintage lens.

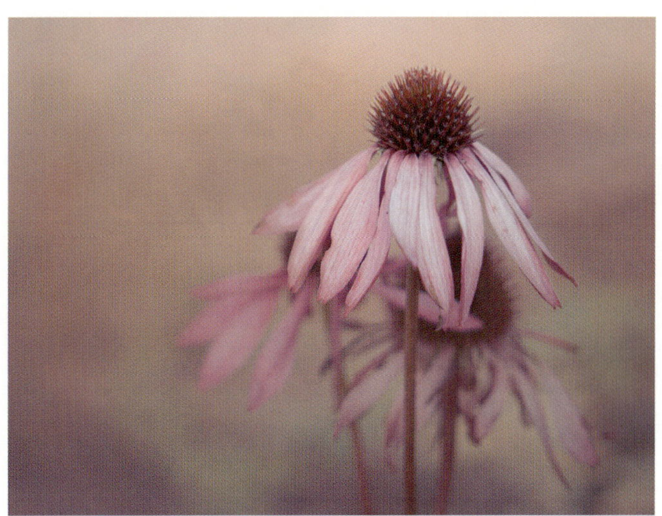

Echinacea – 1/400 sec at f/2, 50mm lens, texture added in the edit.

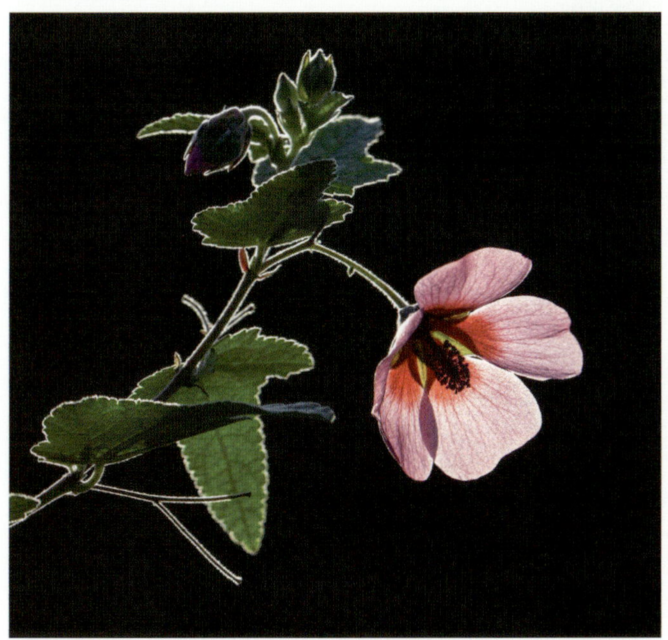

Backlit hibiscus flower – 1/400 sec at f/4, 180mm.

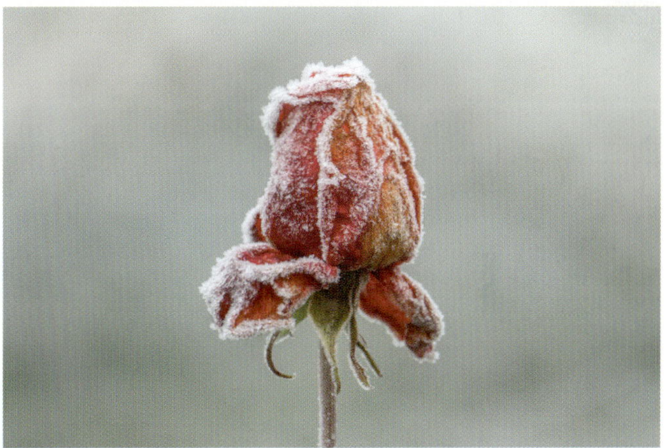

Frosted rose – 1/250 sec at f/4, 210mm.

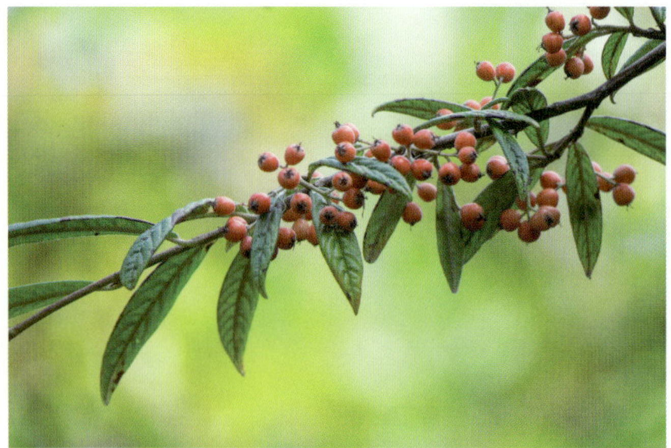

Cotoneaster berries – 1/100 sec at f/4.5, 205mm.

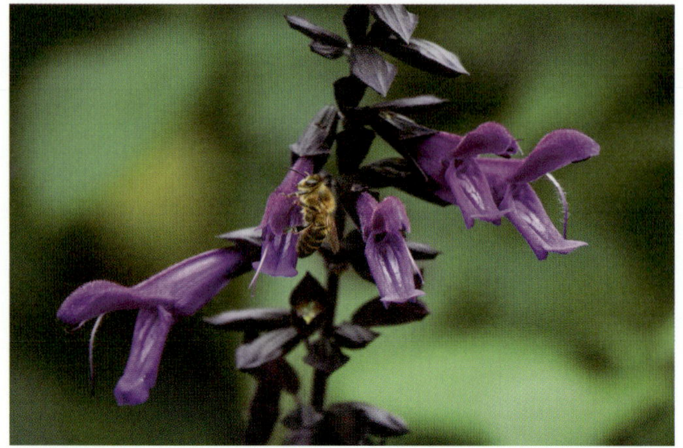

Salvia 'Amistad' – 1/250 sec at f/4, 220mm.

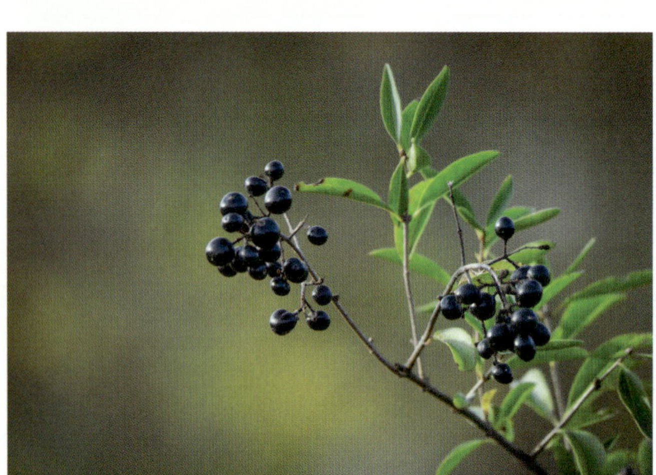

Ligustrum vulgare (wild privet) berries – 1/600 sec at f/4, 220mm.

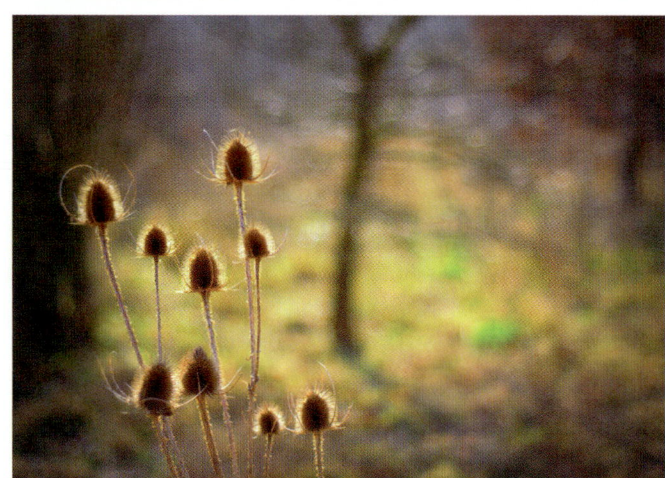

Dipsacus (teasel) – 1/6000 sec at f/1.7, 50mm vintage manual lens.

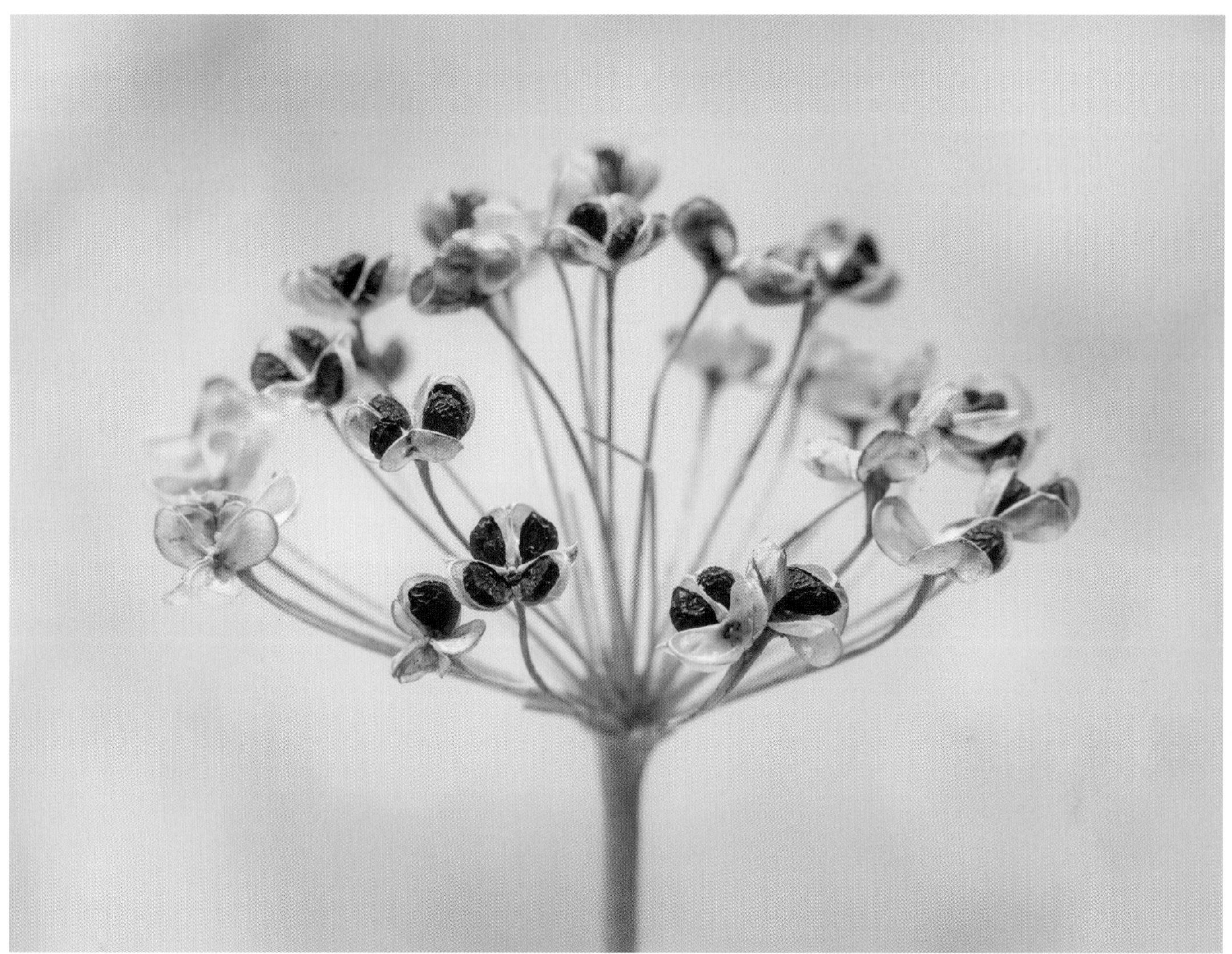

Allium seed head from my garden, photographed indoors with a white background and an overlay added in the edit.
1/8 at f/11, 105mm macro lens.

CHAPTER 12

How to Move Forward

> Which of my photographs is my favourite? The one I'm going to take tomorrow!
> IMOGEN CUNNINGHAM

Developing as a photographer creatively is tricky, as you need to balance the desire to find your own style with the need to experiment and try new things. If anything, I try to avoid adopting a signature style as I like to photograph so many varied subjects, both within the genre of flower and garden photography and outside of it. Having said this, I greatly admire the work of several photographers who have a totally unique style of their own (often this comes down to the way they edit their photos as much as their choice of subject) and this of course is an equally valid approach.

I keep two notebooks with ideas for my future photography; one in my camera bag and one next to my bed as I often get ideas in the night or when waking up. Here I scribble notes about the subjects I'd like to photograph or ideas I'd like to try when editing. After I had photographed the ladybird with a red ranunculus flower background at the beginning of Chapter 8, I had the idea that it could form part of a diptych – if ladybirds are red and black, wouldn't it be interesting to try to photograph another ladybird but with a black background? I couldn't work out at the time how to do this however as I didn't want to bring a ladybird into my house to photograph it against a black background – I hate moving creatures from their natural environment. So I had pushed the idea to the back of my mind (and my notebook) when I recently came across a ladybird on a dahlia that had black foliage. I knew that this could be the shot I was looking for but I only had an extension tube on me at the time (I was in a local public garden) and not my macro lens, and I knew that my non-branded tube with its manual focus was not as reliable. So I tracked the ladybird, taking many, many photos, over a period of about twenty minutes – it was moving about quite a bit and I knew that the shot failure rate would be high as I had to manually focus each time I pressed the shutter. Finally it went down the stalk and disappeared and I knew it was time to stop, not really knowing if I had succeeded. When I viewed the photos later on the computer there was one, out of about eighty, that was sharp, and this is the one you see at the start of this chapter – it has had very little editing, other than the background being darkened just a little more.

Had the weather been hot or rainy I may not have been as tenacious, and I think luck often has a great deal to do with one's success. But the more you can think about your photos and ideas for your photos, the more you will put yourself in

◀ Ladybird on a dahlia bud.

situations where everything comes together, and obviously the more practice you put in the more you will see your 'hit rate' begin to creep up.

BREAKING THE RULES

Once you feel that you've grasped the basic rules of photography it's probably time to break free a bit and be a bit more experimental. Sometimes, for example when you look at the results page of a photo competition and everyone is following the rule of thirds, or presenting perfectly exposed photos, things can get a bit monotonous. So presenting an image that is unique because it has *not* followed the rules can sometimes have real impact, but of course the chances of not pulling this off are high. In this chapter I will look at a few things that you can try to create images that are just a little bit different. Experimenting is key; try to develop the habit of either changing your position or a camera setting between each couple of photos that you take and this will be a good start.

The dark side

If you're faced with very poor lighting conditions, try making it a feature of the photograph. I'm actually very drawn to photos of flowers that would ordinarily be considered to be too dark – for me they often have a hint of mystery and uniqueness and can

Polemonium caeruleum (Jacob's ladder) with an out-of-focus red brick wall behind.

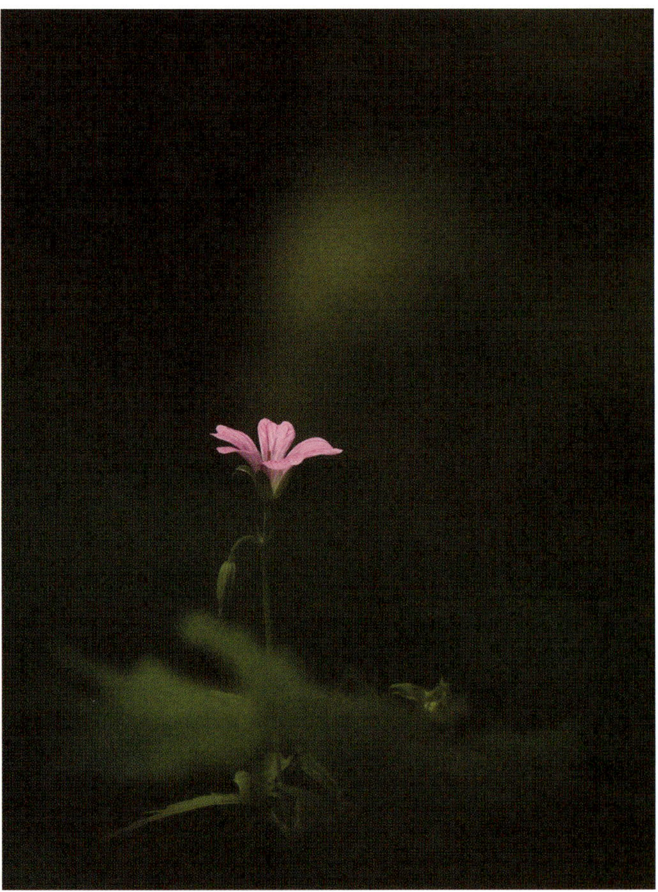

Small geranium in woodland in a patch of sunlight.

therefore connect with the viewer just because they are a bit unusual. Try to ensure that there is at least one point of light and sharpness in the picture, although this may not be part of your main subject. You'll almost definitely need to shoot in manual mode so that your shutter speed can be set faster than it would normally be if your camera were set to 'aperture priority'. This will mean that you can set the light level, rather than the camera.

High key

High key photography is a term for when a photograph is deliberately made overly bright with little or no shadow. Often backgrounds are pure white or a light pastel colour so that the subject is the only thing that commands attention. A high key image will usually have a limited amount of tonal values and limited contrast.

The easiest way to try high key flower photography is either to shoot against a white background and set your exposure to be brighter than you would normally (you can do this in the edit too) or to use a light pad and lay the flower on it. Paler flowers work best, as do those that are a little translucent, however a completely white flower would have little impact as it would get lost in the background. Composition is crucial as we have limited colour or light interplay to respond to, and simplicity here is usually important. To see good examples of high key photography (it is used in many different genres) search the internet or put #highkey into Instagram.

A clematis flower photographed at dusk in my garden. I held a small torch above it to illuminate the centre of the flower.

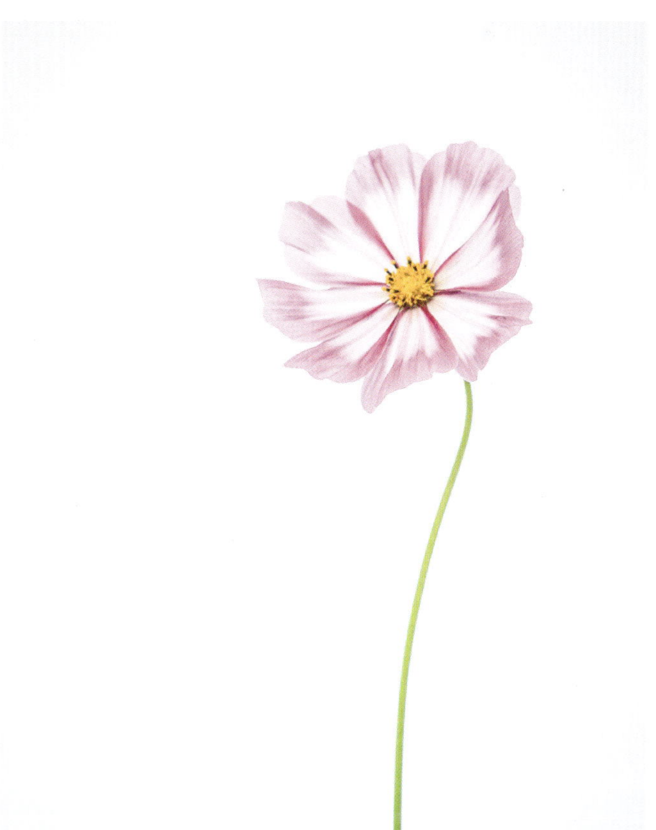

A high-key image of a cosmos flower.

Bright sunlight

Despite my recommendation in the second chapter that flowers work best photographed in diffused or cloudy light, sometimes you just need a hit of bright sunshine, and some flowers, like daffodils, many varieties of grasses, and veronica, just often seem to work better in sunlight. It works especially well with flowers whose petals are a little translucent so that light can shine through from inside or behind. You may need to reduce the highlights slightly in photos like these and sometimes lift the darker shadows.

Flowers which have flattish faces, such as daisies, can work well in sunlight as their petals are not raised up or curved enough to cast shadows back onto other petals. Yellow flowers, such as sunflowers, can also work well as yellow is such a 'sunny' colour.

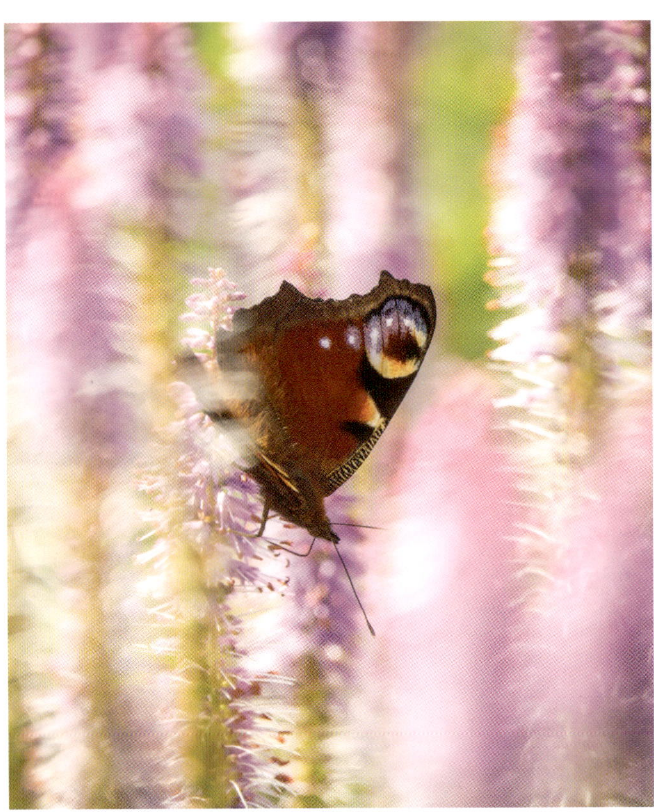

A peacock butterfly (*Aglais io*) in backlit veronica flowers.

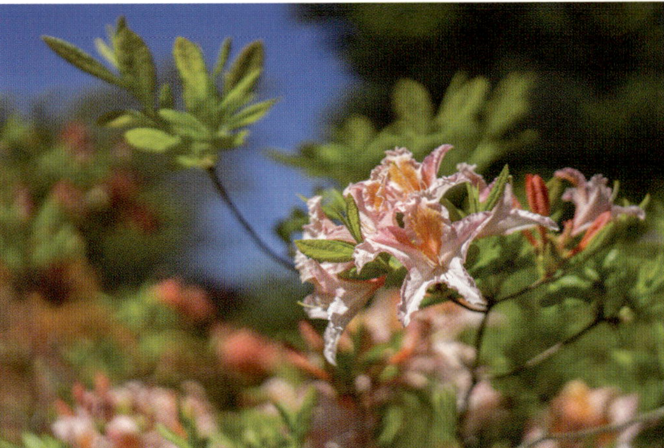

Azalea flowers in sunshine. Out-of-focus colours in the background are often richer in sunlight.

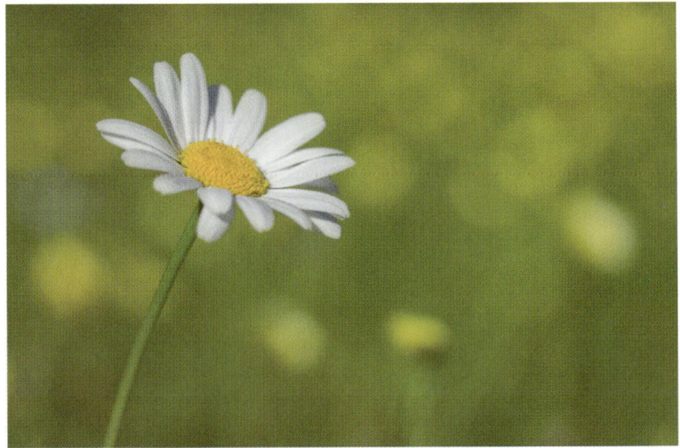

A daisy in sunlight; you can see the out-of-focus blobs of other daisies in the background.

Composition

Sometimes, the rules of composition can be too predictable and you might want to deliberately introduce a sense of imbalance or asymmetry by placing your subject (particularly if it is very small) near a top or bottom corner. This will give an impressive sense of scale (perhaps more akin to how it would be viewed in real life). If there is a patch of light falling on the subject this technique will work even better. I like this trick as it enhances the 'smallness' of the flower (or insect) and puts it in context.

Sometimes you can also choose to crop in quite drastically for maximum impact, like cropping a portrait to exclude most of the head apart from the features. If you do this with petals the textures and petal detail will suddenly stand out. If the photo features an insect it will also allow a closer view.

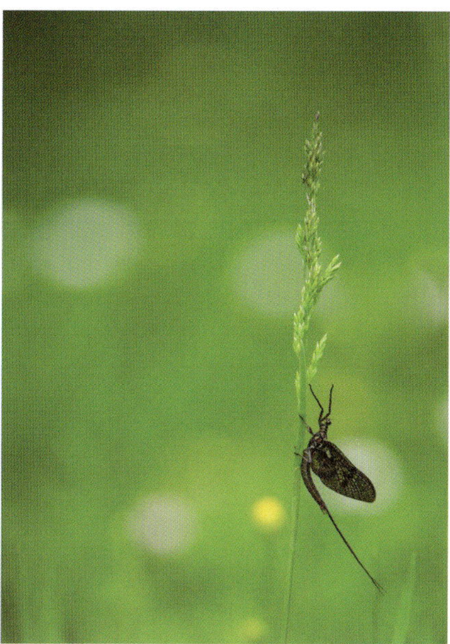

An *Ephemeroptera* (mayfly) on a grass stalk. Placing him in the bottom corner gives narrative – it could suggest he's about to fly upwards, or move further up the grass stalk. A landscape ratio would not have quite the same effect.

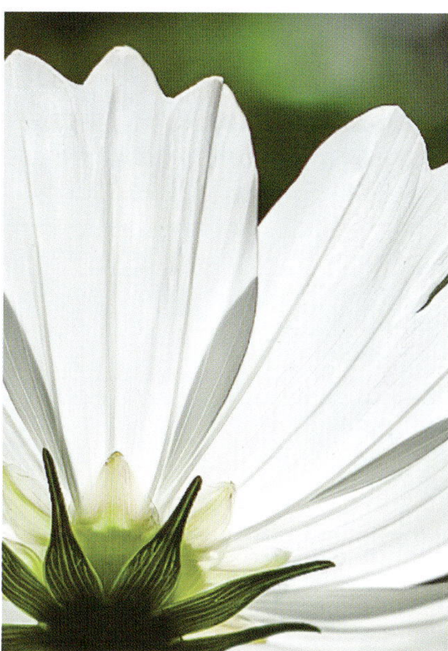

A white cosmos from behind, with a hard crop to feature its attractive sepals.

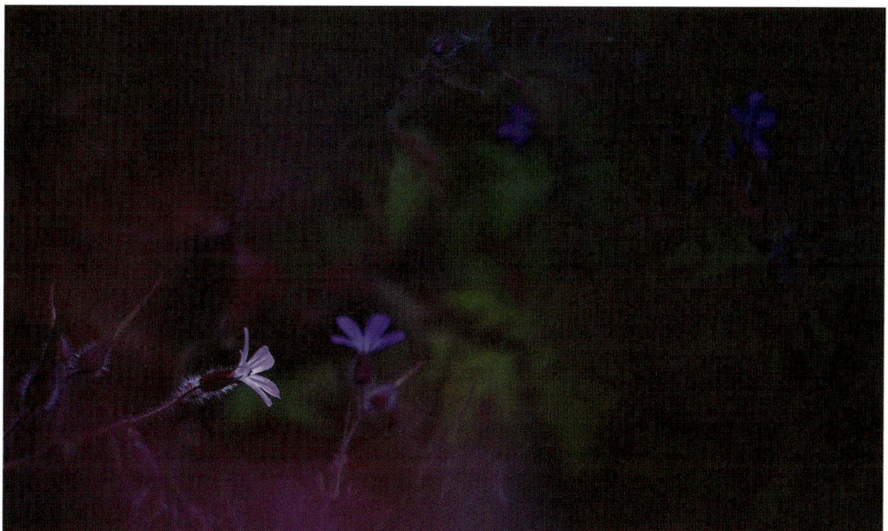

Geranium robertianum (herb Robert) with one flower caught in sunlight in the very bottom left corner. Because of the woodland darkness of the rest of the scene our eye goes straight to the flower. These tiny flowers are favourites of mine; they are so delicate and at certain times of the year, their foliage is a rich magenta colour.

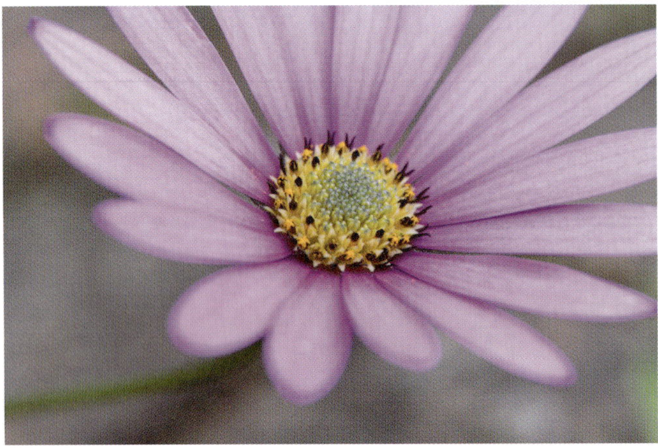

An *Osteospermum* travels into the frame from the left but is cropped from above so that we can see its centre more clearly.

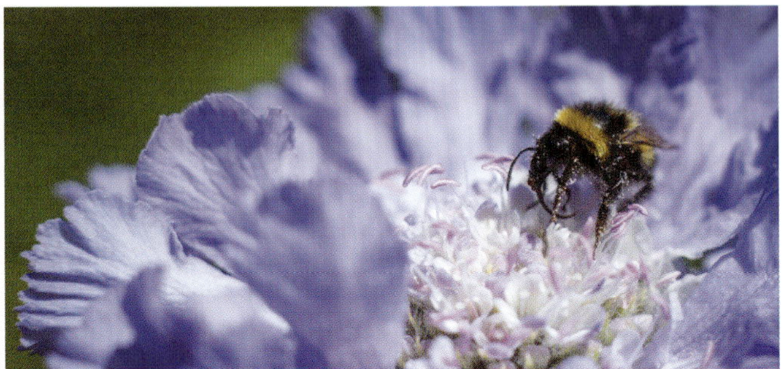

A bumblebee on a *Knautia* flower – this crop allows a closer look at the pollen stuck to the bee, and still gives plenty of flower context.

Unusual perspectives

Consider shooting flowers in gardens from atypical angles (from underneath for example) – sometimes it can really work. This may of course mean that you have to lie on the floor and shoot upwards but it can be worth it if you have the mobility to do this.

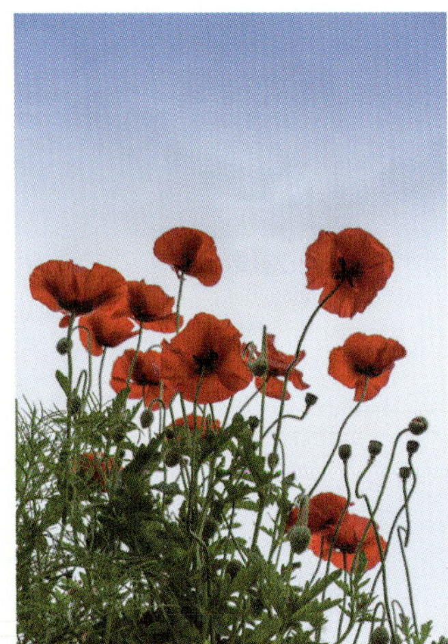

A group of poppies shot from below gives the impression that they're taller than they actually are, and quite imposing.

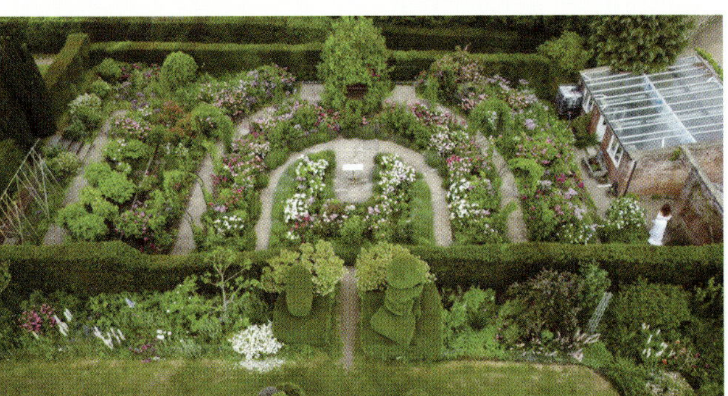

An image taken with my drone camera of a local rose garden – it shows very clearly the stunning symmetry of the garden, which will have been very carefully planned by its designer but rarely comprehended by people walking through the garden at ground level. If I take my drone camera to a garden I always get permission from the garden owner first and I always shoot outside of garden opening times so that no one is disturbed. They can be dangerous and at the least very irritating if you are trying to enjoy the peace and quiet of a garden you have paid money to visit.

Intentional Camera Movement

Intentional Camera Movement (ICM) is all about deliberately breaking the rules concerning shutter speed – it aims to capture the subject in a more Impressionistic or abstract way.

To try ICM I'd recommend switching to 'shutter priority' mode (often 's' on the top dial) and setting the shutter speed to about 0.3 of a second. Ordinarily if you take a photo with a long shutter speed like one second, it will be completely white as so much light enters the camera, so you'll need to balance the shutter speed with a very narrow aperture (I often use the narrowest one available on my camera) and a low ISO of 100 or 64. Review the photos you take on the rear screen and experiment with your exposure triangle – the light on the day will make a massive difference so you'll need to be flexible. You may also need to lighten or darken the photo considerably in the edit so I would definitely shoot in raw. The 'dehaze' slider in Lightroom also works really well with ICM as it gives increased definition to the subject, and the 'contrast' and 'clarity' sliders are also useful. I have listed the EXIF setting of all my ICM photos so you can see how they can vary quite widely.

Some photographers will use a tripod for ICM but I usually handhold, pressing the shutter button just after I have started moving the camera. Success with this technique comes from finding out which direction of movement works best. In nature we often deal with verticals – trees and flower stalks and so on, and vertical lines work really well when trying out this technique for the first time. I usually position my camera above the point of interest, press the shutter and sweep vertically downwards. This technique involves a lot of trial and error – you may need a longer shutter speed (depending on the available light).

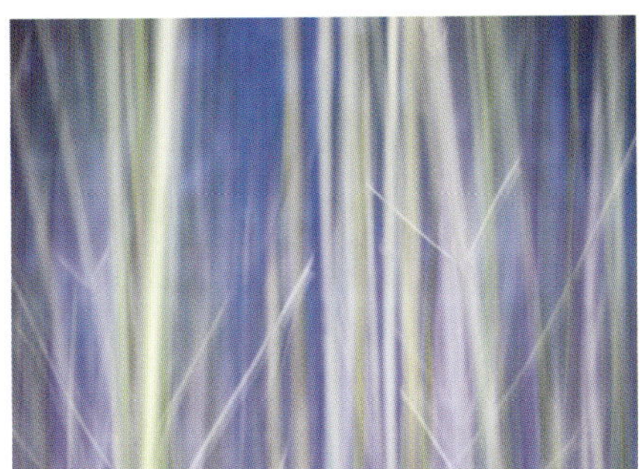

To get this photo of yellow *Cornus* (dogwood) stems, I moved the camera vertically downwards quickly, starting level with the top of my head and ending level with my chest. Moving the camera downwards often works best for things growing upwards. It was quite a gloomy cloudy day in January so I thought I'd try something different. The settings were 1 sec at f/11, 100mm, ISO 64.

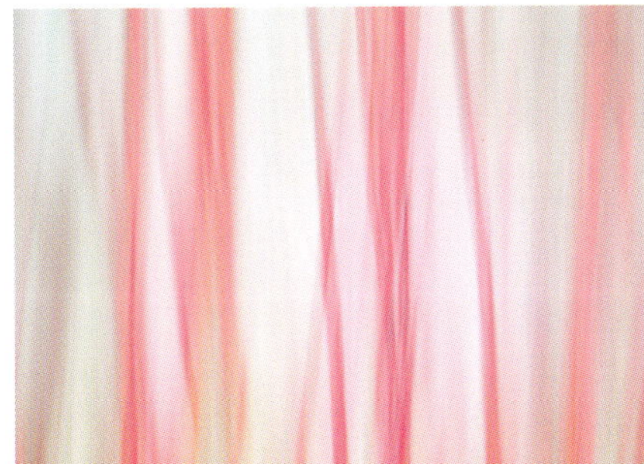

Another dogwood ICM; this time the stems of the shrub were red, with a light brown shrub behind. The settings were 0.6 secs at f/11, 220mm, ISO 64.

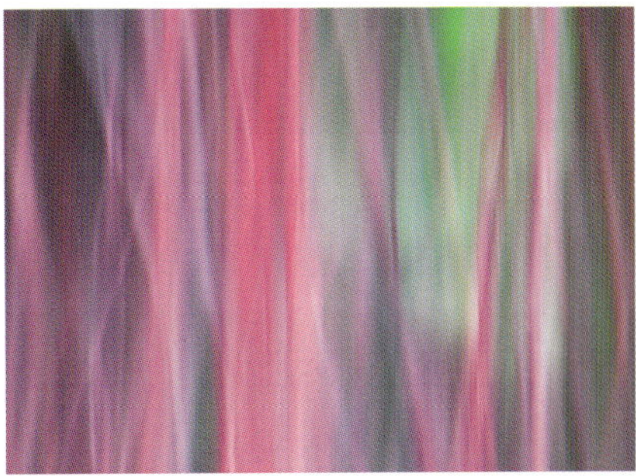

This dogwood had bright red stems with grass behind, which is the green in the photo. I added quite a bit of contrast and saturation to these photos to bring out the colours of this vivid winter shrub. The settings were 0.4 secs at f/5.6, 220mm, ISO 64.

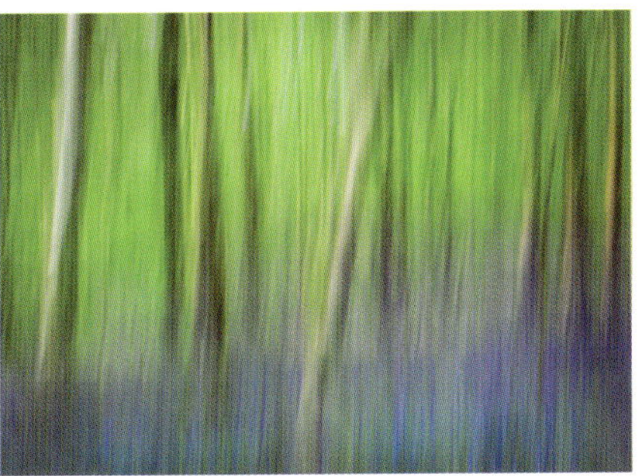

A bluebell wood – ⅓ sec at f/16, 32mm, ISO 64.

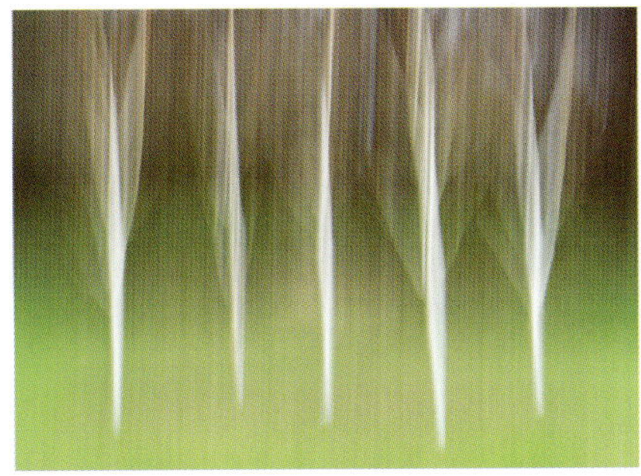

Betula pendula (silver birch) saplings – ¼ sec at f/22, 55mm, ISO 64.

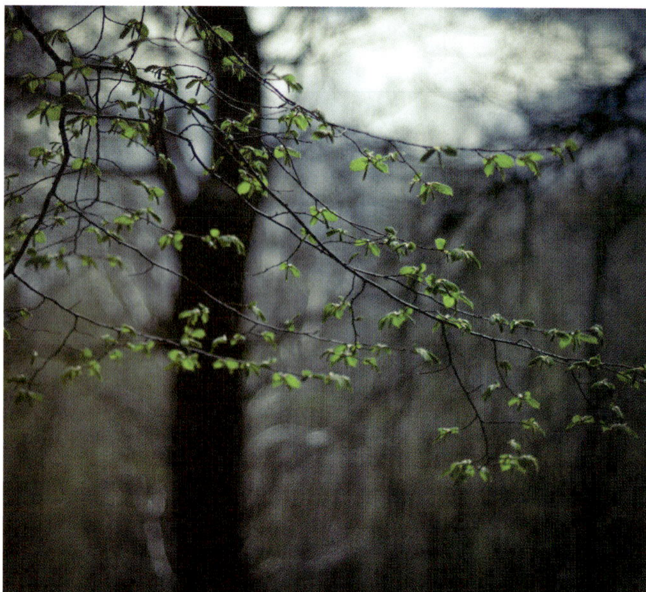

A beech tree in spring photographed with a vintage lens. The focus is on the leaves rather than the trunk and the lens together with the light gives an ethereal effect.

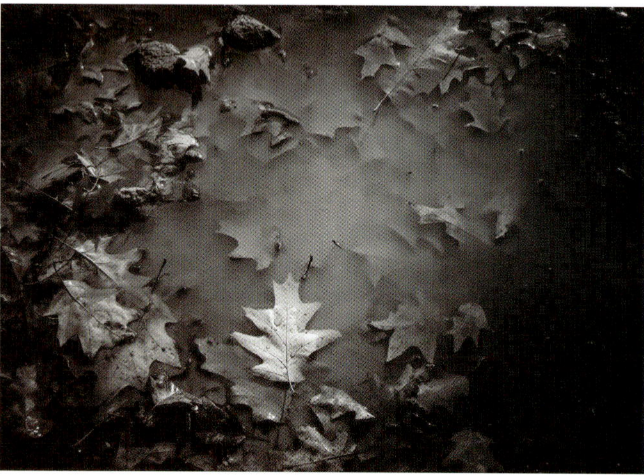

Leaves in a puddle – one lighter one draws our attention near the front.

Be experimental!

OK, so it might not work, but if you don't try you'll never know! The challenge here is often to photograph the mundane and try to make it look interesting... I love to try out new ideas so I don't get stuck in a rut with my photography and lose the creative urge. Just a leaf in a puddle might actually make a good photo but you might need to look at the scene for a little while to decide what to focus on or how to frame the composition. Look for interesting light and ordinary things that have the potential to become extraordinary.

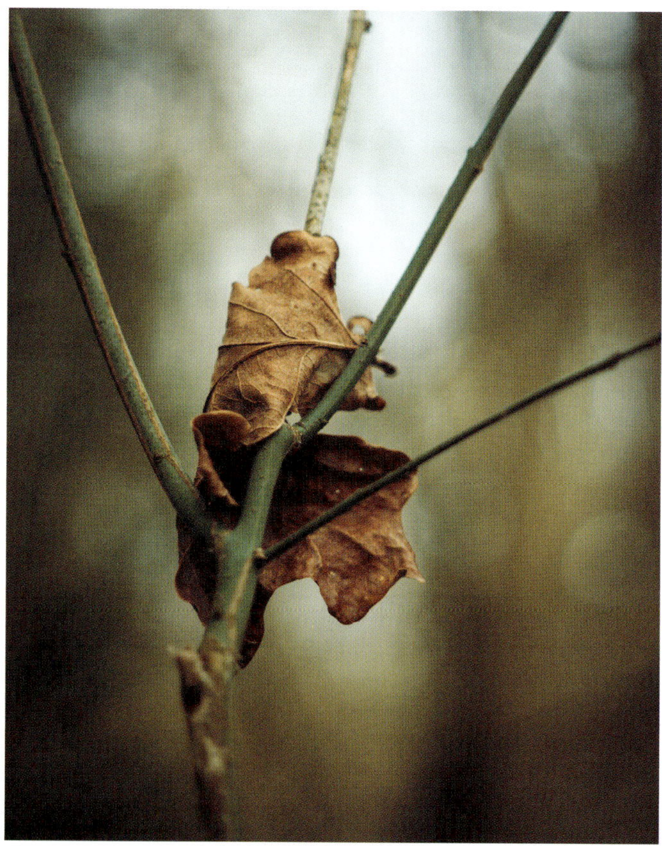

I discovered this leaf that had been shaped around a small branch as a result of being blown repeatedly in one direction by the wind all winter. The light in the wood behind gives a halo effect and the very shallow depth of field gives interesting bokeh; this was taken with another vintage lens at f/1.7.

Inspiration

For me, getting better at photography is about being inspired by art, other photography and nature. It is important to realize that inspiration can come from other genres of art and photography and not just garden and flower photography. A cathedral interior with towering columns might inspire you to take a different kind of forest picture, and so on. Your tastes will develop and it is often emotion rather than skill that creates an excellent photo. Of course, having the skill to react quickly with your camera when you see the shot you want is important too; fiddle around with settings for too long and the amazing light you saw may disappear.

BEING PROUD OF YOUR ACHIEVEMENTS

Every so often, look back at photos you took a while ago. If you've developed as a photographer, this might make you cringe slightly, as you've made progress since then. But it shouldn't stop you acknowledging every stage in your photographic journey. This is extremely important – to develop your craft and your style you have to produce photos that you've enjoyed taking and have been really pleased with when seeing them on a computer, printed or online.

This is one of the first flower photos I took, many years ago.

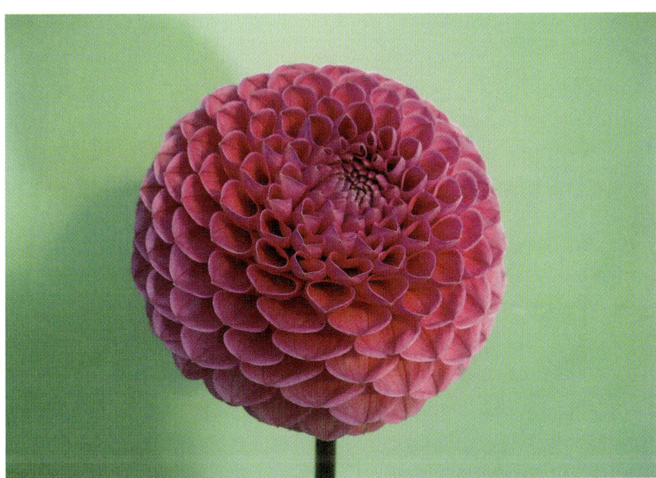

A ball dahlia, photographed against a green wall in my house.

I remember thinking that it was beautiful and being so delighted that I'd taken it. If I were to critique the image now, I'd say that possibly my response at the time was to the beauty of the *flower* rather than the photo itself, and that the two shadows on the left were rather distracting. But it made me happy at the time and this should not be overlooked. Taking pleasure in your own creations will drive you to take more photos, which will become better over time.

While many people enjoy taking photos purely for the enjoyment of it, some go further and build a website to show or sell their work. If you have the Adobe Lightroom and Photoshop subscription, with this (at the time of writing) you get five free

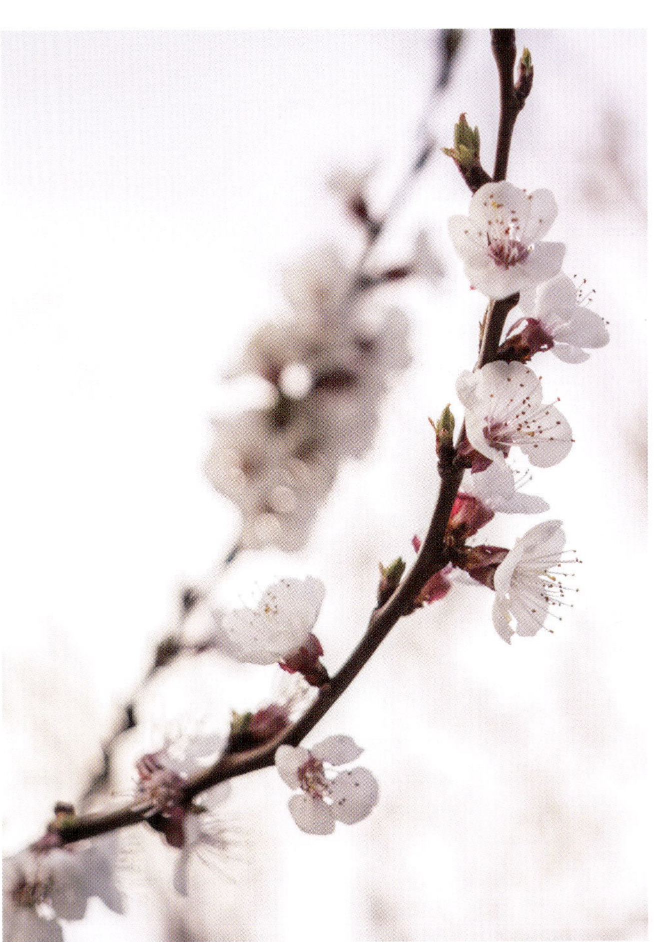

One of my most popular greeting card designs; apricot blossom photographed in my garden. I can never predict which cards will be most popular.

websites, and this is how my own website is created. I watched a couple of YouTube videos at the beginning to understand how to set it up and am now very pleased with the finished result. Alternatively you could print your best photos and hold a mini-exhibition in your local hall or church, perhaps as a joint venture with some friends. These things are usually very easy to arrange once you know who to contact, and seeing your work on a wall is a fantastic experience.

I turn many of my photos into greeting cards; it is nice to always have a supply of cards for birthdays or special occasions. I also sell cards and prints at several local gardens and in local arts and craft shops. Many online card companies will provide a template that makes the card design easier – this way you may not need to do the work in Photoshop. It can seem costly per printed card but if you buy in bulk to keep the cost down and sell at twice the money (or just under) you paid for the card to be printed, you should still earn a reasonable profit.

Competitions

Many photographers are attracted to competitions and this can be a nice way to take part in something national or even international and gain recognition for your work, although becoming successful can take many years. If you do enter your photos into competitions, my only advice would be to enter ones judged by professional photographers, as many others will often be a popularity contest (for example, who can get the most 'likes') rather than a photography contest.

The three big competitions for flower and garden photography are the International Garden Photographer of the Year, the Royal Horticultural Society's Photographic Competition and the Close-up Photographer of the Year, which has a Plants and Fungi section. All are international competitions and have websites but not all are free to enter (although the RHS one currently is). If you plan to enter competitions, my advice would be:

- Never enter in the last few days before the deadline. Be organized and try to enter as early as possible. If you take a stunning photo after you've entered, you can always enter it the following year.
- Read the rules and instructions really carefully. Some allow digital manipulation, some don't, and all will have specific requirements about the size of photo they wish you to upload.
- Scrutinize every inch of your photo zoomed in to 100 per cent before you enter it. Clone out all dust spots and any distractions like dust on the petals (if it's allowed). Even pollen can be a distraction sometimes.
- Look at the photos of previous winners of the competition – not just the previous year, but every year that the competition has run (if the photos are available on the respective websites). This way you'll have a solid understanding of the type of image the judges like. Styles and trends go in and out of fashion but seeing the photography you are potentially 'up against' is very helpful.

Social media, books and magazines

You may already post your photos to social media and use it to inspire you, seeing what other photographers producing similar output are doing. Looking at good photography online or in books or magazines on a daily basis can only help you move forward in your development. It will develop your sense of taste and style, two things that will undoubtedly evolve on your photography journey.

If you're not aware of many photographers working in areas that interest you, try searching for #gardenphotography, or #flowerphotography in the search box on Instagram and then scroll down and browse to find the photographers that interest you. If you click on their profile photo you can then look at their other work. You can search for different flower varieties, for example #daisies or #rose or by their common or botanical names. I also follow many artists and art collections, as for me art is just as inspiring as photography.

You can use the Instagram app on a computer or laptop if you find peering at small images on a phone makes them too difficult to see clearly.

I honestly believe that Instagram can be like getting a new book full of photos that amaze and inspire you every single day. I find it useful to bookmark them to collections so I can view them again later.

If you're thinking of sharing your own photos on Instagram I'd suggest quality over quantity. Your wall should be representative of you and your photography. Posting once a week or fortnight should be more than enough to start with and you may not even wish to share your own photography (lots of people use Instagram solely to find inspiration), in which case you can set your account to 'private'. The most beautiful Instagram

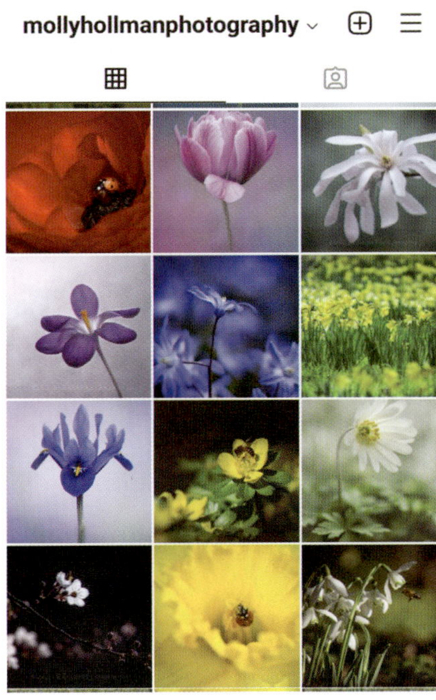

A screenshot of part of my Instagram wall. I only post with current photos as I take them, so my wall is like a chronological journey of my photography. If you decide you don't like one at a later date you can always delete it.

'walls' are connected by a theme and I know photographers who have different accounts on Instagram so they can show their different genres separately. If you want followers (which of course is not a necessity) it's really important to use hashtags in the description and comments. You can watch videos on the internet about how to do this. I watermark the photos I put on Instagram with a very opaque and subtle watermark, near the bottom, for the simple reason that I have had photos stolen (and even found one that had been entered into a competition) before I did this. There are ways to get rid of a watermark of course, but the presence of one might at least make someone think twice.

Aside from social media, books can be just as inspirational, if not more so, and there is something very special about seeing a great photo in print, especially if it's part of a similar collection or genre that interests you. See if you can find copies of the *International Garden Photographer of the Year* book second hand. This book prints the finalists and winners of its annual competition each year and is a large, beautifully produced book. Seek out books about flowers in art – there are many – and see what you like and what inspires you.

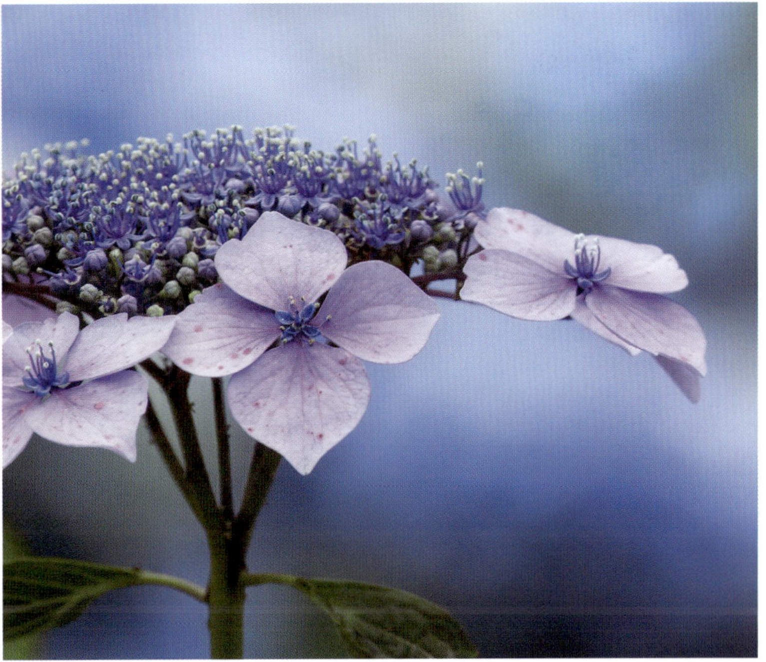

Many people assume that Instagram photos need to have a square crop, but this is no longer true. There is a button made of two arrows < > at the bottom left of the 'add photo' screen that will let you expand the crop to a landscape ratio. Having said this, you might decide you actually prefer it as a square crop, as was the case with this photo.

Flowers and plants to photograph in December

Some flowers such as roses and rudbeckia linger on, but seed heads of the flowers already finished give great sculptural interest.

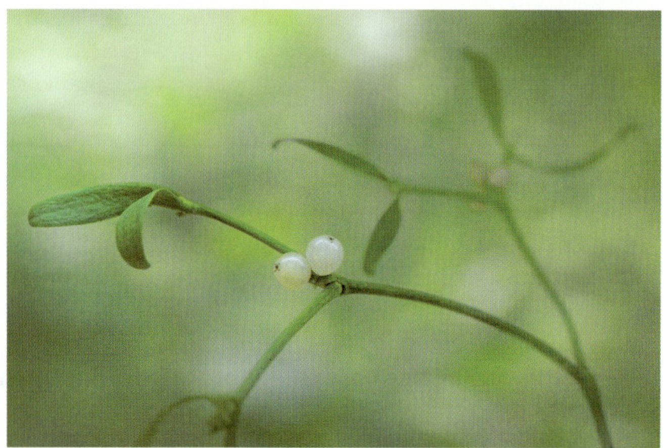

Viscum album (mistletoe) – 1/125 sec at f/2, 55mm with an extension tube.

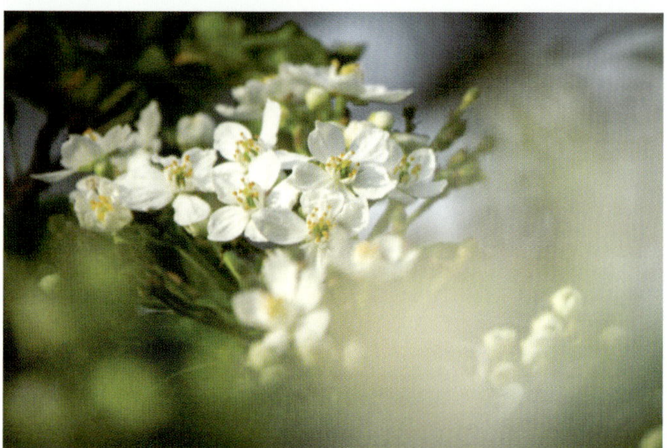

Choisya – 1/200 sec at f/3, 210mm.

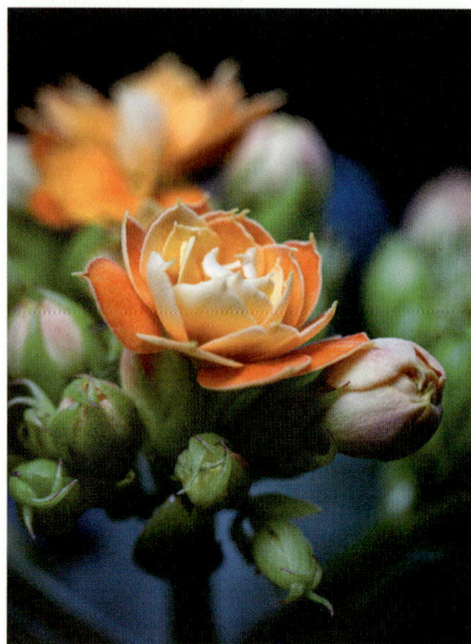

Kalanchoe – 1/180 sec at f/2, 50mm. Photographed indoors (it's one of my houseplants).

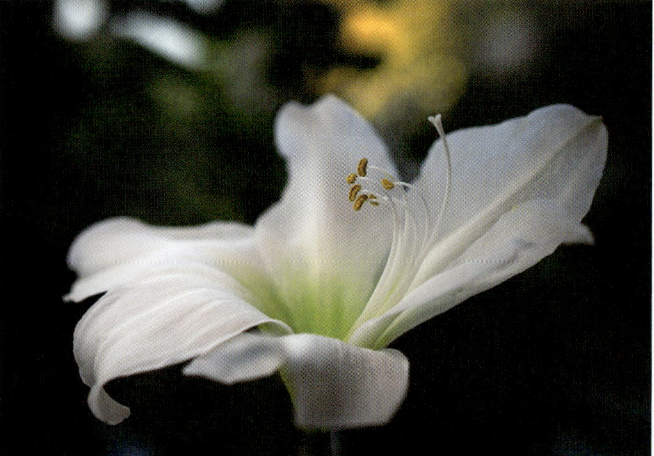

Hippeastrum or amaryllis – 1/800 sec at f/2.5, 55mm. Photographed indoors with my garden through the window behind.

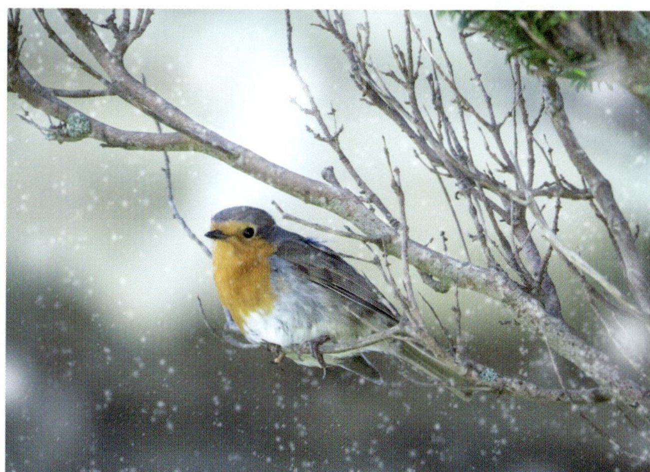

Robin – 1/500 sec at f/4, 220mm. I added a snow overlay purchased on the internet.

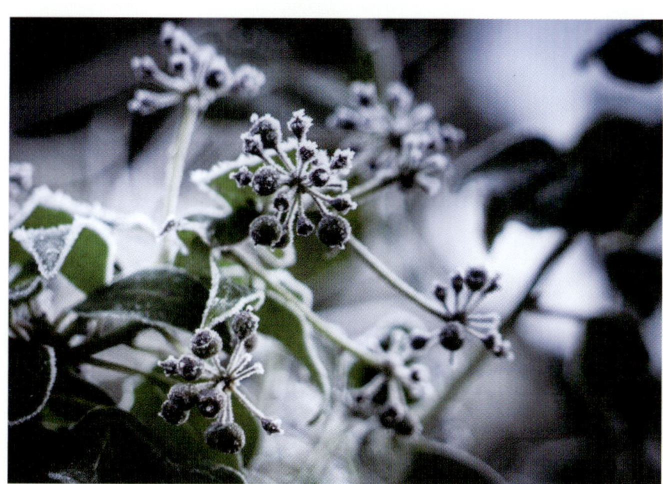

Frosted ivy – 1/400 sec at f/1.7, 50mm vintage lens.

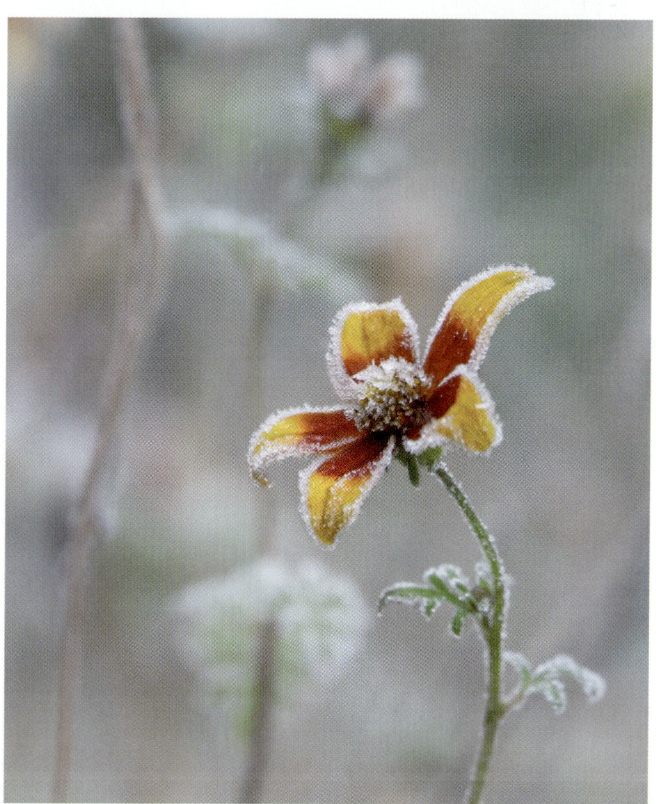

Frosted bidens – 1/250 sec at f/4, 220mm.

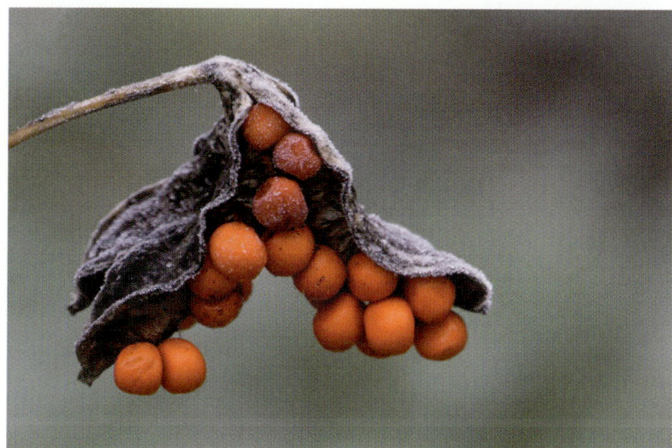

Frosted *Iris foetidissima* berries – 1/250 sec at f/4, 220mm.

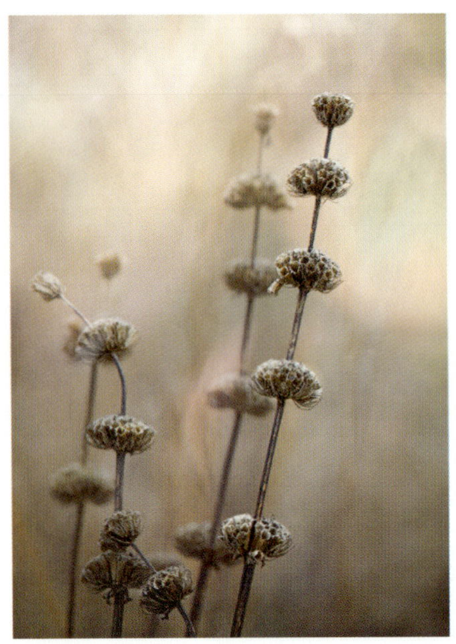

Phlomis seed heads – 1/80 sec at f/4, 140mm. Overlay added in the edit.

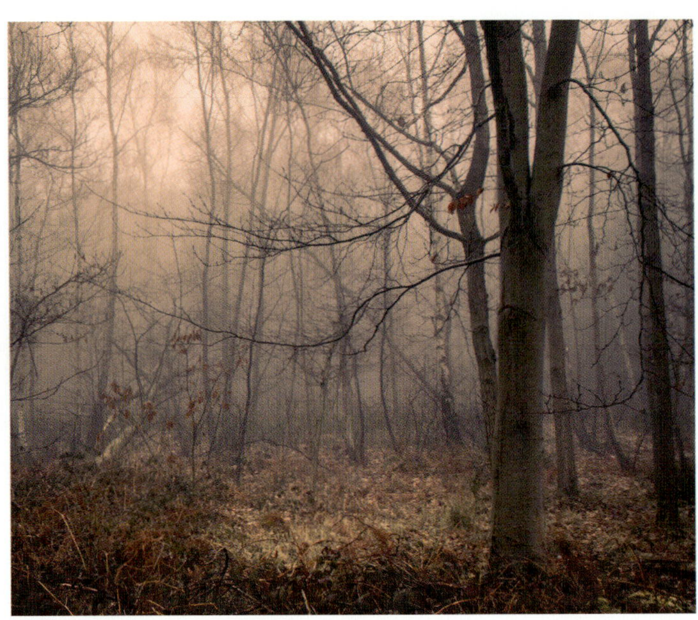

Trees in the mist at sunrise – 1/100 sec at f/8, 50mm lens. Colour changed slightly in the edit.

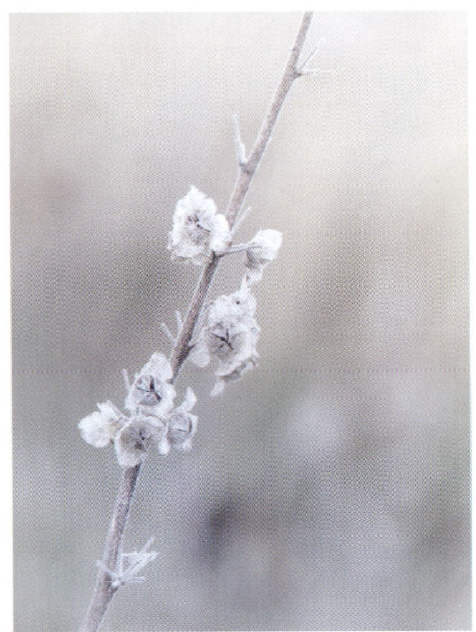

Seed heads – 1/160 sec at f/4, 185mm.

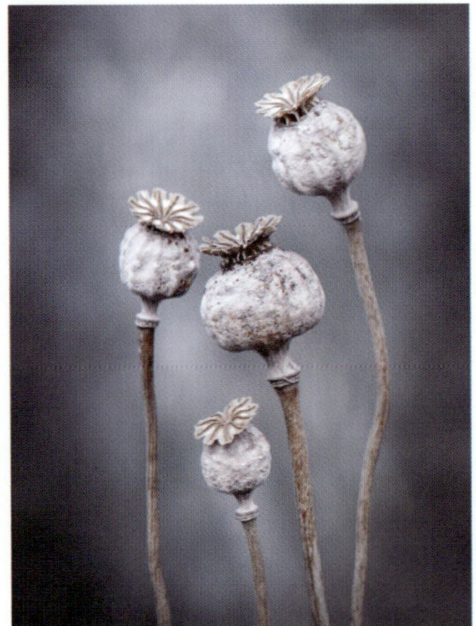

Poppy seed heads – 1/640 sec at f/4, 20mm.

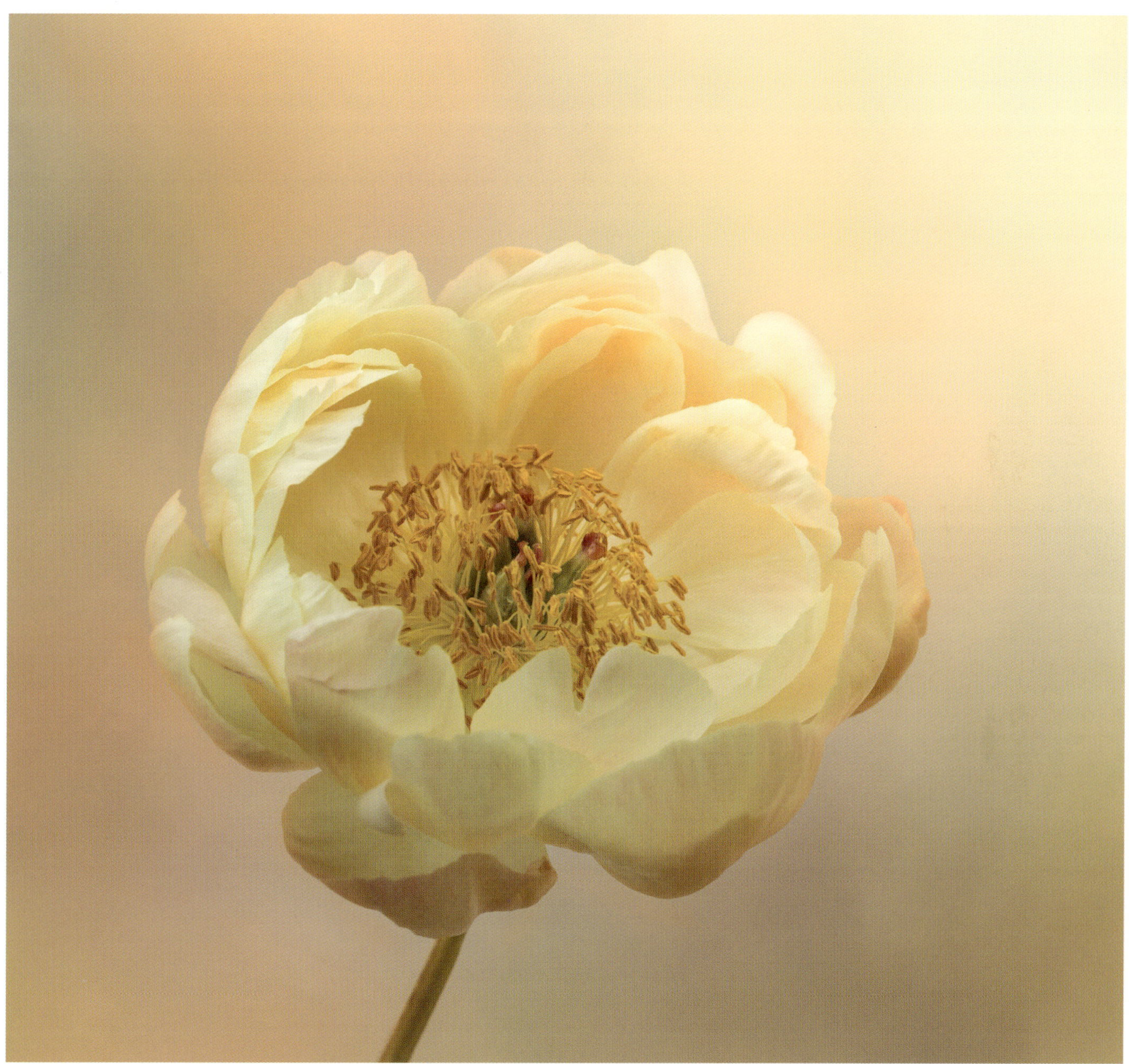

Peony 'Coral Charm', photographed indoors. Overlay added in the edit.

First published in 2022 by
The Crowood Press Ltd
Ramsbury, Marlborough
Wiltshire SN8 2HR

enquiries@crowood.com
www.crowood.com

This impression 2025

British Library Cataloguing-in-Publication Data
A catalogue record for this book is available from the British Library.
For product safety-related questions contact productsafety@crowood.com.

ISBN 978 0 7198 4053 1

Cover design: Sergey Tsvetkov

Dedication
For Ross, Arthur and Edward

Graphic design and typeset by Peggy & Co. Design
Printed and bound in India by Parksons Graphics Pvt. Ltd.

Thank you to:

- Ross, Arthur and Edward Underwood for supporting me and waiting patiently on garden walks
- Len Hollman for inspiring my photographic journey
- Esther Hollman from whom I inherited my love of flowers and gardens
- Poppy Hollman for copy editing
- Graeme Watts for plant advice
- Gary Neville and David Kilpatrick for technical advice
- My Guild of Photographers 'Buddy Group' for their help and encouragement, especially Claire, Jayne and Laura
- Sarah Vinall and Benjamin Arthur for early inspiration when I was starting out as a photographer
- Alex Wilkinson of Wilkinson Cameras
- The Twitter garden and wildlife community for their inspiration and occasional assistance with insect identification.

My favourite local gardens (with thanks to their owners and head gardeners who have been so accommodating over the years):

- Belmont House and Gardens, near Faversham, Kent
- Mount Ephraim, near Faversham, Kent
- Doddington Place Gardens, near Faversham, Kent
- Goodnestone Park Gardens, near Sandwich, Kent
- Godinton House, near Ashford, Kent
- Quex Park and Gardens, near Birchington, Kent

For further information about the author, visit:

- www.mollyhollman.myportfolio.com
- www.instagram.com/mollyhollmanphotography
- www.facebook.com/mollyhollmanphotography
- www.twitter.com/HollmanMolly

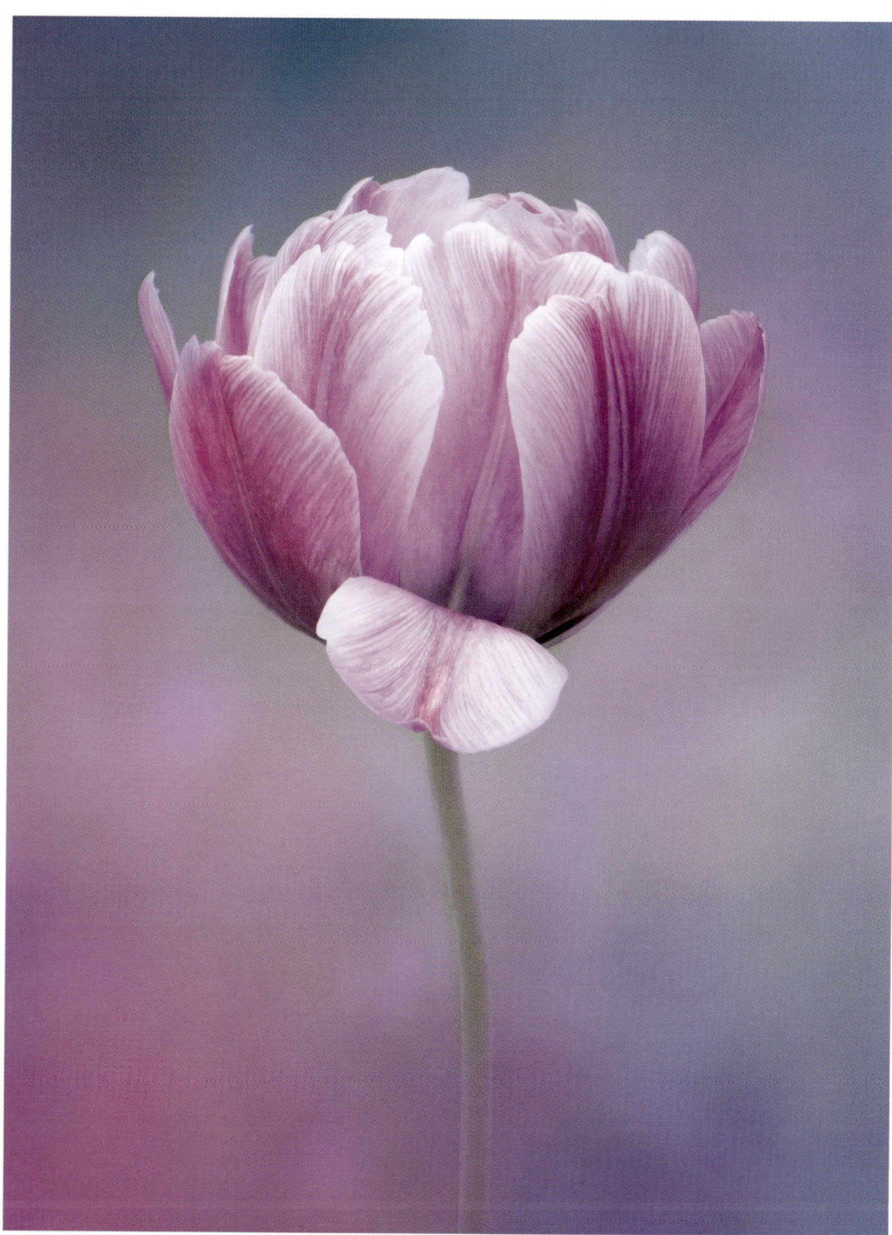

Pink tulip in late spring.

INDEX